Using the MMPI–2 in Forensic Assessment

Using the MMPI–2 in Forensic Assessment

James N. Butcher

Giselle A. Hass

Roger L. Greene

Linda D. Nelson

AMERICAN PSYCHOLOGICAL ASSOCIATION

WASHINGTON, DC

Published by
American Psychological Association
750 First Street, NE
Washington, DC 20002
www.apa.org

To order
APA Order Department
P.O. Box 92984
Washington, DC 20090-2984
Tel: (800) 374-2721; Direct: (202) 336-5510
Fax: (202) 336-5502; TDD/TTY: (202) 336-6123
Online: www.apa.org/pubs/books
E-mail: order@apa.org

In the U.K., Europe, Africa, and the Middle East, copies may be ordered from
American Psychological Association
3 Henrietta Street
Covent Garden, London
WC2E 8LU England

Typeset in Goudy by Circle Graphics, Inc., Columbia, MD

Printer: Edwards Brothers, Inc., Lillington, NC
Cover Designer: Berg Design, Albany, NY

The opinions and statements published are the responsibility of the authors, and such opinions and statements do not necessarily represent the policies of the American Psychological Association.

Library of Congress Cataloging-in-Publication Data

Butcher, James Neal, 1933- , author.
  Using the MMPI-2 in forensic assessment / James N. Butcher, Giselle A. Hass, Roger L. Greene, & Linda D. Nelson. — First edition.
    p. ; cm.
  Includes bibliographical references and index.
  ISBN-13: 978-1-4338-1868-4
  ISBN-10: 1-4338-1868-X
  I. Hass, Giselle A., author. II. Greene, Roger L., author. III. Nelson, Linda D., author. IV. American Psychological Association, publisher. V. Title.
  [DNLM: 1. Expert Testimony. 2. Forensic Psychiatry. 3. MMPI. W 740]
  RA1151
  614'.15—dc23
                                        2014028807

British Library Cataloguing-in-Publication Data
A CIP record is available from the British Library.

Printed in the United States of America
First Edition

http://dx.doi.org/10.1037/14571-000

CONTENTS

ACKNOWLEDGMENTS

The authors would like to acknowledge the following people for their support and guidance during the writing of this book: We would like to express our great appreciation to Susan Reynolds of APA Books for her strong support of our project and David Becker and Robin Easson, from APA Books and APA Journals, respectively, for their editorial contributions. We also would like to express our thanks to Fanny Cheung, Reneau Kennedy, Gloria Morote, and Carlos Saborio for providing case material.

James N. Butcher would like to thank his wife, Carolyn Williams, for her support and thoughtful suggestions for the book; he would also like to thank his daughters, Holly Butcher and Sherry Wickstrom, and his son, Janus Butcher, for their continued support of his writing.

Giselle A. Hass would like to thank Dr. Kari Carstairs for suggestions on the custody and parenting chapter and her husband, Steve Hass, and their daughter, Amanda, for their support and encouragement.

Roger L. Greene would like to extend his deepest gratitude to Stuart Greenberg, who spent years teaching him about the many nuances of forensic assessment.

Linda D. Nelson would like to express her appreciation for the assistance of Thomas Hardey, Elliot Kaye, and Kevin Scheibel in developing the neuropsychological and workers' compensation assessment chapters.

Using the MMPI–2 in Forensic Assessment

INTRODUCTION

The Minnesota Multiphasic Personality Inventory—2 (MMPI–2; Butcher, Dahlstrom, Graham, Tellegen, & Kaemmer, 1989) is a widely researched personality measure that forensic psychologists use for assessing an examinee's mental health and personality adjustment when undertaking forensic psychological evaluations for court cases (see, for example, Bow, Flens, & Gould, 2010; Lally, 2003). The MMPI–2 is the personality measure they use most widely for assessing an examinee's mental health and personality adjustment in making their recommendations for court decisions in several settings, such as family custody and child protection evaluations, personal injury assessments, work compensation and disability decisions, immigration evaluations, and criminal court decisions.

Our goal in writing this book was to develop a guide for interpreting the MMPI–2 in forensic settings that gives the forensic psychologist conducting evaluations and attorneys representing clients who are involved in court cases in which the MMPI–2 has been introduced both a valuable overview

http://dx.doi.org/10.1037/14571-001
Using the MMPI–2 in Forensic Assessment, by J. N. Butcher, G. A. Hass, R. L. Greene, and L. D. Nelson

of contemporary developments and pertinent historical background in using the MMPI–2 in forensic evaluations. We provide a number of forensic case examples throughout the book to illustrate a practical approach on the interpretive strategies for the test. Essential to the use of any psychological test is the need to examine research base support and new developments that influence the application of the instrument. Although some basic background on the MMPI–2 for interpretation of scales in forensic settings is provided, the main goal is to provide a technical resource for using the MMPI–2 in advanced interpretation in forensic evaluations. We assume that the reader has a basic understanding of the MMPI–2.

THE MMPI–2 IN FORENSIC EVALUATIONS

This book was developed to serve as a guide for interpreting the MMPI–2 in these various settings and to provide resource material on the MMPI–2 in order to assist forensic psychologists in preparing for testimony in court cases based upon the instrument. The goals of the book include the following:

1. Describe forensic evaluations and the appropriate role that the MMPI–2 can play in assessing personality and in understanding the credibility of patient report in personality evaluation of examinees in various settings.
2. Provide an introduction to forensic assessment with the MMPI–2.
3. Include an overview of research supporting use of the MMPI–2 in neuropsychological, personal injury, child custody, and family violence cases and in evaluations of criminals.
4. Highlight the demands and challenges that can occur in many forensic evaluations and describe how the MMPI–2 provides valuable personality information that can assist the practitioner in developing hypotheses about the client's behavior and mental-health symptoms in various forensic assessments.
5. Provide an overview of the cultural considerations in interpretation of the MMPI–2 in forensic assessment and provide information and relevant strategies for conducting evaluations in assessing immigrants.
6. Highlight the demands and challenges that may occur in forensic psychology and describe how results of the MMPI–2 assist the practitioner in developing hypotheses about the client's behavior and mental health.

7. Report scientific and legal evidence supporting use of the MMPI–2 in neuropsychological, workers' compensation, personal injury, child custody, family violence, and criminal evaluations.

8. Provide a number of case examples to illustrate the utility of the MMPI–2 in court cases. The case studies included in the book are from actual client cases in which the authors served as expert witnesses. In some situations, the case material was provided by their colleagues. In most cases (except for the Unabomber example, in Chapter 14, which is public information), case material was masked to keep the identifying information confidential.

9. Describe computer-based assessment in forensic cases and illustrate the information that computer-generated interpretations can provide in understanding the client's behavior and problems.

10. Provide a useful report writing strategy for communicating test results in court cases.

11. Describe two controversial measures that were derived from MMPI–2 items, the Lees-Haley Fake Bad Scale (Lees-Haley, English, & Glenn, 1991) and the MMPI–2—Restructured Form (MMPI–2–RF; Tellegen & Ben-Porath, 2008), and their relationship to the original MMPI and MMPI–2. These controversial measures are discussed in some detail because examiners who use the MMPI–2–RF measures in court cases can encounter problems. The measures are new and lack validation research, and their use may potentially provide inadequate support for forensic testimony. *Daubert v. Merrell Dow Pharmaceuticals* (1993) and its relationship to scientific evidence are discussed in this context.

ORGANIZATION OF THIS BOOK

To assist readers in locating the resources available in this book, we provide the following map to guide them through information for using the MMPI–2 in various forensic settings.

In the first chapter we provide general information that can be of value to the psychologist in preparation for court testimony using the MMPI–2. Included in this overview are factors associated with MMPI–2 use that are important to consider in using the test in forensic applications: for example, issues related to appropriate test administration, item and scale interpretation, and report writing and the steps that one can take in the preparation for court testimony. We provide information on test applications in various contexts for use in developing testimony about the MMPI–2.

In the second chapter we give an overview of the important task facing the MMPI–2 test user in determining whether the test results are valid and interpretable. People being evaluated by psychological procedures as part of their testimony in court cases may respond to interview questions or psychological tests in a way meant to influence the outcome of the evaluation. They may respond to items in order to be seen by others as highly virtuous and without problems in an effort to obtain custody of their children; in some criminal cases, clients may respond in a manner suggesting they are mentally disturbed to convince the jury that the crimes for which they are charged were influenced by a mental condition.

The MMPI–2 contains a dozen ways for the psychologist to obtain information on the client's presentation of his or her mental status during the evaluation. The importance of assessing response attitudes in forensic evaluations is presented and the well-established MMPI–2 validity scales are summarized to provide the reader with an overview of this important step in understanding the client's test performance. It is important to note, as we do in this book, that not all scales that have been developed from MMPI–2 items provide valid and important personality-based information on the client. For example, the Fake Bad Scale (FBS), which was recently renamed the Symptom Validity Scale (SVS) by the test publisher, is currently incorporated in forensic evaluations by some psychologists, and is a questionable measure that can disadvantage clients (by labeling them as faking) although they have genuine physical problems or stress-related mental-health problems. The problems surrounding use of this scale—for example, its questionable developmental procedures and its unacceptability in court—are described in Chapter 2.

This book was developed as an advanced text on the use of the MMPI–2 in specific forensic applications. Although we assume that the reader will have a basic background in the structure of the test, we provide an overview summary of the standard scales of the MMPI–2. We include summary descriptions in Chapter 3 of the MMPI–2 clinical, content, and supplementary scales and code types (combinations of score scales) in order for the reader to have close at hand brief descriptions of the basic MMPI–2 measures discussed in this book.

In a multicultural society such as the United States, court cases frequently involve psychological assessments in which the assessment practitioner and the client are from different cultural backgrounds. Therefore, cultural factors in forensic assessment with the MMPI–2, as discussed in Chapter 4, are important variables to appraise and deal with in forensic cases. Cross-cultural variables and the impact they might have on the assessment must be taken into consideration in forensic assessments. The MMPI–2 has been widely adapted cross-culturally (there are over 33 translations in use around the world). There is substantial research showing the test's effectiveness in assessing people from diverse cultures with carefully adapted translations. Psychologists who use translated versions of the MMPI–2 in their evaluations of foreign-born clients may find that there are appropriate norms that have been developed and used to assess clients in different languages and cultures; for example, Belgium, Chile, China, France, Israel, Korea, Italy, Mexico, Spain, and many others.

Psychological assessment and the application of tests are influenced by the setting in which they are employed. The context in which self-report instruments are used is an important consideration, particularly in forensic evaluations. In this book we provide a review and pertinent research background for the application of the MMPI–2 in seven general forensic settings in which it is frequently used. In Chapter 5 we provide a perspective on the application of the MMPI–2 in neuropsychological assessment—a setting in which the MMPI–2 provides a different perspective on the client's personality and behavioral functioning than other tests usually employed by the neuropsychologist to assess potential neurobehavioral problems.

Two very similar settings in which the MMPI–2 is used to evaluate personality and mental-health symptoms of clients with physical or psychologically based injuries are described in Chapter 6 (for personal injury evaluations) and Chapter 7 (for work compensation evaluations). Clients seeking financial compensation for alleged injuries from accidents or difficult life circumstances (e.g., sexual assault or harassment) are often similar in the response approach. Moreover, many of the client's motivational factors and the environmental contexts across the two settings are similar. However, personal injury and work compensation cases are sufficiently different that we thought it was important to deal with them in separate chapters.

In Chapter 8 we provide a summary and discussion of the use of MMPI–2 in immigration evaluations. This assessment service is increasing greatly in contemporary clinical forensic practice. For example, some psychologists are conducting evaluations on immigrants as part of the evidence presented in hearings by individuals who are seeking immigration relief. Assessments of immigrants often have to be conducted in the language of the client rather than in English. In this chapter we provide a discussion of the legal context in which immigrant evaluations are conducted and discuss issues related to understanding the test results. An example of a typical assessment encountered in immigrant assessments is included to illustrate the relevance of the MMPI–2.

One of the most frequent applications of the MMPI–2 in forensic evaluations is in custody or parent capacity evaluations (see Chapter 9). We provide a description of the research on using the MMPI–2 in custody evaluations and discuss the issues involved in conducting child custody evaluations. A relevant case illustration is included to demonstrate how the MMPI–2 can provide information pertinent to custody decisions. In a somewhat related discussion in Chapter 10, on using the MMPI–2 in cases of intimate partner violence, we further examine how the MMPI–2 can provide valuable personality information on this client population and highlight the test's contributions with a case example.

One of the earliest applications of the original MMPI and MMPI–2 in forensic settings involved their use in assessment of people in pretrial criminal cases or those serving time in prison. Many of the early studies on the test included personality appraisals of prison populations and people who are being tried on criminal charges in court cases (see Chapter 11, summarizing use of the MMPI–2 in correctional settings). A number of studies were conducted by evaluating prisoners in determining potentially effective approaches for rehabilitation. In this chapter we provide discussion on pretrial MMPI–2 assessments and on research on prison populations to illustrate the test's utility in these cases.

Two of the authors of this book (Butcher and Greene) have developed computer assessment systems based on MMPI–2. They have cooperated in illustrating the applicability of this interpretive approach in Chapter 12, which describes computer-based interpretation in forensic evaluations from their different perspectives. The chapter provides a discussion of computer interpretation and its general acceptability in forensic assessment. It also provides an example of a computer-based evaluation of a client from an international assessment in a criminal case to illustrate its applicability.

In Chapter 13 we provide a discussion of information that is important to include in developing a forensic psychological report that appropriately summarizes an assessment evaluation of the client.

Forensic psychologists might face questions concerning using the MMPI–2 in court cases as a result of the recent publication of another and rather different instrument (i.e., the MMPI–2–RF) using the MMPI–2 item pool and norms developed for the MMPI–2. The use of the same name implies that this new instrument builds upon the tradition of the original MMPI, but it does not. It is a very different instrument, in terms of method and of the results obtained. We address these issues in the final chapter of the book. Chapter 14 is devoted to a description of the MMPI–2–RF and illustrates through case examples and research studies how these two tests differ.

In Chapter 15 we provide a summary and conclusions of the material included in this book.

We hope that the material provided in this forensic guide can assist forensic psychology experts with an updated and effectively workable knowledge base on MMPI–2 for their practice decisions and contribute to their journey to remain current in psychological assessment. There has been substantial research and development on the MMPI–2 in the past several years. The changes in forensic practice and new developments in research and test development make it necessary for forensic psychologists to be up-to-date and knowledgeable about test-related factors that can influence court testimony.

Many forensic experts feel that there is an unceasing need for current update of research and interpretive strategies based on the MMPI–2, given its broad use. This book was developed to provide the forensic psychologist with MMPI–2 background and to serve this goal in addition to another forensic MMPI–2 book that has been published by the American Psychological Association: *The MMPI, MMPI–2, and MMPI–A in Court: A Practical Guide for Expert Witness and Attorneys* (3rd ed.) by Pope, Butcher, and Seelen, which was last revised in 2006. The present volume should not be viewed as a replacement for the Pope et al. book. Rather, it was developed as a complement to the earlier work as a means of updating the resource and research material on the MMPI–2 that has been published over the last decade. The Pope et al. handbook addresses the legal context in more detail and provides extensive discussion on the legal aspects of test use; for example, it describes the cases in which the MMPI–2 has been included in court decisions. Much of the information described in the Pope et al. handbook is still relevant and is not included here. This book looks more extensively at the application of the test in specific forensic applications and includes past and current research supporting the test.

We now turn our attention to the discussion of general factors for using the MMPI–2 in forensic cases.

DISCLOSURE STATEMENTS

The authors provide the following information concerning their financial involvement with the MMPI products:

James N. Butcher served on the MMPI–2 Restandardization Committee to develop the MMPI–2 and MMPI—Adolescent (MMPI–A). The three members of the original committee, James Butcher, W. Grant Dahlstrom, and John R. Graham, chose not to receive any royalties from the sales of the MMPI–2 and MMPI–A test booklets and manuals, manual supplements, scoring materials, profile sheets, and the like. These authors wrote new items and revised original MMPI items for the MMPI–2 and MMPI–A. They collected the normative sample used in the norm development for the MMPI–2 and MMPI–A and clinical data sets used to validate the revised scales between 1982 and 1989. Butcher co-created several scales for the MMPI–2, such as the content scales; the MMPI–A content scales; the Superlative

Self-Presentation, or S, scale; and the four alcohol and drug problem scales, the MMPI–2 APS and AAS, the MMPI–A ACK and PRO. Butcher also was the co-creator of nine translations of the MMPI or MMPI–2, and he does not receive any royalties for those works. Members of the MMPI Restandardization Committee agreed to forgo any royalties on the new versions of the MMPI resulting from the committee's work during the restandardization project. Butcher does receive royalty payments for some of the books he has published on the MMPI and MMPI–2, although the royalties on some books were donated to the MMPI–2 Symposium and Workshop Series that he directed for 38 years. Butcher receives royalty payment for his development of the Minnesota Reports, a computer-based interpretation system for the MMPI–2 and MMPI–A.

Giselle A. Hass does not have an affiliation with any MMPI–2 products or books published previously and does not receive any royalties related to the MMPI–2. To the best of her knowledge, she owns no stocks or bonds in companies publishing psychological tests.

Roger L. Greene has published several books on personality assessment and the MMPI. He published an interpretive manual for the MMPI–2/MMPI–2–RF and a computer interpretive program for the MMPI–2 and for the MMPI–2–RF from which he receives royalties.

Linda D. Nelson does not have an affiliation with any MMPI–2 products or books published previously and does not receive any royalties related to the MMPI–2. To the best of her knowledge, she owns no stocks or bonds in companies publishing psychological tests.

1

PREPARING FOR COURT TESTIMONY WITH THE MMPI–2

Difficult challenges as well as interesting professional opportunities face psychologists who become engaged in forensic psychological assessments. For over a century, since the pioneering work of psychologists such as Hugo Münsterberg (1908), many psychologists have devoted their professional efforts to understanding the personality and behavior of people undergoing legal processes. Many different psychological tests and procedures have been applied in psychological assessment to address the personal qualities of examinees in forensic cases, although some are less well established and acceptable to the legal community than others.

Over the past 30 years, forensic psychologists have become involved across a broad range of forensic settings. These settings include personal injury litigation; evaluations of criminal and prison populations; and mental-health assessments in determining need for psychiatric commitment, capacity for parents to provide child care, and whether a parent should be allowed custody of children. As a professional subspecialty, assessment of psychopathology in

http://dx.doi.org/10.1037/14571-002
Using the MMPI–2 in Forensic Assessment, by J. N. Butcher, G. A. Hass, R. L. Greene, and L. D. Nelson

forensic settings differs from clinical settings assessment in a number of ways. Psychologists conducting forensic evaluations are confronted with numerous ethical problems and issues that require consideration. Compared with clinical psychologists, forensic psychologists are more likely to be vigorously challenged, to encounter legal-ethical problems, and to have complaints lodged against them (Allan, 2013).

It is essential for forensic psychologists to have a sound knowledge and current understanding of the ethical guidelines, norms, and policies that regulate them (American Psychological Association, 2010a, 2013b; Austin & Drozd, 2012; Knapp & VandeCreek, 2001; Wettstein, 2008). A number of professional associations have recommended guidelines for specific forensic assessment settings. For example, the American Academy of Psychiatry and the Law (2005), the American Psychological Association (2013b), the American Association for Correctional Psychology (2010), and a number of experts have provided information and discussed issues involved in forensic assessment (see Archer & Wheeler, 2013; Austin & Drozd, 2012; Borkosky, 2014; Brodsky, 2013; Gaughwin, 1998; Hemphill & Hart, 2003; Knapp & VandeCreek, 2001; Murrey, 2008; Sparta & Koocher, 2006; Späte & Schirmer, 1987; Wettstein, 2008).

In the following chapters, we provide a discussion of the important factors that forensic psychologists need to consider when conducting evaluations with the Minnesota Multiphasic Personality Inventory—2 (MMPI–2) to enhance their case reports and testimony.

WHAT THE FORENSIC PSYCHOLOGIST NEEDS TO KNOW ABOUT THE MMPI–2 IN PREPARATION FOR REPORT WRITING AND COURT TESTIMONY

Extent of MMPI–2 Test Usage in Forensic Evaluations

As noted above, the MMPI–2 is the personality test most frequently used by forensic practitioners, as reflected in recent surveys and reviews (Archer, Stredny, & Wheeler, 2013; McLaughlin & Kan, 2014; Ready & Veague, 2014); for examples, see Rohrer (2008; battered women), Bow, Flens, and Gould (2010; child custody), and M. A. Martin, Allan, and Allan (2001; Australian court cases). In his survey of forensic diplomates, Lally (2003) found that only the MMPI–2 and Wechsler Adult Intelligence Scale—Third Edition were recommended for insanity evaluations by the majority of respondents and recommended along with the Structured Interview of Reported Symptoms for malingering assessment. Bow et al. (2010) found that 87% of their total sample used the MMPI–2. Respondents almost always (95%) used the full test (567 items) rather than an abbreviated version, and standard instructions were used by 84% of respondents.

Important Points to Consider When Using the MMPI–2 in Court Cases

Psychologists must address several important questions to comfortably and effectively use the MMPI–2 in forensic case evaluations. The following 14 points can provide the practitioner with information to consider in using the test in court cases. (Further information about use of the MMPI–2 in forensic evaluations can be found in Megargee, 2009; Otto, 2002; Pope, Butcher, & Seelen, 2006.)

1. It is important for psychologists to reach a clear agreement with the attorney or the court (preferably in writing) concerning the specific purpose and scope of the assessment, the fees being charged, and the time the evaluation should be completed.
2. Psychologists need to have the relevant education, training, and experience with the MMPI–2 and to be current in interpretative information to be used in the assessment.
3. The psychologist needs to determine that there are no conflicts of interest that would undermine the fairness and validity of the assessment.
4. The psychologist needs to have familiarity with the pertinent research base and contemporary studies that have a bearing on the case.
5. The psychologist needs to determine that the MMPI–2 (or other psychological tests used) have been adequately researched and have been shown to be valid and reliable for the particular use.
6. The psychologist needs to be knowledgeable about any issues or ongoing controversies that could create difficulties with his or her testimony with the MMPI–2.
7. It is important for the psychologist to understand the underlying research on the test and any specific limiting factors to assure that the measure is appropriate for an examinee from this demographic group.
8. The psychologist needs to be knowledgeable about use of the MMPI–2 in assessing response styles and to assure that the examinee has not responded to the instrument in an invalid way in order to appear to be more or less disturbed than he or she actually is.
9. It is essential that the psychologist inform the examinee about the evaluation and obtain appropriate consent forms.

10. The psychologist needs to determine that the examinee is capable of reading at a sixth-grade or higher level and of understanding and responding to the items on the MMPI–2 with the written, computer-administered, or audio version. If the examinee speaks a language other than English, the appropriate version of the MMPI–2 should be obtained.

11. The psychologist practitioner needs to assure that the test administration is monitored adequately and that the test is administered in a private, quiet room that is free from distractions. Examinees should not be given the test to take home and complete.

12. The MMPI–2 has to be properly scored and verified. If the test is computer scored and interpreted, the psychologist needs to assure that the results match the interpretive information available in the literature.

13. In any oral or written report of the MMPI–2 results, including information provided in deposition or courtroom testimony, the psychologist needs to assure that all information relevant to the validity of the assessment is included. Reporting only a portion of the results to support a specific conclusion desired by an attorney is never appropriate.

14. The psychologist needs to ensure that appropriate records of the testing are maintained for as long as the state of residence requires.

ISSUES IN THE ADMINISTRATION, SCORING, AND INTERPRETATION OF THE MMPI–2 IN FORENSIC EVALUATIONS

Administration

Appropriate and standard administration procedures for obtaining the examinee's responses to MMPI–2 items are key factors in using psychological tests in forensic evaluations. Paper-and-pencil booklet, audio, or computer-administered administrations are appropriate for use in forensic evaluations. In the administration of self-report psychological tests it is important to follow carefully the standardized procedures that were used in developing and norming the MMPI–2 to assure that the standardized norms apply appropriately for the case. If, for example, one modified the instructions to read "Please respond to these questions as *you felt before you were arrested for the crime*" (as occurred in a previous case), the MMPI–2 norms would not be an appropriate reference population. No norms are available for such modifications of the instructions.

All 567 of the MMPI–2 items should be administered in order to obtain a complete evaluation of the examinee. Shortened versions should be avoided. The full MMPI–2 should be administered in order to incorporate the research-based set of measures on the test. Administration of all 567 items is particularly important in forensic settings, where altering a standard test administration in an evaluation can come under close scrutiny and result in testimonial problems in cross-examination. As noted above, Bow et al. (2010) found that practitioners in their survey of test usage almost always (95%) used all 567 MMPI–2 items rather than an abbreviated version of the test. Some psychologists, for various reasons such as time restraints or examinee limitations, choose to administer only parts of the MMPI–2. In some instances, psychologists have shortened scales in an abbreviated form, in the assumption that the abbreviated version measures the same constructs as the full form. With regard to brief forms of the MMPI, Hathaway (1975) pointed out,

> If you choose to for any reason to administer only part of the test, you should be aware of how this would affect the interpretations and the consequences which you would subsequently find through your interpretation. I, for one, would never administer only part of the test. I suspect the increment of new information would fall short.

In some cases, an examinee may not be able to complete all 567 items. If the first 370 items have been administered and responded to appropriately, the traditional MMPI–2 clinical scales and validity scales (L, F, K) can be scored and interpreted.

In the United States, immigrant examinees who are not proficient in English may be referred for forensic evaluations. The practitioner, in an effort to employ appropriate psychological tests, may rely upon the MMPI–2 for personality assessment because it has been well validated in numerous languages and cultures. There are over 33 foreign language translations of the test based upon effective translation and adaptation procedures (see Butcher, 1996, for a discussion of many translated versions); in-country norms have been developed in many countries for the translated version. Obtaining copies of many of the foreign language translations is somewhat difficult, because, except for the Spanish-language and Hmong translations (which are available from the test publisher), they are not commercially available in the United States. Translated test booklets are usually obtained by contacting the foreign language MMPI–2 test distributors (see University of Minnesota Press, 2011, for information on licensed, available translations).

Landwher and Llorente (2012) provided a valuable recent review of cultural factors in neuropsychological assessment. More information about cultural factors and the role ethnicity can play in the application of the MMPI–2 is provided in Chapters 4 and 8 of this volume.

Scoring

Accuracy of recording and scoring an examinee's responses to MMPI–2 items is essential in preparing an evaluation for a court case; however, this issue is often minimized or ignored. There are two options for scoring MMPI–2 protocols: hand or computer scoring. When the MMPI–2 is used in forensic evaluations, it is extremely important that mistakes are not made in the scoring. Research has shown that the most reliable method of scoring self-report tests such as the MMPI–2 is by computer rather than by hand (Allard, Butler, Faust, & Shea, 1995; Allard & Faust, 2000; Simons, Goddard, & Patton, 2002), and computer scoring is widely accepted in assessment practice (see, e.g., Federal Aviation Administration, 2013). Regardless of whether hand or computer scoring is used, psychologists should assure accuracy by having another person independently rescore the test or verify the data entry when scored by computer. Moreover, if hand scoring is used, it is important not to be selective in scoring by choosing only a few scales to include in the evaluation (see selective scoring of a case described in Chapter 12). The examinee may have responded to the items indicating problem areas that were not scored; thus, the assessment would be considered incomplete and overly selective.

GENDER DIFFERENCES IN MMPI–2 ITEM RESPONSES

Men and women respond differently to some items in the MMPI–2 item pool. In the development of the original MMPI, Hathaway and McKinley (1940, 1942b) noted the frequency difference between the sexes on some scales, e.g., Depression [D], and chose to use separate norms to assess men and women in order to make the scales more sensitive to psychopathology. Moreover, in conducting research on personality assessment, Cattell (1948) came to similar conclusions with respect to male and female differences in personality and symptoms and used gender-specific norms in the 16 Personality Factor Questionnaire (Cattell, Eber, & Tatsuoka, 1970; Cattell & Stice, 1957).

Mason, Bubany, and Butcher (2012) recently conducted a comprehensive review of gender differences in personality and assessment that concluded that there were clear differences in the symptoms and behaviors of men and women. They reported that there was a robust body of literature on gender differences in personality, psychopathology, cognition, and social behavior that have to be taken into consideration in personality assessment. Han et al. (2013) conducted a cross-cultural comparison of gender differences using the

MMPI–2 and MMPI—Adolescent (MMPI–A) normative samples from the United States and South Korea. They found significant MMPI item gender-related content differences across both cultures, but the gender differences were prominent on a higher portion of the items in the U.S. data than in the South Korean normative samples.

As noted above, in the development of the original MMPI, Hathaway and McKinley (1940) considered it necessary to provide gender-specific norms for the scales. When the MMPI was revised in 1989, separate norms for men and women were maintained (Butcher, Dahlstrom, Graham, Tellegen, & Kaemmer, 1989). Nongendered T scores also were developed for the MMPI–2, based upon the original normative sample, in order to provide a set of specific norms in which men and women were scored according to the same standard. These norms, not recommended for use in forensic settings, were developed for personnel selection applications, in which separate gender-based norms are not considered appropriate for job applicants.

The latest version of the *Diagnostic and Statistical Manual of Mental Disorders* (*DSM–5*; American Psychiatric Association, 2013) focuses substantially on gender differences in some mental disorders. In forensic settings, the response differences between men and women could be problematic if the norms used in profile comparison do not take these differences into account. One example of an MMPI–2 scale that does not take into consideration gender differences is the Fake Bad Scale (Lees-Haley, English, & Glenn, 1991). The same cutoff score is recommended for both men and women, although there are significant gender differences (see the discussion of this scale in Chapter 2). The use of the same cutoff score for men and women results in the scale being biased against women (Butcher, Gass, Cumella, Kally, & Williams, 2008). Some psychological inventories, for example, the Personality Assessment Inventory (Morey, 1991) and the MMPI–2—Restructured Form (MMPI–2–RF; Tellegen & Ben-Porath, 2008), use only nongendered T scores and may be considered insensitive to problem areas in which women and men differ substantially in symptoms expressed. Psychological inventories that do not allow for or compensate for gender differences may be questioned in cases where gender bias might be considered to influence the psychological conclusions.

CLARIFICATIONS OF MMPI–2 BASED HYPOTHESES BY RETESTING OR OBTAINING PRIOR TESTING RESULTS

Psychologists may encounter situations when multiple test results on an examinee are included in a court case as a means of clarifying an examinee's personality performance. This procedure might, in some instances, clarify the examinee's functioning but might actually cloud the performance on the testing procedures in others.

Retesting to Improve Upon Previous MMPI–2 Scores

In some cases, psychologists have chosen to readminister the MMPI–2 as a result of obtaining unusable or problematic results from the initial administration. For example, in one case the examinee had skipped two pages of the item booklet inadvertently because the pages were stuck together. As would be expected, this oversight resulted in an invalid protocol because of the high level of *Cannot Say* scores. In this instance, the examinee was readministered the MMPI–2 in order to obtain complete results. However, other cases have not been as straightforward. Some psychologists have been unsatisfied about their examinee's results and have chosen to readminister the test with clearer instructions as to how to avoid the problem noted in the first administration. In this circumstance, the follow-up administration was challenged because altered instructions were used to provide self-information in a more protective manner, and the second MMPI–2 was not used in the case.

Research has been conducted in some health care and personnel selection settings to readminister the test to enable a more valid result by encouraging the examinee to be more open in his or her symptom endorsement. Butcher, Morfitt, Rouse, and Holden (1997) developed a procedure to reduce test defensiveness among job applicants by allowing those applicants with invalid profiles to retake the test. The applicants were informed that their initial test was invalid and nonusable as a result of their being overly defensive. The instructions recommended that they be more forthcoming in their responses to the items in the retest administration. This procedure was effective in that the majority of applicants produced a valid profile on the retest. Moreover, many applicant profiles showed more elevation among clinical scales, and possible mental-health problems were discovered. This procedure has been cross-validated in a number of studies in personnel and health settings (see Butcher, Gucker, & Hellervik, 2009, for further information). However, the use of altered instructions to obtain more valid protocols has not been examined in forensic settings. The use of standard instructions is recommended at all times in forensic settings, even when a test is readministered.

Locating Prior Testing Results to Clarify Scores in Evaluations

Another circumstance in which multiple test protocols have been used at trial involved obtaining prior testing protocols of the examinee that were administered under different circumstances in order to clarify his or her mental-health status at an earlier point in life. In one situation, the MMPI–2 results from prior records were obtained (from a case) in order to clarify what the examinee's mental-health status was the previous year when he filed a different personal injury claim. It is important to maintain the interpretation of those profiles grounded in the contextual factors of the individual's life at the time of administration.

DETERMINING WHETHER THE EXAMINEE'S MMPI–2 IS DEFENSIBLE IN CROSS-EXAMINATION

As part of an MMPI–2 based personality assessment the practitioner should conduct a thorough evaluation of the examinee's validity, clinical, and supplementary scale profiles to assure that the MMPI–2 information is pertinent for the assessment.

A number of MMPI–2 resources are available for downloading from the website www.umn.edu/mmpi. These files are not exhaustive by any means and represent only an estimate of the full MMPI/MMPI–2 research base. This extensive database has been of immense value in preparing for court testimony. It has been possible to do a literature search of relevant research articles for the problems being presented in the case. For example, in one personal injury case involving an examinee's claim of posttraumatic stress disorder, it was possible to locate 26 relevant articles that shed light on the symptoms and problem behaviors related to the alleged disorder.

MMPI–2 SCALE NAMES SHOULD NOT BE INTERPRETED LITERALLY

Many psychologists who have not been well trained in the interpretation of the MMPI–2 and many attorneys who are examining or cross-examining a psychologist about the MMPI–2 are prone to assume that scale names can be interpreted literally. The names of the scales do not necessarily describe the behavioral correlate information that has been established for MMPI–2 scales. Moreover, some scale names are more general than the established database for the scale. For example, if the examinee has elevated Scale 8 (Sc: Schizophrenia), it is assumed that the examinee must be schizophrenic rather than understood that the examinee shares some behaviors and symptoms that were characteristic of the schizophrenic criterion group. Similarly, elevations of Pa_1 (Persecutory Ideas) in child-custody litigants are assumed to be a natural result of the contentious proceedings. Actually, child-custody litigants (men = 2.13 [52 T]; women = 2.54 [54 T]) and the MMPI–2 normative group (men = 1.74 [50 T]; women = 1.79 [50 T]) have virtually identical scores on this scale (Greene, 2006). Finally, examinees who elevate Scale 4 (Pd: Psychopathic Deviate) are assumed to be psychopaths even though Scale 4 correlates .00 with the Psychopathy Checklist (Hare, 1985).

CAVEATS FOR INTERPRETING MMPI–2 ITEMS

The forensic examiner must keep many caveats in mind when interpreting individual MMPI–2 items to avoid overinterpreting them. First, any single item can be unreliable as the result of momentary lapses of attention in marking the item on the answer sheet, hurriedly reading the item, misunderstanding some key word in the item, and so on. It is not unusual for examinees who are questioned about a response to a specific item to say that they do not remember responding to the item in that manner or they do not know why they responded in the manner that they did. Second, the referent for key words in items may be ambiguous and allow for multiple interpretations. For example, an item such as "I mix well" can be endorsed in the "true" direction because the examinee is a good baker, bartender, painter, chemist, pharmacist, disc jockey, light technician, and so on. This inherent ambiguity in items was one of the rationales for the original emphasis on selecting items empirically for the MMPI scales (Hathaway & McKinley, 1940). Third, the tyranny of adverbs affects the content-based understanding of many MMPI–2 items. Two examinees may endorse an item such as "I have very little back pain" in the "true" direction, one examinee because he has back pain only once a year and another because she has one back pain only once a day. In an empirically based interpretation, the important issue is whether examinees believe that they have back pain rather than the actual frequency or severity of their back pain experienced in a given period. In a content-based interpretation, it would be easy for the forensic examiner to conclude that this examinee does not have back pain, because it is exactly her interpretation of the item. However, the forensic examiner may be missing that an important physical symptom is occurring quite frequently in the examinee's life. Finally, there is ambiguity about the time period that the examinee is using as a referent for responding to an item. This point can be made salient by considering an item such as "Lately I have thought a lot about the bad mistakes I have made in my life." Examinees could endorse this item in the "false" direction because the frequency of such thoughts has decreased over some time period, even though the thoughts are still occurring daily, hourly, and so on.

MMPI–2 CODE TYPES ARE NOT STABLE ACROSS TIME

MMPI–2 code types—that is, the scale scores that are most prominently elevated in the clinical profile—are described in detail in Chapter 3. They are discussed here to give the reader a perspective on their value as well as limitation in the interpretation process. The MMPI–2 code-type literature has proven of great value to the practitioner in understanding the behaviors of clients that are described in multiple MMPI–2 scale score elevations. Code-type research provides important summaries of profiles in which more than one clinical scale is elevated above a *T* score of 65.

However, it is important to realize that clinical profiles change over time. Several studies have examined the stability of MMPI–2 code types (Livingston, Jennings, Colotla, Reynolds, & Shercliffe, 2006; Munley, 2002; Ryan, Dunn, & Paolo, 1995). Livingston et al. (2006) provided information on code-type stability for 94 injured workers who were retested after an average of 21 months. These workers had the same two-point code type only 22% of the time, and the percentage increased to only 24% if the two-point code type was well defined. Munley (2002) reported code-type stability for 114 Veterans Administration inpatients whose MMPI–2s were separated by an average of 688 days. These veterans had the same two-point code type 17% of the time, and the percentage increased to 41% for well-defined, two-point code types. Finally, Ryan et al. (1995) reported code-type stability in a sample of 100 male substance abusers who were retested at an average of 5 and 13 months. They found concordance in two-point code types was 20% at 5 months and 12% at 13 months.

These data on code-type stability suggest several important conclusions. First, forensic examiners should be cautious about making long-term predictions from a single administration of the MMPI–2. It appears that even if well-defined, two-point code types are required, it is more likely than not that the examinee will have a different two-point code type the next time that the MMPI–2 is administered. If the code type is not well defined, the examinee will have a different two-point code type three out of four times. Any MMPI–2 interpretation should be understood as reflecting how the examinee reports his or her behavior and symptoms at this point in time. Second, it is not clear whether the shifts that do occur in code types across time reflect meaningful changes in the examinees' behaviors and symptoms, psychometric instability of the MMPI–2, or some combination of these factors. Finally, research is needed to provide additional information on this issue.

WHO REQUESTS THE EVALUATION?

Whether the prosecution (plaintiff), the defense (defendant), or the court has retained the forensic psychologist may impact the problematic behaviors and symptoms reported by the examinee, but empirical data on this point are minimal. Hasemann (1997) provided data on workers' compensation claimants who were evaluated by forensic psychologists for both the plaintiff and the defendant. There are striking differences between the MMPI profiles that were obtained (see Figure 1.1). The claimant reported more

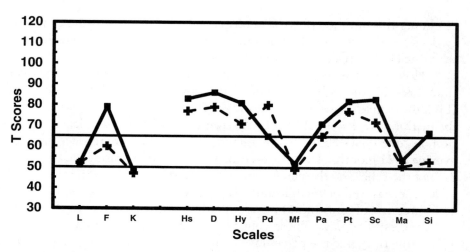

Figure 1.1. Workers' compensation claimants evaluated by defense and plaintiff experts. Solid line: Forensic psychologist retained by the defendant. Dashed line: Forensic psychologist retained by the plaintiff. Excerpted from the *MMPI®–2 (Minnesota Multiphasic Personality Inventory®—2) Manual for Administration, Scoring, and Interpretation, Revised Edition* by Butcher et al. Copyright © 2001 by the Regents of the University of Minnesota. Used by permission of the University of Minnesota Press. All rights reserved. "MMPI®" and "Minnesota Multiphasic Personality Inventory®" are trademarks owned by the Regents of the University of Minnesota.

symptoms and distress to the forensic psychologist retained by the defense attorney. Consequently, some of the differences in examinations performed by forensic psychologists on the same examinee may reflect that examinees actually describe their problematic behaviors and symptoms differently depending upon whether they believe that the forensic psychologist is likely to be sensitive or insensitive to their self-reports. The underlying heuristic of the examinee is likely to be that the "opposing" forensic psychologist will require more proof to be able or willing to perceive and report the examinee as being impaired. These results suggest the possibility that being examined by the plaintiff's expert, by the defense's expert, or by a neutral court-appointed expert over the same psycholegal issue should be considered as different forensic contexts.

Although the forensic psychologist may go to great effort to be unbiased, examinees may have different expectations or may have been provided with different expectations by their legal counsel. Attorneys may remind clients about the diagnostic criteria for the disorder that they are supposed to have, such as posttraumatic stress disorder, or simply remind them to be sure to tell the forensic psychologist about all of the problems that they have experienced and not to forget to report some particularly relevant event or experience. At a minimum, the forensic psychologist should inquire about the examinee's expectations for the examination and about any suggestions that may have been made.

Psychologists should not be advocates for their clients or the attorney who retains them, and they should strive to diminish the influence of personal beliefs, values, and perspectives in their professional work.

RECENT CONTROVERSY OVER THE MMPI–2–RF

The test publisher decided in 2008 to publish a shortened and psychometrically different test under the name of the MMPI–2—Restructured Form, or MMPI–2–RF. Because the new version comprised only 60% of the MMPI–2 items, the scales included are different from those in the original instrument. For example, the measures included are theory based rather than empirically derived, as are the original MMPI clinical scales (Ranson, Nichols, Rouse, & Harrington, 2009). The use of the MMPI–2–RF cannot be supported in court cases on the basis of the empirical research developed on the original MMPI and MMPI–2. Some of these MMPI–2–RF scales were controversial and had been heavily criticized (see Chapter 14). Most of the MMPI–2–RF scales were completely new and have not been researched adequately, particularly by researchers outside the group of investigators who developed the MMPI–2–RF. However, despite the controversies, some psychologists have used the MMPI–2–RF in forensic settings and have learned there were problems with substantiating its use because research support was nonexistent. We review the MMPI–2–RF in more detail in Chapter 14 and further discuss the controversy of its use in forensic settings.

SUGGESTED OUTLINE FOR EXPLAINING THE MMPI–2 IN COURT

This section describes an effective strategy for explaining the MMPI in court:

1. Describe the scientific basis of the MMPI instruments in terms of being an objective, paper-and-pencil personality inventory that has been widely researched and validated since 1940.
2. Describe how widely used the MMPI–2 is in clinical assessment and cite references to support its broad use. The MMPI/MMPI–2 is the most widely used instrument in clinical and research applications. Pope et al. (2006) provided a listing of the extensive use of the MMPI–2 in court (i.e., 320 federal and state citations since 2000).

3. Discuss the rationale for the original development of the MMPI as an objective means of classifying psychological problems with an empirically based scale construction approach.
4. Describe and illustrate how the MMPI–2 has been validated and explain the extensive research base for correlates for the clinical scales.
5. Illustrate how the MMPI–2 is used in personality description and clinical assessment.
6. Describe and illustrate that the clinical scales of the revised versions (MMPI–2/MMPI–A) are composed of largely the same items and possess the same psychometric properties as the original version of the scales. Traditional scale reliabilities and validities have been assured in the revised version.
7. Explain how the credibility and validity of a particular MMPI–2 profile can be determined and the response style revealed on the examinee.
8. Explain the MMPI/MMPI–2/MMPI–A findings for the particular examinee and how they relate to the psycholegal issues of the case.

PREPARATION FOR CROSS-EXAMINATION

In their handbook on the use of the MMPI–2/MMPI–A in court, Pope et al. (2006) provided an extensive description of preparation work that expert witnesses would find helpful in summarizing and presenting information about a examinee's MMPI–2 profile in forensic evaluations.

SUMMARY

For over a century, many psychologists have devoted their professional efforts to understanding the personality and behavior of people undergoing legal processes. Over the past 30 years, forensic psychologists have been actively involved in performing assessments in a broad range of forensic settings including personal injury litigation; evaluations of criminal and prison populations; mental-health assessments in determining need for psychiatric commitment, capacity for parents to provide child care, or whether a parent should be allowed custody of children; evaluation of immigrants, and many more.

The MMPI–2 is the personality test most frequently used by forensic practitioners, as reported in recent surveys. Forensic testimony, based on psychological tests, can be a more difficult application than conducting clinical, counseling, or health psychology examinations. It is important for forensic psychologists to have a sound knowledge and current understanding of the ethical guidelines, norms, and policies that regulate them.

This book was developed to serve as a guide for interpreting the MMPI–2 in these various settings and to provide resource material on the MMPI–2 in order to assist forensic psychologists in preparing for testimony in court cases based upon the instrument. Several important questions must be addressed if psychologists are to comfortably and effectively use the MMPI–2 in forensic case evaluations. Issues in the test administration, scoring, and interpretation of the MMPI–2 in forensic evaluations have been highlighted. A number of important features about forensic assessment using MMPI–2 in court cases have been discussed in this chapter and are considered in detail in this book.

2

IMPORTANCE OF ASSESSING RESPONSE ATTITUDES IN FORENSIC EVALUATIONS

It should come as no surprise that people who are asked to describe their mental-health condition or personality attributes in forensic assessments may make an effort to influence the outcome in their favor. In situations where they need to appear psychologically disturbed or disabled in their claim, they may report many symptoms. Or, in situations where they may lose custody of their children if they show psychological maladjustment, they generally present themselves in a highly favorable and extremely well-adjusted manner. It is not unexpected that a person would respond on self-report inventories in a manner that would advance his or her cause.

Honest and accurate self-portrayal of symptoms and behavior, on the part of the clients, is a crucial factor in personality evaluations on instruments like the Minnesota Multiphasic Personality Inventory—2 (MMPI–2). Invalid performances on personality scales are not unusual in forensic evaluations. Therefore, a key component to any psychological instrument used in forensic evaluations is a means of detecting uncooperative response sets. Several

http://dx.doi.org/10.1037/14571-003
Using the MMPI–2 in Forensic Assessment, by J. N. Butcher, G. A. Hass, R. L. Greene, and L. D. Nelson

invalidating response approaches have been well studied with the MMPI–2, including random responding, all or mostly true or false responding, inconsistent endorsement, admitting to unusual or rarely endorsed symptoms, and responding in an extremely defensive manner. When the examinee's response pattern reaches an extreme level based on these approaches, one can often conclude that the response pattern has likely resulted in test invalidity and the symptom description scales will provide little acceptable information. That is, the pattern of scores may be suggestive of behavior that is often characterized as malingering, lying, or faking because the results of the extreme performances are noncredible. Although this somewhat derogatory terminology may not be acceptable to some, the behavior underlying these response patterns that result in invalid and unusable test results nevertheless constitutes an effort of the examinee to distort his or her actual psychological functioning. The *Diagnostic and Statistical Manual of Mental Disorders* (DSM–5; American Psychiatric Association, 2013) includes a diagnosis of Factitious Disorder that involves falsifying or exaggerating symptoms.

The detection of malingering or uncooperative self-presentation in assessment evaluations can be a difficult process that requires careful considerations. Rogers and Granacher (2011) pointed out that the determination of malingering in forensic evaluations usually involves a careful, multistep process that integrates individualized clinical findings with standardized data. They also called attention to the fact that the assessment of malingering is not a monolithic process but should be considered carefully within specific domains, such as feigned mental disorders, feigned cognitive impairment, and feigned medical complaints.

A thorough evaluation of examinees' motivation and strategy for influencing their evaluation outcome is a basic consideration in a successful forensic assessment. The MMPI–2, with its long-standing research base and effective methodology, can contribute substantially to validity assessment in forensic cases. In forensic cases, the MMPI–2 validity scales can assist the forensic practitioner in determining whether an examinee has provided credible and nondistorted symptomatic information, responded in an exaggerated manner, attempted to present an overly favorable view of adjustment, or responded defensively to the item content in the assessment.

DETECTING RESPONSE SETS WITH THE MMPI/MMPI–2

One of the major advantages of the MMPI/MMPI–2 for forensic psychologists is the availability of well-developed and widely researched validity scales for the appraisal of response sets. Extensive and frequently updated research on the MMPI–2 validity scales can be found on www.umn.edu/mmpi. Response sets are present when an examinee produces answers that are distorted in some important way as a strategy for influencing the outcome of the evaluation. Nichols, Greene, and Schmolck (1989) provided an important distinction in interpreting response sets on the MMPI. They divided response approaches into two major categories: content nonresponsiveness (CNR) and content-responsive faking (CRF). CNR is present when answers bear no meaningful relationship to items. For example, items that are omitted or double-marked and random responding fall into this category. On the other hand, uncooperativeness, poor reading comprehension, or extreme stress may result in CNR responding. The defining feature is that answers cannot be interpreted because they are not meaningfully related to the items. CRF occurs when an examinee distorts responses based on the content of the items. Overreporting of symptoms can often be found in symptom exaggeration among litigants in personal injury claims or in criminal offenders who claim mental-health problems as part of their defense in capital crimes. Underreporting of psychopathology is commonly found in family custody evaluations in which the examinee is attempting to present very positive and favorable adjustment characteristics; thus, he or she answers question in such a way that psychological problems are denied or minimized (Baer, Wetter, & Berry, 1992; Baer, Wetter, Nichols, Greene, & Berry, 1995). In other types of forensic cases (e.g., claiming physical injury in personal injury cases or pleading insanity in a not guilty by reason of insanity case), overreporting of symptoms is more common.

VALIDITY SCALE INTERPRETATION GUIDELINES

One of the most crucial considerations in forensic psychological assessment is to determine the extent of cooperation the examinee has shown in responding to the items on the test. Did the individual respond to all the items? Were the items endorsed in a consistent manner? Were any response sets evident in the pattern of item responding; for example, did the examinee respond in an all true or mostly true or an all false or mostly false manner? Did the examinee attempt to provide an extremely positive or overly virtuous view of his or her personality adjustment that is not credible? Did the examinee attempt to appear more psychologically disturbed or disabled than he or she actually is or to influence the outcome of the evaluation? These and other response set approaches can be effectively evaluated by examination of the MMPI–2 validity scales that are briefly described below. A number of sources can be consulted to obtain more detailed and up-to-date information about assessing MMPI–2 protocol validity (see Butcher, 2011; A. F. Friedman, Bolinskey, Lewak, & Nichols, 2014; Greene, 2011; Pope, Butcher, & Seelen, 2006). The interpretive cutoff scores for the scales included below are consistent with the MMPI–2 manual recommendations (Butcher et al., 2001).

Omitted Items or Cannot Say Scores

The items in the MMPI–2 booklet are written in such a way that either a true or a false response to all the items would be appropriate and relevant to anyone. Persons with a sixth-grade reading level typically do not have a problem understanding the item content, and item omissions are both unusual and unnecessary. Yet, some people omit items, particularly in situations such as personnel selection and forensic settings in which disclosure of information can be viewed as harmful to the person. At the end of the test administration, the forensic psychologist should verify that the examinee has responded to all of the items on the test and has not failed to cooperate with the instructions to answer all of the items. If an examinee fails to endorse any of the items, particularly if a substantial number of items are left blank, the scores on the test will likely be attenuated and suggestive of an uncooperative response pattern. If the examinee fails to comply with the instructions to respond to all of the items, the specific omitted items should be evaluated further. The content of the deleted items can be of particular value in understanding the examinee's concerns; for example, 12 items dealing with family problems were left unanswered in a case of family abuse. The content of unanswered items can often provide important clues to the examinee's motivation or to personality problems that could underlie the invalidating conditions.

Incomplete records can make an MMPI–2 protocol uninterpretable. If the examinee has failed to answer 30 or more items the test is generally considered invalid, although some research (Berry et al., 1997) has found that scales and code types might not be affected with lower levels of the Cannot Say score. Rather than using a 30-item cutoff score to invalidate a protocol, the psychologist can explore further by determining whether each scale has actually been affected by ensuring that all or most of the items on the scale were endorsed. Some computer-scoring programs provide the exact percentage of items endorsed on each scale and thus show those scales that might be impacted by the unanswered items.

Omitted items can be interpreted as follows:

- If the examinee has omitted fewer than six items, the profile is likely to be valid and interpretable.
- If the examinee has omitted between seven and 29 items throughout the item pool, some of the MMPI–2 clinical and validity scales may be invalid.

- The profile is likely invalid if the examinee has omitted 30 or more items throughout the item pool.
- If the examinee has omitted items only at the end of the booklet, information might be sufficient for interpreting the clinical scales and the L, F, and K validity scales because these measures occur in the first 370 items.

All True or All False Response Set

The items on MMPI–2 are written in such a manner as to have an almost equal percentage of both true and false responses that are scored in the pathological direction. That is, the MMPI items were framed in such a way that the pathological direction of scoring would be reflected in a "true" and others in a "false" direction. In general, test takers who respond in either predominantly a true or a false direction usually produce invalid protocols. If about 25% or less of the items are endorsed in either the true or false direction, the protocol is likely to be invalid. Responding to all or most of the items by endorsing the majority of items as true or false is a somewhat uncommon but uncooperative approach to the MMPI–2. However, this approach is occasionally encountered when some individuals try to make a point that they have "no problems" by using the false option or that they are "very sick" by endorsing true, but want to appear as though they completed the examination. Some test takers who want to comply partially with the test will endorse a few items—for example, the first one in each column—in one direction (for example, true) and the remainder in the false direction.

The testing time for this approach to the inventory is usually much quicker than when the examinee actually reads the items. The psychologist should review the examinee's answer sheet carefully. A simple visual inspection of the answer sheet can often reveal these uncooperative response patterns to confirm deviant response approaches.

VRIN and *TRIN*: Measures of Inconsistent Responding

Some test takers do not respond to personality questionnaire items in a consistent manner. A valuable approach to determining the credibility of a person's approach to the items is to examine whether the person has been consistent in responses to items that contain similar content. The evaluation of inconsistent responding to personality questionnaire items is relatively easy to detect if the inventory contains enough items to have some content that is of similar or opposite meaning. The MMPI–2 includes two scales for detecting inconsistent responding to the items: the Variable Response Inconsistency scale (*VRIN*) and the True Response Inconsistency scale (*TRIN*). The scales operate in a similar manner but address different issues.

The *VRIN* scale is a good measure of random responding on the MMPI–2. The *VRIN* is made up of 67 pairs of items for which one or two out of four possible configurations (true–false, false–true, true–true, and false–false) represent inconsistent responses. For example, answering true to a question such as "I usually feel well rested most mornings when I wake up" and true to "I often find that I cannot sleep at night" represents semantically inconsistent responding. The *VRIN* score is the total number of inconsistent responses on the scale.

Inconsistent scores in the true direction on *VRIN* can be interpreted as follows:

- *VRIN* scores between, at, or below a *T* score of 39 are considered to be in an acceptable range of infrequent responding. The examinee may be extremely cautious in responding to items.
- *VRIN* scores between 40 *T* and 64 *T* are considered to be in an acceptable range of infrequent responding.
- *VRIN* scores between 65 *T* and 79 *T* are considered to be valid but suggest some tendency for an inconsistent response set that should be evaluated further.
- *VRIN* scores above 80 *T* are likely to be invalid and to show an extreme number of inconsistently endorsed items. The MMPI–2 profiles are not considered interpretable.

The *TRIN* scale has a somewhat different focus. The scale was developed as a way of evaluating the tendency that some respondents have of endorsing items inconsistently by responding to a number of items as true or false. *TRIN* is made up of 23 pairs of items to which the same response is semantically inconsistent. For example, answering the items "Most of the time I feel moody" and "I am almost always happy" as both true or both false is inconsistent.

If the examinee's *TRIN* *T* score is in the elevated direction (usually *T* > 80), the examinee has endorsed several of the items inconsistently in the true direction. If the *TRIN* score is in the false direction (*F*), the test interpreter can conclude that the person has responded inconsistently in the false direction. Both *VRIN* and *TRIN* have been shown to be effective at detecting invalidating conditions as a result of inconsistent responding (M. E. Clark, Gironda, & Young, 2003).

Inconsistent scores in the true direction on *TRIN* can be interpreted as follows:

- *TRIN* scores between 50 *T* and 64 *T* are considered to be in an acceptable range of infrequent responding.

- *TRIN* scores between 65 *T* and 79 *T* are considered to be valid but suggest some tendency for an all true response set.
- *TRIN* scores above 80 *T* are likely to be invalid and to show an extreme number of inconsistently endorsed true items. The MMPI–2 profiles are not considered interpretable.

Inconsistent scores in the false direction on *TRIN* can be interpreted as follows:

- *TRIN* scores between 50 *F* and 64 *F* are considered to be in an acceptable range of infrequent responding.
- *TRIN* scores between 65 *F* and 79 *F* are considered to be valid but suggest some tendency for an all false response set.
- *TRIN* scores above 80 *F* are likely to be invalid and to show an extreme number of inconsistently endorsed false items. The MMPI–2 profiles are not considered interpretable.

Infrequent Responding: The *F*, Back *F*, and *Fp* Scales

One of the most long-standing, valuable, and widely studied approaches to protocol validity assessment is the evaluation of infrequent responding to the test items. Individuals who are exaggerating their symptom picture tend to endorse a large number of items that are rarely endorsed. The MMPI *F* scale was developed by Hathaway and McKinley (1942a) as a means of detecting invalid records by examining the endorsement of infrequently endorsed items. The value of the *F* scale in detecting symptom exaggeration prompted the MMPI revision/restandardization project to keep this measure (with slight item editing and deletion of four items with religious content that were not continued into MMPI–2) and to develop a second infrequency scale, the Back *F* scale, to address symptom exaggeration occurring toward the end of the item pool (the original *F* items were largely contained in the first 370 items in the booklet; Butcher, Dahlstrom, Graham, Tellegen, & Kaemmer, 1989). Finally, a third infrequency scale, the Infrequency Psychopathology scale, was developed in accordance with a somewhat different strategy: using psychiatric patients to develop a scale that provided a comparison of rare or infrequently addressed symptoms occurring in psychiatric samples rather than the normal population.

Infrequency: F Scale

The underlying development strategy for the construction of the *F* scale reflected Hathaway and McKinley's view that people who attempt to present a more disturbed picture of their symptoms tend to claim an excessive number of rare and unusual symptoms that most people do not acknowledge.

They developed the *F* scale empirically by determining the frequency of item responses to the MMPI item pool that the normative sample endorsed. They defined "rare" as item endorsement by less than 10% of the population. People who endorsed a high percentage of these rarely endorsed items were thought to be exaggerating their symptoms.

The *F* scale has also been shown to be sensitive to patterns of non-content-oriented responding, such as answering in a careless manner or without attending to the item content by simply endorsing items in a random manner. The random response pattern to MMPI–2 items can be readily detected by the *F* scale. The *F* scale contains 60 items; thus, a random performance would result in about half of the *F* items being endorsed. Invalid protocols can also be found in situations in which the test taker gets mixed up or is unable to read and comprehend the items. For example, immigrant examinees who have low English-language skills can produce high elevations on the *F* scale.

The *F* scale has been shown to be one of the most effective means of detecting exaggerated or malingered responding to personality test items (Bagby, Buis, & Nicholson, 1995). The MMPI–2 manual (Butcher et al., 2001) provides interpretive guidelines for clinical inpatients, clinical outpatients, and non-clinical settings. The following guidelines are suggested for use in interpreting the *F* scale elevations in evaluating the credibility of the examinee's responding in diverse forensic applications:

- *F* scores below 54 are considered to be in an acceptable range of infrequent responding. This range of *F* scores can be found with defensive responding.
- *F* scores below 79 are considered to be in an acceptable range of infrequent responding.
- *F* scores between 80 and 89 show moderate responding to infrequently endorsed items. Many people with mental-health problems score in this range. Exaggerated responding can occur, though symptom profiles are likely valid.
- Scores on the *F* scale between 90 and 99 *T* are considered to reflect exaggerated symptom presentation. Extremely high *F* scores are typically found in protocols of test takers who are exaggerating psychiatric symptoms, and the profile may be invalid. However, some genuine psychiatric patients score in this extreme range.
- Scores on the *F* scale between 100 and 109 *T* strongly suggest an exaggerated symptom presentation. The clinical profile is likely invalid.
- Scores greater than $T = 110$ are likely to be associated with individuals falsely claiming mental-health symptoms. The clinical profile is clearly invalid and not interpretable.

Infrequency: The Back F Scale (FB)

The *FB* scale comprises 40 items that are scattered throughout the last part of the MMPI–2 booklet. Thus, the *FB* scale does not address problems of infrequent responding with the MMPI–2 clinical scales because these items appear in the first 370 items. The *FB* scale is most valuable in determining whether there has been infrequent responding on scales (such as the content scales and supplemental scales) that contain items throughout the item pool. The following guidelines are suggested for use in interpreting the *FB* scale elevations:

- *FB* scores below 79 are considered to be in an acceptable range of infrequent responding on the items at the end of the MMPI–2 item pool.
- *FB* scores between 80 and 89 show moderate responding to infrequently endorsed items. Exaggerated responding is possible, but the profile is likely valid.
- Scores on the *FB* scale between 90 and 99 *T* are considered to reflect exaggerated symptom presentation. Extremely high *FB* scores are typically found in protocols of test takers who are exaggerating psychiatric symptoms, and the profile may be invalid. However, some genuine psychiatric patients score in this extreme range.
- Scores on the *FB* scale between 100 and 109 *T* strongly suggest an exaggerated symptom presentation. The content scale profile is likely invalid and is not interpretable.
- Scores greater than *T* = 110 are likely to be associated with individuals falsely claiming mental-health symptoms. The content scales profile is clearly invalid and is not interpretable.

The Infrequency Psychopathology Scale (Fp)

As noted above, the *Fp* scale was developed with a different comparative sample (clinical patients rather than normal individuals) than the *F* and *FB* scales, and the interpretive strategy is different (Arbisi & Ben-Porath, 1995). The *Fp* scale assesses infrequent responding to items that are rarely endorsed by clinical inpatients. Thus, the *Fp* items are highly unusual items for even examinees with severe mental-health problems to endorse. The following guidelines are suggested for use in interpreting the *Fp* scale elevations:

- *Fp* scores below 69 are considered to be in an acceptable range of infrequent responding.
- *Fp* scores between 70 and 99 show exaggerated responding to infrequently endorsed items. The profile may be invalid.
- Scores on the *Fp* scale greater than 100 strongly suggest an exaggerated symptom presentation. The clinical profile is likely invalid.

The K Scale (Defensiveness)

The *K* scale on the original MMPI was developed by Meehl and Hathaway (1946) as a method for detecting patients who were being overly defensive and were responding to the items in a manner suggesting they were extremely well adjusted. The *K* scale was developed empirically by examining the item responses of a sample of psychiatric patients who produced a normal range profile and were assumed to be defensive on the test. The *K* scale is made up of 30 items that address the denial of problems and claiming of overly positive attributes. The *K* scale has been demonstrated by numerous studies to effectively discriminate people who approach the MMPI–2 items in a highly defensive manner (e.g., Baer, Wetter, Nichols, et al., 1995; Bagby, Marshall, Bury, Bacchiochi, & Miller, 2006; Meehl & Hathaway, 1946; Ruch & Ruch, 1967). For an extensive listing of research on the *K* scale, see Butcher (2011).

The *K* scale was also used to correct the profile by adding points (referred to as the *K* correction) to five MMPI clinical scales in order to compensate for the individual's defensiveness. A percentage of the *K* scale was found to improve the effectiveness of some scales in detecting psychopathology. The *K* percentages, known as *K* weights, used in the *K* correction were derived to improve the discrimination of cases in a psychiatric setting. Five clinical scales were thought to be improved by adding a portion of *K*: Hypochondriasis, Psychopathic Deviate, Psychasthenia, Schizophrenia, and Mania. Research has demonstrated that the *K* scale corrections improved the empirical discrimination (Putzke, Williams, Daniel, & Boll, 1999). This approach to correcting the profile for defensiveness has been widely used with the MMPI for decades, and most of the research on the MMPI and MMPI–2 has relied upon *K*-corrected profiles. Some research, however, has found that the correction does not improve empirical discrimination over non-*K*-corrected scores (Archer, Fontaine, & McCrae, 1998; Sines, Baucom, & Gruba, 1979; Weed, 1993).

Although the *K* correction, developed by Meehl and Hathaway (1946), does not function as effectively in improving discrimination as the original authors intended, the practice of correcting for *K* in interpreting profiles still continues in MMPI–2 use because much of the empirical research supporting test interpretation of the clinical scales involves *K*-corrected scores. Although researchers have been encouraged to incorporate non-*K*-corrected scores into their research analyses to evaluate further the relative effectiveness of the two approaches and to build a strong database for empirically based interpretation (Butcher, Graham, & Ben-Porath, 1995; Butcher & Tellegen, 1978), most existing research involves the use of *K*-corrected *T* scores (Wooten, 1984). Much of the research has often demonstrated that there are no differences between *K*-corrected and non-corrected scores when external criteria (therapist's ratings) are used to verify their accuracy (Barthlow, Graham,

Ben-Porath, Tellegen, & McNulty, 2002). When the non-K and K-corrected profiles differ, the forensic psychologist would likely have a stronger research base supporting the K-corrected rather than the non-K-corrected profile, because much of the empirical research has used this approach.

The following guidelines are suggested for use in interpreting the K scale elevations:

- K scale scores at or below 39 T may occur as a result of extreme endorsement of items in the pathological direction with high scores on F.
- K scale scores greater than 40 T but less than 64 T are likely valid.
- K scale scores between 65 and 69 show test defensiveness and possibly invalid profiles.
- K scale scores greater than 70 show extreme test defensiveness and suggest that profiles are likely invalid.

It is important for the forensic test interpreter to keep in mind that the K scale operates successfully as a sign that the person has approached the self-report task in an overly evasive and socially desirable way. When T scores reach the level of 70 or higher, caution should be taken in making decisions about the examinee's personality. Defensive profiles in this range should not be interpreted, because interpretive errors can occur in profiles that have had a lot of K added to them. Keep in mind two key factors: When the elevation on the K scale exceeds a T of 70, one can never feel confident that the examinee has cooperated with the evaluation. Therefore, the most cautious approach is not to rely on the clinical scales in defensive profiles. The interpreter needs also to be aware that, in some cases when K is elevated, clinical scale elevations (e.g., on K-corrected scales such as Schizophrenia or Psychasthenia) can be accounted for by the elevation on K alone. That is, the person may have actually endorsed few of the empirical items on the scale.

The Lie (L) Scale

In some forensic applications, examinees attempt to present a highly favorable view of their psychological adjustment in order to influence the outcome of the court proceedings. For example, it is quite common for parents in family custody disputes to proclaim extensive virtues on the MMPI–2 items in order to gain or retain custody of their children. Moreover, in some personal injury cases, litigants may attempt to show how honest and virtuous they are in an effort to make their physical complaint pattern more acceptable. For information about the frequency of MMPI–2 validity scores in various forensic settings, see Butcher (1997).

The L scale is a 15-item measure that addresses minor flaws or faults that most people are willing to admit. However, people who are attempting to appear virtuous and "without fault" do not endorse these items. A high score on the L scale indicates that the examinee is unwilling to admit to any personal faults in an effort to appear more virtuous than the average person. The L scale has a long tradition of use and a substantial research base supporting its value in detecting people who distort their MMPI responding to present favorably (Baer, Wetter, Nichols, et al., 1995). Examinees with elevated L scale scores are likely described as attempting to create an unrealistically favorable impression, being overly virtuous in self-view, minimizing personal flaws, lacking in insight, lacking in psychological sophistication, and likely showing rigid neurotic adjustment.

The following guidelines are suggested for use in interpreting L scale elevations:

- L scores below 64 are considered to be in an acceptable range of responding. This range of L scores is considered valid, and the profiles are interpretable.
- L scores between 65 and 79 show overly virtuous claims. The clinical profile may be invalid due to defensiveness.
- Scores on the L scale greater than 80 strongly suggest a clearly exaggerated pattern of overly favorable self-presentation. The clinical profile is likely invalid.

The Superlative Self-Presentation Scale

The K scale contains only 30 items and addresses the item responses only within the first 370 or so items. With the inclusion of a large number of new items on the MMPI–2 it became possible to reexamine the potential of the MMPI–2 to assess defensive responding and to possibly examine more closely the different strategies of self-presentation that individuals employ. The Superlative Self-Presentation Scale (S scale) was developed by Butcher and Han (1995) as a means of further examining defensiveness on the test. They employed a known sample of highly defensive airline pilots to contrast with the MMPI–2 normative sample to empirically develop a defensiveness scale. The S scale contains 50 items that differentiated the defensive applicants from the normative sample. The S scale was shown to assess the tendency of some test takers in personnel screenings to claim positive attributes, high moral values, and high responsibility and to deny having adjustment problems. People who score high on S endorse very few minor faults and problems as compared to the MMPI–2 restandardization sample. The S scale is highly correlated with K (.81 for men and .82 for women in the MMPI–2 normative sample).

Further research found that high scores on S were associated with lower levels of symptom reporting and the admission of fewer negative personality characteristics than in even the normative sample report (Sirigatti & Giannini, 2000, 2007). High scores are also associated with extreme endorsement of items addressing self-control in test takers by people who know them. High S responders are also viewed by their spouses as emotionally well controlled and generally free of pathological behavioral features. The larger pool of items on the S scale allows the forensic psychologist to examine different content areas that constitute the S. The items on the S scale were item-factor analyzed. Five component scales emerged:

1. *Beliefs in Human Goodness*. This subscale comprises items that acknowledge unrealistically positive values or goals. High scorers tend to endorse vague and overly positive attitudes about people.
2. *Serenity*. The Serenity subscale includes items that address feeling of being at peace with one's environment, such as having a characteristically low experience of stress and the tendency to never worry about anything.
3. *Contentment With Life*. The items on this subscale address having an extremely positive view of one's life situation and not having any self-doubts.
4. *Patience/Denial of Irritability and Anger*. These items address the view that the person never gets mad or becomes impatient with other people.
5. *Denial of Moral Flaws*. The items on this item cluster assert high moral values and the absence of habits, such as using marijuana or using alcohol excessively.

One important way in which S is thought to improve on K as a measure of test defensiveness is that this scale possesses a greater number of items (50), which allows for a breakdown of items into subscales with homogeneous content. Research has found that examinees in different situations endorse items differently as reflected in the component scales. Airline pilot applicants tended to elevate all five component scales; however, parents in child custody cases tended to elevate on the component subscales of Denial of Moral Flaws or Denial of Irritability.

The interpretive guidelines for the S scale are as follows:

- S scale scores less than 40 T can occur as a result of extreme endorsement of items in the pathological direction.
- S scale scores equal to or less than 64 T are likely valid.
- S scale scores between 65 and 69 show test defensiveness and possibly invalid profiles.
- S scale scores greater than 70 show a high degree of test defensiveness and suggest likely invalid profiles as a result of defensiveness.

FAILURE OF THE LEES-HALEY FAKE BAD SCALE (*FBS*) TO ASSESS MALINGERING

Interest in assessing malingering with psychological tests has prompted the development of a number of assessment measures aimed at discrediting the testing results of examinees in court cases. One measure using MMPI–2 items that has been highly controversial is the Fake Bad Scale (*FBS*) developed by Lees-Haley, English, and Glenn (1991). The *FBS* has been found to be problematic for use in court cases because of the likely bias against people with genuine physical problems, particularly women (Barr, Larson, Alper, & Devinsky, 2005; Butcher, Arbisi, Atlis, & McNulty, 2003; Butcher, Gass, Cumella, Kally, & Williams, 2008; C. L. Williams, Butcher, Gass, Cumella, & Kally, 2009).

In the development of the *FBS*, Lees-Haley et al. (1991) assumed that a very high percentage of people in litigation were actually malingering their symptoms and based the scale's development on the idea that certain MMPI–2 symptom items could identify such individuals. They rationally selected 43 MMPI–2 items for inclusion on the *FBS* using response records of litigants from Lees-Haley's forensic practice that they considered to be malingering (Lees-Haley et al., 1991). Lees-Haley had published another group of "signs, symptoms, and complaints" called the Litigation Response Syndrome (*LRS*), 3 years earlier (Lees-Haley, 1988) to address anxiety that many people encounter during the process of litigation. He actually used a significant proportion of the *LRS* items (23 out of 43, or 53%) for the *FBS* in 1991, even though the constructs were, conceptually, measuring different behavior patterns.

The scale construction strategy that Lees-Haley and colleagues followed in developing the *FBS* differed substantially from the empirical scale derivation of the infrequency validity scales used on the MMPI–2 (*F*, *FB*, and *Fp*). The *FBS* items were not subjected to empirical verification that other validity scales have undergone. Many of the *FBS* symptom items are actually found in people with physical disabilities and mental-health problems such as posttraumatic stress disorder. For example, one third of the items on the *FBS* scale include commonly endorsed somatic complaints (e.g., headaches, fatigue), and other items are symptoms of posttraumatic stress problems (e.g., nightmares). The significant item overlap that the *FBS* items has with several MMPI–2 symptom scales (i.e., the *Hs*, *Hy*, and *HEA* scales in Chapter 3) thus results in high false positive classification rates (Butcher, Arbisi, et al., 2003; Gass, Williams, Cumella, Butcher, & Kally, 2010; C. L. Williams et al., 2009) and assures that people who acknowledge having physical disabilities or stress-related problems score high on the *FBS*. Therefore, people with physical or stress-related symptoms, such as having headaches, can be labeled as "faking" (Law, Schulz, Butcher, Lo, & Ng, 2014).

A recent empirical evaluation of the *FBS* in a Veterans Administration neuropsychological evaluation population provided clear evidence that the *FBS* addresses genuine clinical symptoms rather than "faking bad." Gass and Odland (2014) studied the psychometric characteristics of the *FBS* in a sample of 303 medical patients undergoing a comprehensive neuropsychological evaluation. They identified three prominent sets of characteristics with *FBS*: Factor 1 (Tiredness and Distractibility) was composed of 11 items that focus upon poor concentration, distractibility, tiredness, and low energy; Factor 2 (Stomach and Head Discomfort) was composed of 12 items that address complaints of stomach discomfort, nausea, and headache; and Factor 3 (Claimed Virtue of Self and Others) consisted of 11 items that reflect assertions of truth-telling, altruism, and optimistic views of other people's behavior.

A. F. Friedman et al. (2014) pointed out that the construct validity of the *FBS* has been questioned by a number of researchers. For example, Butcher, Arbisi, et al. (2003) found that, in large samples of psychiatric inpatients, the *FBS* consistently achieved lower correlations with *F*, *FB*, and *Fp*. Guéz, Brännström, Nyberg, Toolanen, and Hildingsson (2005) pointed out the lack of a significant relationship between *FBS* and *F* and *F-K*. A. F. Friedman et al. (2014) also pointed out that the weak construct validity of the *FBS* is shown by a very limited item overlap between *FBS* and two other recent MMPI–2 measures. One of these, the Response Bias scale (*RBS*; Gervais, Ben-Porath, Wygant, & Green, 2007), was constructed to predict failure on neurocognitive symptom validity tests, and the other, the Infrequent Somatic Complaints scale (*Fs*; Wygant, 2008), was designed to measure somatic complaints infrequently endorsed by personal injury and disability claimants with histories of head injuries. *FBS* overlaps *RBS* by only four items and *Fs* by three items, and *RBS* overlaps *Fs* by two items. Thus, the average overlap among these three symptom validity measures is only two items over their average 29-item length (10%), which is unusual for scales purporting to measure such similar constructs.

Moreover, a number of the *FBS* items have a higher endorsement rate for women than for men (e.g., experiencing hot flashes). Thus, there is a potential for gender bias found in the *FBS* scale if the same cutoff scores are used for men and women (i.e., nongendered *T* scores; Butcher, Arbisi, et al., 2003; Dean et al., 2008; Gass et al., 2010; Nichols, Williams, & Greene, 2009). Nichols et al. evaluated the differential response rate of men and women to *FBS* items across 49 samples of participants (78,159) from a broad range of mental health, medical, forensic, personnel, and normative samples to further examine potential gender bias in the scale. They found that many items on the *FBS* show different response patterns for men and for women.

Despite its psychometric problems, the *FBS* (rebranded as the Symptom Validity Scale by the test publisher) continues to be used in personal injury litigation claims and compensation evaluations to address the credibility of examinees' test responses as a means of evaluating the legitimacy of their claims. Moreover, a shortened version of the FBS, the FBS–r, has been added as a key validity measure on the newly published MMPI–2—Revised Form (Tellegen & Ben-Porath, 2008; discussed in Chapter 14). As yet, there have not been published studies that document or verify the utility of the FBS in detecting invalid performance of examinees who are actually malingering. Research has shown that the FBS likely overpredicts "malingering," because patients who are in mental health or health treatment settings (not in litigation) tend to produce high FBS scores (for example, patients with eating disorder; Butcher et al., 2008; Gass et al., 2010; C. L. Williams et al., 2009). Patients with physical problems or disabilities can be adversely affected by inferences that are derived from high scores on the FBS.

Gass and Odland (2012) showed that the FBS–r has two underlying dimensions rather than a single dimension addressing malingering. Persons taking the test can produce an identical high score on the FBS–r for two different reasons: either by consistently denying cynicism and antisocial behavior or by reporting multiple symptoms of anxiety and depression. The Factor of Optimism/Virtue (seven items) was related negatively to the Factor of Somatic Complaints (21 items). FBS–r scores, which purportedly reflect symptom exaggeration, are affected by as much as 23 T-score points on test items that are negatively related to symptom reporting.

Other recent studies have shown further problems with the FBS. Hapidou and Kritikos (2010) focused on determining the effect of litigation on the FBS elevation and identifying differences in outcomes of a 4-week chronic pain management program according to litigation status. They postulated that if the FBS could detect malingering, it would be higher in patients who are in litigation related to their pain problems than in those not in litigation. Moreover, they expected that patients in litigation would report less successful outcomes than would patients not in litigation. They collected data on the MMPI–2 and outcome measures on 288 consecutive chronic pain patients. All litigating patients were funded by their motor-vehicle accident (MVA) insurance companies, as they had been injured in accidents. All nonlitigating patients were funded by the Worker's Safety and Insurance Board as a result of work injuries. Thus, their comparisons addressed behavior resulting from two different sources of funding. Hapidou and Kritikos found that the elevations were significantly higher on FBS and the Hs, D, Hy, and Pt scales for the MVA patients. There were no significant differences between the two groups on positive progress in the program, because all patients experienced the same amount of help from the program regardless of funding source. Hapidou and Kritikos concluded from these results that the FBS cannot be used as a measure of malingering in chronic pain patients. They also concluded that the FBS seems to measure general distress, with insurance-funded auto accident patients suffering more distress than the work injury patients.

Cutoff Scores for the FBS

The use of specific cutoff scores for assessing malingering with the FBS has been a moving target both in past research and in court evaluations. Lees-Haley et al. (1991) initially suggested that a cutoff score for malingering should be a raw score of 20. This recommended cutoff score was increased to 22 in 1992 to reduce the number of false positives (Lees-Haley, 1992). Other shifts in the cutoff score have resulted from criticisms over the high false positive rates; however, the original recommendation of 20 raw score points is still used in some court cases. Greiffenstein, Fox, and Lees-Haley (2007) recommended a variety of cutoff scores depending upon various circumstances. The test publisher (Pearson Assessments, 2007) and the developers of the FBS test manual (Ben-Porath, Graham, & Tellegen, 2009) essentially follow the cutoff score recommendations of Greiffenstein et al. (2007). Ben-Porath, Graham, and Tellegen (2009) recommended the following guidelines for characterizing possible or likely malingering: A raw score of 23 (80 T) or higher for males and a raw score of 26 (80 T) or higher for females for "possible malingering"; a raw score of 30 (100 T score) or higher for men and women for "likely malingering," as recommended by the test publisher.

The FBS has been excluded from use in several court cases, in large part because of the scale's high false positive classification rate and the court's concerns that the FBS is not an objective measure of malingering, exaggerating, or overreporting of symptoms for labeling litigants as "malingering" (*Anderson v. E & S Enterprises*, 2008; *Davidson v. Strawberry Petroleum*, 2007; *Limbaugh-Kirker v. Dicosta*, 2009; *Rodriguez v. Miller Coors*, 2012; *Stith v. State Farm Mutual Insurance*, 2008; *Vandergracht v. Progressive Express*, 2007; *Williams v. CSX Transportation*, 2007). For example, in *Williams v. CSX Transportation* (2007), Judge Bergmann of the Circuit Court of the Thirteenth Judicial Circuit in and for Hillsborough County, Florida, concluded as follows:

> The Court concludes that the FBS is very subjective and dependent on the interpretation of the person using or interpreting it. There is no definitive scoring because the scoring has to be adjusted up and down based on the circumstances and there is a high degree of probability for false positives. Moreover, the scoring assessment has changed over the years from an original cut score of 20 in 1991, with recommended interpretive scores now ranging from 23 to 30; this coupled with the acknowledged bias against women and those with demonstrated serious injuries makes the FBS unreliable.

Despite exclusions of the *FBS* from several court cases and the scale's psychometric weakness, some proponents of its use in personal injury litigation continue to assert its value as a means of detecting malingered responding (Ben-Porath, Graham, & Tellegen, 2009; Ben-Porath, Greve, Bianchini, & Kaufmann, 2009, 2010; Greiffenstein et al., 2007).

Although the false positive research and adverse court decisions have informed many psychologists about the problems with using the *FBS*, the scale continues to be used (in some instances in subtle ways, such as rebranding with a new name: the Symptom Validity Scale; Ben-Porath, Greve, et al., 2009) or included in "indexes" in combination with other scales (Meyers, Millis, & Volkert, 2002). Practitioners need to be aware that this scale can result in examinees being considered to be "faking" when they are not.

We do not recommend the use of the *FBS* to arrive at conclusions about whether an examinee is "faking" symptoms in court cases. The above discussion about the *FBS* was included in this book to call attention to the controversy in the event psychologists are considering using this measure in their MMPI–2 based evaluation.

FACTORS TO CONSIDER IN INTERPRETING VALIDITY SCALES IN FORENSIC EVALUATIONS

Although the MMPI–2 is the most widely used personality assessment instrument and provides generally well-accepted interpretive hypotheses, psychologists need to be aware of a number of issues when incorporating validity scale interpretations in their evaluation. We highlight some pertinent issues.

Certain Response Sets Can Be Anticipated in Some Forensic Applications

Forensic psychologists need to be aware that some types of response distortions by examinees in forensic settings (e.g., high *L* scale in custody cases or high *F* scores in NGRI pleas) are common, given examinees' efforts to influence their case outcome. Such response sets are not specific to the MMPI–2 but would likely be a strong component in all measures administered, including the interview. There is a temptation on the part of forensic psychologists in some cases to simply retest examinees and warn them that their invalidating responses can be detected. There is some research support for this procedure in personnel selection settings. Retesting of an examinee who produced an invalid record has been found to be valuable for obtaining a usable personality protocol in instances in which test defensiveness has invalidated a test. Most of the studies on using the test–retest method have been conducted in health care (Walfish, 2007, 2011) and personnel settings (Butcher, Gucker, & Hellervik, 2009; Butcher, Morfitt, Rouse, & Holden, 1997; Cigrang & Staal, 2001) and not in forensic settings, although this approach has been seen in some court cases as well. Retesting examinees who have produced an invalid protocol would likely result in a more honest self-appraisal. However, retesting under altered instructions has not been sufficiently verified in forensic research to support it in court cases. It is important to keep in mind that the interpretation of MMPI–2 scores is based upon comparison to the normative sample (Butcher et al., 1989). The instructions used in establishing the MMPI–2 norms did not include providing the test taker with information about the test containing validity scales that "watch over the protocol validity." Forensic psychologists need to be aware that the retest method has not been sufficiently validated in forensic settings to warrant its use in court at this time.

The forensic psychologist needs to be aware that an examinee who follows an extreme response approach, such as claiming excessive virtue, is likely engaging in a pattern of symptom reporting that is not meaningful. This response approach is particularly problematic in cases where the scales comprise obvious content, such as the content-based measures. Defensive responding, as reflected in L or K scale elevations, is commonly associated with generally lower MMPI–2 content scales. Thus, the symptom scales are likely uninterpretable.

Influencing Test Results Through Coaching the Examinee

Some psychological test users or attorneys who employ them may attempt to influence the outcome of the examinee's results by modifying the test instructions or providing advice about how to respond to particular items. Standardized tests, like the MMPI–2, have very specific directions for the individual to follow in responding to the items. Alteration of or deviation from these directions can invalidate the results. Research has demonstrated that many forensic test takers are coached on how to respond to MMPI–2 items (Bagby, Nicholson, Bacchiochi, Ryder, & Bury, 2002; Wetter, Baer, Berry, & Reynolds, 1994; Wetter, Baer, Berry, Robinson, & Sumpter, 1993; Wetter & Corrigan, 1995). Other litigants search the Internet or contact MMPI–2 experts by e-mail to find information on how to respond to the test. Psychologists conducting forensic exams should inquire into what information the examinee has been provided about the various tests that are administered in order to determine whether possible "coaching factors" should be taken into consideration in the evaluation. Altered test instruction can result in invalid results that could be challenged in court cases.

What to Do About Conflicting Conclusions From Different Psychological Procedures?

What does the forensic psychologist do about conflicting malingering conclusions derived from different tests? When multiple measures of "malingering" are administered to an individual, it is not unusual to have a variety of conclusions, given the nature and the quality of measures available. In fact, Rosenfeld, Green, Pivovarova, Dole, and Zapf (2010) found that only about half of the conclusions from multiple measures were in agreement. What is the best approach for determining which ones were correct? Using multiple measures that have an established research base can be of clear benefit. Rosenfeld et al. found that the Structured Interview of Reported Symptoms (Rogers, Bagby, & Dickens, 1992) performed well at detecting malingering but that the MMPI–2 contributed significantly to detecting malingering.

Prior Testing, If Available, Can Be of Value in Understanding Invalid Protocols

The forensic psychologist might find that existing data could shed light on interpreting test results of examinees in court cases. The examinee may have been recently tested in a mental health or another forensic setting. The MMPI–2 protocol being evaluated in a forensic case may be only one of several that have been administered to the examinee in the past. It is often of value to obtain MMPI–2 records that may be available from a period prior to the current case.

Cultural Factors in Validity Scale Elevations

Some research has shown that ethnic minority clients might score somewhat higher than Caucasian examinees on MMPI–2 validity scales. Zapata-Sola, Kreuch, Landers, Hoyt, and Butcher (2009) found very similar clinical scale performance between Puerto Rican and U.S. employees in a personnel setting; however, there was a small difference (1.87 T-score points) on the L scale. In settings where test defensiveness is common, such as family custody evaluations, interpreters need to assure that the applicant's L score is within the interpretive range. Cultural factors in psychological test performance are discussed in further detail in Chapter 4.

Clinical Scales Cannot Serve as Validity Indicators

Some psychologists have been noted in court testimony to conclude that an examinee's test results are invalid because one of the clinical scales is extremely elevated. This mistaken conclusion has been made even though no validity scales were extremely elevated. They based their conclusion on the interpretation that the person responded "too extremely" on the *Hs* or *D* scale. There is no MMPI–2 research to support this conclusion. It is important to avoid using the elevation on MMPI–2 clinical scales as an indicator of malingering (see also discussion by Rogers & Granacher, 2011).

SUMMARY

People who are asked to describe their mental-health condition or personality attributes on psychological tests may make an effort to influence the outcome of the evaluation in their favor by responding in mendacious ways. They may respond by endorsing symptoms they do not have in order to appear disabled in personal injury claims or by denying even minor and common attributes to appear highly virtuous in family custody evaluations. Honest and accurate self-portrayal of symptoms and behavior, on the part of the examinee, is crucial in personality evaluations. It is important to include an appraisal of the examinee's response strategies to assure that the test results are interpretable.

One of the most crucial considerations in forensic psychological assessment is the need to determine the extent of cooperation the examinee has shown in responding to the test. The MMPI–2 provides one of the most comprehensive sets of measures to provide information about an examinee's response sets. Various non-content-based response approaches include omitting items (Cannot Say scores), endorsing randomly (*VRIN*) or answering in an all true or all false pattern (*TRIN*), responding in an infrequent manner to claim a high degree of mental health or physical symptoms (*F*, *FB*, or *Fp*), and responding defensively in order to make a good impression by appearing to have high virtue (*L*, *K*, or *S*).

It is important that standardized administration guidelines are followed and that validity scale interpretations are incorporated in the evaluation. Psychologists need to be aware that an examinee might have been coached on responding to test items in order to influence the outcome of the examinee's results. Moreover, psychologists need to be aware that multiple and conflicting approaches to validity evaluation might be included in a forensic evaluation. Some measures with insufficient research background or controversial results might be included by forensic consultants, resulting in courtroom challenges.

3

OVERVIEW OF THE MMPI–2 CLINICAL, CONTENT, AND SUPPLEMENTARY SCALES

Chapter 3 provides a brief overview of each of the Minnesota Multiphasic Personality Inventory—2 (MMPI–2) clinical, content, and supplementary scales in turn. More in-depth information on each of these scales is available in any of the standard MMPI–2 reference books (Butcher, 2011; Butcher & Williams, 2000; A. F. Friedman, Bolinskey, Lewak, & Nichols, 2014; Graham, 2012; Greene, 2011). It should be kept in mind that examinees are reporting their responses to the MMPI–2 items. The accuracy of this self-report will be affected by their insight into and awareness of their behavior, emotions, and thoughts and by their motivation in a specific forensic setting to report or not to report their behavior, emotions, and thoughts accurately. Thus, the interpretive statements for these scales must be understood as being hypotheses to be validated by the examinee's history and background. Throughout this chapter, a high score on a scale is defined as a T score of 65 or higher. A brief discussion of interpretation of code types, profiles in which more than one clinical scale is elevated, concludes the chapter.

http://dx.doi.org/10.1037/14571-004
Using the MMPI–2 in Forensic Assessment, by J. N. Butcher, G. A. Hass, R. L. Greene, and L. D. Nelson

This summary interpretation of each scale will be a general overview of each scale rather than an attempt to make the interpretation specific to the variety of forensic settings in which the MMPI–2 is used. Elevations on specific scales can provide the forensic examiner with indications of which areas should be reviewed with the examinee in the interview and the history and background information. It is particularly important to review those scales whose content is directly relevant to the psycholegal issue. For example, concerns about substance use/abuse can be explored in the Addiction Admission Scale (AAS) and the MacAndrew Alcoholism Scale—Revised. Similarly, concerns about family conflict can be explored on the Psychopathic Deviate and Family Problems scales. The rest of the book illustrates how these scales may be of utility in the different forensic areas.

It is important to consider the impact of the examinee's level of general subjective distress and negative affect and propensity to answer the items as true or false before making a specific interpretation of any of these scales. Table 3.1 provides the correlations of each of the clinical, content, and supplementary scales with the Welsh Anxiety (A) scale, which is an excellent measure of the examinee's level of general subjective distress and negative affect. There are two clinical scales (Psychasthenia [.95], Schizophrenia [.90]), three content scales (Anxiety [.90], Depression [.92], Work Interference [.93]), and two supplementary scales (College Maladjustment [.93], Posttraumatic Stress Disorder—Keane [.93]) that correlate greater than .90 with the A scale. Another five scales correlate greater than .80. The forensic examiner should see the importance of ensuring that these scales are at least 10 T points higher or lower than the A scale before making a scale-specific hypothesis. The forensic examiner also should realize that elevations on these scales are, despite their names, almost entirely due to general subjective distress.

Table 3.1 also provides the percentage of items that are scored true and false on each of the clinical, content, and supplementary scales. There are no clinical scales, six content scales (Obsessions [100.0%], Bizarre Mentation [95.7%], Anger [93.8%], Cynicism [100.0%], Antisocial Practices [95.5%], Type A [100.0%]), and two supplementary scales (Welsh Anxiety [97.4%], Hostility [94.0%]) for which more than 90% of the items have true as the deviant response. A general tendency of the examinee to endorse the items as true will elevate or as false will lower these scales irrespective of their item content.

Forensic examiners are cautioned not to interpret the Wiener and Harmon (Wiener, 1948) obvious–subtle subscales. Forensic examiners should make limited use of the R. E. Harris and Lingoes (1955) subscales or the content component scales (Ben-Porath & Sherwood, 1993) for the content scales,

TABLE 3.1

Correlations With Welsh Anxiety (*A*) Scale and Percentage of True and
False Items for the Clinical, Content, and Supplementary Scales

Scale type	Abbreviation	Welsh *A*	True %	False %
Clinical				
Hypochondriasis	*Hs* (1)	.72	34.4	65.6
Depression	*D* (2)	.75	35.1	64.9
Hysteria	*Hy* (3)	.43	22.8	78.2
Psychopathic Deviate	*Pd* (4)	.72	48.0	52.0
Masculinity–Femininity	*Mf* (5)	.12	44.6	55.4
Paranoia	*Pa* (6)	.66	62.5	37.5
Psychasthenia	*Pt* (7)	.95	81.2	18.8
Schizophrenia	*Sc* (8)	.90	75.6	24.4
Hypomania	*Ma* (9)	.44	76.1	23.9
Social Introversion	*Si* (0)	.81	52.2	47.8
Content				
Anxiety	ANX	.90	78.3	21.7
Fears	FRS	.53	69.6	3.4
Obsessions	OBS	.89	100.0	0.0
Depression	DEP	.92	84.8	15.2
Health Concerns	HEA	.70	38.9	61.1
Bizarre Mentation	BIZ	.66	95.7	4.3
Anger	ANG	.72	93.8	6.2
Cynicism	CYN	.64	100.0	0.0
Antisocial Practices	ASP	.51	95.5	4.5
Type A	TPA	.65	100.0	0.0
Low Self-Esteem	LSE	.87	87.5	12.5
Social Discomfort	SOD	.65	54.2	45.8
Family Problems	FAM	.66	80.0	20.0
Work Interference	WRK	.93	84.8	15.2
Negative Treatment	TRT	.88	88.5	11.5
Indicators				
Supplementary				
Welsh Anxiety	*A*		97.4	2.6
Welsh Repression	*R*	.00	0.0	100.0
Addiction Admission Scale	AAS	.43	76.9	23.1
Addiction Potential Scale	APS	.34	59.0	41.0
MacAndrew Alcoholism	MAC–R	.16	77.6	22.4
Ego Strength	*Es*	−.81	38.5	61.5
Dominance	*Do*	−.71	24.0	76.0
Social Responsibility	*Re*	−.53	20.0	80.0
College Maladjustment	*Mt*	.93	68.3	31.7
Posttraumatic Stress	PK	.93	82.6	17.4
Disorder—Keane				
Marital Distress Scale	MDS	.79	57.1	42.9
Hostility	*Ho*	.74	94.0	6.0
Overcontrolled Hostility	O-H	−.50	25.0	75.0
Gender Role—Masculine	GM	−.79	40.4	59.6
Gender Role—Feminine	GF	−.21	32.6	67.4

using them only to clarify information to the parent scales when the parent scales are elevated because of their lack of independent empirical support.

CLINICAL SCALES

Scale 1, Hypochondriasis (Hs)

The Hs scale focuses upon a wide variety of vague and nonspecific physical symptoms. The MMPI–2 items dealing with physical functioning tend to focus on the abdomen and back; the symptoms persist despite all reassurances and negative medical tests to the contrary. The reader should note that the *Diagnostic and Statistical Manual of Mental Disorders* (DSM–5; American Psychiatric Association, 2013) definition of hypochondriasis emphasizes the fear of or belief in the existence of a serious disease rather than unusual or excessive concern over physical functioning, which is the focus of the Hs scale. Nonspecific somatic symptoms might be considered a more appropriate description for the Hs scale.

Individuals who are actually physically ill tend to produce only a moderate elevation (T score of 55–60) on the Hs scale. They tend to endorse their specific physical symptoms, but they will not endorse the entire range of nonspecific physical symptoms tapped by the Hs scale. The D scale is more likely than the Hs scale to be elevated by physical illness. The relative elevation of the Hs scale above a T score of 65 is a rough measure of how firm or fixed examinees' beliefs are about their physical symptoms. The Hs scale can be understood as a characterological scale (i.e., it reflects a long-term personality style that is stable over time and resistant to change, with higher T scores reflecting individuals' excessive concern about their poor physical functioning).

Scale 2, Depression (D)

The D scale addresses symptomatic depression that is characterized by poor morale, lack of hope in the future, low mood, and general dissatisfaction with one's own status. The major content areas within the D scale focus upon a lack of interest in activities expressed as general apathy, physical symptoms such as sleep disturbances and gastrointestinal ailments, excessive sensitivity, and lack of sociability. The D scale is one of the most difficult clinical scales to interpret in isolation. An elevated score on the D scale reveals that the examinee is reporting general subjective distress and negative affect about something; however, the precise source of this distress and negative affect cannot be determined from the D scale elevation alone. Examinees with elevated scores on the D scale tend to be reporting their general subjective distress and negative affect due either to their current functioning or to circumstances.

Scale 3, Hysteria (Hy)

The Hy scale contains items from two general categories: (a) specific somatic symptoms, typically in the head, arms, and legs, and (b) positive appraisal of and attitudes toward oneself and others. It is imperative that the forensic examiner know which general category of items is contributing to the elevation on the Hy scale. The Harris–Lingoes subscales for the Hy scale can be helpful as an index of which of the two categories is being endorsed. The category of somatic symptoms is found in Hy_3 (Lassitude–Malaise) and Hy_4 (Somatic Complaints), and the category of positive appraisal of others is found in the remaining three subscales. There are 10 items on the Hy scale that overlap with the K scale, and they are scored in the same direction. When a non-K-corrected profile is constructed, the contribution of the K scale to the Hy scale cannot be removed directly because the items are within the Hy scale, not added as a fraction of K. The Spike 3 profile that is encountered frequently when a non-K-corrected profile is constructed reflects the contribution of these 10 items.

Hy high scorers are described as self-centered, immature, and infantile. They are demanding of attention and manipulative in interpersonal relations. They tend to be uninhibited and outgoing in their social relations, although they relate with others on a superficial and immature level.

Scale 4, Psychopathic Deviate (Pd)

The Pd scale addresses behavior problems such as negative interpersonal relations with family and authority figures and self- and social alienation. Some scale content addresses denial of social shyness and the assertion of social poise and self-confidence. The Pd scale does not directly assess psychopathy but rather problematic interpersonal relations, impulse control problems, and alienation. High scorers on the Pd scale are described as showing angry, impulsive, emotionally shallow, and unpredictable behaviors. They are socially nonconforming and disregard social rules and conventions in general and authority figures in particular. They tend to show resentment and hostility toward authority figures, which may or may not be overtly displayed. In the absence of a behavioral history of antisocial behavior, this hostility may have been directed inwardly toward the self. Thus, a marked elevation on the Pd scale indicates the presence of antisocial attitudes and behaviors, but it does not necessarily mean that these behaviors will be expressed openly.

Scale 5, Masculinity–Femininity (Mf)

The Mf scale focuses on several content areas of interests in vocations and hobbies, aesthetic preferences, activity–passivity, and personal sensitivity and restraint. Hathaway and McKinley (Hathaway, 1956) considered masculinity–femininity to be a bipolar dimension, with masculinity at one end and femininity at the other. H. Martin and Finn (2014) developed and established the reliability and validity of seven factors in Scale 5; specifically, denial of stereotypical masculine interests, hypersensitivity/anxiety, stereotypical feminine interests, low cynicism, aesthetic interests, feminine gender identity, and restraint. Their study supports a multidimensional bipolar model of masculinity–femininity and at the same time reveals that the scale measures the related dimension of gender identity. The Mf scale may have limited usefulness in a forensic setting because it does not address psychopathology.

Scale 6, Paranoia (Pa)

The Pa scale assesses several content areas relevant to forensic assessment, such as interpersonal sensitivity, moral self-righteousness, suspiciousness, and unusual ideation. The content of some of the items addresses blatantly psychotic behavior such as the existence of delusions and paranoid thought processes. However, these items are rarely endorsed; four of them are scored on the Infrequency Psychopathology (Fp) scale. High scorers on Pa are generally described as being suspicious, hostile, guarded, overly sensitive, argumentative, and prone to blame others. They often express their hostility overtly and rationalize it as a result of what others have done to them. In addition, an egocentric self-righteousness seems to permeate their behavior. Although they may not actually reflect a psychotic thought disorder, the paranoid suspicious behavior is evident. High-scoring clients believe that life is not fair and that they are getting a raw deal from life.

Scale 7, Psychasthenia (Pt)

The Pt scale assesses psychasthenia, a disorder that was prominently assessed when the MMPI was developed. This disorder is characterized by the person's inability to resist specific actions or thoughts regardless of their maladaptive nature (i.e., the person has weak ideational control that cannot resist these negative thoughts). This diagnostic label is no longer used, and such persons are now typically diagnosed as having obsessive–compulsive disorders. In addition to assessing obsessive-compulsive features, the Pt scale addresses the content areas of abnormal fears, self-criticism, difficulties in concentration, and guilt feelings. The item content does not reflect specific obsessions or compulsive rituals; rather, a characterologic basis for a wide variety of negative self-statements and negative affect is tapped. High scorers are examinees whose characteristic defenses of intellectualization, rationalization, and undoing are no longer capable of controlling their anxiety and tension. They tend to display an extreme concern over their physical functioning; their physical symptoms typically center around the cardiovascular system, although gastrointestinal symptoms are common. Their physical symptoms generally reflect their high anxiety levels and the effects of anxiety on their physical functioning.

Scale 8, Schizophrenia (Sc)

The Sc scale assesses a wide variety of content areas, including bizarre thought processes and peculiar perceptions, social alienation, poor familial relations, difficulties in concentration and impulse control, lack of deep interests, disturbing questions of self-worth and self-identity, and sexual difficulties. Because the total number of the items on the K scale endorsed in the deviant direction is added to the raw score on the Sc scale to plot a K-corrected profile, approximately 20 Sc scale items endorsed in the deviant direction are sufficient to produce a T score greater than 65 when the examinee has an average score (15) on the K scale. Consequently, an examinee can endorse any combination of 20 or more of the 78 items on the Sc scale to obtain a T score greater than 65. Thus, it is important to know the combination of items from the K and Sc scales that the examinee is endorsing to produce a specific T score. For example, men can obtain a T score of 74 by endorsing any combination of 40 items from the K scale and the Sc scale. A man who endorsed 30 items on the K scale and 10 items on the Sc scale will be very different from a man who endorsed five items on the K scale and 35 items on the Sc scale. The former individual has a non–K-corrected T score of 49 on Sc scale, whereas the latter individual has a non–K-corrected T score of 80.

Clients who score high on the Sc scale are typically described as cold, apathetic, alienated, and misunderstood and as having difficulties in thinking and communication, which may reflect an actual psychotic thought disorder. They believe that they are lacking qualities that are essential to being a real person. They tend to prefer engaging in daydreaming and fantasy to enjoying interpersonal relationships. They usually feel isolated, inferior, and self-dissatisfied. High scorers may appear confused and disoriented and may exercise poor judgment. They frequently display associated depressive features and psychomotor retardation. All of these behaviors may be the result of a schizophrenic process, other psychotic conditions, or severe and prolonged stress.

Scale 9, Mania (Ma)

The Ma scale examines a wide variety of content areas including behavioral and cognitive overactivity, grandiosity, egocentricity, and irritability. Scale elevations on the Ma scale reflect the milder degrees of manic excitement, characterized by an elated but unstable mood, psychomotor excitement, and flight of ideas. High scorers are described as being impulsive, competitive, talkative, narcissistic, amoral, extroverted, and superficial in social relations. They typically have problems in controlling their behavior and display hostile, irritable qualities. They are not usually described as depressed. However, they may display actual manic features: flight of ideas, lability of mood, delusions of grandeur, impulsivity, and hyperactivity.

Scale 0, Social Introversion (Si)

The Si scale addresses the social introversion–extroversion dimension, with high scores reflecting social introversion and low scores being associated with extroversion. The Si scale reflects personal discomfort in social situations, isolation, general maladjustment, and self-deprecation. High scorers are described as socially introverted, shy, and withdrawn. They also are considered to be insecure, pessimistic, self-deprecating, and anxious in their interactions with others. Clients with low scores on Si have been found to be extroverted and are described as sociable, friendly, and outgoing in relationships.

CONTENT SCALES

The MMPI–2 content scales (Butcher, Graham, Williams, & Ben-Porath, 1990) can be very useful in clinical settings, particularly when the client has responded in an open and cooperative manner. However, caution must be taken in incorporating the MMPI–2 content scales into a forensic evaluation because the scales are vulnerable to manipulation due to their generally obvious item content. The obvious content of the items makes it very easy for examinees to manipulate their responses in whatever manner is desired. Thus, the forensic examiner must consider carefully the issues of assessing validity that were described in Chapter 2.

The MMPI–2 content scales are organized around four themes: internal symptoms; external or aggressive tendencies; a devalued view of the self; and general problem areas. The internal symptoms cluster, the Anxiety, Fears, Obsessions, Depression, Health Concerns, and Bizarre Mentation scales, is oriented toward symptom disorders. The external or aggressive tendencies cluster, the Anger, Cynicism, Antisocial Practices, and Type A scales, is directed toward the personality-based disorders. The devalued view of the self-category contains only one scale: the Low Self-Esteem scale. The general problem areas assessed include the Social Discomfort, Family Problems, Work Interference, and Negative Treatment Indicators scales.

Anxiety (ANX)

The *ANX* scale focuses upon cognitive and affective aspects of anxiety rather than the behavioral and physiological components. The primary item content in the *ANX* scale is general distress. Clients who score high on the *ANX* scale tend to show excessive worries, nervous tension, disturbed sleep, and problems with attention and concentration. Their subjective stress levels already are so high that decisions and disappointments are felt to carry the risk of total mental fragmentation and collapse. People who score high tend to feel "stressed out" and carry a strong sense both of dread and of vulnerability to upset from almost any quarter. The client tends to feel that all events are potentially disastrous and devastating.

Fears (FRS)

The *FRS* content measure has no counterpart among the standard clinical scales of the MMPI–2 and shares few items with them or any of the other content or supplementary scales. As a result, the *FRS* scale is a unique measure of the presence or absence of fears in MMPI–2 scales. The words *fear, afraid, dread,* and *frightened* appear in more than three quarters of the items. The several groups of items include (a) specific fears of a classically phobic type (darkness, heights, open and closed spaces); (b) loss of physical integrity, particularly through germs and tissue damage; (c) admissions of general fearfulness and a low threshold for feeling fearful that is likely to be incapacitating; (d) animals such as mice, snakes, and spiders; and (e) natural phenomena such as earthquakes, lightning and storms, and fire and water. People who score high on the *FRS* scale show excessive fearfulness (Generalized Fearfulness [FRS_1]) of objects and circumstances in their environment. They generally are apprehensive, anxious, and easily frightened. They also may have more specific phobic concerns (Multiple Fears [FRS_2]) and somatic symptoms. These phobic concerns are multiple in nature when the FRS_2 scale is elevated, as men have to endorse six and women eight of the 10 items to get a T score of 60.

Obsessiveness (OBS)

This content scale addresses obsessive thinking. Individuals who score high on the *OBS* scale tend to have overly busy and quite inefficient cognitive processes. Their decision-making processes become overwhelmed. Moreover, they tend to show timidity, if not dread, when faced with the need to take practical action. They are insecure, anxious, and depressed.

Depression (DEP)

The DEP scale overlaps the D scale by only nine items, indicating that the two scales are likely to have somewhat different empirical correlates. All of the overlapping items are found on the Subjective Depression (D_1) scale, and eight of the nine appear on the Brooding (D_5) scale. Descriptions of being worthless and impotent, along with a view of the self as inadequate or inferior, are primary in the DEP scale but secondary in the D scale. On the other hand, other characteristics commonly found among highly depressed clients (e.g., psychomotor retardation, the inhibition of aggression, and vegetative symptoms such as sleep disturbance, anorexia, and weight loss) make up an important part of the D scale but are not addressed in the DEP scale. High scorers on the DEP content scale tend to report significant despair and a general loss of interest in life. They report feelings of fatigue, apathy, and exhaustion (Lack of Drive [DEP_1]). They are unhappy, blue, and quick to cry (Dysphoria [DEP_2]). They show a low level of self-confidence and self-regard to the point that they feel guilt-ridden, useless, unpardonably sinful, and condemned (Self-Depreciation [DEP_3]). They feel hopeless and contemplate suicide (Suicidal Ideation [DEP_4]). The symptoms they endorse tend to be gastrointestinal symptoms, neurological problems, sensory problems, cardiovascular symptoms, skin problems, pain, and respiratory troubles.

Bizarre Mentation (BIZ)

Clients who score in the elevated range on the BIZ scale are reporting a number of overtly psychotic symptoms (Psychotic Symptomatology [BIZ_1]). High scorers on the BIZ scale, especially when this elevation is primarily the result of the elevation of the BIZ_1 scale, tend to have impaired insight, an inability to enter into collaborative relationships, and a grandiose sense of having been selected or appointed for a secret and lofty mission or endowed with special powers. Individuals with high elevations also report strange, unusual ideas and experiences (Schizotypal Characteristics [BIZ_2]).

Anger (ANG)

People who score in the elevated range on the ANG scale tend to have problems with anger control. They are seen by others as irritable, volatile, and intolerant of frustration. Moreover, they tend to be prone to angry outrages and destructive outbursts that can have potential to be harmful to others or damaging to property (Explosive Behavior [ANG_1]). High scorers may report being a helpless spectator to their angry outbursts. They disapprove of their own destructiveness, yet feel unable to stop themselves (Irritability [ANG_2]). High scorers on the ANG scale have a high urgency to express what they are experiencing. They may also report having family problems.

Cynicism (CYN)

The CYN scale addresses a broad range of feelings, from showing skepticism regarding the motives of others (low scores) to the highly misanthropic conviction that other people are dishonorable, unprincipled, and corrupt (high scores). People with high scores on the CYN scale believe that others are to be distrusted because they act only in self-interest, resort to honesty only to avoid detection, and act friendly only because it makes others easier to exploit (Misanthropic Beliefs [CYN_1]). They see life as a jungle in which they must be constantly on the lookout for any competitive advantage, because others will use any means at their disposal to claim such advantage for themselves if given the opportunity. People with high CYN scores may at times resort to deception, hypocrisy, and manipulation to get away with whatever they can. They tend to justify their exploitive behaviors with the rationalization that others are equally selfish, dishonest, and amoral (Interpersonal Suspiciousness [CYN_2]).

Antisocial Practices (ASP)

People who score high on the ASP scale are reporting a disregard for rules and social conventions along with a cynical perspective on the motives of others (Antisocial Attitudes [ASP_1]). They show little concern or empathy for others. They are prone to abuse substances and to engage in other risky behaviors. They may have a history of antisocial behaviors while they were in school (Antisocial Behavior [ASP_2]). The ASP_2 scale consists of admissions of delinquencies in the past, including theft, truancy, school suspensions, and conflict with school and legal authorities.

Type A (TPA)

Clients who score high on the TPA scale tend to live a pressured existence. They show urgency to get things done, and they become irritated when they have to wait in line or are interrupted at their work (Impatience [TPA_1]). They tend to want to get even with people who oppose or have wronged them, and they are pleased when these people get into trouble (Competitiveness [TPA₂]). They also are described as being depressed and having family problems.

Low Self-Esteem (LSE)

Individuals who score high on the *LSE* scale feel less capable, less attractive, less self-confident, and generally less adequate than others (Self-Doubt [*LSE₁*]). They feel so overwhelmingly incompetent and inferior to others that the independent management of their lives seems out of the question (Submissiveness [*LSE₂*]). They are anxious, pessimistic, insecure, and depressed. The *LSE₁* scale reflects very negative self-attributions that are mostly phrased in such a way as to convey not self-doubt per se but the conviction of personal inferiority and inadequacy. The *LSE₂* scale reflects passivity, a subservient obedience to others, and, by implication, avoidance of responsibility. When both the *LSE₁* and *LSE₂* scales are elevated, examinees are compliant with requests but have little expectation of being competent to carry them out successfully.

Social Discomfort (SOD)

High scorers on the *SOD* scale tend to avoid other people when possible, because they feel uneasy and awkward in such situations and they are happier being alone (Introversion [*SOD₁*] and Shyness [*SOD₂*]). They are described as being insecure, anxious, depressed, and pessimistic. High scores on the *SOD* scale may reflect the kinds of withdrawal and social anhedonia seen in depressive syndromes (high scores on the *D* scale and the *DEP* scale and low scores on *Ma* scale) or the interpersonal aversiveness and social withdrawal seen in those with high *Si* scale scores.

Family Problems (FAM)

Clients who score high on the *FAM* scale not only feel deprived and mistreated by their family (Family Discord [*FAM₁*]) but appear to be antagonistic toward others into adulthood. They are emotionally detached and alienated from family members (Familial Alienation [*FAM₂*]). They are apt to be seen by others as immature and overreactive people who harbor grave doubts about and deeply negative attitudes toward themselves but who are equally mistrustful and disparaging of others.

Work Interference (WRK)

High scorers on the *WRK* scale are experiencing a wide variety of problems that may interfere with their abilities to carry out their work responsibilities.

They find it hard to concentrate on tasks, and they give up easily in the face of adversity. A dysphoric quality permeates their life and interferes with their work. The *WRK* scale is a measure of general subjective distress that has been tied to the context of work. It emphasizes the kinds of problems that would be expected to have adverse effects on productivity. The hypotheses one can make from *WRK* scale elevations include both interpersonal difficulties and the kinds of attitudes and symptoms that impair efficiency and impede output.

Negative Treatment Indicators (TRT)

High scorers on the *TRT* scale appear to be helpless and hopeless in face of their seemingly overwhelming problems (Low Motivation [TRT_1]). They report feeling apathetic, depressive, and impotent. They do not like to talk about their personal problems and are uncomfortable when they have to do so (Inability to Disclose [TRT_2]). Because both the item content and the empirical correlates of the *TRT* scale are so heavily focused upon depression, it is important that the examiner ascertain what role depression has in the client's problem situation.

SUPPLEMENTARY SCALES

The discussion of the MMPI–2 supplementary scales is organized into three groups: (a) the factor scales (Welsh Anxiety, Welsh Repression), (b) alcohol/drug abuse scales (Addiction Admission, Addiction Potential, and MacAndrew Alcohol Scale—Revised), and (c) the remaining supplementary scales.

Welsh Anxiety Scale

Clients who score high on the Welsh Anxiety (A) scale (Welsh, 1956) are described as generally emotionally distressed, anxious, and lacking in confidence in their own abilities. They are characterized as reacting to situational stress or personal distress. The elevation of the A scale reflects their level of discomfort, which usually motivates them to enter into psychological treatment. The general distress syndrome covered by the items in the A scale of the MMPI–2 is more likely to reflect situational stress rather than long-term distress, which is assessed by the *Pt* scale.

Welsh Repression Scale

High scorers (*T* scores of 58 or higher) on the Welsh Repression (R) scale (Welsh, 1956) are seen as being unwilling to share their problems with others, which may reflect conscious suppression, constriction, and inhibition of interests in events around them or actual repression and denial. Those who are denying problems also have elevations on the *K* and *Hy* scales. These persons may appear constricted, inhibited, and overcontrolled, and they lack insight into their own behavior. Clients with high *R* scores tend to be unwilling to discuss any form of psychopathology, even though it may be apparent to everyone but themselves.

Addiction Admission Scale

High scorers on the Addiction Admission (*AAS*) scale (Weed, Butcher, McKenna, & Ben-Porath, 1992) are acknowledging their widespread use and probable abuse of substances. They are likely to have legal problems and problems in controlling the expression of their anger. Because a number of these items are written in the past tense, it is important to determine whether the use or abuse of substances is ongoing or reflects earlier behavior patterns. Two items (489, 511) should be explored with examinees whenever they are endorsed as being true.

Addiction Potential Scale

High scorers on the Addiction Potential (*APS*) scale (Weed et al., 1992) are generally distressed and upset as well as angry and resentful. They describe themselves in negative terms, and they are concerned about what others think of them. They are prone to abuse substances.

MacAndrew Alcoholism Scale—Revised

High scorers on the MacAndrew Alcoholism Scale—Revised (*MAC–R*) scale (MacAndrew, 1965; Weed et al., 1992) are described as being impulsive, risk-taking, sensation-seeking individuals who frequently have a propensity to abuse alcohol and/or stimulating drugs. They are uninhibited, sociable individuals who appear to use repression and religion in an attempt to control their rebellious, delinquent impulses. They also are described as having a high energy level, having shallow interpersonal relationships, and being generally psychologically maladjusted.

Ego Strength

High scorers on the Ego Strength (*Es*) scale (Barron, 1953) describe themselves as experiencing little emotional distress and having few physical symptoms. They have good attention and concentration skills, and they can focus on what they need to be doing. They would seem to have little motivation to engage in a psychotherapeutic process, because of the absence of any emotional distress.

Dominance

High scorers on the Dominance (*Do*) scale (Gough, McClosky, & Meehl, 1951) are described as being able to take charge of and responsibility for their lives. They are poised, self-assured, and confident of their own abilities. They address problems in a realistic, task-oriented fashion and feel adequate in their ability to overcome any obstacles that they may encounter. They tend to show good attention and concentration and to make decisions easily.

Social Responsibility

High scorers on the Social Responsibility (*Re*) scale (Gough, McClosky, & Meehl, 1952) behave in a socially appropriate manner. They are very conventional individuals who interact easily with others.

College Maladjustment

High scorers on the College Maladjustment (*Mt*) scale (Kleinmuntz, 1961) are described as generally emotionally distressed, anxious, and lacking in confidence in their own abilities. They are seen by others as tending to react to situational stress or personal distress, and the elevation of the *Mt* scale reflects their level of discomfort. Because of this discomfort, they are usually motivated to enter into psychological treatment.

Posttraumatic Stress Disorder—Keane

High scorers on the Posttraumatic Stress Disorder—Keane (*PK*) scale (Keane, Malloy, & Fairbank, 1984) are described as generally emotionally distressed, anxious, and lacking in confidence in their own abilities. They are characterized as reacting to situational stress or personal distress, and the elevation of the *PK* scale reflects their level of discomfort. This scale taps into symptoms of distress rather than the specific symptoms of posttraumatic stress disorder. Because of this discomfort, they are usually motivated to enter into psychological treatment.

Marital Distress Scale

High scorers on the Marital Distress (*MDS*) scale (Hjemboe, Almagor, & Butcher, 1992) are experiencing significant distress in their marital relationships. They are alienated from others and are generally distressed.

Hostility

Men with high scores on the Hostility (*Ho*) scale (Cook & Medley, 1954) are rated as being hotheaded, bossy, demanding, and argumentative; women with high *Ho* scores are rated as being nervous, fearful, and depressed and as having paranoid tendencies. High scorers are generally distressed, and they experience negative affect.

Overcontrolled Hostility

High scorers on the Overcontrolled Hostility (*O-H*) scale (Megargee, Cook, & Mendelsohn, 1967) are described as displaying excessive control of their hostile impulses and as being socially alienated. They are reluctant to admit any form of psychological symptoms, even though they are sometimes diagnosed as being psychotic. They are seen as being rigid and as not displaying anxiety overtly. They may be candidates for assertiveness training. The fundamental question with these examinees is whether this is an accurate self-description or a facade. The *O-H* scale tends to measure defensiveness rather than acting-out potential or explicit aggressive behavior. Many normal, non-acting-out individuals score in the moderately elevated range on *O-H*.

Gender Role—Masculine

High scorers on the Gender Role—Masculine (*GM*) scale (Peterson & Dahlstrom, 1992) are self-confident, and they make decisions easily. They have few fears and experience little emotional distress. They have very stereotypic masculine interests and engage in stereotypic masculine activities.

Gender Role—Feminine

High scorers on the Gender Role—Feminine (*GF*) scale (Peterson & Dahlstrom, 1992) have very stereotypic feminine interests, and they engage in stereotypic feminine activities. They are very socially responsible, and they interact easily with others. They do not abuse substances.

CODE TYPES

The MMPI and MMPI–2 have a long history of interpretations based upon the code types that have been established across nearly seventy years of empirical research. The configuration of the scales in the clinical profile came to be as important in MMPI interpretation as the elevation of the single-scale scores. Well-researched descriptors for many of the MMPI code types are available for the two-, three-, and some four-scale elevations (Gilberstadt, 1970; Gilberstadt & Duker, 1965; Gynther, Altman, & Sletten, 1973; Marks, Seeman, & Haller, 1974; J. O. Sines, 1966).

The code type is the basis of any MMPI–2 clinical scale interpretation in which more than one clinical scale is elevated in the clinical range. In fact, many MMPI–2 interpretive systems look no farther than the code type for any profile (i.e., no other scales or configurations are interpreted). For a code-type analysis it is only necessary that two clinical scales or a single clinical scale (spike profile) be elevated at or above a T score of 65 on the MMPI–2. The order of the scales is determined by the more elevated being first or by the numerical order if the scales have identical T scores. However, some empirical data have found that the order does not lead to differences in the correlates of the code type in some code combinations. The validity of MMPI code types has been widely researched and supported (Archer, Griffin, & Aiduk, 1995; Arnold, 1970; Boerger, Graham, & Lilly, 1974; Butcher, Rouse, & Perry, 2000; Fowler & Athey, 1971; Graham, Smith, & Schwartz, 1986; Gynther, Altman, & Warbin, 1972, 1973a, 1973b, 1973c; Lewandowski & Graham, 1972; Persons & Marks, 1971, to highlight a few).

Some code types tend to occur more frequently in certain specific settings. For instance, elevations on scales Hs (1), D (2), and Hy (3) occur more frequently in medical settings, and elevations on scales Pd (4), Sc (8), and Ma (9) occur more frequently in psychiatric settings. We provide two examples of code types that are common in various forensic applications. In Exhibit 3.1 we include a description of the empirical correlate information that is recommended for consideration in interpretation for the 1-3/3-1 profile code type (often found in personal injury and work compensation cases), and in Exhibit 3.2 we include pertinent descriptions for the 4-9/9-4 code type (often found among criminal offenders).

Forensic examiners must remember that the code type is only the starting point for the interpretation of an MMPI–2 profile and is a description of the examinee at this point in time. An MMPI–2 interpretation that is based solely on the code type has the potential of being extremely inaccurate because of the heterogeneity of individual profiles within any code type. The psychologist should also examine the other clinical scales not contained within the code type, as well as the content and supplementary scales, any

EXHIBIT 3.1
Description of the 1-3/3-1 MMPI–2 Code Type

Clients with the profile code of 1-3/3-1 typically are diagnosed with psychophysiological or neurotic (hysterical, hypochondriacal) disorders. The classic conversion syndrome may be present. Severe anxiety and depression are usually absent. These individuals function at a reduced level of efficiency and develop physical symptoms under stress that may disappear when the stress level subsides. In terms of their basic personality characteristics, patients with this profile pattern tend to be overly optimistic and superficial in social situations. They tend to be immature, egocentric, and selfish. They feel insecure and have strong needs for attention and affection. They frequently tend to seek sympathy from others. In addition, they often show a pattern of dependency.

High 1-3/3-1 clients are usually found to be outgoing and socially extraverted, but their interpersonal relationships are superficial. They tend to lack genuine involvement with people and may be exploitive in social relationships. They are reportedly naïve and lacking in skills to deal with the opposite sex. Many clients with this code type appear low in sexual drive but may be flirtatious. They seek attention and may show resentment and hostility toward those who do not offer enough attention and support to them. They are overcontrolled and passive–aggressive and have occasional angry outbursts. They are mostly conventional and conforming in attitudes and beliefs.

These clients are usually not motivated for psychotherapy, and when there they expect definite answers and solutions to their problems. They may terminate their therapy prematurely if their therapist fails to respond to their demands. Individuals who fall into this code-type behavior group tend to prefer medical explanations for their symptoms and to resist psychological interpretations. They tend to deny and rationalize their behavior and to be uninsightful. They may see themselves as normal, responsible, and without fault. They tend to be Pollyannaish about their symptoms and lack appropriate concern, even though their symptoms and problems, if genuine, are extremely disabling.

Note. Adapted from *A Beginner's Guide to the MMPI–2* (3rd ed., p. 196), by J. N. Butcher, 2011, Washington, DC: American Psychological Association. Copyright 2011 by the American Psychological Association.

subscales of all of these scales, and the critical items in developing the interpretation of a specific MMPI–2 profile. It is extremely important to examine these other scales when the code type is not well defined; that is, when it has at least a 5 T-score difference with the next highest scale. In fact, when the code type is not well defined, the psychologist may want to use a single-scale interpretation of the entire MMPI–2 profile.

SUMMARY

This chapter describes the interpretative information available in evaluating the high scores on each of the MMPI–2 clinical, content, and supplementary scales that provide the forensic examiner with a number of potential hypotheses about the examinee in the forensic personality evaluation. The

EXHIBIT 3.2
Description of the 4-9/9-4 MMPI–2 Code Type

Clients with the 4-9/9-4 profile type tend to show marked disregard for social standards and values. They are usually viewed as antisocial; they appear to have a poorly developed conscience, easy morals, and fluctuating ethical values. It is not unusual to find that they have legal difficulties or work problems. They tend to have a wide array of problem behaviors, such as alcoholism, fighting, and sexual acting out.

In terms of personality features, the 4-9/9-4 client is likely to be narcissistic, selfish, self-indulgent, and impulsive. These individuals tend to be viewed as irresponsible. They cannot delay gratification of impulses, and they show poor judgment. They also act out without considering the consequences of their behavior. People with this pattern tend to fail to learn from punishing experiences. When in trouble, they rationalize their shortcomings and failures, blame their difficulties on others, and lie to avoid responsibility. They reportedly have a low frustration tolerance and are seen to be moody, irritable, and having a caustic manner. They are often angry and hostile and may have occasional emotional outbursts.

These clients are also energetic, restless, and overactive. They tend to seek out emotional stimulation and excitement. They are uninhibited, extraverted, and talkative in social situations. They often create a good first impression because they are glib and spontaneous; however, their relationships are usually superficial. Clients with this profile type appear to avoid deep emotional ties. They are considered "loners" who keep others at an emotional distance. They usually present as self-confident and secure but are quite immature. The usual diagnosis for this profile type is antisocial personality.

Note. Adapted from *A Beginner's Guide to the MMPI–2* (3rd ed., pp. 203–204), by J. N. Butcher, 2011, Washington, DC: American Psychological Association. Copyright 2011 by the American Psychological Association.

interpretive strategy of using code-type correlates in developing hypotheses about the client was described. The interpretive hypotheses from the MMPI–2 measures provide areas of interest about which the forensic examiner can query the examinee, use other test data, and use collateral information in order to narrow and individualize the interpretation.

4

CULTURAL FACTORS IN FORENSIC ASSESSMENT WITH THE MMPI–2

The influence of demographic, ethnic, and cultural variables on the Minnesota Multiphasic Personality Inventory—2 (MMPI–2) has been a source of extensive inquiry and research because these factors may modify the way in which psychopathology will be manifested or is interpreted by the examiner. These factors are particularly relevant in forensic cases, because there is an overrepresentation of certain ethnic and cultural groups in the forensic populations pertinent to the evaluations reviewed in this book (Rosich, 2007). Moreover, statistics reveal that ethnic minorities fare poorly in our criminal and legal system, and forensic psychologists are morally and ethically obligated to avoid adding to the burden of bias and discrimination their examinees may face in the forensic arena (American Psychological Association, 1993, Principle 8).

The Specialty Guidelines for Forensic Psychology (American Psychological Association, 2013b) guide forensic psychologists to understand contextual factors including age, gender, gender identity, race, ethnicity,

http://dx.doi.org/10.1037/14571-005
Using the MMPI–2 in Forensic Assessment, by J. N. Butcher, G. A. Hass, R. L. Greene, and L. D. Nelson

culture, national origin, religion, sexual orientation, disability, language, socioeconomic status, and any other difference that may impact the basis for an individual's involvement with the legal system. At the same time, the guidelines ask forensic psychologists to avoid engaging in unfair discrimination and to take action to correct or limit the effects of such factors on their practice. It is quite likely that psychologists conducting forensic evaluations are often evaluating ethnic and language minority examinees with the MMPI–2, and they can expect direct questions regarding the influence of these variables on the MMPI–2 profiles. Members of diverse ethnic and linguistic groups need special attention with the administration and interpretation of the MMPI–2, and forensic psychologists working with them need to be familiar with this information.

As a matter of general recommendation, R. A. Weiss and Rosenfeld (2012) were of the opinion that, in this area, forensic evaluators need to judge their cultural competence case by case. Those cases in which they have the forensic expertise relevant to the psycholegal question but less familiarity with the specific cultural factors of the client require the use of an interpreter, consultant, or both. Forensic psychologists are also obligated to decline or refer cases in which cultural and linguistic differences are unsolvable.

This chapter presents a brief review of the literature concerning the forensic use of the MMPI–2 with ethnic minorities and immigrants and the issues involving the influence of culture and socioeconomic diversity that should be considered when interpreting profiles from forensic examinees who do not neatly fit the normative sample. Psychologists interested in a more in-depth analysis of this topic are encouraged to consult other sources of information and perspectives (e.g., Butcher, 2004; Butcher, Cabiya, Lucio, & Garrido, 2007; Butcher, Mosch, Tsai, & Nezami, 2006; Butcher & Pancheri, 1976; Dahlstrom, Lachar, & Dahlstrom, 1986; Dana, 1988, 2000; Greene, 1987; Pritchard & Rosenblatt, 1980). This chapter concludes with a case study that illustrates the interpretation of an MMPI–2 profile in a forensic case of an ethnically diverse individual.

BACKGROUND

The MMPI was first published in 1942. The normal reference group for its standardization consisted of 724 University of Minnesota hospital and outpatient clinic visitors between the ages of 16 and 65 who were not under the care of a physician for treatment of any illness. Coincidentally, the demographics of this group corresponded to the 1930 Census values of Minnesota in terms of age, gender, and marital status. According to Dahlstrom, Welsh, and Dahlstrom (1972), the typical individual from this group was "about thirty-five years old, was married, lived in a small town or rural area, had had eight years of general schooling, and worked at a skilled or semiskilled trade (or was married to a man with such occupational level)" (p. 8). Smaller normative groups were used in the development of some of the clinical scales in order to assess the influence of age, socioeconomic class, or education on the item endorsement.

The inadequacy of these samples became more relevant over time, as research with the MMPI on newly collected samples of normal individuals repeatedly found that they scored higher than Hathaway's sample (Colligan, Osborne, Swenson, & Offord, 1983; Pancoast & Archer, 1989). There were other issues that made the MMPI problematic and outdated, as the population in the United States became more educated and more culturally and ethnically diverse. The process to restandardize the MMPI aimed to conform to the U.S. Census data of 1980, with the exception of geographic distribution (Nichols, 2001). In the end, the 2,600 individuals who participated in the MMPI–2 restandardization sample met the census in terms of marital status and income distribution. The ethnic diversity representation in the sample was met, but there was some underrepresentation of Hispanics and Asian Americans. There was also underrepresentation of individuals at both ends of the age distribution, in particular men younger than 20 and women older than 70. The sample was found to exceed census estimates for educational level and occupational status. The underrepresentations in the sample have been a source of inquiry that has generated some debate and research (Caldwell, 1997; Helmes & Reddon, 1993). However, a subsequent study with a census-matched subsample of the restandardization sample (Schinka & LaLone, 1997) found that there were no significant differences on the validity, clinical, content, and supplementary scales between the full restandardization and the subsample. These results confirmed that the MMPI–2 does not have a large source of bias in the restandardization sample that could lead to significant errors in measurement or interpretation in those individuals who are similar to the restandardization sample.

Research has found that although ethnic diversity has a small effect on MMPI–2 profiles of ethnically diverse individuals, this factor still has to be taken into consideration because it provides information about the nuances of a person's manifestation of emotional distress and adjustment. It is important to exercise critical thinking when using a standardized assessment measure with a culturally based domain and a reference sample with examinees of a different cultural orientation than the normative sample. Examiners need to consider that in some cases, instead or in addition to reflecting psychopathology, the MMPI–2 scores may reflect the different coping and defense mechanisms that minority individuals utilize in order to manage the special circumstances of their life in an antagonistic society (Dahlstrom et al., 1986).

In particular, profiles from atypical cases that deviate significantly from the normative standards (e.g., recent immigrants, foreign workers, poor African Americans from the inner city, Hispanic migrant seasonal farmworkers, older Asian American individuals, Native Americans from certain tribes) may be susceptible to under- or overpathologizing interpretations when using standard interpretive hypotheses. As stated in the Ethics Code of the American Psychological Association (2002),

> When interpreting assessment results, including automated interpretations, psychologists take into account the purpose of the assessment as well as the various test factors, test-taking abilities, and other characteristics of the person being assessed, such as situational, personal, linguistic, and cultural differences, that might affect psychologists' judgments or reduce the accuracy of their interpretations. (p. 1072)

In addition to determining whether the test's psychometric construction and standardization sample will appropriately fit a diverse examinee, forensic psychologists should begin by paying attention to the administration of the MMPI–2. Velasquez et al. (2000) listed a number of cautionary guidelines that should be considered when using the MMPI–2 to test diverse examinees. Although these recommendations were offered for forensic psychologists evaluating Hispanic examinees, they seem relevant for examinees of other languages and ethnicities as well. Velasquez et al. recommended in particular that forensic psychologists utilize standard procedures, use computerized interpretive reports cautiously, interpret scales in addition to standard validity and clinical scales, and consider the potential impact of acculturative stress. The effects of past oppression, socioeconomic, and other contextual stresses should also be considered in the profile interpretation.

It is ultimately the responsibility of the forensic psychologist to take into consideration all individual differences, including racial, ethnic, and linguistic, in the administration, interpretation, and overall psychological assessment. The MMPI–2 is an instrument that aims to be part of an overall evaluation process and that is integrated with other sources of information that add to the understanding of the examinee's functioning.

Forensic psychologists should not assume that an individual is a member of an ethnic or mainstream group based on the color of his or her skin, surname, or self-description. Measures of identification with the ethnic group and acculturation have been utilized to determine how the individual will fit with the normative sample of the test. A number of measures have been developed with this goal in mind, although most present difficulties due to a lack of consensus in the field about how exactly to define ethnic identity and acculturation and how to measure these constructs. In addition, there are criticisms of determining ethnic identity and acculturation through self-reports, because it is presumed that individuals may be inclined to give socially acceptable responses (J. L. Tsai, Chentsova-Dutton, & Wong, 2002).

Ethnic identity, or the degree to which one views oneself as a member of a particular ethnic group or mixed ethnicities (J. L. Tsai et al., 2002), has been assessed with instruments such as the Multigroup Ethnic Identity Measure (Phinney, 1992) and the General Ethnicity Questionnaire (J. L. Tsai, Ying, & Lee, 2001). Knowing the ethnic group or ethnicities with which the examinee self-identifies, through either a standardized test or an interview, allows the forensic psychologist to know whether the profile of the examinee requires special considerations as recommended by the literature specific for the ethnic group or cultural background.

Knowing the examinee's level of acculturation, or the degree to which he or she feels a sense of belonging to the mainstream American culture (Berry, 1995), helps the forensic psychologist determine if the MMPI–2 with standard American norms is applicable. If a test is preferred over an interview, a test of acculturation specific to the ethnic group of the examinee may be preferred over a general one. Some of the most popular measures of acculturation are the Acculturation Index (Ward & Rana-Deuba, 1999), Native American Acculturation Scale (Garrett & Pichette, 2000), Acculturation Rating Scale for Mexican Americans II (Cuellar, Arnold, & Maldonado, 1995), African American Acculturation Scale (Landrine & Klonoff, 1994), Asian American Multidimensional Acculturation Scale (Gim Chung, Kim, & Abreu, 2004), Brief Acculturation Scale Among Japanese Americans (Meredith, Wenger, Liu, Harada, & Khan, 2000), Abbreviated Multidimensional Acculturation Scale (Zea, Asner-Self, Birman, & Buki, 2003), Stephenson Multigroup Acculturation Scale (Stephenson, 2000), and Scale of Acculturation (Rissel, 1997). Acculturation tests were designed for research purposes, and few have forensic utility. They are also culture specific, and few have published sufficient information about their psychometric properties (Ponterotto, 1996). It is not inappropriate to interview clients regarding their understanding and use of the language, values and norms, customs, and beliefs of their native and host cultures in order to assess their level of acculturation (R. A. Weiss & Rosenfeld, 2012).

Once the examiner knows a person's level of acculturation, a judgment can be made regarding whether the individual belongs to the same population for which the test was designed (that is, the ethnically diverse participants in the normative sample). To date, there are no psychometric adjustments in the MMPI–2 that could correct for a lack of acculturation, despite efforts to develop an index for this purpose (Cuéllar, 2000). Therefore, it is the responsibility of the forensic psychologist to individualize the interpretation of the MMPI–2 when testing individuals with limited acculturation.

Recent immigrants who have not fully acculturated to the United States and who have limited mastery of the English language may benefit from being tested with the MMPI–2 translation and normative population of their home country, if such a translation exists. U.S.-born individuals whose primary language is not English may also prefer to take a translated version of the test. Administering a translation of a test is not the same as ensuring normative equivalence. As noted in the Standards for Educational and Psychological Testing (American Educational Research Association, American Psychological Association, & National Council of Measurement in Education, 2014), "A test should be administered in the language that is most relevant and appropriate to the test purpose" (Standard 3.13, p. 69). The MMPI–2 has been translated into a large number of languages for use worldwide and with immigrants. Pearson Assessments publishes Spanish, French Canadian, and Hmong booklet translations; it also publishes a CD in Spanish, which can be used for individuals who speak Spanish but have limited literacy proficiency. The University of Minnesota has endorsed the following translations: Bulgarian, Chinese, Croatian, Czech, Danish, Dutch/Flemish, French, French Canadian, German, Greek, Hebrew, Hmong, Hungarian, Italian, Korean, Norwegian, Polish, Romanian, Spanish for Mexico and Central America, Spanish for Spain, South America, and Central America, Spanish for the United States, and Swedish (University of Minnesota Press, 2011). Notice that an effort has been made to tailor translations to the different dialects of a language, because the particular conceptual differences between those versions can create a meaningful difference in the construct to be evaluated. There are a number of other translations that have not been published or are not commercially available (Butcher, 1996) and that therefore do not meet criteria for admissibility as scientific evidence set forth in the Federal Rules of Evidence and *Daubert v. Merrell Dow Pharmaceuticals* (1993), to which most states adhere.

Translations must follow the guidelines from the International Test Commission (International Test Commission, 2005), which require that the translation was conducted by teams that, independently of each other, translated and back translated the instrument with special attention to content equivalence. This means that the translated test is not a literal translation of words and that some items may change, especially pairs that require consistency. Then, a bilingual test and retest study is conducted (Butcher, 1996). Forensic psychologists are encouraged to use the formal translation, which has been developed with strict methodological and ethical procedures in the native language of the examinee, rather than use informal translations or read items written in English in a different language. Real-time translations do not comply with the requirements of the Federal Rules of Evidence because they usually cannot be replicated, semantic versus content equivalence cannot be analyzed, and the reliability of the translation cannot be assured. Instructions to the test also must be translated in advance of the assessment session.

A different process is conducted to determine whether the application of the test with a person of another culture has been effective. Cross-cultural relevance is important so the examiner does not apply concepts of normalcy and psychopathology that do not work for the examinee. The test can be administered to well-defined groups, to confirm that the scales are operating properly with the different cultural groups (also called scalar equivalence), and to individuals in the general population, to determine whether the scale scores are within the normal range (Butcher, 1996). The publishers and individuals listed for the MMPI–2 translations in the University of Minnesota webpage can provide information about normative studies for the use of the specific translation in their ethnic and cultural group (University of Minnesota Press, 2011). Resources to consult for a more extensive analysis of this theme are Butcher (1996, 2004), Butcher and Clark (1979), Butcher and Pancheri (1976), and Butcher et al. (2007).

The Cannot Say (CNS) scale, the response consistency scales (VRIN and TRIN), and the infrequency scales (F, FB, and Fp) are relevant to determine if the examinee was able to read and understand the test sufficiently well to provide a valid profile. Because some of these scales also provide information on the examinee's cooperation with the task, forensic psychologists are encouraged to follow up with the examinee during the interview in order to assess whether the difficulties were encountered with understanding, avoidance of certain themes, or denial of symptoms.

Once the forensic psychologist is assured that the immigrant examinee understood the items and that his or her responses were valid as determined by the validity scales, the research in cross-cultural applications of the MMPI–2 provides the forensic psychologist with a strong measure of confidence that even if norms of the examinee's native country were not available, the American norms, when used cautiously, are reliable representations of the examinee's symptoms and acknowledged problems. Cross-cultural studies have shown repeatedly that people in other countries perform similarly to the American normative sample. These findings lend support to the hypothesis that the translations are measuring the same constructs across cultures (Hayama, Oguchi, & Shinkai, 1999; Lucio & Reyes-Lagunes, 1996; Saborío & Hass, 2012; Thatte, Manos, & Butcher, 1987) and that the test is suitable for recent immigrants with limited acculturation.

It is clear that ethnicity, acculturation, and cultural influences are only one aspect of individual diversity that may have an effect on psychological well-being. Diversity within groups has been cited as being more important than variations among groups (A. F. Friedman, Lewak, Nichols, & Webb, 2001). Other factors, such as education, also have a significant if not greater impact for ethnically diverse examinees. Forensic psychologists need to be cautious when the examinee has 10 years or less of education, as both normal and clinical samples have demonstrated substantially higher T scores on the F, Hs, and Sc scales. As years of education decrease, endorsements of symptoms of psychopathology and negative attitudes increase when compared with endorsements by clients with 11 or more years of education (Greene, 2000).

REVIEW OF THE RESEARCH LITERATURE

African Americans

Studies comparing the MMPI and MMPI–2 profiles of African Americans with those of Caucasians have not found significant differences, other than item-level endorsement frequencies that vary in some samples in which a very small number of items consistently differentiate African Americans from other groups including Caucasians. Differences have been reported on the F, Sc, and Ma scales, in which African Americans seem to be scoring somewhat higher than Caucasians. Timbrook and Graham (1994) found that African American men scored slightly higher than Caucasian men on the Sc scale and that African American women had statistically higher scores than Caucasian women did on the Pd, Mf, and Ma scales. This latest finding of higher scores for African American women on the Pa and Ma scales was replicated by Arbisi, Ben-Porath, and McNulty (2002). However, all these differences were half a standard deviation (5 T points), which is not a large deviation (Dana, 2000; Greene, 1987). The statistical differences between ethnic groups seems to diminish in African Americans from higher socioeconomic groups, suggesting that other mediating variables, such as education, age, rural/urban residence, and socioeconomic status (A. F. Friedman et al., 2001), may be having an impact on their scores.

An early study with the MMPI provided information on the effects of race in the Overcontrolled Hostility Scale (O-H; Megargee, Cook, & Mendelsohn, 1967). Studying examinees from a forensic psychiatric hospital, Hutton, Miner, Blades, and Langfeldt (1992) found that African American participants scored more than 5 T points on the O-H scale when compared with Caucasian participants; 43% of Hutton et al.'s African American participants obtained T scores that exceeded the clinical cutoff. This finding has not been replicated in clinical cases (Kay, Duerksen, Pike, & Anderson, 2003). Uninformed interpretation (e.g., interpreting a high O-H scale with African American examinees) may lead to the erroneous assumption that they are more aggressive or inclined toward violence than is the case. The O-H scale does not measure violent behavior. Forensic psychologists who are not aware of this may mistakenly believe that African American defendants with high scores in the *O-H* scale are more dangerous. In the same vein, elevations on the *Pd* and *Sc* scales have been found to be related to estrangement and mistrust of society at large, possibly due to African American historical and contextual realities, rather than to delusional or antisocial ideation (Gynther, 1972). Also relevant to a forensic practice is the finding that MMPI–2 profiles of African Americans and Caucasians with posttraumatic stress disorder do not show significant differences (Frueh, Gold, de Arellano, & Brady, 1997). Another forensically relevant finding was that, compared with Caucasians, African American men in forensic settings scored lower on the *Pd* scale and African American men in a substance abuse setting scored lower on the *Pt* scale (Hall & Phung, 2001).

An important concern, perhaps greater than the score discrepancy between African Americans and Caucasians, is whether examiners make biased interpretations of those scores based on cultural membership, socioeconomic status, and ethnicity (Cohen et al., 1990; Lewis, Crofts-Jeffreys, & David, 1990; Luepnitz, Randolph, & Gutsch, 1982; Neighbors et al., 1999). For instance, Pottick, Kirk, Hsieh, and Tian (2007) reported that clinicians interpreted antisocial behavior as delinquency in African American and Hispanic youths but considered the same behavior to be the result of a mental-health disorder in Caucasian juveniles. The potential for this interpretive bias is diminished by the use of the MMPI–2 in a manner consistent with the empirical literature regarding interpretation (Knaster & Micucci, 2013). When a forensic psychologist interprets the MMPI–2 profile of an African American examinee and finds that the scores are divergent from the norm, the first hypothesis should be to explore whether this finding represents differences in values, perceptions, and contextual factors rather than greater psychopathology.

Hispanic Americans

The MMPI and the MMPI–2 are the most popular instruments when assessing Hispanics (Geisinger, 1992). Prior to assessing Hispanic examinees, the psychologist needs to determine their language dominance. The MMPI–2 has been translated into several versions of Spanish, and some linguistic versions have strong psychometric validity (Boscán et al., 2000; Butcher et al., 2007; Lucio, Reyes-Lagunes, & Scott, 1994). It is recommended that examinees choose which language and version they prefer to answer. In the case of bilingual examinees, it has been noted that there is one preferred language that better conveys the true nature and extent of their psychopathology (Malgady, Rogler, & Constantino, 1987). Thus, an examinee's preferred language version should be honored even if he or she exhibits full competency in

English. Examinees may also be offered both versions, their native language and English, in case they need to refer to one or the other on certain items, given that vocabulary mastery in one language does not always completely overlap with the other language in bilingual individuals.

Hispanics in the United States elevate the F and L scales slightly higher than does the normative sample (Whitworth & McBlaine, 1993). This finding has been interpreted as being related to lower levels of acculturation to the United States and to higher levels of stress. Mexicans and Costa Ricans also presented with elevated L scales (Lucio & Reyes-Lagunes, 1996; Saborío & Hass, 2012), which has been interpreted as the cultural value that incline these individuals to present themselves in the best possible light. A consistent finding is that Hispanics tend to respond in ways that present themselves favorably; when the specific items are analyzed, Hispanics seem to differ in terms of their endorsement of items related to morality rather than those related to psychopathology. When interpreting profiles of Hispanics and Hispanic immigrants in which scales F and L are elevated, forensic psychologists are encouraged to interpret elevations within half a standard deviation (5 T points) as if within the normal range. Greater elevations should be considered in a case-by-case situation, with all aspects reviewed in this chapter being considered before it is determined that a profile is invalid. As noted in Chapter 2, Zapata-Sola, Kreuch, Landers, Hoyt, and Butcher (2009) found that the L scale was somewhat elevated in Puerto Rican compared with Caucasian employees in a personnel setting.

In an extensive review of studies of the MMPI with Hispanic clients, Greene (2011) could not find any clear pattern of differences on the clinical scales. In fact, Cabiya et al. (2000) found minimal differences between Mexican, Puerto Rican, and United States college students. Variability in the Mf scale has been reported for Hispanic men, with higher mean scores found in some studies of Latino men (Lucio, Ampudia, Durán, Léon, & Butcher, 2001) but lower scores found in other studies (Cabiya, Cruz, & Bayon, 2002; Greene, 1987; Hall, Bansal, & Lopez, 1999). Because the Mf scale is heavily impacted by socialization and acculturation, this scale is likely to reflect the individual's cultural influences regarding gender role. The elevation of scale Hy in Hispanics, reflecting an inclination to endorse more somatic symptoms than do Caucasians, has also been noted (Hall et al., 1999).

In the case of Hispanics, as with other ethnic groups, moderator variables such as socioeconomic status, education, and intelligence seem to exert greater influence. Thus, each case has to be considered within its own context of moderator variables. For instance, clients from lower socioeconomic groups, regardless of race or ethnicity, score higher on the F and Si scales, whereas clients from higher socioeconomic background score higher on K

(Dahlstrom et al., 1986). In the same vein, increases in elevations on the *Sc* scales and decreases on the *Mf* scale correlate with lower socioeconomic status, and among women the *D* and *Mf* scales decrease as socioeconomic status increases (Friedman et al., 2001).

Gender also makes a significant difference in the profile pattern of Hispanics in the MMPI–2. Latinas were found to score higher than Caucasian women on the *F, Hs, Pd, Pt, Sc,* and *Ma* scales (Graham, 2006). Mexican men scored higher on the *L* and *Hs* scales, and Mexican women scored higher on the *L, Hs, D,* and *Sc* scales (Lucio et al., 2001).

More specific to forensic applications of the MMPI–2 in Spanish is the finding by Lucio and Valencia (1997) that the Mexican version was able to distinguish those who faked paranoid schizophrenia from normal students and genuine psychiatric patients in scales *F, Fp, L,* and *K.* The response pattern, however, was very similar to what is seen in the U.S. normative sample, as the fake good profiles went to 120 *T* in the *F* scale. Those who faked good were undistinguishable from normal controls. Therefore, the Mexican version of the MMPI–2 does not seem to be sufficiently sensitive to detect those who faked good.

Asian Americans

The Asian American group in the MMPI–2 normative sample was very small; therefore, using the standardized cutoffs has been a source of concern (Graham, 2006). Moreover, the warning that findings from studies with one group do not necessarily generalize to other Asian groups is an important consideration when interpreting MMPI–2 profiles of Asian Americans (Butcher, Cheung, & Lim, 2003; D. C. Tsai & Pike, 2000).

The MMPI–2 has been widely translated and adapted to various Asian languages, including Chinese, Hmong, Korean, and Thai, although most studies have been conducted with Chinese groups. The Chinese MMPI–2 has demonstrated strong psychometric validity (Butcher, Cheung, & Lim, 2003).

Asian Americans have been found to have more elevated profiles than do Caucasians, particularly on the *D* and *Sc* scales (Kwan, 1999). Using Chinese norms, Cheung (1995) found that profiles of Chinese psychiatric patients were less elevated than the standard U.S. norms. When their scores were plotted against U.S. norms, elevations on the *F, D,* and *Sc* scales were found. Elevations on the *D* scale have been noted to possibly reflect the cultural norms of modesty, restraint, and imperturbability (Shiota, Krauss, & Clark, 1996). The *L* scale also appeared vulnerable to higher scores in Chinese female participants, reflecting a tendency to endorse more morally virtuous items (Stevens, Kwan, & Graybill, 1993).

Native Americans

Studies of the MMPI–2 with Native Americans are very scarce, and, due to the diversity of the numerous tribes, findings from a study conducted with one or two tribes cannot be assumed to apply to the ethnic group at large. However, the applicability of the original MMPI normative values with Native Americans has been a source of concern (Pollack & Shore, 1980), particularly given that Native Americans were inadequately represented in the normative sample. A larger sample of Native Americans was included in the MMPI–2 revision (Butcher, Dahlstrom, Graham, Tellegen, & Kaemmer, 1989), thus improving the representation of this group in the MMPI–2.

Robin, Greene, Albaugh, Caldwell, and Goldman (2003; Greene, Robin, Albaugh, Caldwell, & Goldman, 2003) examined the validity of the MMPI–2 with two tribal groups, Southwestern and Plains. They found that Native Americans had statistically significantly higher T scores and significant correlates on several MMPI–2 clinical, content, and supplementary scales than did the MMPI–2 normative group; specifically, on 8 of the 13 basic validity and clinical scales (F, 1, 4, 5, 6, 7, 8, 9) as well as the Welsh Anxiety, Anger, and Antisocial Practices scales. Robin and colleagues concluded that the higher scores appear to reflect actual experiences of the Native American participants, given their adverse historical, social and economic conditions, rather than test bias. Further commentaries regarding this study, from Pace et al. (2006), noted that these elevations may represent the effects of the historical oppression and adversity as well as a different worldview. In sum, psychologists must use a cultural-contextual framework when interpreting MMPI–2 profiles of Native Americans.

CULTURAL FACTORS IN THE CONTEXT OF A FORENSIC EVALUATION

The evidence that ethnic minorities fare poorly in our legal system is overwhelming. African American inmates of Caribbean origin are up to 10 times more likely than Caucasian Americans to be admitted to medium-security units (McKenzie, 2004). Caucasian defendants are more likely than defendants of an ethnic minority to have a successful insanity plea (United States Sentencing Commission, 2008). African American defendants are nearly twice as likely as Caucasian defendants to be referred to a strict security facility for evaluation (Pinals, Packer, Fisher, & Roy-Bujnowski, 2004).

Because cultural values and perceptions influence the manner in which persons see themselves and their relationship with their world, this fact has implications for forensic evaluations beyond their manifestation of psychopathology and adjustment. A general finding from research with ethnically diverse examinees has established the vulnerability of validity scales, particularly F and L, to being affected by cultural values and experiences unique to the examinee. This possibility should be considered during the test interpretation. An examinee may be inclined to present him- or herself in a socially appropriate manner due to cultural values, but the response style may also be affected by immediate experiences. For instance, the forensic psychologist may be perceived by members of certain ethnic groups as an intruder, given the personal and sometimes highly intimate questions posed. As a result, the examinee may be reluctant to engage and collaborate in the evaluation.

Another aspect that may affect the response style in the MMPI–2 is that, in some cultures, exaggeration of experiences is encouraged when reporting symptoms (Garg, Dattilio, & Mazzo, 2011). Attitudes toward truth, deception, and honor are also determined by cultural norms, and these attitudes have an impact in the assessment of malingering, deception, and culpability (Bunnting, Wessels, Lasich, & Pillay, 1996). When an individual has grown up under a harsh and cruel political, legal, or civil society, distortion and deception may have been learned as a self-protective mechanism. The experiences in the country of origin can also shape the manner in which an immigrant relates to authority figures and the U.S. legal system. Having experienced repression or persecution may incline the forensic examinee to be suspicious, guarded, and even paranoid (Tseng, Matthews, & Elwin, 2004), just as has been noted for the response style of African Americans in an environment perceived as discriminating and unfair.

Gender roles and the relationship between genders can come into play in many ways, including the endorsement of socially sanctioned roles; the reluctance of examinees to answer on a self-report, such as the MMPI–2, items that are highly sensitive to the role expected of them; or their editing of what they are comfortable revealing to a stranger (Han et al., 2013). Sexual harassment, sexual abuse, and domestic violence can mean something very different, depending on the culture and socialization of the person, than they do to American society. These differences can influence the manner in which a culturally diverse examinee answers and interprets the items.

When an MMPI–2 profile of an ethnically diverse examinee appears to reflect significant psychopathology, it is important to integrate the interpretations of the MMPI–2 profile with behavioral and observational data in order to arrive at a better appraisal of the examinee's functioning, instead of using automatically traditional interpretations that point toward psychopathology. Similarly, the forensic opinions derived from personality testing should be integrated within the wider cultural and background history of the examinee. For instance, the way in which parents impart discipline, the boundaries set with their children, the role of achievement for the children, and the relationship of the nuclear family with extended family members are affected by the generational and cultural traditions of the family (McGoldrick, Giordano, & Garcia-Preto, 2005). These factors may be extremely relevant when interpreting results of psychological tests in forensic evaluations of custody, child abuse, adoption, and termination of parental rights. The manner in which a person perceives and experiences stress, mental illnesses, depression, and other distressing experiences may be very relevant when one is forming an opinion regarding that person's disability, extent of trauma, and mental status at the time of the offense. Cultural factors are involved in the motives of a crime and determination of criminal responsibility, as well as the sentencing and rehabilitation decisions. Although constructs such as competency to stand trial may be less affected by cultural and ethnic diversity given the basic and practical nature of the knowledge that has to be demonstrated, these aspects may have relevance regarding the accommodations that may be required to ensure the full participation of a defendant and factors that may impact restoration.

Any inferences are quite tenuous when empirically informed decision rules have not been identified and validated in this person's ethnic group. Forensic psychologists need to have a systematic way of reaching conclusions that does not appear biased. They need to generate hypotheses based on the individual's scale scores and code types in a manner that is systematic, impartial, sequential, and comprehensive. This approach minimizes confirmatory biases in the generation of hypotheses. Reviewing the literature is helpful in comparing results of an examinee with those of members of the same ethnic and cultural group. It is important to take into consideration the examinee's acculturation, socialization, educational and socioeconomic background, clinical experience, and knowledge of local cultural norms when interpreting results. A particular interpretation is more likely to be accurate if it is confirmed by several pieces of data, particularly if they come from independent sources and are not disconfirmed by significant evidence (Ganellen, 1996). Because in the forensic field the MMPI–2 is used in conjunction with other assessment instruments and strategies, it is the sum of critical information from diverse sources that helps the forensic psychologist obtain a reliable picture of the examinee's psychological functioning and adjustment.

CASE EXAMPLE

The cross-cultural application of MMPI–2 based assessment is illustrated in the following case in which the computer-based interpretation system, the Minnesota Report, was used to assess the mental-health status and personality problems in a Chinese forensic examinee in Hong Kong (see Chapter 12 for a detailed discussion of computer-based assessment). The case was provided by Butcher and Cheung (2006).

The examinee, Feng, was a 30-year-old, single, and college-educated man who had been arrested multiple times for various sexual offenses (e.g., indecent assault, indecent exposure of his genitals, stealing of female underwear) since 2001. He had been given various sentences, including probation with the condition of undertaking psychological treatment, and he participated in a Christian sex addiction treatment group on a voluntary basis. He was evaluated in a mental-health outpatient setting based on a court referral from his probation officer. His MMPI–2 validity and clinical scale profile is shown in Figure 4.1, and his Minnesota Narrative Report is presented in Exhibit 4.1.

Feng had been court-ordered to undertake psychological treatment in relation to his offending problem. For the first two times, the psychological treatment was terminated, as he had been put into jail because of a relapse in offending. Feng usually appeared compliant in attending the treatment sessions. During his first treatment he also had joined a 12-session sex offender treatment group, which covered topics like combating deviant

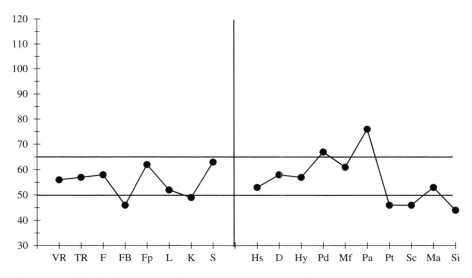

Figure 4.1. MMPI–2 basic validity and clinical scale profile for Feng. Excerpted from the *MMPI®–2 (Minnesota Multiphasic Personality Inventory®—2) Manual for Administration, Scoring, and Interpretation, Revised Edition* by Butcher et al. Copyright © 2001 by the Regents of the University of Minnesota. Used by permission of the University of Minnesota Press. All rights reserved. "MMPI®" and "Minnesota Multiphasic Personality Inventory®" are trademarks owned by the Regents of the University of Minnesota.

EXHIBIT 4.1
MMPI–2 Minnesota Narrative Report for Feng

Profile Validity

This is a valid MMPI–2 profile. The patient was quite cooperative in describing his symptoms and problems. His frank and open responses to the items can be viewed as a positive indication of his involvement with the evaluation. The MMPI–2 profile is probably a good indication of his present personality functioning and symptoms.

Symptomatic Patterns

The behavioral descriptions provided in this report are probably good indications of the patient's present personality functioning. Correlates of *Pd* and *Pa* were used as the report prototype and this configuration shows high profile definition. The patient's MMPI–2 clinical scale profile suggests a pattern of adjustment that might predispose him to psychological and interpersonal problems. He appears to be angry, somewhat sullen, mistrustful, and generally self-indulgent. He seems to have some disregard for authority figures, tends to deny responsibility, and blames others for his problems; In addition, he may become angry or argumentative over seemingly insignificant events.

In addition, the following description is suggested by the patient's scores on the content scales. He may have somewhat naïve ideas compared to others, viewing himself as overly trusting and altruistic. His denial of negative impulses and his proclamation of high moral standards probably influence his attitudes toward others. The patient does not appear to be an overly anxious person prone to developing unrealistic fears. Any fears he reports are likely to be viewed by him as reality-based rather than internally generated.

Profile Frequency

Profile interpretation can be greatly facilitated by examining the relative frequency of clinical scale patterns in various settings. The patient's high-point clinical scale score (*Pa*) occurred in 9.6% of the MMPI–2 normative sample of men. However, only 3.0% of the sample had *Pa* as the peak score at or above a *T* score of 65, and only 2.2% had well-defined *Pa* spikes. This elevated MMPI–2 profile configuration (4-6/6-4) is very rare in samples of normals, occurring in less than 1% of the MMPI–2 normative sample of men.

The relative frequency of this MMPI–2 high-point (*Pa*) score is high in various outpatient settings. In the large NCS Pearson outpatient sample, this high-point clinical score (*Pa*) occurred in 13.6% of the men. Moreover, 8.1% of the male outpatients had this high-point scale spike at or above *T* score of 65, and 5.2% had well-defined *Pa* high-point scores in the range. This elevated MMPI–2 profile configuration (4-6/6-4) occurred in 2.8% of the men in the NCS Pearson Outpatient sample.

Profile Stability

The relative elevation of the highest scales in his clinical profile reflects high profile definition. If he is retested at a later date, his peak scores on *Pd* and *Pa* are likely to retain their relative salience in his retest profile.

Interpersonal Relations

He is likely to demand attention and sympathy from others, but to resent even the smallest demands others place on him. He appears to be oversensitive and irritable and easily becomes very angry with others. Some individuals with this profile have problems forming intimate relationships because of their suspiciousness and aggressiveness.

EXHIBIT 4.1
MMPI–2 Minnesota Narrative Report for Feng   (*Continued*)

The patient's scores on the content scales suggest the following additional information concerning his interpersonal relations. He feels like leaving home to escape a quarrelsome, critical situation and to be free of family domination.

Diagnostic Considerations

Individuals with this MMPI–2 clinical profile tend to have long-standing personality traits, such as aggressiveness and hypersensitivity, that might predispose them to psychological and interpersonal stress. Features of a personality disorder are characteristic of individuals with this profile pattern.

Treatment Considerations

He appears to have personality characteristics that predispose him to interpersonal difficulties that could adversely influence the treatment relationship. He tends to deny problems and to blame others for his own shortcomings. He is not likely to view psychotherapy as an important option for him at this time. Sometimes individuals with this profile are pressured into therapy by outside circumstances. In such instances, their cooperation is minimal and they terminate therapy prematurely.

sexual fantasies, enhancing victim empathy, and learning strategies to prevent relapse. His performance and progress in the group were considered to be satisfactory. He was willing to share his offending history and was compliant in completing some homework assignments.

Despite his involvement and motivation in seeking help, Feng was unexpectedly arrested for reoffending and treatment had to be terminated abruptly. Even though he readily disclosed his past offending history, he usually talked about it in a matter-of-fact and sometimes even slightly animated manner. He revealed no signs of lapses such as increased offending urges during the sessions but was arrested unexpectedly because of reoffending. His therapist was skeptical as to how genuine and motivated he was in undertaking psychological service to eradicate his offending problem.

Feng has recurrent sexually arousing fantasies and behaviors involving the use of female undergarments. He even acted out repeatedly to steal the undergarments for masturbation, and such stealing led to his being arrested a few times over the past few years. As such, he was diagnosed as suffering from Fetishism.

He is the only son in a working-class family, and he has two older sisters. His childhood was uneventful until the time he started suffering from psoriasis, a chronic skin disease, at the age of 11. Because of the disease, his parents, especially the mother, were more indulgent and tolerant to him, satisfying his demands and requests as far as they could. Yet, his school life became unhappy and stressful, as he was mocked and teased by some schoolmates because of his "ugly" physical appearance. He then withdrew from peers and engaged in solitary activities (e.g., reading books, playing computer games).

Subjected to reduced enjoyment from peer interactions and motivated by elevated curiosity about sex during puberty, Feng indulged in watching pornography and masturbating starting at age 13. During that time, he developed some sexually deviant behaviors, such as stealing female underwear and peeping at females by hiding himself in female changing room, touching the thighs of female students on the bus, and exposing his genitals to girls walking alone, a few times in the following years. He was never caught during these years. He stated that such deviant behaviors subsided in 1992, when he changed his living environment and focused more on his studies. Nevertheless, he continued to enjoy browsing pornographic websites. He also started visiting prostitutes for tension release and sexual gratification during his school years.

It should be noted that Feng became more self-confident and related better with his peers after his teenage years, even though he still had psoriasis, which adversely affected his physical appearance. He developed a stable courtship with his girlfriend in 2001, with reportedly a satisfactory sexual relationship. The two of them even started living together in 2006. Even though the girlfriend, as well as his family members, knew of his repeated sexual offenses, they were still forgiving and supportive of him. His girlfriend also helped him financially in setting up his business.

Because of the recurring offenses, the psychologist was skeptical about Feng's motivation to undertake treatment despite his allegation that he did want to continue to seek help. The Chinese version of the MMPI–2 (CMMPI–2) was administered to better understand Feng's current personality characteristics and develop an effective intervention plan. He was expressive and spontaneous in communicating with the psychologist. Most of the time, he presented with stable and calm affect without showing any significant signs of distress.

Feng took a translation of the MMPI–2 in Chinese, which was his native language. There were no concerns regarding his ability to understand the items. The Chinese MMPI–2 has been translated, adapted, and standardized in China. When Feng's scores were plotted with the Chinese norms, the validity scales revealed that Feng was quite cooperative in describing his symptoms and problems. The Chinese profile revealed that Feng's profile fit a 6-4 code type. In order to use the computerized interpretation, the psychologist plotted his scores again with the U.S. norms because that is the population used for the program. It was determined that the profile patterns were almost identical and only slightly higher when the U.S. norms were used; however, the difference was not statistically significant. Therefore, it was considered that the interpretive report based on U.S. norms would be applicable to him and the clinical profile was likely a good indication of his personality functioning and symptoms.

The clinical profile is probably a good indication of his personality functioning and symptoms. The T scores of the clinical scales, except the Mf scale, when using the U.S. norms, were higher than those based on the Chinese norms. Yet, the profile patterns were highly similar, and he obtained a 6-4 code type on both profiles. As such, it is likely that the interpretive report based on the U.S. norms would be applicable to him.

As mentioned in the interpretive report, Feng's MMPI–2 clinical scale profile, with the 4-6/6-4 code type, suggests a pattern of adjustment that might predispose him to psychological and interpersonal problems. People with such profile elevation seem to be immature, narcissistic, and self-indulgent. They are passive-dependent individuals who make excessive demands on others for attention and sympathy, but they are resentful of even the mildest demands made on them by others. They seem to have some disregard for authority figures, tend to deny responsibility, and blame others for their problems.

The assessing psychologist noted that the profile descriptions in the Minnesota Report did remarkably match the clinical impression on Feng. In particular, he failed repeatedly to control himself from reoffending, some of which he even attributed to his having bad moods due to the lack of support and understanding from his family members and girlfriend. He preferred to get more encouragement and support from the Christian group than to be challenged to change in therapy sessions, all of which reflected his narcissistic and self-indulgent characteristics.

The interpretive report cautioned that Feng appears to have personality characteristics that predispose him to interpersonal difficulties that could adversely influence the treatment relationship. His tendency to deny problems and to blame others for his own shortcomings also might pose difficulty in treatment. Moreover, he is not likely to view psychotherapy as an important option for him at this time. Such cautionary remarks were accurate in the therapist's previous encounters with the examinee. To start treatment with him again, the therapist thought that such obstacles to treatment progress should first be addressed and resolved. Otherwise, the pattern of his apparent involvement treatment followed by treatment failure or abrupt termination is likely to repeat itself.

Taking into consideration the cautionary remarks from the Minnesota Report's interpretation of Feng's MMPI–2 results, the therapist spent the first few sessions addressing his personality characteristics that might have adversely affected treatment progress and how he and the therapist would collaborate differently so that he could really benefit from psychological treatment. In addition, he was invited to contemplate the approach goals he had (e.g., what he really desired to achieve in his life and not just what he wanted to avoid getting) and whether and how his recurring sexual offending problems had impacted on his goal attainment so far. After this foundation work, follow-up sessions were arranged with him about every four weeks, with the focus on his enhancing self-monitoring of his offending urges and adopting effective means to cope with such urges. He was supported to keep track on the positive life goals he would like to achieve.

It seemed that addressing Feng's motivation to change and collaborate with the therapist based on his MMPI–2 results had some positive impact. He showed more readiness and cooperation by sharing the fluctuation of his urges to steal female underwear and how he coped with them as the treatment sessions unfolded. Indeed, he had reported a few times that he did go to the area where he used to steal female underwear, but he just looked at the underwear hanging on the laundry line without stealing it. He had frankly disclosed such lapses to his therapist, as well as to the probation officer. Yet, he sometimes did not display any serious concern or worries about his lapses. He even alleged, with a mischievous smile, that it was likely that he would have stolen the underwear if not for the presence of some villagers in the vicinity. In response to such disclosure, he was challenged to recognize that he was the one who was responsible for making the choice in what move he would make next regarding his offending problem. Either he could practice the relapse prevention strategies he had learned in the past or indulge himself in the momentary excitement of reoffending. He would be the one who directly faced the consequence of his choice.

The psychologist noted, however, that Feng still exhibited some problematic personality characteristics reported in his MMPI–2 results by continuing to be self-centered and self-indulgent in his relationship with his girlfriend, which caused some conflict between them. He had also experienced great financial difficulty in his business, and he reported having low mood and resumed spending more time watching pornographic and erotic materials on the Internet. Under such circumstances, he was reminded of the need to recognize and cope constructively with his negative emotions and take great heed of the risk of lapse and relapse. One of the improvements he reported was that he initiated contact with the leader of the Christian group to discuss his mood problem and seek advice to handle it. Further psychological follow-up sessions were needed to continue to keep track of his offending urges and to help him reflect on his responsibility in relationship conflicts and whether and how he would like to change.

SUMMARY

There is a strong body of research that supports the use of the MMPI–2 with African Americans, Hispanic Americans, and Native Americans, and there is adequate basis to use the MMPI–2 with Asian Americans, recent immigrants, individuals of mixed ethnicity, and other special populations that were not a significant part of the normative sample. Cultural factors play a role in many aspects of the forensic assessment with the MMPI–2, from the choice of language version to the administration and interpretation. The literature reviewed indicates that ethnically and culturally diverse examinees may interpret certain items in a different way than the normative sample did, and their profiles may vary slightly from that of the normative sample. The use of the MMPI–2 with ethnically diverse examinees requires that forensic psychologists have knowledge of the potential diversity of profiles they may encounter and the nuances of what differences with normative values represent in the interpretation. This chapter provided a case illustration on the adaptation of a computerized MMPI–2 interpretive report on a forensic examinee in an international setting, Hong Kong, to illustrate the test's broad applicability and utility in assessment.

Forensic psychologists have the responsibility to determine carefully when the profile elevations represent cultural factors and when they are a sign of bona fide psychopathology, as well as when there is a combination of both, and to integrate this information in the report.

5

THE MMPI–2 IN NEUROPSYCHOLOGICAL ASSESSMENT

Brain–behavior relationships are complex phenomena and are not readily understood by lay individuals or nonforensic psychologists. The expectation of a forensic neuropsychologist is to articulate an evidence-based argument for an examinee's test results and then present these results, usually in written form, to professionals and lay individuals. The evidence for or against brain damage generally comes from a number of sources, including scientific research studies, objective test scores, qualitative or process variables, direct observation, physical findings, and historical factors. All of these factors must be woven together to create a preponderance of evidence for or against brain damage.

When neuropsychologists measure and interpret the relationship between known or suspected brain damage and resultant brain dysfunction, emotional functioning is almost always considered. Emotional levels are assessed and studied and compared with other test results to form an expert opinion regarding the presence or absence of brain damage and, ultimately, a clinical

http://dx.doi.org/10.1037/14571-006
Using the MMPI–2 in Forensic Assessment, by J. N. Butcher, G. A. Hass, R. L. Greene, and L. D. Nelson
Copyright © 2015 by the American Psychological Association. All rights reserved.

diagnosis. A strong defense of clinical interpretations related to personality and emotional functioning depends on tests with proven reliability and validity. The Minnesota Multiphasic Personality Inventory—2 (MMPI–2) meets these criteria. This chapter is designed to provide the forensic neuropsychologist with a means of understanding, utilizing, and defending the role of the MMPI–2 in the neuropsychological examination process.

A major purpose in Chapter 5 is to offer a method of decision making designed to render expert opinions. This chapter is organized as follows. It first provides a basic overview of what a forensic neuropsychological examination entails. The specific role of the MMPI–2 in this process is discussed next. Literature related to the MMPI–2 as it applies to brain injury cases is reviewed. Finally, a case study of an examinee suspected of malingering behavior is presented. In this context, supportive literature is provided that will develop the basis for information and opinions expressed. The literature review is not designed to be exhaustive, but it does focus on most, if not all, research designed to examine the relationship between head injury and the MMPI–2. It is acknowledged that not all neuropsychologists were trained or currently practice in the same manner as described in this chapter. A major aim in Chapter 5 is to provide strong empirical and evidence-based support for the role of the MMPI–2 in a forensic neuropsychological examination process.

EXAMINEES IN LITIGATION

Forensic neuropsychological reports or testimony are generally prepared for lay individuals or other professionals. The task of the forensic neuropsychologist is to generate and explain the findings, from both a scientific and a lay standpoint, of the neuropsychological evaluation. In this context, some of the most important data that explain the examinee's impairments are behavioral or qualitative in nature (Lezak, Howieson, & Loring, 2004). Observations of the examinee are ongoing during the appointment(s), from the moment the examinee steps into the waiting room, throughout formal test administration, during the interview portions of the examination, while the examinee takes breaks, and when the examinee interacts with others. Hypotheses are sometimes best supported from persons close to the examinee. Records reviewed for purposes of the examination ideally provide prior test data, premorbid (preinjury) history, educational information, employment history, past treatment, legal information, criminal history, depositions, accident scene data, and medical information, including brain imaging reports. So, the expert examiner acts as a human computer, in a sense, organizing, cataloging, and synthesizing all of this information: the test data, the observations, the interview reports, and subjective descriptions and demonstrations by examinees concerning their problems. Information is synthesized and resynthesized. This product is labor intensive, and reports are generated following many hours of work.

When examinees present for a forensic neuropsychological examination, they typically have had what they or their legal representatives or referral sources consider probable brain damage. *Brain damage* may be a loaded term. It is used interchangeably with traumatic brain injury (TBI), closed head injury, concussion, postconcussive syndrome, head injury, mild brain injury, and likely many more terms that professionals and lay individuals choose to give to any impact to the head that is felt to produce clinical symptoms. These terms are loaded because they imply that any impact to the head is associated with an actual injury to the brain itself. In reality, impacts to the head may or may not result in physical injury to the brain. Alternatively or additionally, cranial impacts may or may not produce clinical symptoms or functional changes associated with impact injuries.

Clinical neuropsychologists render diagnoses that are usually based on *Diagnostic and Statistical Manual of Mental Disorders* (*DSM–5*; American Psychiatric Association, 2013) guidelines. But, in the context of a forensic neuropsychological examination, much more is usually required than the *DSM–5* diagnosis of Major or Mild Neurocognitive Disorder (NCD) associated with traumatic brain injury. As stated in the introduction to the *DSM–5* section on Neurocognitive Disorders, "The criteria for the various NCDs are all based on defined cognitive domains. . . . The domains form the basis on which the NCDs, their levels, and their subtypes may be diagnosed" (American Psychiatric Association, 2013, p. 592).

The NCD cognitive domains listed in the *DSM–5* include general categories of attention, executive function, learning and memory, language, perceptual-motor functioning, and social cognition. Of interest, a category related to emotional or psychological variables is absent from this list. Social cognition criteria are limited to behavioral disturbances that may occur under the rubric of NCD and to what psychologists commonly refer to as *indifference reaction, poor judgment,* or *histrionic tendencies.*

In order to address areas related to emotional or specific behavioral problems and still rely on *DSM* standards, forensic psychologists must now consider additional *DSM–5* diagnoses. The implication of separating out emotional, psychological, and other behavioral symptoms from the NCDs is that traumatic head injuries and other neurological events often fail to produce this type of direct effect. *DSM–5* standards now state that probable outcomes following brain injury that meet criteria for NCDs exclude emotional factors. Clinical neuropsychologists, knowing the importance of considering all types of emotional symptoms and conditions when ruling out or judging severity of head injuries, can certainly still do so. However, more vigilance is required on their part to assure that these variables are not forgotten as the basis for their conclusions.

Why are emotional factors so important in a forensic context? One reason is that litigants are people who respond to situations with conscious intent or unwittingly. They react with apparent disregard for the obvious or in a credible manner, with integrity or without honesty. They may be impatient, unmotivated, unwilling to exert effort, naive, suggestible—all factors that influence test performance. They may have been coached to perform a certain way before the examination and, thus, undermine the evaluation. Their attitude may be positive and cooperative or resistant and guarded. Their demeanor may be friendly or irritable. Emotions may change dramatically based on what is occurring during the evaluation at any point in time. For example, anxiety may be dramatically reduced during test breaks compared with formal test administration. Dramatic improvement in their subjective complaints may be detected outside of the test room, when they feel they are not under observation.

During the examination session, emotional and psychological factors are on constant display in an ever-changing manner. As the evaluation unfolds, they tell a story about a person that is not limited to a diagnosis or by scores from objective tests. They are reflected in every nuance, in behavior and in shifts in behavior, across settings, across different examiners, and in different times of the day. A typical forensic neuropsychological examination takes anywhere from 6 to 16 hours or more. Thus, there is ample time to observe the examinee and gather evidence for conclusions regarding emotional functioning. Symptoms of emotional functioning may be a necessary and sufficient basis for clinical interpretations regarding brain damage, psychopathology, and credibility of the examinee's report. In the forensic neuropsychological context, they may be the key to determining whether the examination process is valid and, ultimately, whether the person has brain damage.

CLASSIFICATION OF BRAIN DAMAGE

Brain damage in the context of any medical evaluation has many descriptors. Variously referred to as *traumatic brain injury*, *mild traumatic brain injury*, *closed head injury*, *head injury*, *brain injury*, *mild brain injury*, *concussion*, and *post-concussive syndrome*, brain damage may or may not be described in the same manner by forensic psychologists or researchers. Many if not most of these terms imply brain damage or a physical injury to the brain when none may have occurred following impact.

The mild traumatic brain injury, or mTBI, is the most common type of traumatic brain injury. In cases of mTBI, an outcome that includes absence of physical evidence may be common. Mild head injury is often used synony-mously with the term concussion. The terms mild brain injury, mTBI, mild head injury (mHI), minor head trauma, and concussion may be used interchange-ably (National Center for Injury Prevention and Control, 2003; Petchprapai & Winkelman, 2007), although the term *concussion* is often treated as a narrower category (Sivák, Kurca, Jancovic, Petriscak, & Kucera, 2005). The term *concus-sion* is still used in sports literature as interchangeable with mHI or mTBI, but the general clinical medical literature now uses mTBI instead (Barth, Varney, Ruchinskas, & Francis, 1999). *Concussion* frequently is defined as a head injury with a temporary loss of brain function that causes a variety of physical, cogni-tive, and emotional symptoms, which may not be recognized, if subtle in nature.

There are standards for judging brain injuries that draw largely from the sports medicine literature. In the Cantu grading system (Cantu, 1998), sever-ity of concussion is based on (a) grade (mild; moderate; severe), (b) duration of loss of consciousness (none; less or greater than 5 minutes), and (c) duration of posttraumatic amnesia (less or greater than 30 minutes; 24 or more hours).

The American Academy of Neurology (AAN; Giza et al., 2013) set practice parameters for determining concussion severity in terms of (a) grade, (b) symptoms (transient confusion; mental status abnormalities) and resolution time of symptoms (less or greater than 15 minutes), and (c) loss of consciousness (none; seconds to minutes or more for severe only). Categories of concussive severity by AAN standards are more liberal than the Cantu system, particu-larly when judging severe head injuries. In cases of suspected mild head injury, a structural imaging technique called diffusion tensor imaging is emerging as important to understanding and examining evidence of damage to white matter regions (Bigler, 2011). Loss of white matter tracts occurs in all grades of head injuries, but diffusion tensor imaging scan results have been particularly sensi-tive to detection of effects of mild brain injury (Belanger, Vanderploeg, Curtiss, & Warden, 2007).

This 2013 modification of the AAN guidelines for severity of brain dam-age specifically calls for computerized tomography imaging (CT) in cases of sus-pected severe brain injuries as an additional determinant for the grade category. Structural imaging techniques, such as CT and magnetic resonance imaging, currently meet *Frye* standards of acceptability in forensic neuropsychological reports and courtroom testimony. Alternatively, some forms of functional brain imaging, such as positron emission tomography, may not currently meet the *Frye* scientific basis for admissibility of evidence for brain damage.

One of the most comprehensive classification systems for judging severity of head injury was reported by Frankowski, Annegers, and Whitman (1985). This system takes into consideration other parameters of brain damage that include (a) grade (trivial; mild; moderate; severe; fatal); (b) loss of conscious-ness (none; 30 minutes to 24 hours; severe: greater than 24 hours) and/or posttraumatic amnesia (same criteria as loss of consciousness); and (c) skull fracture (absence/presence of in moderate, severe) and/or cerebral injuries (none; severe: contusion, laceration, or intracranial hematoma). For forensic neuropsychological examinations, this classification system may be of greater relevance, as it includes alternative guidelines when loss of consciousness or posttraumatic amnesia variables are not available. Additional physical signs of TBI (e.g., skull fracture and intracranial trauma) offer the forensic psychologist greater latitude when grading severity of head injuries.

A clear and brief system of classification of brain damage is based on the Veterans Administration/Department of Defense (VA/DoD) Clinical Practice Guidelines (Department of Veterans Affairs, Department of Defense, 2009). Categories of classification covered under the VA/DoD Guidelines include structural imaging, loss of consciousness, posttraumatic amnesia, and Glasgow Coma Scale score and also differ by level of severity of the suspected brain injury. This classification system was used as a basis for judging brain injury severity in the case example at the end of this chapter.

PSYCHOLOGICAL FACTORS IN NEUROPSYCHOLOGY

Psychological components of brain damage are variously described as neurobehavioral correlates, psychosocial factors, symptoms of emotional functioning, or personality characteristics, to name a few. The psychology aspect of neuropsychology takes in these various descriptors and assigns them meaning based on the outcome of the neuropsychological examination. As symptoms of a mental disorder, they may be observable during the examination process as a qualitative variable. They may represent subjective problems or chief complaints. They constitute diagnostic features of DSM–5 disorders. Their severity and their course are documented as specifiers in diagnostic codes. Their level and type emerge from items and scales that objectively measure them. In short, the sources of information concerning emotional functioning and the manner in which results are integrated into the work product provide the evidence for an examinee's presentation and, ultimately, a diagnosis.

Diagnoses related to emotional and personality functioning fall into different categories within a forensic neuropsychological context. These diagnostic categories may be considered rule outs until and unless sufficient evidence is generated to determine, within reasonable medical probability, whether or not the diagnosis is supportable. Clinical psychologists are generally well aware of the diagnostic categories within the fourth edition, text revision, of the *Diagnostic and Statistical Manual of Mental Disorders* (DSM–IV–TR; American Psychiatric Association, 2000) and the newly revised DSM–5 that are commonly used in psychiatric settings.

However, in the forensic context, clinical neuropsychologists are perhaps more familiar with diagnoses related to conditions involving malingering and factitious behavior, as well as somatic symptoms and related disorders. Issues concerning malingering and factitious behavior are covered in Chapter 2 of this book. Somatic disorders include Somatic Symptom Disorder, Illness Anxiety Disorder, Conversion Disorder (Functional Neurological Symptom Disorder), Psychological Factors Affecting Other Medical Conditions, and Factitious Disorder.

Malingering and Borderline Personality Disorder are among the differential diagnoses offered in the diagnostic nomenclature when ruling out Factitious Disorder. Personality disorders may be diagnosed but no longer on a separate axis. More likely within a forensic neuropsychological context, personality traits, characteristics, or symptoms of a personality disorder are described but are not sufficiently present to qualify as a diagnosis for Personality Disorder, per se. Malingering is not a separate *DSM–5* diagnosis. The main difference between malingering behavior and symptoms of a factitious disorder, by *DSM–5* standards, is that the former implies intent to lie for protection (from liability) or for secondary gain (usually monetary). Factitious disorder implies deception due to the need to appear sick or injured, without any obvious secondary gains present. This distinction is not easy to make in the forensic context, but it is a necessary one when a litigant is suing for millions of dollars.

A cautionary statement is offered regarding use of diagnoses, in general, and the *DSM–5*, in particular, in forensic settings (American Psychiatric Association, 2013) relative to risks and limitations contained herein. An imperfect fit exists between issues related to the law and information contained in clinical diagnoses. A diagnosis of any given mental disorder does not imply that the examinee met legal criteria for the presence of a psycholegal construct. A *DSM–5* diagnosis does not indicate that the person met a specified legal standard for, say, competence, criminal responsibility, or a disability.

THE CONUNDRUM OF CREDIBILITY

Professionals who are qualified to render *DSM–5* diagnoses, such as psychiatrists and psychologists, are trained in the nomenclature and the decision-making process necessary to rule out clinical conditions that may not fit the individual and render a diagnosis that does. In forensic settings, the sum of the evidence in support of expert opinions consists of reasonable probability statements unique to the examinee. As the authors of *DSM–5* state, a diagnostic label does not implicate a person's control over the behaviors associated with his or her disorder. Control, in the forensic neuropsychology context, may be associated with intent, and intent is strongly tied to a rule out of, for example, malingering behavior. Behavioral control of symptoms is considered when evaluating validity of the information and results from the neuropsychological examination.

Because validity of self-report is integral to the evaluation process, the issue of control may create a conundrum for the examiner: Does the examinee exercise conscious or involuntary intent to sabotage the examination? Is the examinee purposely lying or exaggerating to increase the potential for secondary gain? Is the examinee perhaps under the false belief that a physical problem exists when it does not? Do histrionic traits dramatize their problems for effect? Does the examinee like to be dependent on the system to avoid responsibilities? Are there behavioral inconsistencies that support low credibility?

Many of these questions may be addressed from an emotional standpoint. Emotional, because behaviors such as lying, exaggerating, sabotaging, dramatizing, dependency, and credibility are constructs that are on display throughout the examination process. They may be directly observable. They may be testable. Some are inferential. Others are subjective. They vary by type and degree and setting. In the work product produced or in expert testimony, the story is told of an examinee as litigant. It is a story based on facts and opinions, conclusions and interpretations, history and prediction, quantifiable information and subjective inferences. Woven throughout the expert's account is justification for the person's veracity.

Psychologist Lloyd Cripe once said, "The number is not the reality, it is only an abstract symbol of some part or aspect of the reality measured. The number is a reduction of many events in a single symbol. The reality [is] the complex dynamic performance" (L. I. Cripe, personal communication, September 27, 1990). The examination process represents the complex dynamic process. It may include introductions in the waiting room, completion of office forms, discussions with family members, test breaks, review of records—all of which may have bearing on the issue of credibility of an examinee's report, motivational qualities, and emotional levels. When attorneys conduct depositions of examinees or forensic psychologists, they remain vigilant for inconsistent statements, made at different times, by the same person. Inconsistency to an attorney speaks directly to the examinee's or forensic psychologist's credibility. For neuropsychologists, inconsistent remarks made by an examinee may be due to factors like poor memory, low attention, or low credibility. The various opportunities provided to examiners during the medicolegal process allow for direct observation of inconsistent speech and behavior so a determination may be made regarding etiology of an examinee's complaints. The numbers that are crunched and analyzed represent test outcomes that are synthesized and compared to observational data. Consistency remains paramount in this context.

Comparisons of test–retest data, serial brain scans, premorbid and current functioning, and interexaminee performance may all be quantified. Observations are routine and subjective. The forensic neuropsychological examination is thus not just about reporting numbers, as Cripe so aptly stated, but is a synthesis of information from all sources (Cripe, 1996, 1999).

SCIENTIFIC BASIS FOR USE OF THE MMPI–2 IN NEUROPSYCHOLOGICAL ASSESSMENTS

Assessment of personality and emotional functioning has had a place in the field of neuropsychology for over 75 years. We have known of discrete connections between cerebral lesions and the emotional changes they produced from the work of Moniz (1936), Freeman and Watts (1942), Andersen and Hanvik (1950), Mettler (1949), Meier (1961, 1964, 1965a, 1965b, 1969), and others. Ralph Reitan's early research (1955b) comparing performance of patients with and without brain damage showed, in part, that neurotic-like symptoms must be considered when interpreting results. When the movement to consider the concept of brain–behavior relationships took place, it was Manfred Meier and Karl Pribram (e.g., G. A. Miller, Galanter, & Pribram, 1960; Pribram, 1969) who, in the early 1960s, turned neuropsychologists' awareness to the value of localization by associating a brain region with specific behavioral functions (see also Pribram, 1954; Pribram, Lim, Poppen, & Bagshaw, 1966; Pribram & Mishkin, 1955). It took researchers like Meier and Pribram, in the 1960s, to formulate a path that bridged this early research with that of evolving neuropsychological theory. As the process of marrying personality theory to assessment began to unfold, the natural course was to adopt neurological concepts and build the basis for brain–behavior associations.

As history would have it, one of the major measures of personality and emotional functioning was also born around this time: the MMPI. Neuropsychology was taking hold as a distinct field of study within clinical psychology in the 1940s. The MMPI found a natural place in the field and was embraced by researchers as the method to measure personality changes resulting from or associated with structural lesions of the brain. Early efforts to measure cognitive changes and personality correlates utilized the MMPI as early as 1949. Scientists in the early 1950s hypothesized that cephalocaudal lesions were associated with different personality changes in patients with anterior, as compared to posterior, lesions. The anatomical base for localization of personality functions and correlates was beginning to provide a framework for research design. Prefrontal leucotomies were being performed because they reduced anxiety (Meier, 1961, 1964, 1965a, 1965b, 1969). A niche opened up for measurement of outcome variables and response to treatment. The MMPI filled that niche. Serial MMPIs were administered to assess changes in personality functions. Case study reports were published. The *D* and *Pt* scales emerged as particularly sensitive to post-operative changes. Pre- and postfrontal lobotomies also showed high-point code types that shifted dramatically postoperatively and were sustained over serial administrations of the MMPI.

In the 1960s the MMPI was considered the index of psychopathology that combined well with other brain indices. L. K. Sines and Silver (1963) developed a new MMPI scale derived from the *Pa* and *Sc* scales, called *Ip*, that quantified psychopathology. Scores from the MMPI *Ip* scale were compared to electroencephalographic tracings to measure pre- and postoperative lateralized temporal lobe excisions. The MMPI was beginning to be seen as a useful adjunct to early neurological methods of study. For present-day neuropsychologists, the MMPI–2 and its role in a neuropsychological test battery stem from this early work. Data from the MMPI provide the means to judge performance outcome, response to treatment, and other clinical considerations when dealing with examinees with brain injury.

As the field of neuropsychology has grown to become one of the largest branches of psychology, the MMPI and the revised MMPI–2 have grown with it. Stemming from a time when personality theorists were most prolific in helping us understand brain–behavior associations, the MMPI has adapted to a changing field. Its refinements are, as they were in the 1940s, empirically driven. For neuropsychologists, the value and strength of MMPI–2 results to describe personality correlates accurately of an individual with brain injury remain unprecedented. The goal of testing is always to obtain the best performance the individual is capable of producing (Lezak et al., 2004). The "best" performance for some examinees requires optimal effort, given their emotional state while enduring the stress of the examination process, their psychological problems and associated mental disorders, the presence of actual brain damage, side effects of medication, lack of sleep, economic and family worries, pain, and physical injuries and disabilities. The MMPI–2 provides one of the most validated indicators of best performance, because of the strong, actuarial evidence of credibility of its report, as well as personality and emotional functioning.

The MMPI–2 is one of the most researched personality tests available today and, thus, has a well-documented scientific basis for inclusion in a neuropsychological test battery. In a survey of 404 psychologists and neuropsychologists (S. R. Smith, Gorske, Wiggins, & Little, 2010), the MMPI–2 was found to be the second most commonly used test used to measure personality and emotional functioning. The Beck Inventories (Depression; Anxiety) ranked first (Beck & Steer, 1993; Beck, Ward, Mendelson, Mock, & Erbaugh, 1961). A notable distinction between the two rankings was length of the test, certainly a consideration to neuropsychologists within the context of an already lengthy test battery. Test length has been considered prohibitive, with MMPI–2 test-taking time running anywhere from one and a half to three hours, depending on whether the printed or audio version is used. But, as any psychologist or researcher knows, length of a test is directly correlated with reliable outcome (Cronbach, 1970).

Despite its length and the time it takes to administer, the MMPI–2 continues to be the instrument of choice based on surveys conducted among psychologists and neuropsychologists. Sharland and Gfeller (2007), in a survey of 712 neuropsychologists, showed that the most frequently used measures of response bias and credibility of respondent report came from the MMPI–2. Benefits of including a test such as the MMPI–2 involve not only measuring emotional levels and personality characteristics but also assessing for factors of malingering behavior, inconsistent responding, credibility of report, and psychosomatic beliefs. Thus, an inherent danger in discounting a test because of time constraints is to diminish opportunities to assess fully the very factors that require attention in a forensic evaluation.

The MMPI–2, like classic neuropsychological tests, has proven reliability and validity. Both are critical components when selecting a test for inclusion in a neuropsychological test battery. The MMPI–2 has been studied with two methods: clinical research and analog. As shown in Table 5.1, a sample of 23 studies is described using the MMPI–2 as it relates to the field of neuropsychology. Of these studies, two were analog in nature, 13 involved clinical patients, and seven were archival record reviews.

Analog study methods simulate, under controlled conditions, a situation that occurs in real life. In the two studies illustrated in Table 5.1, the participants were instructed to feign a disorder so that their responses could be compared to those of participants who were asked to respond in an honest manner. In these studies, participants were generally suffering from closed head injuries. The definition of closed head injuries varied in terms of severity and depended largely on the source of the classification system used.

Classification of head injury severity level was usually arbitrary and was loosely based on the standard guidelines described earlier in this chapter (e.g., Cantu, 1998; Department of Veterans Affairs, Department of Defense, 2009; Frankowski et al., 1985). Clinical participants were assigned to groups on the basis of their categories of brain damage severity or presence/absence characteristics. Scores from the MMPI/MMPI–2 basic validity, clinical, content, and supplementary scales were then used as a basis for discriminating between groups. Several MMPI–2 scales were found to best discriminate honest responders from people feigning malingering or compensation-seeking behavior based on analog and archival data research. The optimal scales were the basic clinical (*Pa*, *Pt*, *Ma*, *Sc*) and validity (*L*, *F*, *FB*, *Fp*, *Ds*) scales, as well as select validity configurations (e.g., conversion "V") and validity indices (e.g., *F* minus *K*).

TABLE 5.1
Summary of Literature on Traumatic Brain Injury and the MMPI–2

Study	Method	Results
Reitan (1955a)[a]	N = 100. Groups: Examinees with proven brain damage or dysfunction (n = 50) and persons with negative neurological and amnestic findings of organic brain involvement, but with definite neurotic symptoms (n = 50), were administered the MMPI. Clinical research study.	Significant differences between groups on MMPI scales that are ordinarily associated with severe mental disturbances: Pa, Pt, Sc, and Ma. Statistically significant differences between groups of individuals with and without brain damage on F, Pa, Pt, Sc, and Ma.
Doehring & Reitan (1960)[a]	N = 51. Groups: Aphasic brain-damaged (n = 17), nonaphasic brain-damaged (n = 17), and control (n = 17) groups were administered the MMPI. Groups were matched in age and education. Aphasic symptoms were based on results of Halstead–Wepman Screening Test. Clinical research study.	Aphasic brain-damaged groups and nonaphasic brain-damaged groups consisted primarily of persons with traumatic head injuries. Brain-damaged groups were not significantly different across MMPI clinical scales. Both brain-damaged groups were significantly higher on scale L scores than was the control group.
Berry et al. (1995)[b]	N = 99. Groups: Two control and two closed head injury (CHI). No description of head injury classification was reported. The CHI group was split into compensation-seeking and non-compensation-seeking subgroups. The CHI compensation subgroup consisted of people seeking disability benefits or civil actions for their head injuries. Archival data study.	Controls given instructional sets to fake CHI scored significantly higher among all four groups on all MMPI–2 basic clinical scales, except F, Fb, F-K, Fp, Ma, Pd, and Ds2. The latter seven scales were significantly elevated in compensation-seeking CHI examinees over non-compensation-seeking CHI examinees.
Gass & Apple (1997)[c]	N = 63. Closed head injury (CHI). Administered battery of neuropsychological tests (Wechsler Memory Scale—Revised; Wechsler Adult Intelligence Test—Revised Digit Span subtest; Cognitive Difficulties Scale). CHI defined as loss of consciousness, the majority having less than 60 minutes. Clinical research study.	Correlations between cognitive test scores and MMPI–2 variables of depression and anxiety showed significant correlations in the areas of attention and concentration. MMPI–2 scale Pt showed the strongest relationship with cognitive symptoms based on neuropsychological test scores. Unclear whether the MMPI–2 Depression and Anxiety scales related to scales D and Pt respectively or whether they related to content or supplementary scales.

Study	Method	Results
Gass & Wald (1997)[d]	N = 54. Litigating mild closed head trauma cases. Mild head trauma was defined as loss of consciousness of less than 5 minutes primarily due to motor vehicle accident. Data from participants with head injury were compared with data from the MMPI–2 normative sample. The purpose of study was to cross-validate 14 neurologically sensitive MMPI–2 items (correction factor). Clinical research study.	The MMPI–2 items (13 of the original 14 neurocorrection items) that best discriminated participants with head injury from normal examinees were limited to neurologic symptoms.
Youngjohn et al. (1997)[b]	N = 60. Groups: Examinees with moderate to severe head injury (Glasgow Coma Scale > 13, loss of consciousness > 30 minutes, positive imaging, and/or posttraumatic amnesia > 24 hours); subgroups of examinees were litigating, nonlitigating, and those with mild head injury (Glasgow Coma Scale ≤ 15, loss of consciousness < 30 minutes, negative imaging results, and posttraumatic amnesia < 24 hours). Thirty consecutively referred examinees with documented moderate/severe head injuries (18 of whom were litigating) who were capable of completing the MMPI–2 were compared with 30 consecutively referred examinees with symptomatic minor/mild head injuries (all of whom were litigating). Clinical research study.	Results showed that, relative to the severe nonlitigating group, the litigating group had significant elevations on MMPI–2 clinical scales *Hs*, *Hy*, *Sc*, and *HEA*. The mild head injury group had significant elevations on MMPI–2 clinical scales *Hs*, *D*, *Hy*, and *Pt* over both the litigating and nonlitigating severe groups.
Gasquoine (2000)[b]	N = 28. Groups: Examinees with traumatic back pain (traumatic back pain injuries were sprain or strain; most had normal spinal radiographic studies) and examinees with concussion (the majority from motor vehicle accidents). Concussive injuries were primarily posttraumatic amnesia of less than 1 hour. These two groups were combined into one group when MMPI–2 data were examined. Participants were retested about one month later. Simulated neuropsychological impairment was evaluated (≤ 90% on digit memory test). Clinical research study.	Results showed a significant relationship between MMPI–2 scales *D* and *Pt* and degree of change in postconcussion symptoms. Results were interpreted to mean that sudden trauma affected MMPI–2 results, regardless of whether trauma was due to back pain or to concussional pain.

(continues)

TABLE 5.1
Summary of Literature on Traumatic Brain Injury and the MMPI–2   (Continued)

Study	Method	Results
Gass & Luis (2001)[c]	$N = 205$. The majority of the sample was diagnosed with cerebrovascular disease; 20% of the sample was diagnosed with traumatic brain injury. The audiotaped version of the 180-item short form MMPI–2 was used. Archival data study.	Results showed variability across MMPI–2 basic scale scores from the MMPI–2–180 in predicting scores on the MMPI–2. The most accurate score prediction from the MMPI–2–180 occurred on scales L and Hs. Gass and Luis suggested caution regarding use of the MMPI–2 short form in place of the MMPI–2.
Ross et al. (2003)[b]	$N = 381$. Examinees with head injury, the majority of whom were personal injury litigants. 50% of the sample had < 5 minutes posttraumatic amnesia and loss of consciousness. Replication of Gass (1996). Clinical research study.	MMPI–2 scales D, Pt, Sc, DEP, ANX, FRS, OBS, and BIZ all significantly correlated with neuropsychological measures of attention (Wechsler Adult Intelligence Test—Revised Digit Span subtest) and List Learning (California Verbal Learning Test). The neuropsychological tests used in this study were prior versions of current revised tests.
Dearth et al. (2005)[e]	$N = 83$. Groups: Head injury (HI) examinees coached to malinger, HI examinees without coaching, controls coached to malinger, and controls without coaching (HI groups suffered loss of consciousness > 1 hour). Neuropsychological battery included the Controlled Oral Word Association Test, Wechsler Adult Intelligence Test–III Digit Span and Digit Symbol subtests, Finger Oscillation Test, Wechsler Memory Scale–III Word List Immediate and Delayed subtests, Grooved Pegboard Test, the New Adult Reading Test (revised), and Stroop Color–Word Reading Test. Analog study.	Results were unclear regarding group differences on MMPI–2 scales. Conclusions were that scales F and Ds2 helped identify malingering.

Gervais et al. (2007)[e]	N = 1,212. Groups: Workers' compensation and medico-legal referrals. The purpose was to validate the Response Bias Scale. All examinees were administered a test battery containing the MMPI–2 and at least one symptom validity test. The Test of Memory Malingering was not incorporated into the test battery until 1999 and the Medical Symptom Validity Test was incorporated in 2003; hence, there were fewer cases with data for these measures. Archival data study.	The Response Bias Scale discriminated between groups that either passed or failed two neuropsychological tests of malingering behavior.
N. W. Nelson et al. (2007)[c]	N = 122. Participants were considered compensation seeking. Neuropsychological tests used were the Victoria Symptom Validity Test, Test of Memory Malingering, the Letter Memory Test, and MMPI–2 validity scales (L, F, K, FBS, Fp, RBS, Md, Ds-R, S). The purpose of the study was to clarify the meaning of response validity. Archival data study.	Exploratory factor analysis. Results supported use of MMPI–2 validity scales as incremental data to interpret neuropsychological test results when examining civil litigants.
Sharland & Gfeller (2007)[e]	N = 712. Neuropsychology professionals. Survey study.	Most frequently used measures of response bias included MMPI–2 F-K ratio and the FBS among neuro-psychologists.
Wygant et al. (2007)[c]	N = 268. Two groups: criminal defendants and personal injury and disability claimants. Battery of neuropsychological tests administered (Test of Memory Malingering, Word Memory Test, symptom validity test). MMPI–2 scales examined included FBS and Fp. The purpose of study was to test whether criminals who failed symptom validity tests produced elevated psychotic MMPI–2 scales (Fp and FBS). Clinical research study.	Results showed failure on symptom validity tests was associated with (a) type of clinical setting, (b) non-credible reporting of psychotic symptoms in criminal settings, and (c) noncredible somatic complaints in both groups (criminal defendants and personal injury/disability claimants). Wygant et al. concluded that malingering and response bias are expressed differently in criminal settings involving more extreme forms of pathology. Criminals tend to exaggerate symptoms in areas of somatic, cognitive, and psychological complaints. This response pattern was not seen in civil litigants.

(continues)

TABLE 5.1
Summary of Literature on Traumatic Brain Injury and the MMPI–2 (Continued)

Study	Method	Results
Alwes et al. (2008)[e]	N = 308. Sample: Participants with workers' compensation claims and participants with personal injury. Groups: (a) probable psychiatric feigning = evidence for psychiatric feigning based on results of the Structured Interview of Reported Symptoms; (b) probable honest responders. Clinical research study.	Results were significantly higher MMPI–2 scores on scales F and Fb in the group of individuals considered to exhibit probable psychiatric feigning than among the probable honest responders.
Hessen et al. (2008)[b]	N = 41. People with mild traumatic brain injury (mTBI) who sustained their injury in childhood. Their cases were examined, retrospectively, 23 years later. Head injuries were classified according to presence/absence of skull fracture, length of posttraumatic amnesia < 24 hours, and/or pathological electroencephalography (EEG) results. Clinical research study.	Comparison between subgroups with and without skull fracture showed the former scored significantly higher on scales Hs and Hy. Only 4 out of 41 participants with mTBI sustained a skull fracture. Comparisons between subgroups with posttraumatic amnesia > 30 minutes and with pathological EEG showed significant elevations on the HEA, BIZ, and WRK scales. Also, for the mTBI group significant elevations were found on several Harris–Lingoes subscales: Physical Malfunction, Lassitude–Malaise, and Somatic Complaints.
Smart et al. (2008)[e]	N = 307. Two groups: secondary gain and nonsecondary gain. A unique statistical approach was used to provide decision trees that classified degree of effort expended in psychological examination. MMPI–2 validity scales were examined (L, F, K, Fb, VRIN, TRIN, F-K, Fp, S, Ds, FBS, RBS, Md) along with MMPI–2 basic clinical scales. Neuropsychological test battery administered consisting of the Victoria Symptom Validity Test, Test of Memory Malingering, Multi-Digit Memory Test, Word Memory Test, and Letter Memory Test. Archival data study.	Results were summarized to indicate that response validity measures that are psychological in nature (e.g., L, F, K, Fb, VRIN, TRIN, F-K, Fp, S, Ds, FBS, RBS, Md) do not directly correspond with cognitive validity measures. Both are necessary, and they should be considered independently of one another when interpreting test results.

Walters et al. (2008)[e]	$N = 1,211$. Groups: Inmates completed testing as part of a forensic mental health evaluation; other examinees were involved in workers' compensation or personal injury cases. Study design: Measured feigning behavior according to performance on MMPI–2 scales (F, Fp, and Ds). F and Fp scales were considered feigning scales. Malingering was identified by high endorsement rate on these scales. Clinical research study.	Conclusions were that malingering is a complex area and may best be considered in terms of degree of malingering rather than categories of malingerers.
Thomas & Youngjohn (2009)[b]	$N = 83$. Groups were litigating mild traumatic brain injury (mTBI), complicated mTBI, and moderate/severe TBI cases. Moderate/severe TBI included at least two of the following: Glasgow Coma Scale (GCS) < 13; loss of consciousness (LOC) > 30 minutes; positive CT/ MRI results. Complicated TBI defined as meeting one criterion: GCS < 13, LOC >30 minutes, or CT/MRI positive for skull fracture or cranial bleed. The mTBI defined as GCS = 13 to 15 and LOC < 30 minutes and negative CT/MRI. MMPI–2 Restructured Clinical (RC) scales came from the new MMPI–2 restructured form or MMPI–2–RF. The MMPI–2–RC scales were compared with MMPI–2 validity and clinical scale scores. Failure on cognitive symptom validity testing was considered in analyses. Archival data study.	The Conversion V (elevated scales Hs and Hy, lowered D) was the most frequent configuration among examinees with mTBI and examinees who failed symptom validity tests. The $RC3$ scale (the RC equivalent of Hy) did not appear to be a valid measure of somatization and/ or malingering. The MMPI–2 validity scales profile was inversely related to TBI severity. No other MMPI–2 or RC scale was interpreted as clinically significant.
Lange et al. (2010)[e]	$N = 49$. Participants were students (majority female, in their early 20s) at an Australian university. Participants completed the MMPI–2 and Personality Assessment Inventory (PAI) under one of three conditions: control (honest responding), feign posttraumatic stress disorder (PTSD), and feign depression. Analog study.	Participants instructed to feign depression or feign PTSD had significantly higher scores on the majority of MMPI–2 and PAI validity indicators than did controls. Diagnostic-specific MMPI–2 validity indicators, such as the Infrequency-PTSD scales and Malingered Depression scale, were the only MMPI–2 validity scales not effective at detecting participants instructed to feign those conditions. The rest of the MMPI–2 validity indicators (scales F, Fb, Fp, $F-K$, FBS, $Ds-R$, and RBS) were clearly superior to those on the PAI at identifying feigned versus honest responding in this sample.

(continues)

TABLE 5.1

Summary of Literature on Traumatic Brain Injury and the MMPI–2   (Continued)

Study	Method	Results
Misdraji & Gass (2010)[c]	N = 197. Groups: Veterans with no or suspected brain dysfunction. No additional information provided to define the sample relative to brain damage. Primary neuropsychological measure was Trail Making Test (A and B). Archival data study.	Results showed nonsignificant relationships between MMPI–2 scales of Depression and Anxiety and Trail Making Test performance. Misdraji and Gass concluded that poor performance on the Trail Making Test (Grapple-motor speed) should not be attributed to symptoms of anxiety or depression as measured by the MMPI–2.
S. R. Smith et al. (2010)[c]	N = 404. Psychologists, of whom 20% were board certified in neuropsychology; the majority were in private practice. Respondents were surveyed on types of personality tests most commonly used (MMPI–2; MMPI–A; Millon 3rd ed.; Rorschach; Thematic Apperception Test). Survey study.	The most commonly used test was the Beck Depression Inventories (Anxiety and Depression). The second most commonly used personality test was the MMPI–2/MMPI–A. Smith et al. concluded that neuropsychologists do not make use of personality assessment tests with older adult populations but instead tend to use them more with children and adolescents.
Gass & Odland (2012)[c]	N = 303. Veterans with multiple medical conditions. Primary complaints were memory and concentration. The majority had mood disorders. Results of MMPI–2 symptom validity Fake Bad Scale (FBS) were examined. The relationship between MMPI–2 content scales and the FBS was examined. Clinical research study.	Gass and Odland stated that the FBS measured noncredible symptom reporting or somatic malingering. Anxiety was the most powerful predictor of FBS item endorsement rate. Anxiety was more powerful than level of physical health and somatic symptoms (HEA). Results supported that some FBS items reflect emotional distress. Fake Good responses were less efficient in predicting emotional distress.
Gass & Odland (2014)[e]	N = 303. Male veteran mental health referrals. The purpose was to examine the validity of the 12-item Fake Bad Scale (FBS). The FBS was described as a measure of exaggerated or malingered distress and non-credible symptom reporting. Clinical research study.	Modest internal consistency (reliability) of FBS. Variance of FBS scores largely accounted for by ANX scale scores and ASP scale scores. High ASP scores were associated with low FBS results. Anxiety appeared to be the most powerful predictor of FBS item endorsement. Thus, FBS items seem to reflect emotional distress.

Note. The primary areas of focus for each study are denoted by superscripts: [a]Localized brain damage; [b]Traumatic brain injury; [c]Forensic neuropsychology and the MMPI–2; [d]Neuro-correction; [e]Malingering and faking bad. CT = computerized tomography imaging; MRI = magnetic resonance imaging; TBI = traumatic brain injury; MMPI–A = Minnesota Multiphasic Personality Inventory—Adolescent. Basic scales: D = Depression; Hs = Hypochondriasis, Hy = Hysteria; Ma = Hypomania; Pa = Paranoia; Pd = Psychopathic Deviate; Pt = Psychasthenia; Sc = Schizophrenia. Content scales: ANX = Anxiety; ASP = Antisocial Practices; BIZ = Bizarre Mentation; DEP = Depression; FRS = Fears; HEA = Health Concerns; OBS = Obsessional; WRK = Work Interference. Validity and bias scales: Ds = Dissimulation; Ds2 = Dissimulation–2; Ds-R = Dissimulation–revised; F = Symptom Exaggeration; Fb = Back F; FBS = Fake Bad Scale; Fp = Infrequency-Psychopathology; K = Defensiveness; L = Lie; Md = Malingered Depression; RBS = Response Bias Scale; S = Superlative Self-Presentation; TRIN = True Response Inconsistency; VRIN = Variable Response Inconsistency.

TABLE 5.2
The Top 15 MMPI–2 Items Differentiating Closed-Head Trauma
Examinees From Normal Examinees

MMPI–2 item	MMPI–2 scales
40	Hy, HEA
180	F, Sc
101	Hs, Hy, HEA
229	Sc, Ma
31	D, Hy, Pd, Pt, Sc, ANX, WRK
175	Hs, D, Hy, Pt, HEA
325	Pt, Sc
147	D, Pt, Sc
39	Hs, D, Hy, ANX
170	D, Pt, Sc, ANX
165	Fall; D, Pt, Sc
308	Pt, Si
149	Hs, HEA
299	Sc, ANX, WRK
247	Hs, Sc, HEA

Note. Items in this table represent MMPI–2 correction items for closed head trauma. All items, except for Item 165, are scored in the true direction. Items are listed in order of importance (i.e., in terms of power of differentiating patients with closed head trauma from normal patients). From "MMPI–2 Interpretation and Closed Head Trauma: Cross-Validation of a Correction Factor," by C. S. Gass and H. S. Wald, 1997, *Archives of Clinical Neuropsychology, 12*, p. 202. Copyright 1997 by Oxford University Press. Adapted with permission.

In contrast, clinical studies using the MMPI–2 involved participants with well-documented brain injuries and normal controls. When individuals with suspected brain injury were compared to controls, results supported MMPI–2 scales *Hs, D, Hy,* and *Pt* and 14 neurocorrection items (see Table 5.2) as best discriminating between groups. The approach taken in these studies was to examine the relationship among cognitive test scores, results of malingering measures, and data from the MMPI–2 basic validity, clinical, and content scales.

The process of qualifying emotional distress from credibility of response involves two very different questions. Studies using clinical patients appear to best address how the MMPI–2 measures psychopathology in individuals with brain injury, whereas analog research seems to better address the issue of malingering behavior. Pseudo-brain-injured individuals are represented in analog research, and those results may be pertinent to answering questions regarding credibility of responding. Analog and archival data offer assistance in distinguishing between someone who exaggerates or is faking bad and someone who is responding in a credible manner. Clinical studies, on the other hand, may help direct neuropsychologists as to MMPI–2 response patterns in persons with brain injury, especially mTBI, and how people with different levels of severity of brain damage score on the MMPI–2. For example, if one considers analog and archival research methods, the controversial *FBS* appeared to serve as a valid basis for discriminating honest responders from noncredible ones. However, when individuals with brain injury were compared to controls, the *FBS* served as a measure of anxiety and not response validity (as Lees-Haley found in his 1988 use of the items that were incorporated into the *FBS*). So, it seems that a combination of the two types of research designs should be considered by researchers when making determinations about "faking bad" compared to psychosomatic factors that may drive the elevation of MMPI–2 scale scores. Ultimately, all decisions, as neuropsychologists know, include the entire context of the examinee's clinical information. The rule of thumb when referring to and relying on research, such as that represented in Table 5.1, is to qualify the studies that best pertain to the case at hand and the results of those MMPI–2 scales that best represent the examinee. This decision-making process is illustrated in the case example that follows.

CASE EXAMPLE

Hector is a 24-year-old, left-handed, high-school-educated, married Hispanic man who was referred for an independent medical examination (neuropsychological). The examinee was involved in a motor vehicle accident on December 6, 2009, in which he was found unresponsive at the scene. Glasgow Coma Scale scores ranged from 3 to 13 (out of 15) within 24 hours following this event. The independent medical examination was conducted 3 years postevent. He was found to have suffered probable mild to moderate level closed head injury based on VA/DoD standards (Department of Veterans Affairs, Department of Defense, 2009).

The content of the neuropsychological examination included (a) interviews with Hector and family members; (b) administration of a neuropsychological test battery; (c) behavioral observations of Hector throughout a 16-hour evaluation period; and (d) review of medical and school records. Tests that measured credibility of response, effort, and malingering behavior were administered. The MMPI–2 was used to assess personality and levels of emotional functioning, as well as response validity.

Clinical decision making applied to this case incorporated several steps within the evaluation process. Decisions were made as to what tests would best measure cognitive and emotional functioning. This case was a high-profile, multimillion-dollar lawsuit in which secondary gain was at issue. So, credibility, motivation, effort, and veracity of his test responses and behaviors required close and careful consideration. Tests commonly used to measure these factors were thus incorporated into the test battery. Tests were also selected for inclusion that duplicated those administered by other neuropsychologists, so that performance could be evaluated across examiners. Records were carefully reviewed, and inconsistencies in Hector's test results and his report across different examiners and across different settings were noted. Behavioral observations were made continuously: while the examinee was in the waiting room, prior to the evaluation process, during the interview portion of the evaluation, and on test breaks. Educational records were carefully inspected for grades, special education placement, involvement in alternative schools, and teacher comments. His school's psychological records required a separate subpoena directly to the neuropsychologist, as it is privileged information distinct from school transcripts. In this case, school psychological records helped establish malingering behavior on the examinee's part. Comparisons were made between what the examinee reported during the interview and what his family independently reported in their interviews. Tests completed by family members about the examinee were compared to results of the same tests completed by the examinee.

Emotional and personality functioning was examined through interview, observation, and testing. Hector's behavior was erratic, spontaneous, and surprisingly inconsistent at various points. For example, when he was caught in an apparent lie, he would appear anxious. At one point, he abruptly got up and left the exam room when he "failed to recall" being in special education throughout elementary school. When asked to complete an office form, his wife claimed he did not know his address or telephone number. Yet, on a test in which he was asked to "address an envelope to himself," he accurately addressed it. On one test, and in his wife's deposition testimony, it was reported that Hector required assistance using the bathroom, that he was unable to use a telephone to make or receive calls, and that he depended on others to put soap on a washcloth. Yet, behavioral observations showed him as using the bathroom facilities without anyone present, as performing well on fine motor tasks, as able to demonstrate activities of daily living, and as routinely texting and calling using his cell phone during breaks.

Personality and emotional functioning were tested with the audiotaped version of the MMPI–2. The audiotaped version (in this case, English) is ideal in medicolegal contexts where reading ability may be at issue, where attention may be low, and where standardized administration is optimal. At least five 15- to 20-minute stretch breaks were allowed. The MMPI–2 was interpreted with several sources and methods. The extended score report and the Minnesota Report were obtained through Pearson Assessments.

Unrealistic claims of virtue ($L = 74$), as shown in this profile (see Figure 5.1), reflect conscious attempts to influence the outcome of litigation by giving the appearance of having extremely high moral virtue and honesty. This interpretation, which is based on Caucasian patients, must be tempered about 10 T points because of his Hispanic ethnicity (see Chapter 4). (The slight elevation on the Fp scale was partially a function of the four

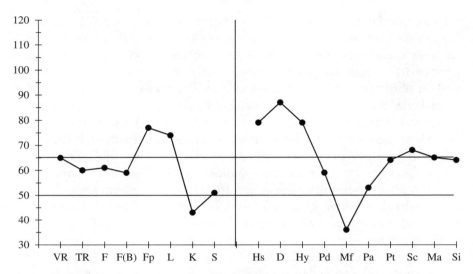

Figure 5.1. Profile of MMPI–2 basic validity and clinical scales for Hector. Excerpted from the *MMPI®–2 (Minnesota Multiphasic Personality Inventory®—2) Manual for Administration, Scoring, and Interpretation, Revised Edition* by Butcher et al. Copyright © 2001 by the Regents of the University of Minnesota. Used by permission of the University of Minnesota Press. All rights reserved. "MMPI®" and "Minnesota Multiphasic Personality Inventory®" are trademarks owned by the Regents of the University of Minnesota.

items shared with the *L* scale and thus can be ignored.) Despite his virtuous responding, he still elevated five clinical scales at or above a *T* score of 65.

The MMPI–2 computerized report was augmented by separate interpretations based on actuarial sources (Butcher, 2011; Greene, 2000). Code types and individual elevated scores were examined across basic clinical, validity, content, and supplementary scales. Harris–Lingoes subscale results were particularly useful in this case to help determine what was driving basic clinical scale scores. In this case the *Sc* scale was significantly elevated, but psychotic symptoms were not borne out in other aspects of this examination. The elevated Sc_4 subscale pointed to factors, other than bizarre mentation, as accounting for Hector's high *Sc* score.

The high-point code type (1-2/2-1) suggests mild to moderate levels of emotional distress characterized by tension, anxiety, and dysphoria. Hector endorsed items indicating physical symptoms that are reflective of anxiety. The elevated content scale, *HEA* ($T = 68$), offered additional support regarding motivational features and the examinee's attitude toward health issues. He responds like others who are grouchy, easily frustrated, and irritable.

There was a lack of insight into somatic symptoms and behavior and often refusal to acknowledge that symptoms were related to emotional conflict and are used as a means of coping with psychological problems. Hector is scoring like others who are overly concerned about their health. He endorsed a variety of physical and neurological symptoms and some general pain. Individuals with this profile often report nausea, vomiting, weakness, insomnia, and fatigue. Dizziness is a frequent symptom among similar-scoring individuals. Psychosomatic symptoms are usually focused around the alimentary system, particularly the abdomen. Physical symptoms are usually vague, nonspecific, and difficult to isolate medically. Hector's scores indicate that, even if he has real physical symptoms, he may exaggerate their severity. Others who share this profile will return to their physicians repeatedly, with limited change in their physical condition due to lack of follow up (treatment noncompliance). Hector endorsed feeling tired a good deal of the time and having little energy.

The case was taken to court and tried before a jury of Hector's peers. The examiner presented evidence that, within reasonable medical probability, supported the conclusions and opinions that Hector was not a credible respondent. Indeed, he had suffered brain damage, but now, 3 years following his motor vehicle accident, he could be considered back to baseline from a neurocognitive standpoint. Should Hector be awarded monetary damages? That was the decision that jurors were, in part, considering. The MMPI–2 profile was explained to the jury as part of the expert trial testimony. A clinical picture of a young man who had psychiatric and psychological issues emerged. The MMPI–2 allowed for a clear and compelling explanation of the psychopathology present in this case. Woven into the testimony and the written report was evidence based on all other aspects of the neuropsychological evaluation process: tests, interviews, observations, and records. A diagnosis was then established that was well supported from this body of evidence. Malingering is not a diagnosis, by *DSM–IV–TR* or *DSM–5* standards. But, given the information obtained on Hector, malingering behavior was clearly present. The MMPI–2 helped establish this opinion. Was Hector making a deliberate attempt to be dishonest, to sabotage the examination process, to give up without trying, to purposely appear dysfunctional? Perhaps, but motivation is not easy to measure. What neuropsychologists conclude, as in this case, is sufficient evidence weighing toward a malingering performance.

This case example illustrates that face-value MMPI–2 results are not always going to be a close match to data based on the neuropsychological examination. Observations of inconsistencies in behavior were therefore stressed, although inconsistent responding was not represented within the MMPI–2 (e.g., *VRIN/TRIN* scale results). In fact, this individual's MMPI–2 results were surprisingly different than observational data, test data, and self- and other (family) report. This is not necessarily a malingering profile. Rather, it is an example of how the MMPI–2 shows someone who, with reasonable medical probability, was faking bad. In this case, faking bad meant exaggerating symptomatology. The extent of exaggeration was apparent because it was so out of sync with all the other neuropsychology indicators. It was obvious the client was trying to portray himself in the worst possible manner. This was how the MMPI–2 was interpreted. And this interpretation was what served as the basis for the disconnect between actual clinical presentation and the client's interest in appearing "damaged."

SUMMARY

When faced with conducting an independent medical examination, neuropsychologists engage in a decision-making process. Components of the evaluation take into consideration aspects of examination content and process. The MMPI–2 plays an important role in terms of ruling out malingering behavior, determining response validity, and measuring psychosomatic factors—all of which contribute to a diagnosis and expert opinions. Reasonable medical probability serves as the legal and clinical basis for summarizing results. Several standards that a neuropsychologist may use to base opinions of brain injury severity were described. Thus, a major purpose in this chapter was to offer a method of decision making designed to render expert opinions. The importance of underlying scientific and empirical bases for integrating results of the MMPI–2 was a point of emphasis. Utility of the MMPI–2 within a forensic neuropsychological examination was supported. The case example described here took the reader through a method of how neuropsychologists may build a case regarding the impact of brain injury on cognitive and emotional functioning, as well as the identification of malingering behavior, in a medicolegal context.

6

THE MMPI–2 IN PERSONAL INJURY EVALUATIONS

Personal injury evaluations are among the most frequent assessment applications in forensic psychology today. In this book, we provide two chapters to deal with injury-based evaluations. This chapter addresses the general topic of personality injury evaluations, and Chapter 7 addresses the specific topic of personal injury in the workplace and work compensation evaluations.

In personal injury cases, the litigant's personality (both pre-injury and post-injury adjustment) is often an important consideration for the court to address in determining the impact of the alleged injury on the claimant's adjustment resulting from the incident in question. Although a large number of psychologists specialize in personal injury assessments and devote their practice to injury litigation cases, some psychologists who work in other areas may be asked by an attorney to testify in a case. Psychologists trained in areas such as clinical or health or counseling psychology may serve as expert witnesses in a court case and testify about a personality evaluation they have conducted. Psychological testimony about the mental-health status of examinees

http://dx.doi.org/10.1037/14571-007
Using the MMPI–2 in Forensic Assessment, by J. N. Butcher, G. A. Hass, R. L. Greene, and L. D. Nelson
Copyright © 2015 by the American Psychological Association. All rights reserved.

in personal injury cases has become highly acceptable in court cases over the past 30 years. Thus, being able to provide a professional evaluation in forensic cases can result in a strong source of income for psychologists in practice. However, there are some clear problems that practitioners may face.

Unlike many other court cases in which a court-ordered evaluation is requested (e.g., custody or not guilty by reason of insanity), personal injury cases typically involve partisan-based assessment. It is rare in personal injury cases that forensic assessment psychologists function as independent medical examiners appointed by the court to evaluate examinees in litigation. In most cases, expert witnesses in personal injury cases are hired either by the examinee's attorney to evaluate the examinee's alleged impairments or as an expert for the defense whose role involves finding flaws with the examinee's case or claimed mental-health status (L. Miller, Sadoff, & Dattillo, 2011). Psychologists need to be aware of the often-contentious nature of personal injury cases and at times grueling questioning that can occur during cross-examination and to prepare for their participation in advance.

FACTORS TO CONSIDER IN CONDUCTING PERSONAL INJURY EXAMINATIONS

Guides for Incorporating Psychological Evaluations in Personal Injury Cases

It is important to consider the appropriateness and effectiveness of procedures used in personal injury evaluations. Several resources are available to guide the practitioner in understanding the context for the forensic evaluations and how the Minnesota Multiphasic Personality Inventory—2 (MMPI–2) can contribute to the evaluation (see Arbisi & Butcher, 2004; Heilbrun, DeMatteo, Marczyk, & Goldstein, 2008; Varela & Conroy, 2012). The specialty guidelines for forensic psychology provide important information to follow in conducting forensic evaluations (American Psychological Association, 2013b).

Appropriateness of the Forensic Expert's Background

Credible expert testimony requires that psychologists conducting personal injury evaluations have the necessary educational background and professional experience in working with examinees in injury-related contexts. Simply having a graduate degree in psychology is insufficient for conducting credible personal injury case evaluations. For example, clinical or counseling psychologists, who largely provide mental-health treatment to patients in which they provide a supportive role with their patients, may not have the broader perspective required for understanding an examinee's problems within the post-injury context. It is critical that the psychologist conducting personal injury litigation have both work-related experience with the population of examinees and a psychometric understanding of the specific procedures being used as the basis for conclusions.

Psychometric Understanding of the Psychological Tests Used in Assessing Examinees in Personal Injury Cases

Psychologists conducting forensic examinations need to be conscientious about choosing instruments that have demonstrated validity, broad acceptance in the field, and appropriateness for the application in question. Hundreds of tests are commercially available; however, availability alone is not an acceptable criterion for use in forensic evaluations. It is very important to choose well-established measures that are valid and acceptable to the broad community of experts and not rely upon nonstandard or individually accumulated experience. In order for tests to be acceptable in court, the standards governing their use must be followed. Tests and conclusions drawn about them can be challenged if procedural requirements are not followed.

Assurance That Standard Administration Procedures Have Been Followed

Be aware that some personal injury evaluations can be viewed as one-sided evaluations. It is very important to follow standard test administration procedures in assessing examinees in the process and not modify or be selective in dealing with the results by choosing only part of the test results to use.

The primary goal of the attorney employing a psychologist to conduct personal injury evaluations is to make the best case possible to support the case foundation, whether for the client or for the defense against the client's allegations. It is not unusual for attorneys to provide input into an evaluation and to make suggested edits for reports concerning their client's adjustment. It is critical that psychologists avoid making biased interpretations in order to make the case stronger. The test conclusions, particularly if objective procedures are used, should be consistent with standard interpretations for the instruments used and not tailored to meet the specific goals of the employing attorney (i.e., test results should be conclusive and not selective). Important test results, even if they seem to weaken the case, should be considered. Drawing selective conclusions can be challenged by the experts on the other side. See the case of Mr. B. at the end of this chapter.

Level of Cooperation of the Examinee

As noted in other chapters of this book, it is important to assess the examinee's level of cooperation in the evaluation. An examinee's uncooperativeness (e.g., withholding key information in order to make a particular impression) can result in questionable or invalid results (see Chapter 2).

Context in Which Personality Test Data Are Being Used

In most personal injury cases, the evaluation of the examinee involves the use of a number of assessment approaches for gathering information. These include conducting an interview, obtaining a personal history, and reviewing medical records in cases where physical injury is involved. Thus, reliance upon a single instrument is not common. Even very widely used tests such as the MMPI–2 are usually incorporated in a battery of personality measures in order to obtain a comprehensive picture of the examinee's symptoms and behavior. For example, the Structured Interview of Reported Symptoms and Test of Memory Malingering provide additional perspectives on validity assessment, and behavioral rating scales such as the Symptom Checklist—Revised can provide additional information on symptoms and behavior.

VALUE OF THE MMPI–2 IN PERSONAL INJURY EVALUATIONS

As described in Chapter 1, the MMPI–2 is the most widely researched and used personality measure in personal injury evaluations, in large part because of the utility of the scales that were developed using the empirical validation test construction approach. McKinley and Hathaway (1940) published the Hs scale as a means of understanding physical symptoms reported by the patient. They also developed the Hy scale (McKinley & Hathaway, 1944) to measure the expression of physical complaints in the context of hysteroid personality characteristics (e.g., denial). Hundreds of articles have been published on the use of the MMPI and MMPI–2 scales in assessing examinees in medical contexts (see Arbisi & Butcher, 2004). Numerous research studies with the original MMPI and MMPI–2 have shown the value of the instrument in personal injury cases. Several examples are cited below.

Pollack and Grainey (1984) compared the MMPI scores of state disability applicants, private industrial insurance applicants, and applicants for adoption in order to investigate the effectiveness of the MMPI in predicting successful outcomes (attainment of disability benefits or adoption of a child). The adoption group had the most normal MMPI scores, and a lower or normal MMPI score increased the likelihood of a positive outcome. In addition, significant gender differences were found for the Hs, D, Hy, Mf, Pt, and Sc scales. The effects of injury had a more damaging effect on the psychological status of men. Hersch and Alexander (1990) compared MMPI profiles of employees referred for psychological evaluation and a sample of employees from a study of Repko and Cooper (1983), who had been seen for evaluation related to workers' compensation litigation. In the two samples, an almost identical percentage of MMPI profiles reflected significant psycho-pathology (85 vs. 83%). Three of these code types (12/21, 13/31, and 23/32), which involve the Hs, D, and Hy scales, represented 38% and 26% of the two groups, respectively. Gandolfo (1995) conducted a study to determine whether the MMPI–2 differentiated between workers' compensation claimants with psychological problems who presented with work-related harassment or with nonharassment complaints. The MMPI–2 mean scores revealed that those in the harassment group scored significantly higher than the claimants in the nonharassment group on the Pa scale.

Fordyce, Bigos, Batti'e, and Fisher (1992) conducted a workplace evaluation of people with back injury using the MMPI–2. They evaluated the extent to which the Hy scale served as a predictor of back injury. They found that both job task dissatisfaction and elevations on the Hy scale were statistically related to back injury reporting. DuAlba and Scott (1993) conducted a post hoc study of Hispanics and Caucasians who had filed workers' compensation claims. They examined cross-cultural differences of somatization and malingering as assessed by the MMPI. Somatization was assessed by analyzing two- and three-point code types based on the Hs, D, and Hy scales. Hispanics were more likely to somatize problems. Minimal differences were found between Hispanic and Caucasian claimants on the scales and indexes of malingering. Dush, Simons, Platt, and Nation (1994) compared examinees with chronic pain who either were or were not involved in litigation over settlement for their injuries. They found a significant difference between litigators and nonlitigators. Gatchel, Polatin, and Kinney (1995) evaluated whether a comprehensive assessment of psychosocial measures can be useful in characterizing those acute low back pain examinees who subsequently developed chronic pain disability problems. They found that scores on the Hy scale of the MMPI were associated with those injured workers who are likely to develop chronic disability problems. Similarly, Vendrig (2000) found a specific subset of the items on the Hy scale was related to the report of lassitude and malaise ($Hy3$) was related to failure to return to work after participating in a chronic pain program in the Netherlands. Personality factors associated with the Hy scale, such as somatic preoccupation and a naive denial of emotional or interpersonal difficulties, lend a vulnerability to the individual toward developing a chronic pain condition and becoming disabled.

Colotla, Bowman, and Shercliffe (2001) examined the stability of MMPI–2 scores over time in a test–retest study of injured workers. Ninety-four workers completed the MMPI–2 on two separate occasions. The MMPI–2 provided consistent and stable results across time in these injured workers. Livingston, Jennings, Colotla, Reynolds, and Shercliffe (2006) also examined the retest stability of MMPI–2 code types in a sample of injured workers. They found congruence rates for undefined code types were 34% for high-point codes, 22% for two-point code types, and 22% for three-point code types. The data provided evidence suggesting that defined code types are more stable than undefined code types. However, as noted in Chapter 1, the majority of profiles will shift somewhat in terms of high points at retest.

Lanyon and Almer (2002) tested whether the personal characteristics, as measured by the MMPI–2 scales related to attention-seeking behavior through somatization, would differ between compensable personal injury claimants who choose to go to litigation and those who choose not to litigate. The differences between the two groups were accounted for by the litigating examinees' significantly higher scores on the Hs, D, and Hy scales. The Hs and Hy differences held up separately in claimants with physical injuries and in claimants whose injuries were psychological only. The differences also persisted after severity of injury was held constant.

Some of the differences in reported impairments between examinees in general and personal injury claimants appear to be related to whether litigation is involved. Gatchel, Polatin, and Mayer (1995) evaluated whether a comprehensive assessment of psychosocial measures would be useful in characterizing those patients with acute low back pain who subsequently develop chronic pain disability problems. Their study revealed the importance of three measures: self-reported pain and disability, the presence of a personality disorder, and scores on the Hy scale. These results demonstrated the presence of a psychosocial disability variable that was associated with those injured workers who were likely to develop chronic disability problems.

Long, Rouse, Nelson, and Butcher (2004) studied MMPI–2s produced by women and men who initiated legal claims of ongoing emotional harm related to workplace sexual harassment and discrimination. The MMPI–2s were administered as a part the forensic evaluation of the claimants' current psychological condition. Among the women, 28% produced a "normal limits" profile that provided no MMPI–2 support for their claims of ongoing emotional distress. Analysis of the validity scales of the remaining profiles produced four distinctive clusters of profiles representing different approaches to the test items.

Value of the MMPI Validity Measures in Detecting Malingered Protocols in Forensic Cases

Sternbach, Wolf, Murphy, and Akeson (1973) showed that the presence of a pending compensation action served to exaggerate the psychophysiological and psychopathic scales of the MMPI. Repko and Cooper (1983) assessed a group of examinees seen for psychiatric evaluation that involved workers' compensation litigation. They found that the MMPI validity scales provide useful information to forensic psychologists involved in the diagnostic evaluation process with workers' compensation cases. Likewise, Jarvis and Hamlin (1984) found the MMPI to be valuable in determining the possibility of malingering in disability claims.

Berry et al. (1995) compared the MMPI–2 validity scales in different four groups: nonclinical participants answering under standard instructions; nonclinical participants instructed to fake closed-head injury (CHI) symptoms; non-compensation-seeking CHI examinees; and compensation-seeking CHI examinees. They found that MMPI–2 overreporting scales were sensitive to fabrication of CHI complaints and possibly to exaggeration of CHI complaints. Youngjohn, Davis, and Wolf (1997) compared the MMPI–2s of patients with moderate/severe head injury with those of symptomatic minor/mild head injury examinees. Their results are discussed in terms of the influence of litigation and injury severity on symptom endorsement on the MMPI–2.

Assessment of Posttraumatic Stress Disorder Relevant to Personal Injury Cases

It is important to be aware of the MMPI posttraumatic stress disorder literature in personal injury cases, because stress is often a key component in clients who are litigating following an injury. Fairbank, McCaffrey, and Keane (1985) administered the MMPI to Vietnam veterans with posttraumatic stress disorder (PTSD) and to two control groups instructed to fabricate the symptoms of PTSD. Both groups with fabricated PTSD produced elevations on the F scale and on the PTSD scale developed by Keane, Malloy, and Fairbank (1984) higher than those of the veterans with actual PTSD. The analysis of selected scale scores and an empirically derived decision rule correctly classified over 90% of the three groups. Chaney, Williams, Cohn, and Vincent (1984) evaluated MMPI scores of posttrauma patients, patients with organically based illnesses, and patients with psychogenic pain or functional complaints. They reported differences among the groups on the Hy, Ma, and F scales. The MMPI profiles of patients with posttraumatic stress disorder more closely resembled the MMPI profiles of patients who had organic disease with pain caused by organic pathology than they did the profiles of patients with psychogenic pain and/or hypochondriasis.

Jordan, Nunley, and Cook (1992) examined the relationship between service-connected disability and exaggeration of PTSD symptoms. Inpatient Vietnam combat veterans in PTSD treatment comprised three groups: veterans financially compensated for PTSD; veterans financially compensated for physical or other mental problems; and veterans not financially compensated. Jordan et al. found that those veterans who were service connected exaggerated their symptoms on the F scale more than those who were non-service connected. Also, the F scores reported for inpatients with PTSD were higher than previously established cutoff criteria found chiefly in outpatient populations. Frueh, Smith, and Barker (1996) studied differences between compensation-seeking veterans and non-compensation-seeking veterans on the MMPI–2 and other psychological measures who were evaluated for post-traumatic stress disorder at an outpatient Veterans Affairs PTSD clinic. The veterans were grouped on the basis of their compensation-seeking status, with 69% classified as compensation seeking for PTSD. The compensation-seeking veterans achieved significantly more elevated scores across a wide range of psychological inventories and MMPI–2 validity indices. Elhai, Gold, Frueh, and Gold (2000) studied veterans in an outpatient PTSD treatment program to distinguish genuine from malingered PTSD on the MMPI–2. They identified F, |F-FB|, F-K, Ds, O-S, and OT as the best malingering predictors. A predictive discriminant analysis yielded good hit rates for the model, with impressive cross-validation results. Franklin, Repasky, Thompson, Shelton, and Uddo (2003) studied response styles of veterans seeking compensation for PTSD. Veterans were classified as having a valid or overreporting response style based on their scores on three MMPI–2 validity scales that measure over-reporting (F, Fp, F-K). Finally, Vilariño, Arce, and Fariña (2013) found that the MMPI–2 was effective at assessing feigning strategies and also showed convergent validity and discriminant validity in cases of PTSD.

Other contributions to forensic assessment can be found in a more extensive listing of references on the MMPI/MMPI–2 in personal injury cases on the MMPI–2 research website (see Butcher, 2012).

MMPI–2 BASED TESTIMONY

In personal injury litigation, whether testifying on behalf of the injury claimant or for the defense, the expert should provide an objective and defensible evaluation of the data and should not ignore important features of the examinee's performance. One important feature of using the MMPI–2 in personal injury litigation is its objectively established and widely researched test correlates and MMPI–2 interpretive statements that are well substantiated and generally accepted by the profession. Testimony about the MMPI–2 can be objective, widely accepted, and readily explainable to nonpsychologists (e.g., jurors) in court cases. Using the MMPI–2 in personal injury cases is straightforward in that one can simply use standard research-based correlates and avoid subjective and nondefensible opinions. The MMPI–2 can be objectively interpreted whether it is for the defense or the litigant. The interpretive conclusions and behavioral descriptions of the client should be the same: that is, based upon the examinee's responses and not dictated by outcome motivation. For example, when one of the authors of this book (JNB) is approached by an attorney to serve as an expert witness on the MMPI–2 in a personal injury case, he follows the same strategy. Before knowing much about the case and what the attorney's approach to the case involves, he asks for the MMPI–2 answer sheet in order to do a blind interpretation; he interprets the scale scores and also verifies his clinical interpretation in comparison to a computer-based interpretation and then provides the contacting attorney with the information on the examinee and what his testimony about the MMPI–2 would be. Of course, the information provided may not be what the attorney had hoped. Needless to say, in some cases he is not retained as a witness, as occurred in the case presented below.

The attorney for a claimant in a personal injury case provided the MMPI–2 answer sheet for the following case (see the validity scale profile in Figure 6.1). The claimant, Barbara, a 42-year-old woman who alleged that she was sexually harassed by her employer, was administered the MMPI–2 by a psychologist as part of her mental-health treatment following the incidents at work. The MMPI–2 was scored, and the attorney was provided the following preliminary information about the claimant's MMPI–2 protocol. No useful personality symptom information was available from the claimant's test performance because she was uncooperative with the evaluation. She presented an overly virtuous picture of her personality and tended to be overly defensive in her self-portrayal. Her extreme score on the L scale indicates that the symptom picture she provided is likely to be a false statement and not a frank, open presentation of her mental health status.

Interpretation of MMPI–2 protocols in personal injury cases can be complicated by the fact that individual motivation to present in a particular manner is more complex in this setting than in other forensic evaluations such as family custody, where presentation of self in a highly positive manner is common. In personal injury cases, some litigants are motivated to present themselves in a defensive manner, but others are motivated to present themselves as much more disturbed psychologically than they actually are to appear disabled yet virtuous.

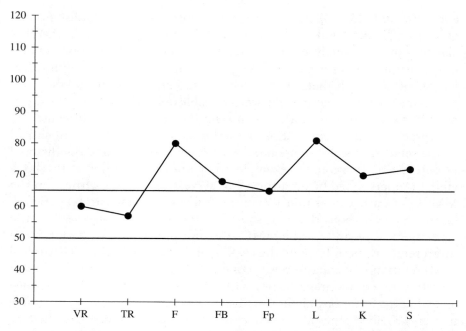

Figure 6.1. MMPI–2 validity scale profile for Barbara. Excerpted from the *MMPI®–2 (Minnesota Multiphasic Personality Inventory®—2) Manual for Administration, Scoring, and Interpretation, Revised Edition* by Butcher et al. Copyright © 2001 by the Regents of the University of Minnesota. Used by permission of the University of Minnesota Press. All rights reserved. "MMPI®" and "Minnesota Multiphasic Personality Inventory®" are trademarks owned by the Regents of the University of Minnesota.

Validity Patterns in Personal Injury Litigation Cases

In order to obtain a clearer idea about the interpretive meaning of profiles in personal injury cases, as described in Chapter 2, one should evaluate possibly differing motivations presented by examinees in personal injury cases. The data on personal injury cases can be difficult to interpret because of the low degree of cooperation on the part of many persons being evaluated. One situation often encountered is that in which the examinees produce extremely defensive profiles; that is, deny psychological problems in order to produce a credible physical problem. Another situation that can occur is that the examinee endorses an extreme number of symptoms, resulting in an overreporting response pattern with extensive scale elevation. What then do the base rates of personal injury cases tell us about the relatively defensive or exaggerated profiles found in these cases?

Frequency of Various MMPI–2 Scores in Forensic Settings

Knowing the relative frequency of MMPI–2 profiles in various settings can be of value in developing hypotheses about examinee's personality performance. Butcher (1997) provided base rate information on examinees who were being assessed in a broad range of personal injury cases to examine typical profiles occurring in a variety of lawsuits including workplace harassment, sexual harassment, age discrimination, "slip and fall" injury complaints, and posttraumatic injury from incidents such as accidents, rape, and workplace trauma.

When the total sample is considered without regard to response attitudes, three scales receive high prominence. The *Hy* scale is the highest peak score, with 17.2% of the cases producing elevated and well-defined peak scores; the *D* scale is the second most frequent peak, with 7.6% frequency as an elevated and well-defined peak; the *Pa* score is the third highest spike score, occurring with 6.4% frequency as an elevated and well-defined score. However, when the response attitudes are taken into consideration—that is, when the profiles are grouped according to defensive (likely feigned) versus exaggerated (likely malingered) psychological symptoms—the picture changes markedly. The frequency of well-defined *Hy* scores increases to 22.2% in the defensive (possibly feigned symptom group); however, when the exaggerated (possibly exaggerated-malingered) profiles are grouped together, the profile peak becomes one of high *Pa* (14.6% have well-defined scores at or above a *T* of 65). These data suggest that it is important to keep the examinee's motivation in perspective when interpreting MMPI–2 profiles in personal injury cases (see Butcher & Miller, 2005; Long et al., 2004).

MMPI–2 RESEARCH THAT CAN BE OF VALUE IN FORMULATING HYPOTHESES FOR PERSONAL INJURY EVALUATIONS

Several MMPI–2 personality variables that can assist the psychologist in addressing pertinent personality variables in personal injury cases are described below; references reflecting research on each variable are provided. The following sections include an overview summary of research that provides support for these areas of evaluation.

Assessment of Protocol Validity in Examinees

As discussed in Chapter 2 and other places in this book, the MMPI–2 validity scales (*Cannot Say, VRIN, TRIN, F, FB, Fp, L, K,* and *S*) can provide valuable information about the manner in which the examinee approached the test. Often, there is an effort to sway the outcome of the testing—a test strategy not uncommon in personal injury litigants. It is important to determine whether the examinee has responded in an honest manner in self-reporting his or her symptoms. The MMPI–2 can point to efforts at overly virtuous self-perceptions or efforts to manipulate test results to show symptom endorsement that is highly unlikely and thereby not credible in the evaluation (pertinent research includes Archer, Fontaine, & McCrae, 1998; Baer, Wetter, & Berry, 1992; Bagby, Buis, & Nicholson, 1995; Bagby, Sellbom, Costa, & Widiger, 2008; Jordan et al., 1992; Moyer, Burkhardt, & Gordon, 2002; Nichols & Greene, 1997; Perl & Kahn, 1983).

Appraisal of Disabling Response to Stress

In some cases, as noted earlier, in which the examinee has experienced severe trauma, the MMPI–2 scales may have prominent elevations. Posttraumatic stress assessment can provide important hypotheses about an examinee's functioning in personal injury cases in which traumatic experiences have been alleged. Symptoms of psychological injury in response to trauma, such as depression or anxiety as addressed in the D, Pt, and ANX scales, can result from severe life changes, physical injury, grief over loss of a close relative, or other traumatic events such as loss of a job or an automobile accident. Moreover, the PTSD scale PK, developed by Keane et al., provides informative clues as to the level of stress an examinee is experiencing, perhaps in response to major stresses (see, e.g., Chaney et al., 1984; Elhai, Gold, Mateus, & Astaphan, 2001; Fairbank et al., 1985; Greenblatt & Davis, 1999; Morrell & Rubin, 2001; Munley, Bains, Bloem, & Busby, 1995; L. A. Neal et al., 1994; Penk, Rierdan, Losardo, & Robinowitz, 2006; Shercliffe & Colotla, 2009; Vilariño et al., 2013).

Assessment of Mental-Health Symptoms

In some cases, particularly when the examinee may have a history of mental health problems such as depression or anxiety, the MMPI–2 depression indices, such as the D scale or the content scale DEP, can be prominent in the profile. A number of MMPI–2 clinical and content scales have been found to measure symptomatic behavior. For example, depressed mood can be a long-term problem or the result of recent life circumstances (see Archer, Griffin, & Aiduk, 1995; Biondi, Picardi, Pasquini, Gaetano, & Pancheri, 2005; Elhai et al., 2001; Elwood, 1993; Greenblatt & Davis, 1999; Gross, Keyes, & Greene, 2000; Infrasca, 2003; Munley, Busby, & Jaynes, 1997; L. D. Nelson, Pham, & Uchiyama, 1996; Pospisil, Kirsten, Chuplis, Conger, & Golden, 2002; Ruttan & Heinrichs, 2003; Streit, Greene, Cogan, & Davis, 1993; Ward, 1997).

Assessing Behavioral or Personality Factors Occurring Among Examinees With Traumatic Brain Injury

Behavior and personality issues among examinees with brain disorders and injuries have been widely studied with the MMPI–2. Particular scale elevations, such as *Hy, D, Pd, Pt,* and *Sc,* are often reported among patients in neuropsychology settings (Anderson, 2001; Andreetto & de Bertolini, 1999; Bardenhagen, 2006; Cripe, 1999; Gass, 2009; Gass & Brown, 1992; Golden & Golden, 2003; Hessen, Anderson, & Nestvold, 2008; Novack, Daniel, & Long, 1984; Palav, Ortega, & McCaffrey, 2001; Patch & Hartlage, 2003; Pospisil et al., 2002; Ruttan & Heinrichs, 2003; Warriner, Rourke, Velikonja, & Metham, 2003; Wheatley, 1984; Youngjohn et al., 1997). Also see the discussion in Chapter 5 for further information.

Evaluation of Suspicion, Mistrust of Others, and Problems of Cognitive Distortion

It is not unusual in some forensic evaluations to find the client appearing cautious and unwilling to share personal information. This is particularly a marker in family custody evaluations and in some personal injury assessments and criminal investigations. Symptom patterns of suspicion, mistrust of others, and problems of cognitive distortion can be found in elevations on MMPI–2 scales such as the *Pa, Sc,* and *BIZ* scales. These scales might also provide a reliable assessment of long-term, chronic mental health problems (relevant articles include Adams & Foulds, 1963; Blackburn, 1968; Caine, 1960; Caldonazao, 1963; Chalus, 1976; Collet, Cottraux, & Juenet, 1986; Costa, Zonderman, McCrae, & Williams, 1986; Dahlstrom, 1960; Eisenman & Coyle, 1965; Fracchia, Sheppard, Merlis, & Merlis, 1970; R. J. Harris, Wittner, Koppell, & Hilf, 1970; Heilbrun & Norbert, 1972; Hersen & Sudik, 1971; Vestre & Watson, 1972).

Assessment of Somatization and Chronic Pain Disorders

Chronic pain populations have been widely studied with the MMPI/ MMPI–2 scales. Several MMPI–2 measures address long-term psychological adjustment problems such as somatization (*Hs, Hy, HEA*) or chronic pain (*Hs*). The MMPI–2 clinical scales have been found to be effective in describing examinees who somatize conflict and develop physical conditions even though there is no or little organic basis for the disorder. Chronic pain, with minimal physical basis, occurs frequently as a symptom condition underlying some personal injury claims (see, e.g., DuAlba & Scott, 1993; Fordyce et al.,

1992; Gatchel, Polatin, & Mayer, 1995; L. S. Keller & Butcher, 1991; Kinder, Curtiss, & Kalichman, 1986; Kleinke, 1994; Koretzky & Peck, 1990; Lanyon & Almer, 2002; Lemmon, 1983; Lichtenberg, Skehan, & Swensen, 1984; Murray, 1982; Prokop, Bradley, Margolis, & Gentry, 1980; Sternbach et al., 1973; Vendrig, 2000).

The Examinee's Personality Characteristics Might Have Influenced the Events Initiating the Case

The personality characteristics and behavior patterns of the examinee might be associated with his or her everyday functioning in ways that could be influential in the case. The MMPI–2 scale elevations and scale patterns can provide possible personality factors of the examinee. For example, the repression–sensitization dimension has been shown to be related to the experience of impending painful stimulation (Scarpetti, 1973). Other persistent personality characteristics can provide information that might be of great value in a personal injury evaluation. Examples include social alienation (*Si, SOD*; Chang & Wright, 2001; Sieber & Meyers, 1992; Ward, 1998; J. L. Williams, 1971), anger-control problems (*ANG, Pd, Pa, Ma, O-H*; Goldstein et al., 2005; Mittag & Maurischat, 2004; Schill & Wang, 1990; Uluç, 2008), and issues with self-esteem (*ALN, LSE*; Brems & Lloyd, 1995; Englert, Weed, & Watson, 2000; Gurman & Balban, 1990; Moriconi & Martinez, 1995). Personality characteristics such as extreme introversion, low self-esteem, or reliance upon denial to deal with stressful situations can be important factors in understanding the client's ability to deal with stressful situations in forensic cases.

Assessment of Antisocial Behavior

It is not unusual, in evaluations across a number of forensic settings, to find the client displaying underlying maladjustment and personality dysfunction. The MMPI–2 can be of value in addressing these factors. Long-term personality disorders can be detected in MMPI–2 patterns. A client's acting-out potential and antisocial attitudes and behavior can be found in several MMPI–2 scales (*Pd, Ma, ASP*) and code types, such as 4-3, 4-9, 4-8, 8-9, addressing long-term personality problems (Campanella, Vanhoolandt, & Philippot, 2005; Gacano & Meloy, 2009; Hale, Goldstein, Abramowitz, Calamari, & Kosson, 2004; Lilienfeld, 1996; Matsuoka, Kim, Toshida, & Ohshima, 2000). Chronic behavior problems as shown by some MMPI–2 personality scales that attain high profile elevation should be addressed in the personality evaluation even if other factors, such as physical symptoms, are more prominent.

Evaluation of the Examinee's Potential for Substance Abuse Disorders

An important area to consider in the assessment of examinees in personal injury cases is whether substance use is a factor for the examinee. Many clients with substance abuse problems do not address them in interviews. However, these problems may emerge from the personality information provided in the MMPI–2. Several scales for assessing substance abuse problems are available on the MMPI–2 (*MAC-R, APS, AAS*). These scales often detect problems that are central to the evaluation and have not been sufficiently addressed in other areas of the assessment (Craig, 2005; Elwood, 1993; Matsuoka et al., 2000; Weed, Butcher, McKenna, & Ben-Porath, 1992).

CASE EXAMPLE

The following case study illustrates the importance of using standard and acceptable MMPI–2 interpretation procedures in forensic evaluations. The assessment psychologist in this case did not follow standard administration procedures and did not incorporate all the available information that was important to understanding the examinee's test performance.

Mr. B., a 56-year-old divorced man who has been unemployed for the past 2 years, feels unable to return to work because of his long history of depression resulting from abuse he suffered as a child. He reportedly has long-standing depression and PTSD as a result of being abused by a Catholic priest when he was 9 years old. He filed a personal injury lawsuit against the church to compensate him for the mental health problems he alleges have caused his adjustment problems. Mr. B. claims that the abuse he suffered as a child has affected his capability to function on his job and care for his family.

A number of psychological tests were administered to evaluate his mental status in order to substantiate his mental health problems resulting from the injury that he reportedly experienced as a result of the abuse. He was administered the MMPI–2 as part of the battery of tests to evaluate his mental status.

Although Mr. B. was administered the full MMPI–2, the psychologist conducting the evaluation chose to hand-score the test and used only a portion of the available scales in his assessment and did not examinee's the full test performance. The psychologist did not incorporate in his assessment several key scales that provided information as to the examinee's invalid test performance. Moreover, several of the scales he included in his evaluation were misscored: He had failed to recheck carefully the counted scores. These discrepancies in scale scores were found when the defense psychologist rescored the answer sheet with computer-based scoring. Research has generally shown that machine scoring of MMPI–2 answer sheets is more accurate than hand-scored protocols (Allard & Faust, 2000; Simons, Goddard, & Patton, 2002). Consistent with the research, some summary differences in his scoring were noted when compared with computer-scored protocol.

Two important scale omissions in the plaintiff psychologist's MMPI–2 interpretation were the inconsistency scales, *VRIN* and *TRIN*. As a result of his selective approach to interpretation of the MMPI–2 scales he failed to detect the random nature of the examinee's responding to the test. The psychologist's conclusions about the examinee's psychological adjustment were incomplete and incorrect. He used extremely exaggerated and invalid clinical and content scale scores without acknowledging that the examinee likely responded in a random fashion. In his report, the psychologist attempted to explain away the elevated *F* scale and invalid MMPI–2 profiles by using item content to show Mr. B.'s problems more clearly. However, in an invalid test performance, the psychologist should not rely upon item content measures such as the content component scales or critical items in an effort to provide information about the examinee's mental state. Invalid MMPI–2 profiles, with the examinee's level of elevation on *F* and *VRIN*, cannot be rehabilitated through a superficial examination of "critical items."

The MMPI–2 profiles summarizing the examinee's test performance are shown in Figure 6.2. As shown, Mr. B. endorsed an extreme number of MMPI–2 items covering a wide range of mental health symptoms and behaviors. His extremely high score on the MMPI–2 *F* scale ($T = 95$) resulted in an invalid test performance. This type of indiscriminate endorsement of items shows an exaggerated response pattern of claiming an unusual number of symptoms not found in genuine mental health examinees. The test performance shown in this protocol can occur with examinees who are unable to read the items, who respond randomly, or who endorse extreme items to give a picture of severe mental health problems. The examinee's high score on the *VRIN* scale ($T = 84$) indicates that he endorsed a number of similar items in an inconsistent manner in his response to extreme items. Thus, his performance on the validity scales is more likely than not the result of a desire by Mr. B. to appear more psychologically disturbed than he really is. His MMPI–2 protocol is invalid and does not allow for interpretations of mental health problems. His score on the *VRIN* scale, like his elevation on the *F* scale, indicates an invalid protocol and should not be interpreted. His response to MMPI–2 items did not show the necessary level of cooperation in responding to the items to allow for a confident personality assessment.

The MMPI–2, or any personality measure, cannot verify whether an alleged event actually occurred or serve as evidence to refute the events claimed. However, the response attitude measures on the MMPI–2, as this case shows, can add significantly to understanding the ways these assertions are

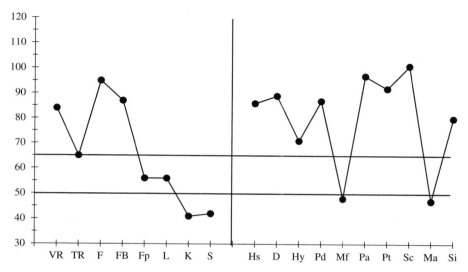

Figure 6.2. MMPI–2 validity scale profile for Mr. B. Excerpted from the *MMPI®–2 (Minnesota Multiphasic Personality Inventory®—2) Manual for Administration, Scoring, and Interpretation, Revised Edition* by Butcher et al. Copyright © 2001 by the Regents of the University of Minnesota. Used by permission of the University of Minnesota Press. All rights reserved. "MMPI®" and "Minnesota Multiphasic Personality Inventory®" are trademarks owned by the Regents of the University of Minnesota.

being presented by the claimants—as an exaggerated and overstated picture of his mental health symptoms.

SUMMARY

The research background on the MMPI–2 relevant for supporting the test in personal injury evaluations was described in this chapter. The material includes brief summaries of some of the special contributions that describe the instrument's utility in assessing behavior that is pertinent to compensation seeking or personal injury litigation cases. Several areas in which the MMPI–2 can provide information on aspects of the examinee's test performance to assist the practitioner in developing interpretive hypotheses were included.

7

THE MMPI–2 IN WORKERS' COMPENSATION EVALUATIONS

Workers' compensation is a form of insurance providing wage replacement and medical benefits to employees injured in the course of employment. Employees are awarded appropriate levels of compensation based on fixed formulas. In the United States, the first statewide workers' compensation law was passed in Maryland in 1902, and the first law covering federal employees was passed in 1906. By 1949, all states had enacted some kind of workers' compensation system. Injured workers may bring to a workers' compensation setting industrial injuries that include aspects of their emotional and cognitive functioning. According to the Bureau of Labor Statistics 2010 National Compensation Survey, workers' compensation costs represented 1.6% of employer spending overall. For instance, workers' compensation accounted for 4.4% of employer spending in the construction industry, 1.8% of employer spending in manufacturing, and 1.3% of employer spending in service jobs.

http://dx.doi.org/10.1037/14571-008
Using the MMPI–2 in Forensic Assessment, by J. N. Butcher, G. A. Hass, R. L. Greene, and L. D. Nelson
Copyright © 2015 by the American Psychological Association. All rights reserved.

When injured workers file a claim, the task of the qualified medical evaluator is to affirm or disaffirm one or more of the following: (a) Is the worker suffering an industrial injury that met an arbitrary percent threshold for compensability (percentages differ from state to state)? (b) If so, what caused the industrial injury? (c) Are there apportionable, nonindustrial factors that may be accounting for the industrial injury? (d) Has the industrial injury reached maximum medical improvement and is thus considered permanent and stationary? and (e) What, if any, are recommendations for future medical treatment?

Industrial injuries that result in psychiatric disabilities or neurocognitive deficits add a layer of complexity to the routine examination process for psychologists and clinical neuropsychologists, who may serve as, for example, qualified medical evaluators (e.g., the term used in the State of California). Issues addressed by examiners may relate to information regarding the permanence of the disability (e.g., Permanent Disability Rating Schedule), predisability impairment factors (e.g., apportionment), issues of causation, and impairment ratings (e.g., whole person impairment percentages; WPI). Psychological tests are routinely considered for inclusion in a workers' compensation evaluation, and test results often become the basis for interpreting the various complexity factors. Permanent disability status is typically determined first, along with one or more impairment ratings (e.g., WPI). Permanence of the disability is a term usually applied following the evaluation to help determine diminished future earnings capacity.

Interwoven into the workers' compensation evaluation process are traditional aspects of psychological and neuropsychological testing, such as a clinical interview, ongoing behavioral observations of the claimant during the evaluation, and direct test administration. The duration of a qualified medical evaluation is usually longer than the typical psychological or neuropsychological examination, because more information is required to render conclusions made with "reasonable medical probability" about a claimant. The work product or report is also typically longer, largely due to the need to address various complexity factors and the additional review of records. Reports are typically read by lay individuals and not professionals, so the language of the report is written accordingly.

The area of workers' compensation, as it pertains to a psychologist, is largely tailored to the field of psychiatry. Psychologists may be referred to as physicians. Qualified medical evaluations performed by psychologists are typically termed psychiatric evaluations. A claimant's disability is usually referred to as a psychiatric disability. The former version of psychiatric diagnostic standards, the *Diagnostic and Statistical Manual of Mental Disorders* (DSM–IV–TR; American Psychiatric Association, 2000), is heavily relied on in formulating opinions and addressing various factors of complexity (e.g., WPI percentages). In short, the medical model more or less controls the manner in which information is collected and results are communicated to the parties involved in a workers' compensation case. As a result, psychologists adapt their manner of professional communication to a system that may be more familiar to medical doctors than psychologists.

Industrial injuries that result in psychiatric disabilities have been problematic in some states, such as California, largely because of changes made in terms of rating psychiatric disabilities over the past 25 years. In 1997, for example, the Permanent Disability Rating Schedule (PDRS) significantly altered protocols for rating permanent psychiatric disabilities to require that each qualified medical examiner evaluate a person's psychiatric condition along eight work function impairments. Claimants who were disabled or filed complaints prior to 1997 were subject to those guidelines.

In 2005, the PDRS guidelines changed radically. The examiner in California, for example, is no longer required to evaluate a person's psychiatric condition along eight different work function impairments. In the revised rating system (S. 899, 2004), the fundamental requirement for compensability of a psychiatric industrial injury is now "preponderance of the evidence that the actual events of employment were predominant as to all causes combined of the psychiatric injury" (Cal. Labor Code, Bender 2014).

In the decision *Rolda v. Pitney Bowes* (2001), the question of whether actual events of employment were the predominant cause of the psychiatric injury is now a question regarding medical evidence. It is a question that psychologists are asked to address on the basis of results of qualified or independent medical evaluations.

Psychiatric and neuropsychiatric injuries are currently evaluated under American Medical Association (AMA) guidelines (see the discussion in AMA, 2012). Issues of compensability are mostly generated according to categories of impairment, such as visual acuity. Percentages as applied, say, by a neuro-ophthalmologist examiner are based on a classification system in which physical (not psychiatric) impairment (e.g., visual acuity) is typically rated in terms of level of severity. For example, a Class 5 rating for visual acuity impairment implies a 70% to 89% profound visual loss from baseline. Percentages are typically used in cases involving affected organ systems, where precise measures of impairment exist.

Mental impairment percentages have a weak empirical basis and low clinical utility in workers' compensation evaluations performed by psychologists. The use of percentages implies a certainty that does not exist in mental health, because many factors influence emotional functioning and behavior. Mental health impairment percentages have little to any empirical basis or clinical utility in workers' compensation evaluations performed by psychologists. Nonetheless, psychologist examiners are required, by law, to lay out conclusions based on percentage breakdowns and to support these conclusions with medically probable evidence. The evidence-based approach to medicine and the AMA guidelines for workers' compensation thus determine the manner in which results of qualified medical evaluations are considered, interpreted, and communicated within the work product or psychological report.

Application of percentages to denote degree of impairment is a requirement that may seem to run counter to the way psychologists practice. Most neuropsychologists, for example, are trained in empirical and objective means of calculating impairment based on standardized test results and baseline and normative comparisons. The percentage system for workers' compensation purposes can be fluid and subjective, which makes formulating and providing opinions with reasonable medical probability—at least according to the way statistical probability is typically considered by psychologists—more difficult.

Similarly, whole person ratings of psychiatric injuries are considered within the scope of practice for qualified medical evaluators. Whole person ratings are currently based on *DSM–IV–TR*. Once a Global Assessment of Functioning (GAF) score is determined and reported on Axis V, it is converted to an equivalent WPI rating with a standard conversion table provided in the 2001 edition of the American Medical Association *Guides* (Cocchiarella & Andersson, 2001). As clinical and neuropsychologists know, the GAF score is considered arbitrary and subjective in many instances. Indeed, the GAF and its accompanying Axis V reporting mechanism have since been eliminated in the revised *Diagnostic and Statistical Manual of Mental Disorders* (*DSM–5*; American Psychiatric Association, 2013) nomenclature. Arguably, reliability for making judgments, based on the GAF rating system, is subject to considerable differences among qualified medical evaluators, and this may be one reason the GAF is now obsolete. It may take years for the legal system to update its role in workers' compensation settings.

Notwithstanding elimination of the GAF from *DSM–5*, psychologists know that a reliable GAF comes down to how well it can be supported through medical evidence from interviews, tests, and records. In conjunction with use of rating schedules (e.g., PDRS, WPI, GAF), medical determination of the psychiatric or neurological condition must be based on substantial medical evidence. Medical evidence for a disability is typically based on results of the clinical evaluation, test data, information from medical records, and the claimant's history. Activities of daily living, for example, constitute a primary source of information concerning the nature of the claimant's alleged mental, behavioral, or psychiatric industrial injury. The activities of daily living are based on forms administered to the claimant and serve to support ratings for the PDRS, WPI, and GAF (Cocchiarella & Andersson, 2001).

Mental status, cognition, and highest integrative function disturbances originating in verifiable medical impairments (e.g., stroke, head injury) are assessed with criteria based on the amount of interference with ability to perform one or more activities of daily living (e.g., sleep, sexual activity, attention and concentration). Instrumental activities of daily living are included in this category and pertain to functions like shopping, use of the telephone, and traveling. Claimants may be required to rate whether, for example, they can use a telephone independently, use one with assistance, or are completely dependent on another to use this device. So the questions and, by implication, the response choices are written in a general manner, leaving a great deal of room for subjectivity and misperception on the claimant's part.

In the conduct of workers' compensation evaluations, the psychologist may also be responsible for determining causation. In this sense, the psychologist is asked to decide whether personnel actions substantially caused, say, between 35% and 40% of the claimant's psychiatric condition. Thus, the psychologist offers a medical opinion as to what percentage of the psychiatric condition is caused by personnel action (industrial factors) and what percentage, if any, is due to nonindustrial factors. The predominant cause threshold of compensability standard holds for all types of psychiatric and neuropsychiatric claims (e.g., physical–mental; mental–mental; mental–physical injuries), including those arising from a physical injury (e.g., pain; *Lockheed Martin v. Workers' Compensation Appeals Board*, 2002).

To meet the standard of causation, wherein a disability is considered to be caused by industrial factors, the threshold may vary (in the State of California it is 50% or more of the disability). Causation must be accounted for by industrial factors. For example, a neuropsychologist may need to state that 40% of the diagnosis (e.g., cognitive disorder not otherwise specified) was caused by the physical injury (e.g., cumulative head trauma) suffered during the course of employment (e.g., playing professional football) and that 60% of the injury was caused by other factors (e.g., normal age-related decline, preexisting medical conditions, socioeconomic problems).

Apportionment of permanent disability to causation (Cal. Labor Code, Bender 2014) is a different matter under consideration by the qualified medical evaluator. Determination of causation is usually made (e.g., 40% industrial, 60% nonindustrial factors), and then apportionment is opined in terms of what factors may be accounting for the claimant's industrial injury outside of the industrial injury. In other words, what were the preexisting factors accounting for the claimant's current industrial injury? What preexisting factors were maintained at the same level postinjury? Was the preexisting pathology or disease aggravated (i.e., permanently worsened)? Or was there exacerbation of the preexisting medical condition (e.g., a transient or temporary elevation)?

In the example of the professional football player discussed below, cumulative head trauma was believed to have been suffered during the course of professional play. In this example, the examiner estimated that 40% of the injury was due to industrial factors and 60% of it was due to nonindustrial factors, then made a separate determination that 60% of the industrial injury was caused by preexisting conditions, such as prior head injuries, chronic medical conditions, or long-standing personality traits that may have been highlighted or exacerbated, aggravated, or worsened by the person's industrial injury.

In summary, specific areas of psychiatric and neuropsychological assessment and evaluation within workers' compensation form the basis for a qualified medical evaluation (or independent medical examination, as it is termed in other states). These areas of focus include compensability, causation, and apportionment. Within this context the examiner is expected to answer questions regarding whether or not the injury is compensable, by workers' compensation standards. If the answer to this question is yes, percentage breakdowns of how much an industrial injury is accounted for by industrial versus nonindustrial factors are determined. Written reports are expected to include conclusions opined within reasonable medical probability. Substantial medical evidence is considered within the context of evidence-based medicine and serves as supporting evidence underlying expert conclusions within workers' compensation.

Results of a qualified psychological or neuropsychological evaluation are thus expected to tell the story of how a claimant's emotional problems or cognitive impairments came about, how they affect day-to-day functioning, and what caused them. Occupational health and safety standards within workers' compensation for areas of mental and behavioral disorders may be loosely connected, subjective, and unreliable. It is up to the psychologist, in this context, to provide a clear, objective, and valid clinical presentation of the claimant's mental health. Substantial evidence to support clinical interpretations and diagnoses is presented, and opinions regarding the various industrial issues are rendered within a probability framework.

USE OF THE MMPI–2 IN WORKERS' COMPENSATION

When a claimant presents for a qualified medical evaluation in the workers' compensation setting, several issues must be addressed. The injured worker typically presents with multiple physical complaints associated with what he (or she) believes was an industrial injury incurred during the course of his employment. Injuries may be physical or psychiatric in nature. They may range from a nail through the skull when a nail gun misfired or posttraumatic stress disorder from being tied up and pistol whipped in the course of a store robbery. These injuries come to the attention of the psychologist, who then examines the claimant for perceptual problems (because the nail affected the eye), personality changes (because the nail also penetrated the frontal lobe), and emotional disorders (because the claimant is traumatized by the entire event and blindness to one eye).

The Minnesota Multiphasic Personality Inventory—2 (MMPI–2) is typically the standard measure of personality and emotional functioning used in workers' compensation evaluations involving mental and behavioral industrial injuries. These types of alleged injuries are often referred to as stress claims. Stress on the job may consist of, for example, verbal harassment, a physical beating, or loss of a limb. The question of what constitutes stress lies in the eye of the beholder. When a stress claim is presented, the degree to which the claimant is responding adversely to perceived job stress is under consideration. Results of the MMPI–2 are used to address and operationalize the person's response to the stressor.

Qualified psychologist medical examiners may also administer the MMPI–2 because credibility of the informant is at issue. As illustrated in Chapter 5, neuropsychologists are frequently faced with addressing the issue of respondent credibility and veracity of complaints. Such is true of workers' compensation settings, where secondary gain in the form of a pronouncement of permanently disabled status, for example, may ensure lifelong workers' compensation benefits. Results of analog studies (e.g., Alwes, Clark, Berry, & Granacher, 2008) demonstrated high *F* scale scores among individuals asked to feign psychiatric problems. N. W. Nelson, Sweet, Berry, Bryant, and Granacher (2007), using an archival study design, showed that specific validity scales (*L, F, K, FBS, Fp, RBS, Md, Ds-r*, and *S*) added incremental validity to standard MMPI–2 profile interpretations in compensation-seeking individuals. The basis for using these scales to judge profile validity in neuropsychological examinations is described in greater detail in Chapter 2. Using an archival research design, Berry et al. (1995) found that scales *F, Fb, F-K, Fp, Ma, Pd*, and *Ds2* were significantly elevated in compensation-seeking patients with closed head injury compared to non-compensation-seeking patients with head injury.

Secondary gain undoubtedly remains a major consideration for psychologists in the workers' compensation arena. As the MMPI–2 literature suggests, validity, credibility, and effort of the applicant's report should be strongly considered in this setting. Issues of malingering behavior, overreporting, and exaggeration, discussed in Chapter 2, remain paramount in this regard. Conditions or problems that existed prior to the date of injury require consideration. Long-standing personality traits and chronic, lifelong conditions do not all arise when an industrial injury occurs. They must be identified by the qualified medical evaluator, who decides whether they were exacerbated by the alleged injury or remain unchanged. If the claimant has personality characteristics that are interpreted as traits, an argument may be made for either an exacerbation of these symptoms or stability of symptoms from pre-injury to postinjury states.

The MMPI–2 may also be used to determine long-standing personality traits that figure into the person's claim. Distinguishing traits from state dispositions has a long history in the psychology literature on assessment and evaluation. In the workers' compensation setting, identifying traits on the basis of, for example, sociopathic tendencies, paranoid ideation, and histrionic behaviors, may assist in assessment of preexisting conditions. Personality correlates that characterize trait-like mechanisms, rather than strictly state conditions, are important to consider in this regard. Once the psychologist defines traits through scale analysis, changes in personality functioning from pre-injury status may be better determined. It may be that traits are highlighted or exacerbated by the industrial injury. Alternatively, there may be no basis for the industrial injury's connection to existing traits, and that may be considered as well. The claimant may always have been paranoid and mistrustful of others. The industrial injury had little to no impact on this trait.

Forensic psychologists often deal with individuals who may have had years of enduring chronic pain. Many if not most claimants present with multiple physical problems affecting one or more body parts. These physical problems affect their day-to-day functioning, as indicated by their responses on activities of daily living. Often, they are precluded from lifting, bending, or standing for periods of time. They may be using assistive devices. Driving is a challenge. They may be homebound. Subjective pain is typically rated 10 on a scale of 1 to 10 when certain activities are performed. It is not uncommon to see ratings of 8 to 10 across all kinds of physical activities. Individuals may be on a number of medications to control pain. These medications keep them sedated and help them sleep and carry on throughout the day. They are likely to have undergone medical procedures to either diminish or eradicate pain symptoms. Surgeries, especially, tend to cause increased pain responses during periods of recovery. The process of filing and appealing claims is lengthy, and claimants often find themselves dealing with the system for years, postinjury. It is not unusual for many claimants to present to the psychologist with psychiatric issues 3 to 5 years after the alleged injury.

CASE EXAMPLE

Mark is a 56-year-old retired professional football player who presented with a history of cumulative head trauma and multiple physical injuries over the course of his 9-year professional career. He estimates sustaining over 300 industrial (closed head) injuries while playing professional football, as well as numerous fractures, contusions, and postoperative complications. Body parts affected include head, neck, back, spine, shoulders, elbows, hands, wrists, legs, ankles, knees, feet, and internal organs. Two of the traumatic brain injuries are considered moderate to severe because of associated loss of consciousness, sensory dysfunction, and transient amnestic episodes. In many of the head injuries sustained during the course of play, symptoms of altered consciousness and postinjury confusion were ignored or minimized to facilitate return to play.

The claimant now presents with memory and attention problems that are negatively impacting his current work performance in the field of real estate and his activities of daily living. He reported that he is unable to work on most regular work duties for longer than an hour because of pain and fatigue. He often has to go back and retrace steps while performing routine tasks. Memory problems interfere with his completing paperwork assignments. He experiences occasional headaches.

The MMPI–2 was administered to Mark, and the results are shown in Figure 7.1. His performance on the MMPI–2 validity scales was well within the normal range, indicating that the profile is valid and interpretable. He cooperated sufficiently with the evaluation to provide useful personality information for the evaluation. It should be noted that his approach to the MMPI–2 items was somewhat inconsistent, and he tended to endorse items as false at times, regardless of their content. However, this approach did not invalidate his profile, and the MMPI–2 results provide valid personality information.

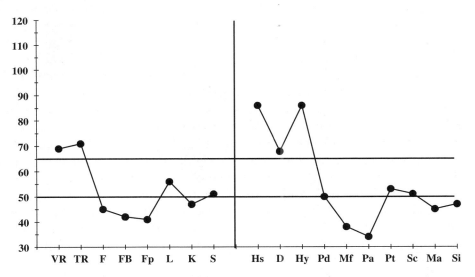

Figure 7.1. MMPI–2 basic validity and clinical scales profile for Mark. Excerpted from the *MMPI®–2 (Minnesota Multiphasic Personality Inventory®—2) Manual for Administration, Scoring, and Interpretation, Revised Edition* by Butcher et al. Copyright © 2001 by the Regents of the University of Minnesota. Used by permission of the University of Minnesota Press. All rights reserved. "MMPI®" and "Minnesota Multiphasic Personality Inventory®" are trademarks owned by the Regents of the University of Minnesota.

Mark's MMPI–2 clinical profile pattern, in which the *Hs*, *D*, and *Hy* scales were extremely elevated, shows very high profile definition. His current MMPI–2 pattern would likely be prominent in his profile if he is retested at a later date. Thus, a high degree of confidence can be placed in the behavioral descriptions from the MMPI–2 scales. The client presents a picture of multiple physical problems and a reduced level of psychological functioning. His elevated scores on *Hs* and *Hy*, for example, occur in less than 2% of the normative sample of men.

His MMPI–2 pattern is one of extensive but somewhat vague persistent attention to his pain symptoms, fatigue, weakness, or unexplained periods of dizziness. The client reports some symptoms that might occur from stress. Some individuals with this pattern show long-term physical symptoms and may become incapacitated and dependent on others. His physical problems may be vague, may intensify after a period of stress, and may be persistent over time. With a history of cumulative head traumas, some severe, the likelihood that actual organic changes were evident is high. True chronic pain is more likely with his pattern of symptoms and is consistent with the information reviewed in medical records on this case.

Given that the MMPI–2 addresses current functioning, the snapshot presented in this case example, thus far, suggests that Mark demonstrates a picture of multiple physical problems and a reduced level of psychological functioning. The 1-3-2 code-type profile was further examined in terms of Harris–Lingoes subscale analysis. This type of analysis helps determine what is elevating the basic clinical scales. In Mark's case, the Mental Dullness (*D4*) and Subjective Depression (*D1*) subscales, together with Lassitude–Malaise (*Hy3*) and Somatic Complaints (*Hy4*), were significantly elevated. Interpretive evidence based on this analysis suggests that feelings of mental slowness, slowed processing, and psychomotor retardation are part of his clinical picture. Mark's presentation involves chronic pain. The effects of ongoing, unremitting pain (and pain medication treatment) would certainly dull the senses and create the experience of clinical depression. We have evidence, based on the MMPI–2, that emotional levels are mild for depression and worry. So, the level and type of emotional response seen here appear closely tied to this individual's physical ups and downs. A strong argument for symptoms of a mood or anxiety disorder, per se, based on *DSM* standards was not upheld.

Positive personality characteristics were demonstrated that lend credence to stable emotional functioning and a healthy attitude toward life. Mark tends to think in a very concrete manner and to focus on his physical ailments, but he values being seen as logical and without psychological problems. His judgment is better than it ever was. He finds it easy to make decisions. He is self-confident.

The psychologist had corroborative evidence congruent with the MMPI–2 information from outside sources. Mark's physical health was not as good as that of his friends, and he worries constantly about his health. He reports a wide variety of physical and neurological symptoms such as gastrointestinal difficulties, chest and neck pains, hay fever or asthma, and balance and coordination difficulties—all corroborated in medical record. Mark tires quickly and feels tired a good deal of the time. He has sleep difficulties.

The MMPI–2 allows for ideas regarding how to formulate the section of the workers' compensation report that addresses future medical care. Mark was shown as not naturally introspective, which would complicate the implementation of any therapeutic intervention. Individuals with this MMPI–2 clinical profile pattern tend to be defensive toward psychological interpretations of their physical symptoms and show reluctance to engaging in self-exploration. They are generally not very open to the idea that their own thinking may be influencing their problems. They show little anxiety about their symptoms and are not motivated to improve their personal adjustment.

Conservative medical treatment is recommended because his physical ailments are numerous. Some are difficult to document. Short-term interventions focused on providing symptomatic relief from his physical ailments may be beneficial and can provide the foundation for more traditional psychotherapy.

SUMMARY

Workers' compensation is a form of insurance providing wage replacement and medical benefits to employees injured in the course of employment. This chapter addressed the use of the MMPI–2 in evaluating clients in workers' compensation cases. The role of the psychological examiner serving as a qualified medical evaluator and the task of the psychological examiner in contributing to work compensation decisions were described. The workers' compensation evaluation process includes a range of information, such as traditional psychological and neuropsychological testing, a clinical interview, and ongoing behavioral observations of the claimant during the evaluation.

Forensic psychologists are responsible for developing a comprehensive analysis and description of the claimant's symptoms and behavior and may also contribute to determining causation of the alleged disability. The injured worker typically presents with multiple physical complaints associated with what he or she believes was an industrial injury incurred during the course of employment. Injuries may be physical or psychiatric in nature. A case study is provided to illustrate the utility of the MMPI–2 for understanding the symptomatic behavior of an injured worker in a workers' compensation case.

8

THE MMPI–2 IN IMMIGRATION EVALUATIONS

The use of psychological assessment in immigration cases has emerged as an area of specialty in the last 20 years. This new field involves the use of psychological assessments as part of the evidence presented in hearings by individuals seeking immigration relief. Psychological assessments can provide information about a number of issues that are relevant to the psycholegal framework of an immigration case. This chapter presents the literature relevant to these types of cases, albeit its limited scope, and describes how the Minnesota Multiphasic Personality Inventory—2 (MMPI–2) can be a useful tool in many of these assessments. The chapter ends with a case example that illustrates how the information derived from the MMPI–2 supports the collective data required to meet the psycholegal constructs in these types of evaluations. The rather detailed review of the legislature and legal foundations behind this topic is presented first to familiarize the forensic psychologist with this newer forensic field.

http://dx.doi.org/10.1037/14571-009
Using the MMPI–2 in Forensic Assessment, by J. N. Butcher, G. A. Hass, R. L. Greene, and L. D. Nelson

The term *immigrant* refers to a person born outside the United States. A subset of immigrants is refugees, who have been forced to flee their country because of persecution, war, or violence. Another subset of immigrants is economic migrants, individuals who leave their country voluntarily to seek a better life. They can return to their country of origin and continue receiving the protection of their government, whereas refugees cannot return safely to their homes (United Nations, n.d.).

The need for immigration evaluations is increasing rapidly, yet the number of psychologists conducting them is limited. According to the Psychologists for Social Responsibility website (http://www.psysr.org/about/programs/humanrights/projects/asylum, PsySR's Political Asylum Project, para. 4), several factors prevent psychologists from properly fulfilling the demand for these types of evaluations: a lack of familiarity with immigration law; limited multicultural competence; and poor understanding of the political, social, and cultural context of immigration and refugee experiences.

Indeed, these evaluations differ in many ways from other types of forensic evaluations because the psycholegal constructs focus on many issues beyond the psychological state of the individual, such as family dynamics and social context. In addition, proceedings in immigration courts differ significantly from those in criminal, civil, and family courts, with which forensic psychologists are more familiar and for which training is more readily available. These evaluations are challenging, because these victims are often extensively traumatized and require a great deal of expertise from psychologists to elicit the information needed for the purpose of the assessment. In many cases, victims may come from countries where they have already been abused or exploited without legal or community protections, and they may have difficulty trusting an authority figure and articulating victimization that they may not identify as such. Further, they usually are recent immigrants who may have limited mastery of English and have limited acculturation to U.S. society; thus, they require specialized psychological instruments and assessment procedures. These factors combine to make the field very demanding in terms of professional knowledge and training, as well as ability required to deal with the vicarious suffering of being exposed to unspeakable human tragedies.

LEGAL CONTEXT OF IMMIGRATION EVALUATIONS

The United States is home to a complex and diverse population of immigrants from various ethnic, cultural, and national groups whose migration was motivated by a host of reasons. The experience of immigration can be difficult when leaving behind family support and known environment and culture. The risks of an unfamiliar environment and barriers to integration are often compounded by discrimination and prejudice (Narayan, 1997). Adding to these risk factors are the dangers that accrue when the person migrates without legal authorization to reside, study, or work in the United States. In many cases, these immigrants have escaped from difficult situations or crimes in their countries, such as war, civil strife, repressive regimes, environmental disasters, persecution, gender violence, or striking deprivation. Some are drawn to the United States by economic opportunities (Shetty & Kaguyutan, 2002) or to reunite with family members. Some of these immigrants are unable to obtain appropriate visas. Undocumented status leaves an individual vulnerable to revictimization and may prevent the person from accessing community and government services and resources. To fulfill its human rights values, the U.S. Congress has passed a number of laws that provide protections to these vulnerable groups. These pieces of legislation also strengthen the ability of law enforcement agencies to investigate and prosecute crimes in order to prevent perpetrators from victimizing vulnerable immigrants.

Accordingly, many undocumented immigrant victims of crimes or persecution committed in their native countries or in the United States may be eligible for protection and relief from deportation and can apply for various types of immigration relief, such as the Nonimmigrant Visa for Victims of Crime (U visa) or the Visa for Victims of Human Trafficking (T visa), cancellation of removal, asylum, withholding, and relief under the Convention Against Torture. A grant of immigration relief in some instances may provide the person and often his or her immediate relatives legal work authorization and the ability to remain in the United States without fear of deportation. In addition, such immigration relief may provide the ability to convert that legal status to lawful permanent residency and, in some cases, eligibility for other social service benefits such as housing, food, income and employment assistance, English-language training, health care, mental health services, and foster care.

The Department of Homeland Security (DHS) is the executive agency responsible for overseeing the immigration processes. For some types of relief, including asylum, DHS officers may adjudicate the petition or refer the case to a federal immigration court for a charge such as being present in the United States without authorization (Ramji-Nogales, Schoenholtz, & Schrag, 2009). If the applicant is denied immigration relief, he or she can apply to the Board of Immigration Appeals, and if this board sustains the deportation, the individual can appeal to the U.S. Court of Appeals. In other cases, an individual may file an affirmative petition for immigration relief, including in response to the Violence Against Women Act ([VAWA], 1994) self-petitions such as U visas (that give victims of certain crimes temporary legal status and work eligibility in the United States) and T visas (visas provided to persons who are victims of trafficking). U visas and T visas are administered by the U.S. Citizenship and Immigration Services (USCIS), a division of the DHS. Immigration laws are complex and under constant revision. The following is a brief explanation of some of the major types of immigration cases and the role that psychological factors play.

Asylum

In this type of immigration petition, an individual who has been subjected to mistreatment or abuse—persecution—in a foreign country files a claim for political asylum. The mistreatment is usually related to an individual's politics, religion, ethnicity, nationality, membership in a particular social group, or gender (Ramji-Nogales et al., 2009). The U.S. Congress has ratified the international Convention Against Torture and Other Cruel, Inhuman or Degrading Treatment or Punishment (Burgers & Danelius, 1988), which provides that it will not expel, return, or extradite a person if this person is believed to be in danger of being subjected to torture. The assessment regarding the potential for future torture includes a determination that the fear is well founded and that torture is systematically practiced in the country where the person would be sent. According to the law, the individual has a year after arriving in the United States to file for asylum. The individual must show that he or she is unable or unwilling to return to or cannot obtain the protection of his or her home country due to a well-founded fear of persecution. If the individual voluntarily applies to the DHS, a psychological assessment can aid in determining whether the individual was the victim of a traumatic experience and whether he or she continued to suffer from psychological symptoms related to the abuse or mistreatment after his or her arrival. If the individual applies for asylum after having been apprehended and placed on removal proceedings in immigration court, in addition to assessing the trauma, the psychologist has to assess whether the psychological consequences of the abuse prevented the individual from filing the asylum claim within the 1 year allowed.

Relief Under the Violence Against Women Act (VAWA Self-Petition)

If there is domestic violence in a marriage, a battered spouse who is an undocumented immigrant may be deterred from taking action to protect himself or herself (such as filing a civil protection order, filing criminal charges, or calling the police) because of the threat or fear of deportation (VAWA, 1994). Therefore, Congress specifically included an immigration protection

(VAWA) to allow a battered alien to file for immigration relief without the help of the U.S. citizen batterer. In these cases, an alien spouse of a U.S. citizen or legal permanent resident can file a petition for residency independently when the noncitizen or the children have been battered or subjected to extreme cruelty by an abusive spouse. The psychologist in these evaluations assesses the psychological state of the victim in order to provide psychological evidence regarding allegations of battering and *extreme mental cruelty* (required for family petition cases), as well as opinions regarding other aspects of the legislation such as having entered the marriage in *good faith* and having *good moral character*. These italicized words are the psycholegal constructs under VAWA (2013).

The legal definition of extreme cruelty includes any act or threatened act of violence, including any forceful detention, that results or threatens to result in physical or mental injury. Psychological or sexual abuse or exploitation, including rape, molestation, incest (if the victim is a minor), or forced prostitution, shall be considered acts of violence. Other abusive actions may also be acts of violence under certain circumstances, including acts that, in and of themselves, may not initially appear violent but that are a part of an overall pattern of violence (8 C.F.R. 204.2(c)(1)(vi) (2004)).

The meaning of "abusive actions that in and of themselves may not appear violent" has been the focus of attention of a study that reports how some offenders tailor the abuse to the victim's vulnerabilities and cultural idiosyncrasies; thus, small actions may have a traumatic meaning for the victim (Hass, Dutton, & Orloff, 2000). When there are patterns of maltreatment, each incident cannot be treated as a discrete event because the multiple incidents and multiple types of maltreatment over a prolonged period multiply the emotional impact exponentially. Ultimately, seemingly minor incidents bring back the memories of previous ones, which, together with the ongoing fear, results in overwhelming levels of anxiety and an environment of fear.

Good moral character has been legally defined by the lack thereof, meaning the presence of conditions that oppose being considered a person of good moral character. These conditions include engaging in murder, aggravated felony, persecution, genocide, torture, or severe violations of religious freedom. For a conditional bar, the factors to consider include committing certain crimes (particularly involving a controlled substance or immigration crime, prostitution, or gambling), being an alcoholic, failing to support dependents, committing adultery, failing to file tax returns, defrauding the government with public benefits, and other unlawful acts (United States Citizenship and Immigration Services [USCIS]; http://www.uscis.gov/policymanual/HTML/PolicyManual-Volume12-PartF.html).

T Visa, or Relief for Victims of Trafficking

The T visa is available for victims of severe forms of trafficking, defined as

> a) sex trafficking in which a commercial sex act is induced by force, fraud or coercion, or in which the person induced to perform such an act has not attained 18 year of age, or b) the recruitment, harboring, transportation, provision, or obtaining of a person for labor or services, through the use of force, fraud, or coercion for the purpose of subjection to involuntary servitude, peonage, debt bondage, or slavery. (Victims of Trafficking and Violence Protection Act of 2000 [TVPA], § 103(8), 22 U.S.C. § 7102(8))

Trafficking victims must provide evidence of these elements to be defined a victim of a severe form of trafficking under the TVPA (§ 103(80), 22 U.S.C. § 7102(8)). This form of immigration relief allows victims to apply for a temporary visa and then adjust their status to legal permanent resident, provided that they cooperate in the investigation against the traffickers. This legislation interacts with the Violence Against Women Reauthorization Act of 2005 ([VAWRA], 2006), because it allows trafficking victims whose physical or psychological trauma impedes their ability to cooperate with law enforcement to seek a waiver of the cooperation requirement of the T visa.

The psychological evaluation in these cases may provide evidence that force, fraud, or coercion occurred. Under the definitions of this legislation, *psychological coercion* is included as fraud or coercion under the TVPA and T visa regulations. Coercion in this sense includes (a) threats of serious harm to or physical restraint against any person; (b) any scheme, plan, or pattern intended to cause a person to believe that failure to perform an act would result in serious harm to or physical restraint against the person; and (c) the abuse or threatened abuse of the legal process (TVPA, § 103(2)C, 22 U.S.C. §7102(2)(C)).

The concept of trafficking under this law is quite complex and contemplates the possibility that what started as smuggling progressed to trafficking once the individual entered the United States and then was forced or coerced into a situation of labor or sex exploitation (The Human Smuggling and Trafficking Center, 2006). The core concept to evaluate in this type of psychological evaluation is coercion that usually consists of psychological threats that are meaningful to the person, as defined by the patterns or schemes that would make a person feel like he (or she) may be harmed if he fails to perform the act demanded of him (TVPA, 28 C.F.R. § 1100). The psychological evaluation in immigration cases may support the victim's experience of the psychological harm he or she suffered as a trafficking victim.

U Visa, or Relief for Victims of Criminal Activity

In these types of cases, victims of criminal activity are granted temporary immigration benefits if they "a) have suffered substantial mental or physical abuse as a result of having been a victim of criminal activity, b) have information regarding the criminal activity, and c) assist government officials in the investigation and prosecution of such criminal activity" (Federal Register Publications, 2007, Background and legislative authority, para. 15). Therefore, the psychological factors in these evaluations relate to the nature and characteristics of the impact of crime on the victim and provide psychological evidence to meet the criteria of having suffered *substantial mental or physical abuse*. DHS regulations require that when determining whether a U visa applicant has suffered substantial abuse, the USCIS must consider the nature of the injury inflicted or suffered; the severity of the perpetrator's conduct; the severity of the harm suffered; the duration of the infliction of the harm; and the extent to which there is permanent or serious harm to the appearance, health, or physical or mental soundness of the victim, including aggravation of preexisting conditions (8 C.F.R. § 214.14(b)(1)).

Cancellation of Removal

To be eligible for cancellation of removal, the Immigration and Nationality Act (1952) provides that a person in deportation proceedings may be spared deportation, at the immigration judge's discretion, if he or she has been physically present in the United States for a certain period of time and has not committed an aggravated felony. Cancellation of removal is also available for individuals who are not legal permanent residents in removal proceedings if they have lived in the United States for at least 10 years, are individuals of good moral character, have not been convicted of crimes or offenses that would make them removable, and do not pose a national security threat. The noncitizen must also show that deportation would cause *extreme hardship* (for a current legal permanent resident) or *exceptional and unusually extreme hardship* (for a noncitizen nonresident) to the alien, his or her spouse, parent, or children who are U.S. citizens or lawful permanent residents.

The concept of extreme hardship has been clarified with case law (Board of Immigration Appeals, 1978) as including the following factors: (a) length of residence, (b) conditions of health, (c) conditions in the country to which the alien is returnable (economic and political), (d) financial status (business and occupation), (e) the possibility of other means of adjusting status, (f) whether the person is of special assistance to the United States or community, (g) immigration history, and (h) position in the community.

The standard of extreme hardship has to be met with hardship beyond the normal caused by deportation such as decline in standard of living or loss of employment.

These psychological assessments tend to assess the family member who would be most affected by separation from the individual being deported. The point is to provide evidence of the harm or potential harm to a U.S. citizen or legal permanent resident if his or her relative is deported. The psychologist describes the nature of the relationship the alien has with the qualified relative (Vaisman-Tzachor, 2012), reflecting that the individual being deported plays an extremely relevant role and one that cannot be easily replaced in the life of his or her relative. In addition, the psychologist describes the anticipated damage to the qualified relative if the alien is removed from his or her life.

The concept of conditions of health was clarified in *Jara-Navaretta v. Immigration and Naturalization Service* (1986) as including factors such as prolonged or geographic separation from children or removal of children to a country with a different language or culture. In these cases, the evaluation would assess the psychological impact of breaking the attachment or enduring a prolonged separation from a parent or the difficulties in adjustment if the child is moved to another country. Other cases typical of this type of immigration relief that a psychologist may assess would be if a U.S. citizen or permanent resident child or wife might have a mental health condition for which the individual being deported was a primary caregiver and for which treatment would not be of equivalent quality if treated outside the United States. This psychological assessment diagnoses the psychological disorder and assesses the potential of treatment in the country to which the person would have to move. The psychological evaluation may also evaluate alien examinees to assess whether they would suffer extreme hardship involving unusual and severe harm if they were removed from the United States and returned to their country of origin.

EVALUATING PSYCHOPATHOLOGY IN IMMIGRANT AND REFUGEE INDIVIDUALS

In conducting immigration evaluations, the psychologist must consider the impact of human suffering on both an individual's internal and external circumstances and background. It is recommended that the psychologist also pay attention to the individual's changes in functioning within the family, community, and cultural context (Frumkin & Friedland, 1995).

At the core of the psychological assessment in immigration cases is the individual's current psychological functioning and its application to the psycholegal constructs of the particular visa. Evaluations that focus on a relative to the alien in cases of extreme hardship benefit from assessment not only of the relative's overall mental state and functioning as well as health status but also of the attachment and relationship to the alien. An understanding of this relationship is central to answering the questions regarding the damage if the relationship is interrupted. There is a strong body of research that addresses the evaluation of psychopathology in ethnically diverse and immigrant populations and that helps the forensic psychologist formulate the issues in these evaluations. A review of this literature is included in Chapter 4, together with an analysis of its implications in personality assessment.

Immigration evaluations focused on asylum petitions, VAWA, T visa, and U visa involve an assessment of the distress the person suffered due to the crime committed against him or her. These evaluations involve the detection of trauma sequelae. Fortunately, there is a solid body of literature that assesses trauma-related psychopathology for immigrant and refugee groups, including exposure to traumatic events.

Trauma-based presenting problems have been cited as highly prevalent among first-generation immigrants (American Psychological Association [APA], Presidential Task Force on Immigration, 2012). While reviewing the trauma literature for immigrants, Foster (2001) identified several areas in which traumatic experiences leading to psychological distress may occur: (a) events experienced prior to migration that were a determinant of the relocation; (b) events experienced during transit; (c) events that happened during asylum seeking and resettlement; and (d) inadequate living conditions in the host country related to unemployment, limited supports, and ethnic discrimination. In addition, for the purposes of immigration evaluations, it is important to consider the distress caused by becoming a victim of a crime in the host country. These are the areas that the psychologist would focus on when looking for psychological data in an immigration evaluation.

Although precautions should be taken when applying U.S. diagnoses to people from non-Western cultures, there is considerable research evidence that posttraumatic stress disorder (PTSD) and depression are found in immigrant and refugee groups and are related to events at different points in the immigration process. Premigration trauma may include persecution on the basis of political, gender, ethnic, or religious factors, as well as victimization such as rape, domestic violence, genital mutilation, natural disasters, and famine. Although research studies in this field are plagued by conceptual, methodological, and design inconsistencies, they support a relationship between traumatic events and different clinical manifestations of trauma.

For instance, Jaranson et al. (2004) tried to differentiate between 1,134 adult Somali and Oromo refugees, some of whom were tortured and some of whom escaped before they were tortured. Jaranson et al. found PTSD in

25% of those participants who reported being tortured compared with 4% in those who did not. Asgary, Metalios, Smith, and Paccioni (2006) studied 89 men who presented at the Bronx Human Rights Clinic for medical and mental health services. Eighty-seven percent were found to have experienced multiple types of torture due to political opinion or activity, ethnicity, and religion. They found that approximately 40% were diagnosed with PTSD at the time of the interview and 5% were diagnosed with major depressive disorder (MDD). An 8-year follow-up study of 44 refugee men diagnosed with war injuries (Hermansson, Timpka, & Thyberg, 2002) found PTSD in 50% of their cases. The men represented nine different nationalities, and their histories included having experienced long periods of guerrilla life or other political activities, interrupted schooling and working life, death and separation of family members, a high frequency of imprisonment and torture, and negative circumstances related to their migration.

Other studies have found an even higher prevalence of mental health problems among refugees. Sixty-one refugees admitted to psychiatric outpatient clinics in southern Norway (Teodorescu, Heir, Hauff, Wentzel-Larsen, & Lien, 2012) were examined with structured clinical interviews and self-report psychometric instruments. PTSD was diagnosed in 82% of the refugees, and Disorders of Extreme Stress, Not Otherwise Specified were present in 16%. Sixty-four percent of the refugees had both PTSD and MDD, and 80% of those who had PTSD had three or more additional diagnoses. Similarly, A. Keller et al. (2006) evaluated over 300 survivors from a torture treatment clinic in New York. More than 80% of these survivors had clinically significant anxiety, 84% had clinically significant depression, and just under half of them had significant levels of post traumatic symptoms, with women having higher levels of symptoms than men.

A 3½ year study of the evolution of trauma-related symptoms in a group of 21 Bosnian refugees (Vojvoda, Weine, McGlashan, Becker, & Southwick, 2008) using standardized psychological assessments found that 76% of the refugees met the diagnostic criteria for PTSD at baseline, 33% at 1 year, and 24% at 3½ years. At the 3½ year evaluation, 44% of women and 8% of men met the criteria for PTSD.

A community sample of 258 immigrants from Central America and Mexico were compared with a sample of 329 native-born Mexican Americans and Anglo Americans (Cervantes, Salgado de Snyder, & Padilla, 1989) for depression, anxiety, somatization, generalized distress, and PTSD. The diagnosis of PTSD was applied to 52% of Central American immigrants who reported their emigration as motivated by war or political unrest, 49% of those who emigrated for other reasons, and 25% of Mexican immigrants. Cervantes et al. also found higher levels of generalized distress for all immigrants when compared with native-born Americans.

PTSD following natural disasters has also been studied across borders. De la Fuente (1990) evaluated 573 individuals who underwent Mexican earthquakes and found that 32% warranted the diagnosis of PTSD, 19% that of generalized anxiety, and 13% that of depression. PTSD reactions following a paint factory explosion were studied by Weisaeth (1989). The study found that 80% of these individuals with high stressor exposure had immediate PTSD reactions and 5% had delayed PTSD responses.

Differences in prevalence of trauma-related diagnosis and depression may be related to diverse methodologies, assessment instruments, length of time after migration, and adjustment in the host country, among other variables. However, it is important to note that researchers may have focused on the symptoms of trauma as we know them in the United States and not on assessing other forms of maladjustment. For instance, in their 2006 study, Asgary et al. acknowledged that the low percentage of depression diagnoses (5%) among victims of torture may have resulted from a bias to look for MDD and preferentially diagnose PTSD or confusion due to the overlap of several symptoms of major depression with PTSD. Despite these confounds, there appears to be a clear universal link between premigration trauma and PTSD-related psychopathology that remains over time and can be detected.

Victimization that happens in the host country after resettlement has also been the focus of study as it relates to potential immigration benefits. Chaudry et al. (2010) surveyed undocumented immigrants detained in the immigration raids of the Postville and Grand Island meat plants and the New Bedford factory and found that 10% to 15 % of these workers could qualify for temporary or permanent residency based on being a victim of crime or abuse, a cooperative witness, or an asylum claimant.

Intimate partner violence for immigrant women as it relates to their undocumented immigration status has been widely studied (Abraham, 2000; Ahmad, Riaz, Barata, & Stewart, 2004; Ammar, 2000; Ammar, Orloff, Dutton, & Aguilar-Hass, 2005; M. A. Dutton, Orloff, & Hass, 2000; Hass et al., 2000; Orloff, Dutton, Hass, & Ammar, 2003; Raj & Silverman, 2002a, 2002b; R. Rodriguez, 2004; Srinivasan & Ivey, 1999). With a general population sample of 280 immigrant Latinas, the survey conducted by Hass et al. (2000), which the U.S. Congress relied upon when reauthorizing VAWA in 2005 (VAWRA, 2006), demonstrated that 31% of the battered women reported an increase in the incidence of abusive incidents after their immigration to the United States. For 9%, the abuse began with their immigration. More specifically, 47.8% of the women who reported physical, sexual abuse, or both, were married to a U.S. citizen or a lawful permanent resident. When abusers controlled the immigration status of a spouse, 72.3% never filed immigration papers on behalf of the immigrant victim spouse. Those who filed immigration papers on behalf of the spouse had an average delay of almost four years.

As described above, there is solid research demonstrating the presence of trauma and depression in refugee and immigration groups. The knowledge of this literature is important to the psychologist, because the core issue for many psychological evaluations in the context of immigration proceedings is the assessment of trauma impact. There is considerable evidence that trauma produces lasting biological changes that are reflected in symptoms and behaviors that change a person and should facilitate diagnosis, especially when the premorbid functioning is known to the forensic psychologist.

However, the use of a PTSD diagnosis with cross-cultural and immigrant groups has been questioned (M. Friedman & Jaranson, 1994) because the experience and expression of trauma is impacted by cultural factors. PTSD and depression are not necessarily typical or the only possible signals of distress and suffering when traumatized immigrant and refugee individuals are being assessed. A percentage of the refugees in the research studies previously reviewed who did not show diagnosable PTSD or depression may have had other idioms of distress that were not targeted. Other symptoms or deficits in functioning may be present together with or instead of PTSD and depression.

Idioms of distress vary according to education, social class, cultural factors, and past knowledge and experiences (Pedersen, 1997). Somatic symptoms are reportedly more consistent with idioms of distress in some African and other ethnic groups. For instance, the assessment of clinical responses to trauma in various African subgroups has found somatic symptoms to be more prevalent than psychic symptoms (Peltzer, 1998). Similarly, health deterioration has been found to be related to trauma. A study of Armenians after an earthquake found that mortality peaked 6 months after the disaster. An association was found between loss of family members or material possessions and risk of developing heart disease, hypertension, diabetes mellitus, and arthritis (Armenian, Melkonian, & Hovanesian, 1998). A sample of 795 adults who survived Typhoon Xangsane in Vietnam was found to show MDD, panic disorder, and lower self-rated health postdisaster (Conrad et al., 2010). Similarly, studies have found high prevalence of alcohol use as a response to traumatic events. For instance, when studying the psychological problems related to the September 11 terrorist attacks, Ford, Adams, and Dailey (2007) found increased alcohol use as a risk factor for psychological problems.

In addition, the literature notes that some groups may show their psychological distress in a culturally specific manner (Guarnaccia, 1993; LaBruzza & Mendez-Villarrubia, 1994). Culture-bound syndromes is the name given to a broad assortment of psychological, somatic, and behavioral symptoms that present in certain cultural contexts (Trujillo, 2008). These symptoms and signs are recognized as illness behaviors by the participants in that culture, often masking mental illness in groups where mental health problems are stigmatized (Juckett & Rudolph-Watson, 2010). It is important to assess for the presence of particular symptoms and behaviors that signal in the examinee's culture that something is amiss regarding his or her psychological functioning. The *Diagnostic and Statistical Manual of Mental Disorders* (*DSM–5*; American Psychiatric Association, 2013) outlines a cultural formulation that is meant to add to the diagnostic assessment and to address difficulties that may occur in applying *DSM–5* criteria with foreign-born examinees. Observation of cultural variants assists forensic psychologists with the prevention of bias during the diagnosis of mental disorders among examinees born outside the United States.

In sum, it behooves the forensic psychologist when conducting an evaluation for immigration purposes to use strategies and instruments that open a wide net to capture the different signs of distress with which a examinee may present, as well as to carefully assess the potential biases that an instrument may bring to the evaluative process.

ROLE OF PSYCHOLOGICAL ASSESSMENTS IN IMMIGRATION EVALUATIONS

Because psychological constructs are at the core of this immigration legislation, mental-health professionals are becoming more relevant and provide invaluable contributions to this field. As in other forensic settings, psychologists practicing immigration law have specialized knowledge that can assist the trier of fact to understand the evidence (Federal Rules of Evidence; see also Melton, Petrila, Poythress, & Slobogin, 2007). Psychologists may act as expert witnesses in cases in which they examined the petitioner and are able to provide a report and testimony about the claims of the individual. Psychologists may also provide an opinion when they did not personally conduct the evaluation of the petitioner. In these cases, the expert witness may testify about psychological knowledge that may be relevant to the case. However, the strength of psychological testimony lies in using psychological tests that help clarify the psychological state and behavior of the target individual.

Psychological assessments of the petitioner or the petitioner's relatives are useful in most immigration cases, and their use as part of the evidence provided by the claimant has become customary. Psychological assessments for immigration cases are usually requested by the legal representative or other agent of the petitioner. A psychological assessment may be introduced during affirmative or defensive processes. The affirmative process is when the individual voluntarily applies for the immigration relief. This process is non-adversarial; however, the petitioner has to have complied with all admissibility requirements. In these cases the psychologist completes a report that, if it is favorable at the discretion of the applicant's attorney, is attached to the application. The defensive process is automatic for individuals placed in removal proceedings. This hearing is adversarial and demands that the individuals defend themselves from removal (De Jesús-Rentas, Boehnlein, & Sparr, 2010). Psychologists who provide expert testimony in these cases need to testify and will be cross-examined.

Although the evidentiary rules in immigration court are different than those in other courts and in many ways are more flexible, psychological testimony admitted into evidence follows federal rules of evidence (Vaisman-Tzachor, 2012). Psychologists' opinions should have a reasonable degree of psychological certainty based on the scientific method, including testability and acceptance in the field (Melton et al., 2007). Psychological tests used by immigration psychologists need to be reliable, commercially available, relevant to the legal issue, applicable to the population, administered in a standardized fashion, and used for the purpose for which they were developed (APA, 2010a). During cross-examination, the attorney representing the DHS may question the psychologist expert on the merits of the methodology utilized, including psychological tests such as the MMPI–2 when used, and may also contest the expert's findings by using either social science literature or the opinion of a consultant.

The use of structured interviews is typical of immigration evaluations. A number of structured interviews have been developed to target the specific nuances of trauma sequelae and can aid in the assessment of immigrants and refugees who feel comfortable verbally explaining their experiences. Some of the more popular are the Clinician Administered PTSD Scale (Blake et al., 1995), the Acute Stress Disorder Interview (Bryant, Harvey, Dang, Sackville, & Basten, 1998), the Structured Interview for Disorders of Extreme Stress (Pelcovitz et al., 1997), the Structured Clinical Interview for DSM–IV Dissociative Disorders—Revised (Steinberg, 1994), and the Detailed Assessment of Post Traumatic Stress (Briere, 2001). These interviews are helpful to address the idiographic aspects of psychological disturbances related to difficult life experiences. However, they can be challenging if the psychologist does not speak the petitioner's language, and they do not offer an objective way of measuring deception. Good practice indicates that opinions be formed on data from several sources (Ganellen, 1996). Therefore, structured interviews are helpful but should be used in combination with other information, such as review of files, collateral information, and objective psychological tests such as the MMPI–2.

Conducting psychological testing to support the expert opinion enhances the credibility of the report (De Jesús-Rentas et al., 2010). Psychological tests not only provide rich information but are a more solid and valid foundation for testimony (Lally, 2003). Psychological testing can strengthen a case made by the applicant for immigration relief. However, there are opinions on both sides about the advisability of using psychological tests in immigration cases.

Pope (2012) argued that psychological testing can be intrusive, alien, and disturbing, particularly as perceived through the cultural lenses of some immigrants and refugees, who are more reserved regarding disclosures about their inner lives. Further, Pope noted that psychologists need to be mindful that, for some torture victims, the test-taking situation may be too evocative of the torture situation or may raise concerns that they are being exploited or used as guinea pigs. On the other hand, the manual for examining asylum seekers by Physicians for Human Rights (2012) reported that individuals who survived torture (or other traumatic experiences) may have difficulties putting their feelings and symptoms into words and may benefit from a paper-and-pencil instrument that helps them describe their symptoms. In this sense, the MMPI–2 can be not only helpful but even more productive than other assessment methods when administered to individuals who prefer a less intimate way of reporting their functioning.

Just as in any other psychological evaluation, there is no one-size-fits-all approach for immigration evaluations. The psychologist needs to carefully evaluate every assessment instrument and strategy as to whether it is going to work for the specific referral question, person, and situation. Psychologists conducting psychological assessments with immigrants and refugees need to be thoughtful about not retraumatizing the individual during the evaluation process. It is important to use sound clinical judgment based on their knowledge of the trauma literature and training, as well as to always check with the examinee about his or her level of comfort, understanding of the process, and desire to continue.

The standards regarding psychological testing (American Educational Research Association, American Psychological Association, & National Council of Measurement in Education, 2014) recommend the use of validated instruments that are language and culturally appropriate and that are normed for the group to which the claimant belongs. Some of the literature on the assessment of ethnic minorities or foreign-born examinees stresses that these individuals cannot be readily or effectively compared with the members of the dominant culture group on conventional assessment measures (Dana, 2000). Culture-specific measures are considered by many the only way to tap properly into the ethnic experience. In her discussion about choosing psychological instruments for the assessment of refugees and asylum seekers, Okawa (2008) noted that Western tests may not capture indigenous, culturally constructed disorders that differ from those classified in the DSM (American Psychiatric Association, 2013) but that are relevant to the person's functioning.

A number of self-report rating scales have been developed in different languages to meet the need of evaluating refugees and immigrants. These include the Hopkins Symptom Checklist–25 (Mollica, Wyshak, de Marneffe, Khuon, & Lavelle, 1987) and the Harvard Trauma Questionnaire (Mollica et al., 1992), which are part of a toolkit to use with culturally diverse populations traumatized by mass violence and natural disasters. The Symptom Checklist–90 (SCL-90; Derogatis, Lipman, & Covi, 1973) has been utilized in cross-cultural validation studies in different countries and in populations of immigrants and refugees (Hauff & Vaglum, 1994; Kisac, 2006; Noh & Avison, 1992). The State–Trait Anxiety Inventory has been translated into 41 languages and has been developed for cross-cultural utility (Novy, Nelson, Goodwin, & Rowzee, 1993; Spielberger, Diaz-Guerrero, & Strelau, 1990; Spielberger, Gorsuch, Lushene, Vagg, & Jacobs, 1983). The Beck Depression Inventory (Beck & Beck, 1972) is another self-rating scale that has been translated into numerous languages. These rating scales are useful for the purposes for which they were created and complement other sources of information such as the MMPI–2, which measures factors not addressed in these instruments.

MMPI–2 ASSESSMENT OF REFUGEE AND IMMIGRANT INDIVIDUALS

According to Otto (2002), the utility of the MMPI–2 in forensic assessments lies on its ability to assess reliably the type of constructs that constitute the foundation to the psycholegal issues at hand. Following Otto's logic, many steps are needed to connect the findings from the MMPI–2 regarding psychopathology, emotional state, and reliability of presentation to the legal concepts of extreme hardship, substantial abuse, extreme mental cruelty, experience of torture or victimization, psychological coercion, fear to return to the country of origin, conditions of health, and good moral character, which are key to immigration evaluations and ultimately relevant to the court.

Generic tests, or those that are designed to assess general psychological functioning, have the advantage of detecting many nonspecific symptoms as well as comorbid disorders and overall adaptive functioning. According to Briere and Scott (2012), a good psychological test battery to assess trauma should include at least one generic measure in addition to trauma-specific tests. The MMPI–2, as the most widely used and researched measure of adult psychopathology (see the discussion in Chapter 1), has solid research backing up its cross-cultural (Butcher, 1996) and forensic applicability (Lally, 2003). There is extensive literature showing that the MMPI–2 has sufficient test generalizability and validity for different types of purposes with ethnically diverse and cross-cultural populations and many specific settings, including the assessment of immigrants and refugees, torture victims, and asylum seekers. The MMPI–2 not only counteracts the limitations of tests with narrower foci but also provides a strong assessment of response style, which is an important aspect to assess in immigration evaluations.

Many adaptation programs for the MMPI–2 have demonstrated the equivalence of the instrument for use across languages and cultures (Butcher, Coelho Mosch, Tsai, & Nezami, 2006). In fact, although many researchers have developed separate norms for their culture, it was found that those scales' scores are within the standard error of measurement for the U.S. normative population scales. Internal factor analytic studies and external validity studies of the MMPI–2 scales have demonstrated generalization validity for different populations in other countries and minority populations in the United States, as explained in Chapter 4.

Although the MMPI–2 has been translated into different languages for worldwide use (Butcher, 1996), not all translations have been adequately developed. A translated test requires its own validity and reliability testing and standardization norms for the particular group, and there are some versions of the MMPI–2 that have questionable linguistic equivalency or that lack adequate norms. Psychologists need to decide if it is more appropriate to use the normative data from the country or region where the examinee comes from rather than the U.S. norms. Please refer to Chapter 4 for more detailed information regarding the translations and norms that have shown greater research foundations.

The MMPI–2, both in English and in adequate translations, has been successfully used in assessing victims of torture (Pope & Garcia-Peltoniemi, 1991). According to Pope (2012), the Center for Victims of Torture in Minneapolis currently uses the MMPI–2, in conjunction with the SCL-90 (Derogatis et al., 1973) and the Beck Depression Inventory (Beck & Beck, 1972), in its assessment of victims of torture.

Efforts to use the MMPI with immigrants and refugees started with the original version of the MMPI. S. Clark, Callahan, Lichtszajn, and Velasquez (1996) compared the MMPIs of refugees from Guatemala and El Salvador with those of Mexican immigrants. Clark et al. expected that the refugees from Guatemala and El Salvador would have higher scores on the F, D (2), Pa (6), and Sc (8) scales, because they came from war-torn countries. However, a multivariate analysis yielded no significant differences between the three groups on any scales. It was found that many of the items of the MMPI original version caused language confusion and were difficult to translate, which was solved with the MMPI–2.

An international translation of the MMPI–2 specifically designed with refugees in mind was conducted with first-generation Vietnamese refugees living in the United States (Dong & Church, 2003). MMPI–2 mean profiles and items showing extreme endorsement rates were found, suggesting that certain symptom tendencies and cultural values may be reflected in responses to some MMPI–2 items. Older age, lower acculturation, greater experienced premigration-postmigration traumas, and military veteran status were all associated with elevated MMPI–2 profiles, which Dong and Church (2003) interpreted as suggesting that the MMPI–2 functions in a reasonably equivalent and valid way with this population.

Many of the constructs assessed in immigration evaluations are a good match for the information provided by the MMPI–2. In evaluations of extreme hardship, information about general psychopathology and social adjustment provided by the MMPI–2 can be used as a basis for predictions regarding future adaptability to new and difficult circumstances, thus helping to predict the psychological response a person may have to the removal of a loved one from his or her life or having to be forcibly returned to the native country. The MMPI–2 is also helpful when providing evidence regarding good moral character, because it provides information about the presence or lack thereof of antisocial tendencies and other socially undesirable traits. The information the MMPI–2 provides regarding the impact of chronic and acute trauma in a person's functioning and current stress is helpful when forming opinions regarding substantial abuse, such as having experienced torture, mistreatment, or psychological coercion or being the victim of a crime.

No less important is the ability of the MMPI–2 to explain why a person may testify about his or her history of trauma in ways that may not appear logical to the official or judicial audience. The issue of altered emotional presentation when testifying about the experience of brutal violence or oppressive hardship is riddled with confusion. Although people may expect the victim to break down emotionally when relating a history of trauma, the opposite, a flat or dissociated affect, is also congruent with genuine psychological injury. The information from the MMPI–2 on the individual's psychological reaction and processing of the trauma together with his or her personality and cultural characteristics can help explain resilience, self-protective strategies, and bona fide traumatic reactions that the court may find confusing.

Further, because the results of the person's MMPI–2 are compared with those of thousands of other individuals, the psychologist has an objective measure of the extent of the problems and areas of intact functioning (Butcher & Perry, 2008), which helps when opining about whether the psychological injury is substantial. The MMPI–2 also provides information for the person's treatment planning. Such information helps to prevent the worsening of the trauma symptoms, once these have emerged, and to predict the person's receptivity or resistance to treatment as well as change over time.

ANALYSIS OF RESPONSE STYLE AND ASSESSMENT
OF MALINGERING

In all of the immigration forums, the credibility of the applicant is key to the outcome of the process. The adjudicator seeks testimony that is consistent and without contradictions and a history that matches the known information (De Jesús-Rentas et al., 2010). The variability in adjudications based on the opinion of the adjudicator about the truthfulness of the applicant has been a subject of concern due to the subjectivity of such perception (Ramji-Nogales et al., 2009). In particular, the adjudicator's discretion is key in suspension of deportation proceedings.

Psychologists conducting immigration assessments are also particularly interested in the credibility of claims made by individuals seeking immigration relief, as any good report must specifically evaluate the possibility of malingering (De Jesús-Rentas et al., 2010). The evaluation of malingering is a particular area of difficulty in immigration evaluations. Such an evaluation often requires the assessment of the psychological impact of past events, which is complicated by the interference of culture, language differences, and the confounding presence of other traumatic experiences. Moreover, the secondary gains of malingering in an immigration evaluation can be extremely valuable to the applicant. For instance, if individuals genuinely fear returning to their country of origin, they may try to present their best case and may feign greater distress than what they are actually experiencing. The MMPI–2 has the most extensive research base in detecting malingering (Rogers, Sewell, Martin, & Vitacco, 2003). Chapter 2 provides a review of the studies exploring response styles and how they affect the reliability of the profile.

Research regarding profile validity for immigrants and refugees is limited, but studies of ethnic minority groups and cross-cultural populations suggest that profiles from some cultural groups may present higher elevations in validity scales than psychologists are used to seeing in the MMPI–2 norms (Greene, 1987). For instance, the L scale (Butcher, Cabiya, Lucio, & Garrido, 2007; Zapata-Sola, Kreuch, Landers, Hoyt, & Butcher, 2009) and the F scale (Cheung, Song, & Butcher, 1991) may tap into a more diverse construct than the traditional interpretation indicates. It is important to note that elevations in the F scale in some cases may reflect severe psychological disturbance and symptoms atypical of Western diagnostic constructs rather than faking bad. Elevations in these scales, when research supports an alternative interpretation, do not invalidate the profile. Please refer to Chapter 4 for a complete review of cross-cultural issues that should be taken into consideration when interpreting MMPI–2 validity profiles of immigrants and refugees. Elevations in the MMPI–2 validity scales in immigration evaluations should be interpreted as a hypothesis to be corroborated with other information. The stakes of false positives are very high, as they may contribute to the deportation of an individual to a place where his or her life and mental health could be at great risk. Use of multiple measures is recommended as a gold standard of psychological testing to minimize the error caused when using one source alone.

Evans (2004) recommended four elements to ensure comprehensive assessment of the psycholegal issues in immigration evaluations: a comprehensive clinical interview, an appropriate psychological test battery tailored to the psycholegal questions, collateral materials relevant to the claims of the individual, and a formal assessment of malingering and deception. It can be appropriately added to this model that the forensic psychologist should use measures that are independent of one another, use both structured and unstructured methods of data collection (Ganellen, 1996), and use both nomothetic and idiographic methods of data gathering. Idiographic methods of gathering data are important, because this type of assessment requires a contextual approach to understanding the person's construction of reality in his or her own terms.

CASE EXAMPLE

The following case is from a psychological evaluation requested to support a VAWA petition. Oksana was an immigrant bride paired with her U.S. citizen husband by a matchmaking agency. Her husband refused to file papers for Oksana to attain legal immigration status in the United States. After Oksana had spent 5 years in a violent marriage, police placed her and her son in a shelter, and she was advised to self-petition as a battered wife.

Oksana described her childhood in Kiev, Ukraine, as "very happy." When she was 20, she married a fellow Ukrainian. This marriage lasted 3 years before they drifted apart. At the time they separated, she learned she was pregnant. After their son, Viktor, was born, her ex-husband disappeared from her life and that of their son. Shortly after registering with a matchmaking agency, Oksana received a message from John that he was on a bride tour and wanted to meet her. John had a PhD in mathematics, and Oksana was impressed with his intelligence and professional status and thought he seemed like a nice person. After corresponding over the Internet, John proposed and she happily accepted. She believed that because John was 28 years older and had a previous marriage, he was a mature individual who would love, appreciate, and support her. Oksana arrived in the United States on a bride visa with her son a few months later, and she and John got married 3 days later. Oksana indicated that the marital conflict began immediately after her arrival. She stated that she felt as if John wanted her to be a housekeeper and a sexual object but had no interest in her as a person. The violence escalated over

5 years until the violent beating that led to the police removing her from her home and placing her in a shelter.

Oksana reported that John was abusive sexually, physically, and emotionally. She said he demanded sex at all times and was a sexual sadist, who forced unwanted sex and bizarre painful sexual activities that she detested. If she refused, he raped her and let his anger out on her or her son. When she rejected his sexual demands he became violent, including beating her up with his fists or whatever was handy. He relentlessly abused her psychologically. For instance, although John signed an Affidavit of Support declaring his intent to support Oksana and her child economically for 2 years, he told her he could not afford her and that the money he gave her was a loan she had to repay. John put black tape across the house, dividing it into two different areas, his and hers. He threw away what she bought, turned off the electricity when Oksana was enjoying a television show, locked her out and turned off the lights when she went outside to smoke. John made fun of her friends and did not like her to see or talk to them. He restricted her use of the phone and ability to leave the house. John threatened to divorce her and to make her life miserable; to cut her off the medical and car insurance; to take away the phone, the computer, the Internet, and the cable television. He accused Oksana of being an unfit mother and threatened to call social services and the police and to put her in jail. He threatened to call immigration officers and have her deported. Oksana believed John's threats and was alarmed by his anger and emotional instability. John began therapy when he became suicidal at the time of the divorce from his previous wife, and when upset, he sometimes cried and threatened to commit suicide. He displayed and bragged about his rifles and two shotguns. At times Oksana became so scared of his rages that she hid in the closet with her son for hours.

Oksana said John either ignored or abused Viktor. Oksana reported that John would rip toys from Viktor's hands and throw them in the garbage. Oksana reported that when John was upset with her, he would retaliate by harassing or mistreating Viktor. In addition, he exposed Viktor to the violence toward Oksana, ignoring Oksana's pleas not to do it in front of Viktor.

Oksana coped with the abuse by being as compliant as she could, trying to avoid him when he was upset, reasoning with him to calm him down, and not doing anything that would provoke him. On occasion, she answered back, protested, complained, argued, and rejected his sexual advances. Oksana reported that she became very depressed and had numerous medical symptoms that she attributed to the stress in the marriage.

Oksana's psychological evaluation for a VAWA self-petition aimed to help document her story of multiple types of abuse at the hands of her U.S. citizen husband and the psychological consequences of such violence in order to prove *extreme cruelty*. Oksana was administered the MMPI–2 in

Russian, as translated in 1999 by Mera Atlis. This is an unofficial translation, which nonetheless has been carefully done with translation and back-translation. No Russian norms of the MMPI–2 exist, and thus the American norms were utilized.

Oksana elevated several validity scales; specifically, a 72 *T* score on scale *F*, a 71 *T* score on scale *L*, and a lower score of 56 on scale *K* (see Figure 8.1). Her score on the *TRIN* scale (78) indicate that she was somewhat inconsistent in her responding, endorsing some items inconsistently in the False direction. This pattern of elevation reflects some distress with an effort to present well but also a cooperative attitude. This is an interpretable and valid profile. Her slight elevation on *L* and her *TRIN* responding could be the result of cultural differences, because this pattern has been found in other culturally and ethnically diverse individuals.

Oksana presents a 3-2-1 profile on the clinical scales, with elevations on the *Pd* (4), *Pa* (6), *Pt* (7), and *Sc* (8) scales. This profile suggests that Oksana presents a high level of anxiety and depression that includes varied symptoms revealing overwhelming stress and coping difficulties. Oksana's depression takes the form of pessimism, inertia, demoralization, and decreased self-esteem. Oksana's emotions tend to be labile, and she may suffer from periods

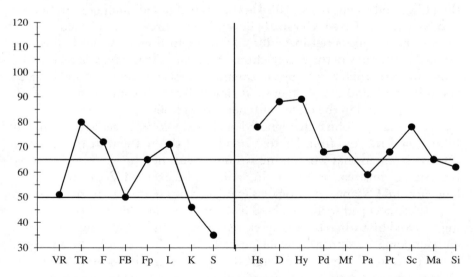

Figure 8.1. MMPI–2 basic validity and clinical scale profile for Oksana. Excerpted from the *MMPI®–2 (Minnesota Multiphasic Personality Inventory®—2) Manual for Administration, Scoring, and Interpretation, Revised Edition* by Butcher et al. Copyright © 2001 by the Regents of the University of Minnesota. Used by permission of the University of Minnesota Press. All rights reserved. "MMPI®" and "Minnesota Multiphasic Personality Inventory®" are trademarks owned by the Regents of the University of Minnesota.

of dejection and crying. She feels unhappy and dissatisfied with herself and her life. She does not take pleasure in activities that were pleasurable in the past. Oksana also suffers from low mood in that she is easily distractible and has problems with inattentiveness and indecisiveness. Oksana's mental functioning is compromised due to her rumination and excessive preoccupations. Her chronic worry leads her to constant self-recrimination. Oksana deals with life stresses by developing physical illnesses and complaints. She seems to have a strong tendency to use physical malfunctioning as a way of channeling her distress. She suffers from marked eating and sleeping disorders, including overeating. Some of her symptoms include bizarre sensory experiences and gastrointestinal, neurological, and general health symptoms of a vague nature. Oksana tends to have some symptoms that are quite dramatic.

The MMPI–2 reveals that, at times, Oksana's high levels of anxiety can get out of control. Indeed, a follow-up interview revealed that she suffers from panic attacks and freezes, has chills, or has experiences of panic when she thinks about John. Given that Oksana does not have a history of antisocial behavior, the elevation in *Pd* (4) suggests that she perceives herself as distant and alienated from herself and from her social environment and is experiencing problematic interpersonal relations. She is possibly angry and is having difficulty adjusting to the social rules and dealing with the authority figures in her life. Oksana presented an elevation in *Pa* (6) revealing some paranoid ideation and significant thought disorganization, as suggested by *Sc* (8). During the interview, Oksana reported numerous physical symptoms, anxiety, and depression as highly perturbing and related to her stress to family and work conditions.

In sum, the results of this MMPI–2 support the allegations that Oksana likely suffers from psychological symptoms that are usually associated with trauma. The results corroborate that the psychological, physical, sexual, and child abuse that occurred in her marriage constitute extreme mental cruelty, given the intensity of psychological suffering revealed in the MMPI–2. With these results and extensive collateral information and other testing data, Oksana was able to present to immigration court a petition to remain in the United States under VAWA legislation.

SUMMARY

The MMPI–2 is an assessment instrument that offers a great deal of valuable data in many different types of immigration evaluations, because it provides information on general psychological constructs that are the foundation of the legal questions. Unfortunately, there are no empirical studies regarding the use of the MMPI–2, or almost any other psychological instrument, in immigration court. Research about the use of the MMPI–2 with immigrants and refugees is very limited, as explained above. However, when used as a measure of general psychopathology, adaptive functioning, and response style, the MMPI–2 is appropriate to the legal questions in immigration court evaluations. The MMPI–2 can provide a general personality profile for cases of extreme hardship, reveal moral character, and counteract claims of ineligibility. In asylum cases and petitions for VAWA, U visa, and T visa, the MMPI–2 can be useful in assessing the impact of trauma, especially because it captures a wider range of trauma manifestations, which go beyond typical measures of PTSD and depression and may identify cultural variations of distress. The MMPI–2 allows the forensic psychologist to match the victim's account of the traumatic experience and the psychological findings and assess their consistency. It also provides an evaluation of response attitude that helps the psychologist present issues of credibility, which are of paramount importance in these evaluations. It is our hope that, as this branch of forensic psychology continues to progress and develop, greater attention will be paid to the scientific foundations of this practice.

9

THE MMPI–2 IN CUSTODY AND CHILD PROTECTION EVALUATIONS

Both custody and child protection evaluations, also called parent capacity and parent fitness evaluations, are forensic psychological services that assist the court in understanding the dynamics of a family in such a way that the most appropriate plan for care of the minor children can be determined. Although there are significant differences between these two types of evaluations, the overall focus is the same when evaluating parents; that of assessing their parenting practices as well as their perceptions of their children and the children's needs. The identification of broad psychological constructs, such as clinical and personality psychopathology, substance abuse, and impulse control, is an important part of the foundation to understanding parenting lapses, risks to the children, and continued acrimony with the other parent or animosity against the state. In both of these evaluations, parents are interested in portraying themselves in the best possible light, are defensive, and are undergoing extremely stressful experiences and real or potential losses.

http://dx.doi.org/10.1037/14571-010
Using the MMPI–2 in Forensic Assessment, by J. N. Butcher, G. A. Hass, R. L. Greene, and L. D. Nelson
Copyright © 2015 by the American Psychological Association. All rights reserved.

Custody evaluations involve the evaluation of the needs of the children in relation to the parents' divorce (Stahl, 2010). Johnston (1994) reported that only 20% of divorcing or separating families take the case to court. Approximately 80% of divorce cases are settled up front or during the process, and 4% to 5% ultimately go to trial. This small percentage of cases that could not settle their disputes without court intervention often involve issues such as family violence, serious parenting deficits, substance abuse, or serious psychopathology, and they are often the cases referred to custody psychologists.

Custody evaluations provide the courts with impressions about alliances and conflicts within the family, opinions regarding present and past intensity of the marital conflict, and information on the role of each parent, among other factors. These data assist the psychologist in predicting the probability of success of various conditions of custody and visitation (Melton, Petrila, Poythress, & Slobogin, 2007). The psychological functioning of the parties in custody cases is directly connected to decisions related to custody and visitation, as family courts typically try to determine which parent is more likely to fulfill the child's physical, emotional, intellectual, and basic health and safety needs (National Council on Disability, n.d.).

Child protection cases include parents who are fighting the custody of their children against the government following substantiation of child maltreatment or neglect. These evaluations have as a broad aim to assess the parenting skills and capacities of caregivers suspected or found to have committed child abuse, maltreatment, or neglect (Condie, 2003). The psychological status of the offending parent is one of many aspects that the court and social service agencies look at when making decisions about treatment and rehabilitation, reunification, and termination of parental rights. Similarly, psychological factors play a role in understanding mitigating and aggravating issues that provide a framework to better define the role that courts and social services agencies need to play in the rehabilitation of the offending caregiver.

An important distinction in parenting fitness of custody litigants versus child protection cases is that in child custody, unlike child protection, there is a presumption of minimally adequate parenting (Budd, Clark, & Connell, 2011). Custody evaluations include a comparison of parenting skills among the custody litigants, while child protection evaluations compare the parent against a standard of minimally adequate caregiving. Although technically it could be argued that the presumption of psychopathology does not apply to divorcing parents, but rather to offending caregivers who are part of the clinical population, in reality both types of parents who are involved in legal disputes regarding their children's custody and were unable to resolve the issue out of court are likely to present relationship dysfunction and clinical psychopathology, among other psychosocial problems. Care should be taken not to minimize the psychopathology of divorcing parents, because doing so may lead to ignoring risk factors that may end up harming their children. In particular, the presumption of adequate parenting for custody litigants when allegations of child or spouse abuse or neglect are raised should be eliminated. Studies have found that parents in custody disputes are not more inclined than people in the general population to make unfounded complaints (Johnston, 1992; Johnston & Campbell, 1988; Johnston, Lee, Olesen, & Walters, 2005).

LEGAL AND ETHICAL BASIS FOR PSYCHOLOGICAL EVALUATIONS IN CHILD CUSTODY AND PARENT CAPACITY CASES

The Uniform Marriage and Divorce Act (1987, § 402) provides the legal basis for using psychological evaluations in child custody cases. Based upon the most recent modifications to this document, the court is expected to assure, as much as possible, that custody decisions in court are to be made in the best interests of the child. The court must consider all relevant factors, including the wishes of the child's parent or parents as to his or her custody; the wishes of the child as to his or her custodian; the interactions and interrelationship of the child with his or her parent or parents, the siblings, and other persons who may significantly affect the child's best interests; the child's adjustment to his or her home, school, and community; and the mental and physical health of all individuals involved.

Similarly, in parent capacity evaluations involving child protection, there are various state statutes that qualify child abuse and neglect. The legal, social services, and mental-health systems have different definitions regarding what constitutes abuse and neglect. However, at the core of these evaluations are the care and protection of a minor embedded in the best interest standard. In addition, family preservation is a fundamental principle of child protection legislation and asserts that children need to be cared for by their families if at all possible (American Psychological Association, 2010b; Family Preservation and Support Services Program Act, 1993). The ultimate goal of a parent capacity evaluation is usually to provide a path for reunification, even if the report is used later as forensic evidence for a termination of parental rights when remediation did not happen within the temporal parameters established by statutes. When an evaluation is requested to determine incompetency as a parent, the focus is on the severity of the impairment and lack of rehabilitation of the parent when dispatching his or her parenting responsibilities.

The best interest of the child should be the primary concern of psychologists conducting parent capacity evaluations, either for custody or for child protection matters. When evaluating parents and caregivers, psychologists gather information with the purpose of identifying how these parents met or failed to meet the psychological needs of the children. Therefore, recommendations are also geared toward rehabilitation or restructuring of parental responsibilities in relation to children's best interests.

There are ethical guidelines that pertain to clinical and counseling psychologists performing these types of evaluations (American Academy of Matrimonial Lawyers, 2011; American Psychological Association, 2010a, 2010b, 2013a; Association of Family and Conciliation Courts, 2006). Among those guidelines two stand out as pertinent to this review. The American Psychological Association (APA) has provided oversight guidelines for these professional activities to aid practitioners and to assure that the most effective and appropriate procedures are followed. The goal of these guidelines is to promote proficiency in the conduct of these evaluations. Psychologists conducting family custody or parent capacity evaluations should be familiar with and competent in following these guidelines. Among the important issues mentioned in the guidelines is that child custody evaluations should include multiple sources of information and multiple methods for gathering information. Forensic psychologists who conduct custody evaluations need to address a number of issues, such as the parents' and child's mental health, the child's adjustment to home and school, the emotional bonds between the parents and child, and the parents' ability to nurture the child.

The Guidelines for Psychological Evaluations in Child Protection Matters (APA, 2013a) warn psychologists about the finality of termination of parental rights and the responsibility they have in these cases. The guidelines note that psychologists "gather information on family history, assess relevant personality functioning, assess developmental needs of the child, explore the nature and quality of the parent–child relationship, and assess evidence of trauma" (APA, 2013a, p. 21). It is also recommended that psychologists consider risk factors, such as substance abuse or chemical dependency, domestic violence, and health status of family members, and the entire family context.

Psychologists conducting custody or child protection evaluations require specialized training and education regarding the specific factors involved in parenting, child development, family dynamics, and psychopathology. In addition, psychologists need to include in these assessments an integration of cultural, educational, religious, socioeconomic, gender, and community factors.

Another ethical issue is the importance of psychologists using only well-established and validated measures in conducting psychological assessments in custody cases. If a psychological test is marketed for custody evaluations by a test publisher, there is no guarantee that the test is valid in predicting parenting behavior and acceptable to the court.

EVALUATION OF THE PERSONALITY AND BEHAVIORAL CHARACTERISTICS OF PARENTS

A healthy family environment should ensure that the child's needs are appropriately responded to and attended to. The child's best interest involves the provision of an ideal environment for the child in relation to the specific developmental and idiosyncratic needs of the child and the family's dynamic and culture. According to Haynes (2010), there are three major types of parental competence, including capacity to care, capacity to protect, and capacity to change. These competences are tied to the parent's own mental stability and personality. No single personality trait is associated with child maltreatment, although certain characteristics, including low self-esteem, poor impulse control, lack of personal power, negative emotions, and antisocial behavior, have been found to correlate with poor parenting and child maltreatment (Pianta, Egeland, & Erickson, 1989).

Significant mental disorder in a parent may or may not have an impact on the parent's parenting practices, the parent's ability to co-parent, and the child's development. When a mentally ill parent is sufficiently incapacitated and as a result fails in protecting his or her child from harmful situations, the parenting role is severely compromised. This may lead to loss of custody. The psychologist is tasked with making the connection about how exactly the mental-health problems impact the parent's parenting role and functioning, if at all. When parenting capacity evaluations are conducted, the results of psychological tests should be matched to the particular characteristics associated with adequate parenting and the child's needs.

Mental disability alone is insufficient to establish parental unfitness (Americans With Disabilities Act of 1990; Rehabilitation Act of 1973), but some aspects of mental illness have been considered by some states when deciding on loss of custody or parental rights. Parent capacity evaluations in cases of severe mental illness can describe the characteristics and patterns of the diagnosis, provide potential explanations for mental-health problems, identify the potential for change and determine the interventions needed to help stabilize the mental state, and identify individual or environmental factors that influence behavior (White, 2005). However, this analysis has to be done in the context of how these mental-health issues interact with the caregiving system and parenting behaviors and responsibilities. Determining parenting capacity from a psychiatric diagnosis is not possible without a direct measure of daily parent–child interaction and actual parenting functioning.

There are numerous studies of parental psychopathology associated with poor parenting behaviors that provide pathways to further explore in a case-to-case basis. For instance, depression has been found to be linked to greater difficulties in attending to and interacting with the infant, as well as insensitivity and unavailability, which provoke anger and distress in the child and disrupt the minor's ability to modulate affect and arousal (Cummings & Davies, 1999; England & Sim, 2009). Depressive symptoms such as lack of motivation, withdrawal, and detachment have been found to be damaging to the child–parent relationship (Downey & Coyne, 1990), and diminished judgment in parents with schizophrenia is associated with accidents or neglect of the child (Cassell & Coleman, 1995). Anxiety has been found to contribute to altered patterns of interaction between mothers and babies, particularly a lack of responsiveness (Nicol-Harper, Harvey, & Stein, 2007), as well as to confer a significant risk of anxiety and depression for the children of anxious parents (Micco et al., 2009). With obsessive–compulsive disorder, if the obsessions involve the child directly there may be risk of using poor judgment (Cassell & Coleman, 1995). Unrealistic concerns about the child's weight and body shape have been found in mothers who are bulimic (Stein & Fairburn, 1996). Children have higher rates of psychiatric disorders and are more likely to suffer abuse and enter the care system (Zoccolillo & Cloninger, 1985) when their parents suffer from somatization disorder. Suicidality has been indirectly associated with child abuse (Roberts & Hawton, 1980), and parents who were suicidal and acutely psychotic have been involved in filicide-suicide (Hatters-Friedman, Hrouda, Holden, Noffsinger, & Resnick, 2005). Personality disorders and traits of personality disorders in parents have also been found to contribute to engagement in high-conflict divorce that harms the children (Johnston & Campbell, 1988). These psychopathological conditions cannot always be attributed to the stress of litigation, separation from children, or divorce. Often, these are bona fide, long-term conditions that should be properly identified and treated to improve parenting fitness.

The forensic psychologist needs to determine whether the psychological effects of the mental-health problems reach the level of significant harm to the child's psychological development (Cassell & Coleman, 1995). This analysis has to be done after the psychologist has compiled extensive data to place the psychiatric disorder in context. Some of the critical factors that play a role in the intractability of mental illness and potential harm to the child include denial of the illness versus cooperation with treatment, history of treatment compliance, denial of parenting problems, presence of suicidal and homicidal ideation, substance addiction, high levels of stress and chaotic home environment, and support in the parenting role (Jacobsen, 2004). With regard to this latter issue, an important consideration for taking custody away from parents with mental-health problems is the severity of the illness in relation to the absence of another competent adult in the home who would compensate for the parent disability (Sands, 1995).

SCOPE OF THE CUSTODY AND PARENTING CAPACITY EVALUATION

Evaluations of parenting capacity in both child protection and custody usually include interviews of the parents, traditional psychological testing including measures of both personality/psychopathology and cognitive/ intellectual functioning, specialized tests, and often observations and testing of the children (Gould, 2005; Melton et al., 2007; Otto, Edens, & Barcus, 2000; Stahl, 2010). These evaluations also often include a review of records and both clinical and home visits (Budd, Poindexter, Felix, & Naik-Polan, 2001). Evaluations of caregivers can be brief or comprehensive, depending on the referral question, individuals involved in the evaluation, resources available to the psychologist, and what judges and attorneys expect in terms of depth and scope (Condie, 2003). There is little consensus about what constructs are involved in minimal parenting competence (Budd et al., 2001; Condie, 2003; Melton et al., 2007). Because there is not a standard to define what is minimally adequate parenting, forensic psychologists have to use their knowledge of child development, child psychology, and adult psychopathology to match the capacity of the parent against the characteristics and needs of their child.

The evaluation of parents typically includes an in-depth interview that assesses the parents' own development and the parenting they experienced as children; clinical symptoms and personality traits, substance abuse, management of aggression, motivation for change, mental state, and general coping mechanisms; and information about finances, housing, hygiene, occupational and recreational activities, routine of child care, and supervision and discipline of the child. Careful attention should be paid to assess not only personality and intelligence but also behaviors linked to parental care. The latter include providing resources for growth and development, such as nutrition, shelter, medical care, and adequate supervision, and showing sensitivity to the child's needs for sensory stimulation, positive emotional expression, child-centered interaction, predictable routines, a safe environment, and appropriate boundaries and limits in family interaction (Azar, 2002). Factors such as reflective functioning or mentalization, emotional attunement, and sensitivity, which facilitate attachment and emotional development, are also at the core of parenting behaviors and should be assessed (Sharp & Fonagy, 2008; Slade, 2005). In the same manner, vulnerability factors should be carefully explored. For instance, parents who were abused as children have been found to be more likely to abuse their own children than are parents who were not abused (Egeland, Jacobvitz, & Sroufe, 1988; Merrill, Hervig, & Milner, 1996). Additional parental vulnerability factors include poverty, ongoing stress, failure to understand a child's needs, relationship instability, violence, substance abuse, lack of social support, and job loss (Cicchetti & Olsen, 1990). Parenting styles of abusive parents have been described as less flexible and more overreactive and authoritarian (C. M. Rodriguez, 2010).

In addition to diagnostic and background interviews, other structured interviews focus on the assessment of a parent's values and internal representations, bond with the child, and reflective functioning in relation to the parenting role and interactions with the child. The Parenting Development Interview (Slade, Aber, Bresgi, Berger, & Kaplan, 2004) and the Working Model of the Child (Benoit, Zeanah, Parker, Nicholson, & Coolbear, 1997) target these specific constructs. Because the availability, sensitivity, and responsiveness of the caregiver are key to the development of an attachment with the child (Ainsworth, Blehar, Waters, & Wall, 1978), observations of the interaction between parent and child are utilized to augment the data regarding the health of the relationship and attachment bond between caregiver and child.

There are many specific tests that assess parenting skills and capacities or risk vis-à-vis the relationship with the child. The most widely supported are the Parent–Child Relationship Inventory (Gerard, 1994), the Parenting Stress Index (Abidin, 1990), and the Child Abuse Potential Inventory (Milner, 1986). However, because these tests have not been empirically connected to parent capacity (Budd, 2005), the information derived from these tools has to be critically considered. There are many tests that look at factors specific to custody, including the Parent Awareness Skills Survey (Bricklin, 1990b), the Bricklin Perceptual Scales (Bricklin, 1990a), the Perceptions of Relationship Test (Bricklin, 1989), and the Custody Quotient (Gordon & Peek, 1989). These and other such measures have limited utilization and have usually poor empirical support and commercial availability. In addition, these measures do not evaluate general psychopathology and do not have validity scales to assess the parent's response style. Examiners need to be careful about using measures that are unreliable, because doing so may lead to inaccurate data and erroneous opinions (Flens, 2005).

To complement those specific tests and techniques, a thorough evaluation of personality and emotional status is essential to the determination of parental capacity, particularly to identify risks of parental lapses and maintenance of parental fitness in the long run. This emphasis led to the inclusion of the Minnesota Multiphasic Personality Inventory—2 (MMPI–2) in the Ackerman–Schoendorf Scales for Parent Evaluation of Custody (Ackerman & Ackerman, 1997).

RESEARCH BASIS FOR USING THE MMPI/MMPI–2

As noted in Chapter 1, the MMPI–2 has been found to be the most frequently used personality measure in child custody evaluations. Keilin and Bloom (1986) reported that 70.7% of assessment psychologists used the MMPI in child custody evaluations as compared with 41.5% for the Rorschach and 37.8% for the Thematic Apperception Test. Wangberg (2000) found the MMPI–2 was the most widely used measure (76%) in custody evaluations. Bow, Flens, Gould, and Greenhut (2006) found that 87% of their sample used the MMPI–2 in child custody evaluations, and Hagen and Castagna (2001) found that 84% of practitioners used the MMPI–2. Quinnell and Bow (2001) explored the current status of psychological testing in custody evaluations using a national survey of 198 psychologists. The participants were more discriminating in their test selection, particularly in the use of parent inventories and rating scales, and showed a greater focus on objective assessment. Among the self-report personality tests, the MMPI/MMPI–2 was by far the most frequently used in custody cases, with the MMPI–2 used in 94% and the original MMPI version used in 7% of the cases. Finally, King (2012) conducted a comprehensive review and analysis of the research and theoretical perspectives on child custody evaluation from a research-practitioner's perspective. She reviewed several tests that are used in this forensic application and concluded that the MMPI–2 is the most effective and acceptable instrument for assessing parents in custody evaluations. She cautioned about using measures such as the Millon Clinical Multiaxial Inventory—III, which was not designed for this application, and the MMPI–2—Restructured Form (MMPI–2–RF), as a new measure that has not been empirically validated for this application (see Chapter 14).

One important reason for this wide acceptance of the MMPI–2 in parent capacity and custody evaluations is the extensive research detailing the instrument's validity and effectiveness. Early research with the MMPI on parental behavior established the test's utility in understanding parent problems. Hundreds of studies on personality and behavior of parents in relation to their children in which the MMPI/MMPI–2 were used have been published over the past 75 years. The following review describes a small sample of the specific research findings that support using the MMPI/MMPI–2 for assessing couples in custody cases and parents who have mistreated their children. For a more extensive listing of research articles on the MMPI–2 in custody cases, see Butcher (2013a).

A number of studies conducted with the original MMPI have provided strong support for its use in assessing parents (Hafner, Butcher, Hall, & Quast, 1969). Sopchak (1952) studied whether there is a relationship between parent personality, as measured by the MMPI, and the children. For both men and women, identification with parents is associated with normality and good adjustment rather than with abnormal trends; tendencies toward abnormality are in general associated with failure to identify with the parents, especially failure to identify with the father. Sopchak concluded that knowing the relationship between children and their parents is valuable for determining their adjustment. Liverant (1959) found that the MMPI scales strongly supported the clinical impression that both fathers and mothers of disturbed children are more maladjusted than the fathers and mothers of nondisturbed children. Loeb (1966) and Loeb and Price (1966) studied parental personality and the difficulties of children from broken homes. Divorced and separated mothers scored much higher on the *Pd* (4) scale and higher on the *Sc* (8) and *Ma* (9) scales, suggesting impulsiveness, anger, and nonconformity usually associated with conduct disorders. Inflated mean *Pd* (4) scores were also obtained by remarried mothers and by fathers with histories of marital disruption (see also Bradley, 1974; Murstein & Glaudin, 1968). The MMPI has been found to be a useful instrument for detecting the potential for child abuse. Paulson, Afifi, Thomason, and Chaleff (1974) conducted an evaluation to determine whether the MMPI can aid in the identification of potentially abusive parents. They found characteristic MMPI profiles that differentiated between abusive and nonabusive parents. Wright (1976) administered a battery of psychological measures (e.g., the Rorschach and the MMPI) to convicted child batterers. He concluded that battering parents were psychopathically disturbed but whenever possible presented a distorted picture of themselves as healthy and unlikely to abuse their children; thus, the label "sick-but-slick syndrome." Egeland, Erickson, Butcher, and Ben-Porath (1991) used the MMPI–2 in assessing personality characteristics of women who had a high potential for abusing their children. The women from the high-risk sample closely resembled child-abusing parents on the MMPI–2 clinical scales. Moreover, these women differed significantly from all of the comparison groups on a number of MMPI–2 clinical and content scales. Erickson (2005) provided a comprehensive review of studies of battered women's MMPI/MMPI–2 scores to determine whether elevated MMPI/MMPI–2 scores of battered women represented characterological traits or reactive states. This survey supported the hypothesis that the MMPI–2 profiles of battered women often are a result of the abuse they have suffered, a reactive state, rather than an indication that these women have personality traits indicating that they would not be fit parents. Schmidtgall, King, Zarski, and Cooper (2000) found that family conflict can result in depression when the child becomes an adult. Several studies have found that the MMPI–2 supplemental scales provide valuable information in custody evaluations in addition to the clinical scales (see Ben-Porath & Sherwood, 1993; Bosquet & Egelund, 2000; Ollendick,

1984; Posthuma & Harper, 1998). The triad of *Hy* (3), *Pd* (4), and *Pa* (6) and validity and underreporting scales were found to be significantly higher in high-conflict custody litigants than the normative sample and even previous studies of custody litigants (Siegel, Bow, & Gottlieb, 2012).

Otto and Butcher (1995) evaluated the use of computers in evaluation of parents in child custody assessments, which has played an increasing role in mental-health practice in recent years, including in the administration, scoring, and interpretation of a number of tests. They pointed out that computer-assisted testing has the potential to improve the validity of child custody and other types of forensic and nonforensic "therapeutic" evaluations.

Bathurst, Gottfried, and Gottfried (1997) developed specialized norms for parent MMPI–2s based on 508 child custody litigants. Defensive underreporting and self-favorability were often exhibited, along with an elevation on the Overcontrolled Hostility (*O-H*) scale. The highest mean clinical scale scores were on the *Hy* (3), *Pa* (6), and *Pd* (4) scales. Differences were not found among mothers, fathers, and stepparents, indicating that a single set of norms is suitable. Their findings highlight the importance of context specificity in personality assessment. Proper interpretation of personality inventories in child custody disputes should involve considering both the norms of the standardization sample and the litigants' reference norms.

A number of researchers have evaluated the impact of defensive responding on MMPI–2 evaluations. The bias of parents in parent capacity evaluations to present themselves favorably in the MMPI–2 was found to generalize to all other tests utilized in the assessment, and elevations are more substantial than those of parents in custody evaluations (Carr, Moretti, & Cue, 2005). Leib (2006) found that child custody litigants who provided an accurate self-description in the MMPI–2, indicated by *T* scores of less than 65 on the validity scales *L, K, Sd,* and *S,* and who lacked an emotional connection to their children scored higher on FAM_2 (Familial Alienation) than FAM_1 (Familial Discord). Further, the *Pd* (4) scale demonstrated a high correlation with FAM_2, suggesting that both these scales are highly sensitive to problems in family of origin.

Ezzo, Pinsoneault, and Evans (2007) evaluated MMPI–2 profiles for three types of child custody samples: child maltreatment, unmarried, and married. The child maltreatment group was differentiated from the two nonmaltreatment groups (collapsed into one group) with *T* scores significantly higher on the *F, Pd* (4), *Pa* (6), *Sc* (8), *Ma* (9), and *Si* (0) scales and lower on scale *K*. Discriminant analysis provided a formula that successfully identified 79% of the profiles as maltreatment or nonmaltreatment. Implications of these findings were discussed in relationship to psychosocial and demographic variables in child maltreatment cases.

Cooke (2010) conducted an evaluation of a sample of parents in child custody disputes to determine the utility of the MMPI–2 given the proclivity of some parents to produce defensive invalid records. K scores in the Cooke study were 62.4 for males and 62.0 for females. The mean S score was 63.5 for males and was 61.5 for females when the custody litigant was of higher educational/socioeconomic level (particularly college graduate or above). Cooke concluded that the psychologist who does the evaluation should not describe the individual as having a defensive test-taking attitude, consider that the test is invalid, or attribute the personality characteristics typically associated with such elevations unless the scores are at least one standard deviation above these means. Ollendick and Otto (1984) conducted an evaluation of couples who received joint custody versus those undergoing contested disputes completed through court decision. They found that custodial parents tended to represent themselves in a healthier fashion than did those in contested cases, tended to cope with feelings of anger and impulsivity more effectively, were more trusting and open toward others, and received lower alcohol use scores than noncustodial parents.

Cross-cultural generalizability of the MMPI–2 in parental competency evaluations has been supported. Carstairs, Richards, Fletcher, Droscher, and Ecob (2012) compared the MMPI–2 profiles of a sample of United Kingdom (UK) parents who had undergone court-ordered parental competency evaluations with a sample from the United States (Stredny, Archer, & Mason, 2006). The MMPI–2 results for the UK sample were found to be largely consistent with those for the U.S. sample, with a near-significant elevation on the L scale and peaks on the Pd (4) and Pa (6) scales. The elevations on the Pd (4) and Pa (6) scales in the British sample and the U.S. sample were noteworthy and highly similar to the results reported by Bathurst et al. (1997), who also obtained elevations on the Pd (4) and Pa (6) scales, along with Hy (3), in their child custody sample.

DEVELOPING HYPOTHESES FROM THE MMPI–2 IN CONDUCTING CUSTODY AND PARENT CAPACITY EVALUATIONS

The MMPI–2 can provide the psychologist with substantial information about the mental-health adjustment and personality characteristics of parents that can give a perspective on their ability to carry out their parental roles and potential problem behaviors that might influence their daily lives. Several important areas in which the MMPI–2 can provide hypotheses about a parent's behavior that can have an impact on custodial roles are listed below.

Did the Parent Cooperate With the Evaluation to Provide Useful Information?

The parent's approach to the psychological assessment is one of the most important areas to evaluate. Did the parent present himself or herself accurately, or were there extensive efforts to present in an overly favorable manner to influence the decision-making process about parent fitness? Child custody and child protection psychologists commonly have to deal with the strong tendency of parents to be overly positive in the way they present themselves. The defensiveness that these parents show in the evaluation process is not just a problem that occurs with personality tests like the MMPI–2 but is characteristically present in other data as well. Psychologists must make efforts to obtain the most cooperative participation to determine the parent's situation as accurately as possible.

The MMPI–2 validity scales, described in Chapter 2, are extremely valuable in providing information as to response approaches to the items the parent may have used to create a particular impression in the custody evaluation. The parent's level of cooperation with the evaluation can also be determined through the validity profile. For example, a common pattern of defensiveness (high K and L scale scores) occurs in cases where the parent seeks to present a well-adjusted and problem-free mental-health status (Baer & Miller, 2002; Bagby, Nicholson, Buis, Radovanovic, & Fidler, 1999; Butcher et al., 2001; Cooke, 2010; Posthuma & Harper, 1998; Siegel, 1996). However, it is important to consider also that socioeconomic and educational status may have an impact in custody litigants' response style (Cooke, 2010).

If disclosure is only partial or is not present, it is important to incorporate this lack of cooperation in the interpretation of test data and note it in the report or expert testimony (for instance, by noting that the examiner's formulation is a minimal representation of the entire psychological picture). As noted in Chapter 2, reliability of the test data can be compromised when the parent tries to fake good. In many cases, however, it is still possible to obtain clinically significant data that corroborate data points from other sources.

Is There Suspicion or Mistrust on the Part of the Parent?

Examining the attitudes of the parent during the evaluation is a key consideration for determining the credibility of the parent's self- and family descriptions. Suspicion and mistrust about the evaluation process and concern about not feeling properly understood by the psychologist or the courts are important considerations in the appraisal. The MMPI–2 clinical and content scales, particularly the Pa (6) and CYN scales, can provide information as to the parent's attitudes toward new events or situations the parent encounters and how he or she faces challenges (Butcher et al., 2001; Butcher, Graham, Williams, & Ben-Porath, 1990). Elevated Pa (4) scores occur commonly in child custody evaluations (Bathurst et al., 1997; Resendes & Lecci, 2012). Higher elevations of these measures can reflect the parent's situational concerns and show a personality tendency toward suspicion and mistrust in others, which may not be solely a product of the transitional stress of litigation and risk of losing contact with the children.

Is the Parent Undergoing a High Degree of Stress at This Time?

Central to any custody evaluation is whether the parents are undergoing a high degree of stress and adjustment difficulties that could negatively impact their functioning and the child's adjustment. The MMPI–2 can provide information about a parent's stress level and potential adjustment difficulties that could lessen his or her ability to properly deal with the children (Morrell & Rubin, 2001; Ritzler, 1981). In addition to the Pt (7) scale and the content scale ANX, the $PTSD$ scale (PK) can provide hypotheses about a parent's stress level that should be further evaluated with current background information (Butcher et al., 2001; Keane, Malloy, & Fairbank, 1984).

Does the Parent Manifest Mental-Health Symptoms?

The psychological assessment must address the possibility of mental-health symptoms shown by the parent that might influence his or her parenting behavior just as it disturbs other aspects of functioning. The impact of parental mental illness on family life and children's well-being can be significant. Children whose parents have a mental illness are at risk of developing social, emotional and behavioral problems (American Academy of Child and Adolescent Psychiatry, 2000). These symptom patterns could have a severe impact on the parent's daily behavior and the child's environment. Mental-health symptoms that affect the way a parent behaves toward the children can be detected by the MMPI (Bradley, 1974; McAdoo & Connolly, 1975). Depression among parents and its negative impact on children's behavior is a widely researched area (Otto, Buffington-Vollum, & Edens, 2003), and it can be detected in the D (2) scale, among other scales. Anxiety can be identified in the ANX and Pt (7) scales (Butcher et al., 2001). The scales assessing depression and anxiety contain subtle items that are difficult to disguise for defensive litigants (Caldwell, 2005). The Pd (4) scale offers information on a parent's self-interest and narcissism (Caldwell, 2005) as well as family problems and conflict. These are important considerations when conducting an evaluation of parenting.

Did the Parent Show Unrealistic Attitudes About His or Her Ability to Manage Problems?

It is important in custody examinations to determine whether the parent has realistic attitudes when dealing with everyday problems or situations that could impact his or her parenting behavior and relationship with the children. The MMPI–2 validity scales K and L can reflect problem denial; however, denial of problems that can occur in various circumstances with some parents can also be reflected in elevated Hy (3) scores. Elevations on the Hy (3) scale, for example, can reflect that the parent may tend to deny his or her mental-health symptoms including parenting stress (for discussions of problem denial of psychopathology, see Baldwin & Roys, 1998; Donnelly, Murphy, & Waldman, 1980; Grossman & Cavanaugh, 1990; Haywood & Grossman, 1994; Lim & Butcher, 1996). In addition, the Es scale provides indications about a parent's ability to manage the day-to-day demands of parenting and whether this capacity is compromised (Caldwell, 2005).

Does the Parent Experience Problems in Social Relationships?

Obtaining information about possible interpersonal difficulties that the parent might experience, such as extreme social withdrawal, introversion, or extraversion, can be valuable in developing hypotheses about the environmental context in which children are raised. The MMPI–2 can be a valuable instrument in describing interpersonal relationships. The parent might have high elevations on several MMPI–2 scales that address social relationship issues: the Si (0), SOD, Pd (4), and Ma (9) scale (for details, see Butcher et al., 1990, 2001). In particular, the Pa (6) scale provides information regarding a parent's difficulties in trusting and collaborating with others including an ex-spouse, a child, a social worker, or a case manager (Caldwell, 2005).

Is There a History or Presence of Antisocial Behavior?

Evaluating parents for antisocial behavior is an extremely important consideration in the process of assessing parents in a custody or parent capacity examination. Although past extreme antisocial behavior in some parents might be documented in arrest records, some individuals may not have been arrested or charged with a crime even though they have participated in antisocial acts. They may possess the personality characteristics that are often associated with engaging in impulsive acts, high risk taking, rule breaking, immature behavior, and narcissistic and self-centered activities that can have a highly negative impact on their parenting practices and their children's adjustment. The MMPI–2 has a strong research base for several scales (e.g.,

Pd (4), *Ma* (9), ASP, AGGR) that address antisocial attitudes (Bosquet & Egelund, 2000; Carstairs et al., 2012; Egeland et al., 1991; Erickson, 2005; Ezzo et al., 2007; Loeb, 1966; Loeb & Price, 1966; S. R. Smith, Hilsenroth, Castlebury, & Durham, 1999; Wright, 1976).

Does the Parent Experience an Unusual Degree of Anger, Hostility, and Temper Control Problems?

Open anger or aggressive behavior can have a damaging effect on a person's daily functioning and be harmful to parent–child relationships. In child custody and parent capacity evaluations, it is important to determine if anger and temper control problems are present in the parent's behavior and examine whether this problem has been a factor in his or her relationship with the child and the child's adjustment as well as the relationship with the other parent or the government. The MMPI–2 has a number of scales (e.g., *Pd* (4), *Pa* (6), *Ma* (9), ANG) that examine the manner in which people deal with anger (Butcher et al., 1990; Faunce, Mapledoram, & Job, 2004; Harkness & McNulty, 2006; Murstein & Glaudin, 1968; Ollendick & Otto, 1984; Schill & Wang, 1990). The combination of high scores on the *Pd* (4) and *Pa* (6) scales should alert the practitioner to the possibility of abusive temper outbursts (Caldwell, 2005).

Are There Elevations on MMPI–2 Scales That Have Been Found to Be Associated With a Potential for Child Abuse or Neglect?

In conducting custody or child protection examinations, psychologists evaluate any personality factors that might suggest a potential for behavior that could have a negative impact on children, such as impulse control problems or extreme narcissism. Several MMPI scales (e.g., *Pd* (4), *Pa* (6), *Sc* (8), ANG, Ho) have been found to be elevated in child abuse cases. Elevations on scales that address potential aggressive behavior should alert the psychologist to examine this possibility further (Han, Weed, Calhoun, & Butcher, 1995; James & Boake, 1988; Korbanka & McKay, 2000; Land, 1986; Lucenko, Gold, Elhai, Russo, & Swingle, 2000; Lundberg-Love, Marmion, Ford, & Geffner, 1992; Paulson et al., 1974).

Does the Parent Appear to Experience Emotional Detachment Problems?

Emotional detachment in a caregiver leads to potential problems with child care and interferes with children's development of attachment behaviors. Difficulties in establishing or maintaining relationships and difficulties in emotional engagement can be detected in several MMPI–2 scale elevations including the *Pa* (6) scale (Caldwell, 2005; Velligan, Christensen, Goldstein, & Margolin, 1988). Parents who are experiencing alienation are likely to engage poorly with their children, have problems as a co-parent, and have problems engaging with social services (Nardi & Pannelli, 1997; Pianta, Egeland, & Adam, 1996; Siegel & Langford, 1998).

Is the Parent Experiencing Marital Adjustment Problems or Family Conflict in His or Her Present Relationship?

Marital adjustment problems in the parent's current living situation and the resulting family conflict can have a deleterious effect on children's development. A number of studies with the original MMPI and with the MMPI–2 have addressed the role of marital maladjustment in producing family conflict (Ollendick, Otto, & Heider, 1983; Osborne, 1971; Richard, Wakefield, & Lewak, 1990; Schmidtgall et al., 2000). The Marital Maladjustment (*MDS*) scale (Hjemboe, Almagor, & Butcher, 1992) provides a well-validated description of marital problems.

Does the Parent Have a Substance Abuse Problem?

Substance abuse problems in one or both parents can have a deleterious impact on parenting behavior and a child's behavior and adjustment. It is thereby important to assure that alcohol or drug use is not a causal factor in the family situation. The MMPI–2 contains several scales (*AAS, APS,* and *MAC–R*) that can provide information with respect to substance use or abuse conditions in parent evaluations (Craig, 2005; Craig, Ammar, & Olson, 1998; Knisely, Barker, Ingersoll, & Dawson, 2000; Ollendick, 1984; Ollendick & Otto, 1984; Sher & McCrady, 1984; Svanum & McAdoo, 1991; Workman & Beer, 1992).

Are the Mental-Health Problems Treatable or Amenable to Rehabilitation?

An important aspect of the parent evaluation is to include opinions about the parent treatability or rehabilitation when parenting is compromised. Negative Treatment Indicators (*TRT*) is a scale that helps understand when the parent feels helpless and hopeless in face of his or her seemingly overwhelming problems. The particular aspects of this scale, Low Motivation [TRT_1]), and Inability to Disclose [TRT_2], provide insight into the particular difficulties the parent may be having. The psychologist also needs to take into account how remediation's secondary effects may interfere with the parenting role. For instance, sedating medications and frequent attendance to therapy and treatment that may impair memory, decrease initiative, and consume energy and time for the parent can also indirectly harm the children (Seeman & Göpfert, 2004).

Are There Positive Personality Characteristics and an Absence of Mental-Health Problems in the Assessment Results?

The positive aspects of the parent's personality functioning should be highlighted in order to provide a balanced picture of the assessment process, provided that the testing performance was cooperative and valid. If there is a notable absence of mental-health problems and if the parent shows a strong motivation to maintain a positive functioning environment for the child that fulfills the child's needs, this should be indicated as much as the potential problem areas. The absence of scale elevations on the validity, clinical, and supplementary scales of the MMPI–2 can be an important starting point in exploring positive features of parenting responsibility. Finding no mental-health problems or fractious personality characteristics in parents in custody or parent capacity assessments is an important consideration for an affirmative description.

CASE EXAMPLE

The following case is one in which both issues of custody and child neglect were at the source of the court investigation and litigation. Robert, age 44, received a notice of divorce and custody petition by his wife of 10 years, Anne, age 38. Anne alleged that, since having a car accident 2 years earlier, Robert had stopped working and contributing to the family, both financially and with the care of the children. Robert fell asleep at the wheel of his car when coming home at midnight after working a double shift as supervisor in a fast food restaurant. He suffered only bruises caused by the deployment of his air bag, but his car was totaled when he crashed into the road median. Due to the economic hardship, Anne, who is a nurse, took a second job while trusting Robert to care for their children, ages 7 and 6. However, Anne reported that Robert's parenting was inadequate and neglectful. Anne reported receiving frequent calls from school authorities because Robert failed to pick up the children from school or did not drop them off in the morning because he overslept. Reports from the school also stated that the children arrived unclean, with dirty wrinkled clothes, without lunches, without homework, and unprepared for field trips. After school the children were often at neighbors' houses all afternoon, including for suppertime, and Robert sat them in front of the television instead of having activities with them or supervising their play.

Robert reported that he has been experiencing significant marital difficulties for the past couple of years, and that the marital situation worsened after he had to quit his job due to medical problems, which he believed had not been properly diagnosed. Robert said that his wife has grown increasingly intolerant of his illness and unemployment, and these issues were the cause of constant conflict between them. Robert is completely dependent on his wife in that he has been unable to drive for the past 2 years after he lost his license. A constant source of conflict between the couple was money. Because Anne managed all her income without consulting Robert, he felt that he had to ask for money item by item. Robert reported that when he asked his wife for $50 to pay for transportation to and from doctors, she told him to be happy with $20 because that is all she was going to give him.

Robert felt that the role of housekeeper fell on him because he did not work, while his wife had two jobs and was the only breadwinner in the family. He said he cooked, cleaned the house, did all household chores, and took care of the children. This is an issue that brought constant conflict, as Robert believed that he was expected to perform these duties even when he was sick or overwhelmed. Once, an argument ensued because when Anne came home from work he had not taken the children to school or changed them out of their pajamas because he was feeling tired. When faced with this situation, Anne called the police and accused him of child neglect, which opened an investigation by child protective services. Robert acknowledged that he did not feel competent or supported in caring for his children. Robert said that his wife came home from work to watch television and expected him to serve her dinner. She did not make conversation with him and did not share much about her life. Robert indicated that his wife never made time for him and did not go out with him other than to do grocery shopping. However, Robert did not want to divorce his wife because he feared losing contact with his children if he moved out of the house. Because he did not work or drive, he would have to move in with his parents or relatives, and they live in another state.

Robert's MMPI–2 is valid (see Figure 9.1) but shows a pattern consistent with underreporting of symptoms in that he attempted to portray a very positive picture of his emotional and personality functioning. His validity scales also suggest that he is emotionally reserved and moralistic. He is not introspective or psychologically minded, and he denies his faults and trivializes his moral deficits. His lack of awareness regarding how others perceive him rises to a level of being socially problematic, as he wonders why others feel put off by him.

Despite his defensiveness, Robert generated a prominent elevation on the *Hs* scale, which is associated with somatic and bodily problems and strong concerns with his physical health. It seems that Robert tends to react to stress by developing or becoming overly concerned with physical symptoms,

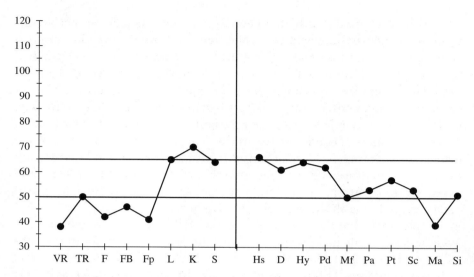

Figure 9.1. MMPI–2 basic validity and clinical scales profile for Robert. Excerpted from the *MMPI®–2 (Minnesota Multiphasic Personality Inventory®—2) Manual for Administration, Scoring, and Interpretation, Revised Edition* by Butcher et al. Copyright © 2001 by the Regents of the University of Minnesota. Used by permission of the University of Minnesota Press. All rights reserved. "MMPI®" and "Minnesota Multiphasic Personality Inventory®" are trademarks owned by the Regents of the University of Minnesota.

complaining about his health, and viewing himself as being physically ill. Emotional reactions are given a physical expression, but his concern for his somatic complaints is not genuine. It seems that Robert may be using his physical symptoms to secure secondary gains, such as obtaining attention and sympathy and not fulfilling his responsibilities.

Robert's profile also depicts him as a passive-dependent individual in his relationships and as someone who seeks excessive nurturance from others and fears being negatively judged. Although he seeks social approval, he also tends to make demands on others, complains a great deal to get attention, and may be somewhat cynical and hostile if his wishes are not met. The results of this test also suggest that Robert is dissatisfied with his life and suffers from a mild to moderate level of anxiety, depression, and nervousness. Demands to perform and pressures from others increase his anxiety. He has low tolerance for frustration and tends to externalize problems and blame others. He seems to alternate between emotional overcontrol and relatively intense emotional outbursts.

Regarding the implications of these findings on Robert's parenting skills, these findings suggest that Robert may spend an inordinate amount of time concerned about himself and his desire for attention, which may interfere with the time and energy he has to dedicate to his parenting role. Feeling needy, Robert may have difficulties caring for his children or may expect that they meet his emotional needs. His personality traits may interfere with his ability to meet the children's needs properly before he meets his own. Robert's MMPI–2 confirms the dynamic described by both parties; specifically, Robert's deficits in his parenting role and his feeling emotionally deprived and behaving self-protectively. The MMPI–2 provides a new understanding of the dynamic inherent in his medical complaints, his expectations from his wife, his emotional needs, and the chronicity of his personality traits. Robert is in need of both a psychiatric consultation and psychotherapy intervention in order to decrease his high level of anxiety and self-focus. The MMPI–2 provided a good explanation of the internal dynamics behind Robert's behavior and attitude. Together with the rest of the information acquired in this evaluation, this can help the psychologist develop a parenting plan that allows Robert to find help for himself and to engage in his children's lives in a way that would benefit them and does not place them at risk.

SUMMARY

This chapter described forensic psychological services to assist psychologists in understanding the dynamics of family custody and child protection evaluations. The assessment goals and evaluation strategies for these programs differ in many respects, and the distinctions were clarified. The legal bases for psychological evaluations in custody and parental capacity evaluations were summarized, and the evaluation procedures and goals were detailed.

This chapter also provided a historical perspective on the research basis of the MMPI–2 scales in evaluating parents. A number of these studies were highlighted to illustrate the empirical basis of the test in this application in a number of family-oriented contexts. Early research with the MMPI on parental behavior and problems established the test's utility in understanding couple's problems, and hundreds of studies on personality and behavior of parents and their children using the MMPI/MMPI–2 have been published over the past 75 years.

The MMPI–2 can contribute substantially to a family custody or a parent capacity evaluation by providing the practitioner with relevant information about the parent's mental health adjustment or personality characteristics. Such information can give a valid perspective on the likelihood of the parent's carrying out parental responsibilities.

Finally, this chapter discussed several issues that are pertinent for forensic practitioners to consider in determining which psychological measures to include in a parental custody examination.

10

THE MMPI–2 IN CASES OF INTIMATE PARTNER VIOLENCE

There are forensic cases in which intimate partner violence (IPV) is a central component to understanding the individual being assessed. This situation may be found in different types of forensic evaluations, and the issue can either be at the core of the evaluation or be an ancillary factor. This concern may be raised in all forensic settings: personal injury, child custody, victim impact, immigration, parental capacity, work compensation, criminal (most notably the criminal defense based on battering and its effects), and correctional settings, among others. This topic has been separated from the other forensic evaluations examined in this book due to the need to look more closely at the issue. IPV cuts across populations and can be the focus of different forensic evaluations for several reasons. It is a significant and widespread social problem, and issues of safety and professional ethic mandates trump other concerns. Also, IPV usually involves trauma, which can be an organizing experience that forms the core of an individual's identity rather than an isolated event (M. Harris & Fallot, 2001). Forensic evaluators are

http://dx.doi.org/10.1037/14571-011
Using the MMPI–2 in Forensic Assessment, by J. N. Butcher, G. A. Hass, R. L. Greene, and L. D. Nelson

encouraged to screen for this issue routinely in their forensic practices, particularly when practicing in family law.

The American Psychological Association ([APA], 1996) defined *family violence and abuse* as "acts of physical abuse, sexual abuse, and psychological maltreatment; chronic situations in which one person controls or intends to control another person's behavior, and misuse of power that may result in injury or harm to the psychological, social, economic, sexual, or physical well-being of family members" (p. 3). The literature on domestic violence and IPV has focused extensively on the different types of abusive behavior; namely, physical, sexual, psychological/emotional/verbal, and economic abuse. These categories leave out some other abusive strategies, such as endangering children (Edleson, 1999; Tajima, 2004) with threats to kidnap, exposing children to violence, taking custody of or deporting children, or harming children. Immigration-related abuse (Hass, Dutton, & Orloff, 2000) consists of threats to call immigration authorities, threats to have the partner deported, or refusal to support a visa application. Although the identification and description of IPV is essential to the understanding of its role and dynamics, the central feature of this phenomenon, especially for forensic psychologists, is its function, being a tool of control of one person over another (M. A. Dutton, 1992). Outside the context of control, abusive behaviors in and of themselves may not necessarily qualify as IPV.

The most up-to-date model for understanding domestic violence was borne out of the need to reconcile the disparate perspectives and research data between the battered women movement and family social researchers in order to settle on a framework that would be useful to the court system (Johnson & Ferraro, 2000; Ver Steegh & Dalton, 2008). Four patterns of domestic violence emerged from this new formulation of IPV (Graham-Kevan & Archer, 2003; Holtzworth-Munroe, 2005; Johnson & Ferraro, 2000; Johnston & Campbell, 1993; Kelly & Johnson, 2008): separation-instigated violence, conflict-instigated violence or situational couple violence, violent resistance to violence, and abusive controlling violence or coercive controlling violence.

- In *separation-instigated violence*, one or two incidents of IPV emerge with the couple's separation without a previous history of power and control issues in the relationship. This type of incidental violence is a response to the trauma, humiliation, and loss of control and can be demonstrated by both men and women (Johnston & Campbell, 1993; Kelly & Johnson, 2008).
- In *conflict-instigated violence* or *situational couple violence*, the incidents emerge from conflict escalating out of control, but power, coercion, and control are not central to the dynamic. This type of violence can be initiated by either gender, and partners are

not afraid of one another. Serious injuries are uncommon. This type of violence decreases over time and with age, and it often stops after separation (Babcock, Costa, Green, & Eckhardt, 2004; Capaldi & Owen, 2001; Ellis & Stuckless, 1996; Gelles & Straus, 1988; Holtzworth-Munroe, 2005; Jaffe, Crooks, & Bala, 2005; Kelly & Johnson, 2008; Ver Steegh, 2005).

- *Violent resistance* includes the use of violence as self-defense against an abuser who is using violence as a form of coercive control (L. Frederick, 2001; Johnson & Ferraro, 2000). This type of violence includes women in shelter samples and victims who killed their batterers (Jaffe, Johnston, Crooks, & Bala, 2008) and were using violence to prevent imminent harm. This group also includes individuals with a history of previous abuse who use physical violence to send the message that they will not tolerate abuse in their current relationship (L. Frederick, 2001).

- *Abusive controlling violence* or *coercive controlling violence* includes what is traditionally known as classical battering. It is characterized by a unilateral pattern of using intimidation, coercion, control, and emotional abuse to dominate the other partner (Kelly & Johnson, 2008). Although primary perpetrators of this type of violence are male, there are reports of female offenders. Injuries incurred by victims are more frequent and severe, as this violence often includes severe physical and sexual abuse. This type of abuse usually does not stop with separation and often continues into custody battles (Jaffe et al., 2005; Johnson, 2006a; Johnson & Ferraro, 2000; Johnston & Campbell, 1993).

Categorical labeling of complex phenomenon such as IPV has its limitations, as it does not incorporate the role of factors such as substance abuse and mental illness. The complexity of the dynamic in IPV makes it clear that forensic psychologists evaluating this issue need to pay close attention to assessment of specific behaviors, context, and nuance in order to obtain the most comprehensive picture possible. It is important to remember that the fact that domestic violence has not been mentioned in previous records or interviews is not evidence that the issue does not exist in a particular case, as there are many reasons why individuals may hesitate to bring it up. Factors to assess when performing a forensic evaluation that involve the possible presence of IPV include the frequency, intensity, and recency of the violence; the presence of sexual coercion or abuse; the existence of nonphysical coercive strategies including verbal abuse and intimidation, threats, isolation, and financial control; the presence of an established history of violence; the mutuality of violence; criminal activity, substance abuse, or mental health issues; the impact to the victim(s); the victim's fear of imminent danger and the victim's vulnerability; the extent to which the violence is consistent with a recognized pattern with proven implications for ongoing risk or lethality; and the utility or impact of previous interventions (Hass, 2014).

ASSESSMENT OF IPV

The presence of IPV has to be established with methods independent of the Minnesota Multiphasic Personality Inventory—2 (MMPI–2). The context to interpret the results of the MMPI–2 in cases of IPV has to be established with data collected through different forensic methods that build around the aspects of the psycholegal construct or issue to be opined.

Standardized Measures of IPV

The Conflict Tactic Scales (CTS and CTS-2; Straus, 2007; Straus, Hamby, Boney-McCoy, & Sugarman, 1996) is claimed to be the most widely used instrument for measuring intimate violence. The survey assesses the use of reasoning, verbal aggression, and violence, ranging from low in coerciveness to high in aggressiveness, including injury and sexual coercion. The CTS measures behaviors of both the respondent and the respondent's partner. This test is widely accepted in the professional community, is commercially available, and has strong psychometric properties published in hundreds of articles (Straus, 2007). It thus meets criteria for admissibility as scientific evidence set forth in the Federal Rules of Evidence and *Daubert v. Merrell Dow Pharmaceuticals* (1993), to which most states adhere.

The Psychological Maltreatment of Women Inventory (PMWI; Tolman, 1999) measures the extent and nature of abuse toward women in a relationship. The PMWI subscales of dominance/isolation and emotional/verbal discriminate among three groups: physically abused women (BW), who score higher than the other groups; relationship-distressed/nonabused (RD) women; and relationship-satisfied/nonabused women (RS). A 14-item short version of the PMWI also successfully discriminated between the BW, and RD, and RS groups. Both the short and long versions of the PMWI have demonstrated good convergent and discriminate validity and internal consistency (Tolman, 1999), have been utilized by a large number of empirical studies, and are available for free (University of Michigan School of Social Work, n.d.). These characteristics also fulfill criteria for admissibility in court.

The assessment of coercive control is key to the determination of risk and issues of safety in IPV. Coercive control is the construct that differentiates the abusive behaviors that are situational and transitory from those instrumental to the establishment of power and control over the other person

(M. A. Dutton & Goodman, 2005). Two instruments address this issue: the Domestic Violence Evaluation (DOVE; Ellis & Stuckless, 2006) and the Coercive Control Survey (M. A. Dutton, Goodman, & Schmidt, 2005). The DOVE measures coercive control in general and specific relational or behavioral acts in particular. The research that tested this scale revealed that all three types of controlling behaviors were related to pre-separation assaults and emotional abuse and to post-separation abuse. General controlling behaviors were associated with serious physical harm. The Coercive Control Survey (M. A. Dutton et al., 2005) includes questions to assess coercion on the basis of determining the threat of noncompliance, which removes the victim's ability to make a free choice. The items in this survey focus on the context of the demand in order to distinguish it from other forms of persuasive behaviors that are not rooted in the dynamic of control. Both instruments have been supported in empirical studies published in major professional journals.

Another critical aspect to assess in cases that present IPV is the level of risk for the victim, particularly in custody cases, because the stress of separation has been cited as a dynamic index of future risk (Hanson & Harris, 2001). Risk has been the subject of a few actuarial instruments, specifically the Danger Assessment instrument (DA; Campbell, Webster, & Glass, 2009), the Spousal Assault Risk Assessment Guide (SARA; Kropp, Hart, Webster, & Eaves, 1999), and the Ontario Domestic Assault Risk Assessment (ODARA; Hilton, Harris, & Rice, 2010). The DA is utilized in a variety of settings including battered woman's shelters, criminal justice, and health care settings. A strength of this instrument is that internal consistency did not vary significantly among different ethnic groups in the sample (Campbell et al., 2009). The SARA contains risk factors of predictive value according to clinical and empirical studies, and it attempts to determine the degree to which the threat of a physical assault to an intimate partner is still present (Kropp et al., 1999). The ODARA places the abuser in a level of risk category regarding recidivism (Hilton et al., 2010). The Mediator's Assessment of Safety Issues and Concerns (Holtzworth-Munroe, Beck, & Applegate, 2010) is a behaviorally based measure of intimate partner violence and abuse focused on coercive control, stalking, and physical violence throughout the relationship and over the past year. This measure also assesses lethality and offers procedural changes for mediation based on the level of risk.

These and other inventories that measure different dimensions of IPV have numerous limitations, and their use isolated of other types of evaluations may incline the forensic psychologist to make precipitous decisions without having a complete understanding of the complexity of the situation (D. Dutton, 2006; M. A. Dutton & Goodman, 2005; Johnson, 2006b; Stark, 2007). These instruments can be useful adjuncts to a measure of general psychopathology, such as the MMPI–2, in cases in which the specific dynamics of alleged victimization through partner abuse is at the core of the evaluation of psychological functioning or psychological impact.

Models of Assessment for Domestic Violence in Custody Evaluations

Due to the critical role of allegations of IPV in custody evaluations, some models incorporating the different dimensions of domestic violence have emerged. The focus of these models is by necessity to assure the safety of the children for determining custody and access. The safety first model (Drozd, Kuehnle, & Walker, 2004) proposes to assess the children's safety in relation to parents' violence, substance abuse, mental illness, credible threats, and other forms of violence within the family. Affinity and bond of the children with each parent are also assessed to screen for child alienation. The potency, pattern, and primary perpetrator model, developed by Jaffe et al. (2008), looks at types of violence and how they relate to parental behaviors. The specific factors to assess are *potency*, or the severity, dangerousness, and risk of serious injury and lethality; *pattern*, or the coercion and domination dynamic; and *primary perpetrator*, to determine the initiator of the violence, if it is mutual or initiators alternate. Jaffe et al. believe that, all other factors being equal, this information guides which parent is most likely to provide a nonviolent home. As a "working hypothesis" (Jaffe et al., 2008, p. 506), this model provides a systematic structure of inquiry to evaluate the type of violence and the factors to consider when recommending different interventions to reduce risk.

The MMPI–2 can be a useful adjunct instrument when utilizing these models of assessment in custody cases. It provides information regarding the clinical and personality functioning of the parties including aspects relevant to the safety of the self and other family members, such as substance abuse, mental illness, risk for violence and impulsivity, and credibility.

ASSESSMENT OF THE IMPACT OF IPV

Once the occurrence and role of IPV have been established through independent data, assessing the impact that such a critical event has on the lives of its victims is crucial to the evaluation. Forensic psychologists are tasked with differentiating between emotions of loss and resentment that will heal in time, as may be the case in situational couple violence, and traumatic reactions that will progress negatively without prompt intervention, as may be the case in coercive controlling violence. Victims of coercive controlling IPV have characteristics that set them apart from individuals traumatized in other ways because of the nature of the abuse, which occurs in an intimate setting and capitalizes on vulnerabilities that the abuser knows intimately. In general terms, it can be said that victims of coercive controlling IPV have an increased sense of vulnerability, shame, guilt, fear, and helplessness that becomes a dominant framework and leads them to organize their lives around these traumatic memories and self-protection strategies.

In terms of clinical syndromes, posttraumatic stress disorder (PTSD) and depression have been overwhelmingly cited as disorders common among victims of IPV (Anderson, Saunders, Yoshihama, Bybee, & Sullivan, 2003; Basile, Arias, Desai, & Thompson, 2004; Campbell, Kub, Belknap, & Templin, 1997; Campbell & Soeken, 1999; Gleason, 1993; Golding, 1999; Weaver & Clum, 1995). A significant factor when interpreting these findings is that the type of abuse seems to shape battered women's response and reaction. For instance, PTSD has emerged as strongly correlated to psychological abuse (Arias & Pape, 1999; M. A. Dutton, Goodman, & Bennett, 1999; Taft, Murphy, King, Dedeyn, & Musser, 2005). Severe and broad psychopathology has been found when sexual coercion or assault was present in addition to the physical violence (Bennice & Resick, 2003; Pico-Alfonso, Echeburua, & Martinez, 2008). Emotional and verbal abuse has emerged as a significant single predictor of depression (Mechanic, Weaver, & Resick, 2008).

The assessment and accurate identification of the psychological impact of IPV are crucial to decisions and interventions with victims of IPV. The knowledge obtained from an appropriate assessment can help in determining forensic issues, such as custody and access of children, sanity at the time of the offense for victims who injure or kill their abusers in self-defense, or the extent of compensation in civil cases, or in meeting the standard of substantial mental harm in immigration evaluations. In addition, treatment planning for victims of IPV greatly benefits from the understanding that comes with an effective assessment of IPV impact in order to tap specific cognitions and emotions generated by the trauma. In particular, delivery of services to trauma victims should be modified on the basis of an understanding of the vulnerabilities or triggers that traditional service delivery approaches may aggravate, so as to avoid retraumatization and promote healing (Substance Abuse and Mental Health Services Administration, 2014).

Psychological testing has been used to identify symptoms of trauma from IPV and their severity and to assess the credibility of battered women. Although much of what has been written regarding IPV impact has referred to PTSD as a major type of sequelae, the psychological impact of IPV can be expressed through many different symptoms and disorders. No two persons experience IPV in the same manner or have the same vulnerabilities. The MMPI/MMPI–2 is widely used in research and clinical practice with battered women as part of a multimodal assessment battery.

LITERATURE ON THE MMPI–2 WITH BATTERED WOMEN

A literature search revealed that there are more studies on the use of the MMPI and MMPI–2 with abusers than with victims. However, this chapter focuses on victims of IPV, as the analysis of abusers is considered to fit better in the criminal arena.

Widely cited has been the seminal work of Rosewater (1988), who was the first to publish an MMPI study rebutting Palau's (1981) research suggesting that battered women were high on the Masochistic Scale and thus to blame for their own predicament. Rosewater found that battered women had elevated profiles, particularly on the Pd (4), Pa (6), and Sc (8) scales, with T scores above 70. For victims of IPV, the elevated scores on the Sc (8) scale are reinterpreted as representing the disruptions in their boundaries and reality testing characteristic of the trauma picture. Rosewater's study began the accumulation of empirical support for the notion that MMPI elevations are usually reactions to IPV rather than reflections of underlying psychopathology. In particular, the Sc (8) scale has been found to be highly sensitive to depressive cognitions, helplessness, PTSD, and other severe and potentially disabling anxiety disorders that have an impact on self-esteem and identity.

Rhodes (1992) focused her MMPI research on the Pd (4) scale and the Harris and Lingoes subscales with a clinical population of battered women and a nonbattered group drawn from a similar clinical setting. She found that the battered group scored higher on the full Pd (4) scale and more specifically on the Authority Problems (Pd_2), Social Alienation (Pd_4), and Social Imperturbability (Pd_3) Harris and Lingoes scales, but there was no significant difference on the Self-Alienation scale (Pd_4). The score on Family Discord (Pd_1) was the most elevated for the battered group, although just below moderately elevated. These findings support the association between elevated scores on the Pd scale and victimization by domestic violence.

Using the MMPI–2, Khan, Welch, and Zillmer (1993) studied the psychological functioning of battered women who were shelter residents. In addition to taking the MMPI–2, the 31 participants provided information regarding the length, severity, and types of abuse they suffered. Khan et al. found elevated MMPI–2 profiles in 90% of the women, and the most frequent code type was a combination of the F, Pd (4), Pa (6), and Sc (8) scales. Of interest, the D (2) and Pt (7) scales, which reflect depression, anxiety, and other forms of subjective distress, were not consistently elevated in this study. The analysis of supplementary MMPI–2 scales revealed elevations on the MAC–R, Mt, PK, and PS scales. Khan et al. also found significant relationships between length and severity of psychological forms of abuse and overall levels of psychological distress as evidenced in elevations of the F scale and average clinical T scores.

Perrin, Van Hasselt, Basilio, and Hersen (1996) studied the validity of the Keane PTSD Scale (*PK*) validity in battered women. Sixty-nine battered women were assigned to PTSD-positive and PTSD-negative groups and then compared on measures of PTSD, distress, social support, and history of abuse in and out of the battering relationship. The PTSD-positive group scored significantly higher across all measures of PTSD and distress, which corroborated the concurrent validity of the *PK* scale in a population of battered women. However, the *PK* scale appeared to be only mildly sensitive to the level of trauma exposure. Lower levels of perceived social support were found in the PTSD-positive than the PTSD-negative group. In a follow-up study with a segment of this sample, Perrin, Van Hasselt, and Hersen (1997) determined that a cutoff raw score of 22 on the *PK* scale correctly classified 80.4% of the sample of PTSD sufferers, suggesting that the scale is moderately sensitive to many of the PTSD symptoms from the *Diagnostic and Statistical Manual of Mental Disorders* (3rd ed.; *DSM–III*; American Psychiatric Association, 1980), especially intrusion and psychological arousal. This investigation provided further support for the validity of the MMPI *PK-PTSD* scale and its utility in screening battered women for PTSD.

Morrell and Rubin (2001) administered the MMPI–2 to 93 women domestic violence survivors from shelters, support groups, outreach centers, and other social service agencies. These women were diagnosed with or without PTSD through an independent measure. Multivariate analysis of variance with nine MMPI–2 scales found significant differences between women domestic violence survivors with and without PTSD on the *F, K, Hs* (1), *D* (2), *Pa* (6), *Sc* (8), and *PK-PTSD* scales. A discriminant function using the *K* and *Hs* scales had a 78% correct classification rate and sensitivity and specificity of 88% and 60%, respectively. The *PK-PTSD* scale correctly classified 68% of all cases, and sensitivity and specificity of 81% and 45%, respectively, were found. In sum, the MMPI–2 appeared to be sensitive to PTSD symptomatology and capable of discriminating between domestic violence survivors with and without PTSD.

A review of the raw data from 13 past research studies of the MMPI–2 with battered women, conducted by Erickson (2005), reported the following code patterns: *482, 426, 486, 648, 376, 489, 648, 463* (below 65), *681, 468, 486, 6824,* and *642*. There is significant consistency in elevations of the *Pa* (6), *Sc* (8), and *Pd* (4) scales. When reasons for these elevations are examined, it seems clear that they point to fearfulness, suspicion, confusion, the feeling of being overwhelmed, resentment, irritability, projection of blame, and family problems. Erickson emphasized that MMPI–2 scores tended to normalize after the end of abuse, when data of current versus past abuse were compared. Erickson made a cogent case to support the notion that battered women were not mentally ill before the abuse, but their pathological scores in the MMPI are a representation of the impact of the trauma and are thus reactive and temporary.

EXPERT TESTIMONY CONCERNING BATTERING AND ITS EFFECTS IN CRIMINAL TRIALS

The effects of being in an intimate partner violent relationship, previously called battered woman syndrome and now associated with PTSD, are sometimes used in court cases as mitigation in diverse situations. Examples include women who defended themselves against their abuser and have been charged with assault or homicide; have been coerced into criminal activity; have been charged with a crime as a result of "failing to protect" their children from their batterer's violence, abuse, or both; have fled with their child (or children) to protect themselves and their children and been charged with parental kidnapping or custodial interference; or have been charged with a crime directly related to battering. This defense may be raised when facing trial or considering a plea, going through a trial, waiting to be sentenced, or when the case is on appeal.

The law does not currently accept battered woman syndrome as a defense because of its lack of validity as a psychological disorder. Many states allow expert testimony on the effects of intimate partner battering and its effects to explain the victim's behavior in claims of duress, coercion, or self-defense, which would excuse the defendant from criminal liability under certain circumstances or lessen a charge. This expert testimony has been proffered to defend against charges of international and interstate kidnapping. Prosecutors have also used this argument to explain victims' behavior, such as recantations (Michelson, 2001).

According to Kaser-Boyd (2004), expert testimony after the forensic assessment of an IPV victim is typically used to establish that the person has been battered, that the person displays common symptoms that result from battering, and that there is a nexus between the legal issue and the experience of battering. This type of testimony is important to educate the trier of fact and dispel erroneous beliefs about victims of domestic violence, because many of the symptoms and behaviors battered women present defy logic.

The MMPI–2 is the personality instrument most widely employed in court cases to provide clinical information when psychological adjustment factors and psychopathology are crucial to the case and the psycholegal question. The MMPI–2 is particularly suited to be utilized in IPV court cases because it has a strong research base and is easy to explain effectively to lay audiences. However, it is important to remember that the MMPI–2 assesses current mental state and adjustment, not the mental state at the time of the offense. Current mental state may be relevant to the psycholegal issue but is not dispositive by itself (Otto, 2002). Moreover, the MMPI–2 may provide information about the impact of trauma but not about the root cause of such. That is why it is very important to utilize a multimethod approach to assess IPV in the context of forensic examinations.

CASE EXAMPLE

The following case is that of a 22-year-old woman, Tenesha, who was battered by her same-sex partner during their 3-year relationship. The forensic evaluation of Tenesha's psychological state was requested to assess her state of mind at the time when she stole a car, which she used to escape from her partner and drive to her sister's home in another state. Tenesha has a history of childhood abuse through exposure to IPV with her parents. Tenesha said that ever since she can remember her father was a controlling alcoholic who would come home to fight and beat her mother. Her father ran the house with an iron fist, physically abused the children with a horsewhip, and verbally abused everyone in the family. She said her mother did not protect her from the child abuse because her mother did not want to make things worse for everybody. When little, Tenesha did as her siblings did, hiding under the bed or behind the furniture, crying, until the beating of someone in the family stopped. However, by age 6 she had started trying to defend her mother or the sibling being abused. Tenesha said that her father became so angry at her interference that he increased the severity of the abuse by threatening the family with knives or a gun and making the children strip naked before being beaten. In addition, Tenesha reported that the family was very poor, as they had money to eat but not for less essential items such as clothes, television, or a phone. When Tenesha was 16 years old, her mother had an episode of mental illness, was hospitalized, and was diagnosed with schizophrenia. Tenesha said her mother had recurrent episodes in which she would wander the streets speaking about God and the Bible and neglecting herself. Until her father's death by cirrhosis when Tenesha was 19 years old, she lived at home with him and her mother, morally obligated by her desire to be there to protect her mother from further abuse by her father.

Tenesha met Helen during her freshman year in college, and the two started a romantic relationship. Helen was a college professor in another department and 20 years her senior. Tenesha reported that she moved in with Helen after dating her for 3 months and the violence began shortly thereafter. The violence began with arguments, provoked by Helen's jealousy, that included shoves and pushes and escalated to slaps and struggles in which Helen pulled her hair and grabbed her arms in a lock and twisted her hand.

Tenesha reported that Helen was the primary perpetrator, and she defended herself only by trying to break free and then locking herself in the bathroom. Tenesha did not know who to tell or how to seek help. She said that she was under the wrong assumption that battered women hotlines and shelters were only for women in heterosexual relationships. One night after a violent fight she went for a walk and saw a car with the keys in the ignition. She impulsively took it and drove to her sister's home 5 hours away.

An MMPI–2 was administered to Tenesha as part of this evaluation of mental status at the time of the offense. Her profile (see Figure 10.1) shows elevations on the *TRIN*, *F*, and *L* scales and all of the clinical scales with the exception of *Pa* (6) and *Si* (9).

The validity scales showed Tenesha as mildly attempting to present herself as functioning better than she is. She seems to make attempts to deny or ignore bona fide symptoms of emotional distress, discomfort, and negative traits and attitudes. At the same time, the Gough *F-K* index shows such a large positive difference that it suggests that Tenesha dramatized her distress and may be quite disorganized psychologically. Her elevated score on the *TRIN* scale suggests some inconsistency in her responding. Given that this combination of response styles is incongruent with someone who may

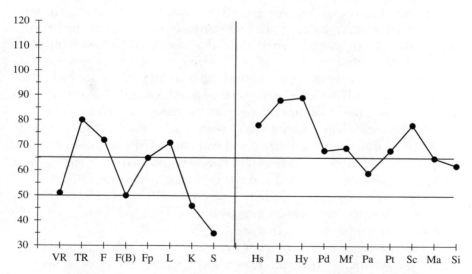

Figure 10.1. MMPI–2 profile for Tenesha. Excerpted from the *MMPI®–2 (Minnesota Multiphasic Personality Inventory®—2) Manual for Administration, Scoring, and Interpretation, Revised Edition* by Butcher et al. Copyright © 2001 by the Regents of the University of Minnesota. Used by permission of the University of Minnesota Press. All rights reserved. "MMPI®" and "Minnesota Multiphasic Personality Inventory®" are trademarks owned by the Regents of the University of Minnesota.

try to deceive and malinger to obtain a better outcome in her legal case, it was hypothesized that Tenesha was honest and this naive defensive style reflects both a personality trait and her mental status. Given her background, it seems that this elevation in *L* reflect her indomitable spirit and survival mechanisms to keep her going in spite of the challenges she encountered. Finally, the ratio between *F* and *K* suggests that, under her façade of doing well, Tenesha is actually quite disregulated emotionally and is suffering from a variety of important clinical symptoms.

Tenesha's profile is considered to fit a 3-2-1 code type (*Hy*, *D*, and *Hs*; not-well defined) which is associated with weakness, fatigue, stress-related medical symptoms, general concerns with health and physical functioning, aches and pain with emotional distress, dysphoria, discomfort, and lack of interest in leisure and recreation. The preoccupation with somatic symptoms in Tenesha is considered a mask to obscure signs of depression. Deep inside, Tenesha feels hopeless and pessimistic, is uncomfortable with herself and her environment, is a worrier, and suffers from a chronic sense of sadness. However, Tenesha places strict controls over her emotions to avoid experiencing the full extent of her distress, trying to appear upbeat and carry on. Her depression is reactive and not endogenous and is rather a reaction to difficult life conditions.

Moreover, the elevation in the *Sc* (8) scale suggests that Tenesha also suffers from cognitive confusion, her reasoning becomes blocked at times, and there are lapses in her reality testing and appraisal of boundaries to appropriate behavior. Tenesha perceives herself as damaged, alienated, estranged, and incompetent.

Tenesha's personality style as revealed in her MMPI–2 code type appears as immature, passive, dependent, and avoidant. She also presented with personality characteristics that cause some functioning difficulties. She is self-deprecating, is filled with self-doubt, and has low self-esteem. At the same time, she can be naive and concrete, try too hard to please, and be lacking in insight. The MMPI–2 code type also suggests that Tenesha wants to be seen as self-confident, upbeat, friendly, cheerful, trusting, responsible, and seeking harmony. She has difficulty and confusion about identifying herself with the traditional feminine role. Dealing with gender expectations makes her very anxious because she is not interested in appearing feminine or behaving in a feminine manner.

Elevations on the *F*, *Hs* (1), *D* (2), *Pd* (4), *Pa* (6), and *Sc* (8) scales are congruent with research findings that these symptoms are associated with trauma-related reactions to IPV. The elevation on the *Sc* (8) scale, supported by all other clinical data in Tenesha's MMPI–2 profile, reflects her difficulties in making and executing rational plans, especially when under the emotional arousal of a critical situation such as a violent episode with her partner. Therefore, the MMPI–2 can contribute to the defense of having had an altered mental status during the commission of a crime and allegations of being victimized in a relationship with IPV.

SUMMARY

This chapter provided an empirical perspective of the state of the IPV field and the intricacies of interpreting the MMPI–2 with victims of IPV. Because IPV trauma includes a constellation of diverse symptoms and signs that interact with personality traits and previous trauma, this part of the field tends to be riddled with confusion and misinterpretation. However, when utilized as part of a multimodal battery of interview and tests, IPV surveys, and actuarial instruments, the MMPI–2 provides an effective appraisal of the victim's credibility and psychological functioning. This knowledge is useful in forensic evaluations where the issue of IPV is raised, because it provides empirically validated information that assists the psychologist to formulate an opinion in a variety of psycholegal matters.

11

THE MMPI–2 IN CORRECTIONAL SETTINGS

Personality evaluations of people being tried as criminal offenders have a long history in assessment psychology. Over 100 years ago, the psychologist Hugo Münsterberg conducted research and substantially enhanced our understanding of the process of testimony in court cases (Münsterberg, 1908; see also Vaccaro & Hogan, 2004). As personality assessment measures began to be developed in the 20th century, tests came to be widely used to assess personality factors in criminals (Symonds, 1934). Shortly after the Minnesota Multiphasic Personality Inventory (MMPI) was published in 1942, it became a component of personality evaluations in court cases with both adults and juveniles. The extensive research that accumulated with the MMPI in correctional settings during this period served as a strong support for its use after the role of psychologists in forensic settings was more soundly established in the 1970s (Archer, Stredny, & Zoby, 2006). Archer, Buffington-Vollum,

http://dx.doi.org/10.1037/14571-012
Using the MMPI–2 in Forensic Assessment, by J. N. Butcher, G. A. Hass, R. L. Greene, and L. D. Nelson
Copyright © 2015 by the American Psychological Association. All rights reserved.

Stredny, and Handel (2006); Borum and Grisso (1995); and Lally (2003) found that the MMPI–2 was one of the most widely used and accepted personality measures in forensic assessments.

Assessments of people undergoing criminal investigations, those who have been convicted of crimes, or severely disturbed mental health examinees considered to be dangerous to themselves or others are prominent in forensic practice today. Forensic psychologists conducting assessments for the court usually provide an evaluation that includes a record review, examination of the defendant, interviews of collaterals, psychological testing, and the preparation of a written report (L. Miller, 2013). This chapter is devoted to describing the various contexts in which personality-based information is needed for important decisions, reviewing the historical use of the MMPI/MMPI–2, and examining the MMPI–2 as it is used in these applications.

CONTEXTS FOR PSYCHOLOGICAL ASSESSMENT IN CRIMINAL CASES

There are several legal contexts in which psychological tests are used to determine the mental health status of examinees. Each of these different applications requires special considerations and behavioral focus to address the referral questions involved. In the sections that follow we address several situations in which the MMPI–2 is used in evaluating clients in pretrial assessments. Moreover, we include a description of MMPI–2 applications in which incarcerated offenders are evaluated in preplacement or treatment-planning circumstances.

Competence to Stand Trial

It is a well-established legal precedent that the 14th Amendment to the U.S. Constitution prohibits the criminal prosecution of a defendant who is not competent to stand trial. If someone is charged with a crime and is considered to be unable to understand the trial proceedings as a result of an intellectual deficit or severe mental health problems, he (or she) can be hospitalized until his mental state is determined to be improved sufficiently for him to be competent to stand trial. It has been estimated that 5% of all criminal cases appear to be vulnerable to competence challenges, though only about two thirds of those cases were actually referred for evaluations (LaFortune & Nicholson, 1995). A typical example occurred in May 2011, when a federal court judge ruled that Jared Loughner, who shot Congresswoman Gabrielle

Giffords and killed six people, was not competent to stand trial (C. Harris & Kiefer, 2011). This court ruling was based upon the opinion of several expert witnesses for the defense and prosecution who examined the defendant. Loughner was then held in a federal hospital and received treatment until it was determined that he was able to stand trial. In August 2012, Loughner was considered to be mentally able to stand trial. He then pleaded guilty to the criminal charges (Santos, 2012) to avoid the death penalty and was sentenced to life in prison.

A meta-analysis by Pirelli, Gottdiener, and Zapf (2011) of contemporary research on persons who were found not competent to stand trial reported that defendants diagnosed with a psychotic disorder were about eight times more likely to be found incompetent than defendants without a psychotic disorder. Moreover, unemployed people were twice as likely to be found not competent as defendants who were employed. Pirelli et al. also found that defendants with a previous psychiatric hospitalization were twice as likely to be found not competent to stand trial as those without a history of psychiatric hospitalization.

Several factors can influence a court decision that the defendant in the case is not competent to stand trial. Both cognitive abilities (e.g., being capable of making decisions, having a working memory, being able to attend to proceedings, being able to process events successfully) and psychiatric symptoms (e.g., psychosis, withdrawal, depression, hostility) can be crucial factors in a person's being able to stand trial. A mental health diagnosis does not establish whether a person is or is not competent to stand trial, but the mental health evaluation can assist the court in gaining an understanding as to why a defendant is not competent.

The value and impact of psychological evaluations to assess people charged with major crimes to determine if they are competent to stand trial have been widely studied (Bagby, Nicholson, Rogers, & Nussbaum, 1992; Bonnie, 1992; DeMatteo, Murrie, Anumba, & Keesler, 2011; Faust, 2012; R. I. Frederick, 2012; Grisso, 2003; Grisso, Cocozza, Steadman, Fisher, & Greer, 1994; Heilbrun, 2001; Megargee, 2006a, 2006b; Melton, Petrila, Poythress, & Slobogin, 2007; L. Miller, 2013; Stafford & Sadoff, 2011; Zapf, Boccaccini, & Brodsky, 2003). Psychological evaluations to appraise the sanity of defendants in court cases require careful consideration and meticulous attention to detail. Some research has found that psychological evaluations in sanity determinations often show disparity (Gowensmith, Murrie, & Boccaccini, 2013). Gowensmith et al. (2013) pointed out that agreement appears more likely in some cases than in others. The frequent disagreements between psychologists suggest a need for experts in the field to further develop appropriate standards and for practitioners to follow acceptable procedures for accurate psychological assessment. It is equally important for forensic psychologists to use psychological measures that are objective and not reliant on the practitioner's clinical judgment.

Psychological Assessment in Civil Commitment

Courts have been empowered to commit some mentally ill citizens to psychiatric institutions in order to protect them from harming themselves or others. The legal power of courts to commit citizens to mental health facilities was restricted somewhat in the 1970s, and the commitment process now requires much more judicial oversight with many more constitutional protections. People cannot be committed to a mental hospital simply because they are experiencing psychiatric problems. More legal oversight is now in place to ensure that a person's constitutional rights are protected.

The process of determining whether to utilize civil commitment laws is complex due to variation in case-specific factors, limitations in forensic psychologists' ability to predict future violent or suicidal behaviors, and the impact on establishing a therapeutic alliance with the examinee. The importance of determining an examinee's need for psychiatric treatment and the need to guarantee that the examinee's civil liberty rights are not violated must be carefully understood by the forensic psychologist. Within this context, forensic psychologists must be prepared to evaluate the examinee's current symptoms and collect relevant historical information when an examinee may be unable or unwilling to cooperate fully with the examination. A number of resources are available to provide the practitioner with further information about the commitment process and the process of evaluating examinees in this context (Burke, 2010; Mrad & Watson, 2011; Quinsey, Lalumière, Rice, & Harris, 1995).

Mental health practitioners may be called upon to evaluate the possibility that a psychiatric examinee might be dangerous, and there is strong evidence that psychologists can contribute to such an assessment (Cunningham & Sorensen, 2007; McNiel & Binder, 1994; Quinsey, Harris, Rice, & Cornier, 2006). The determination that an examinee is potentially dangerous can, however, be difficult to make (Bauer, Rosca, Khawalled, Gruzniewski, & Grinshpoon, 2003). Some have asserted that this is one of the most important decisions that forensic professionals can make (Burke, 2010). However, Scott, Quanbeck, and Resnick (2003) pointed out that the accuracy of predicting future violence is influenced by many factors, such as the circumstances of the evaluation and the length of time over which violence is predicted. When asked to perform an evaluation of dangerousness, a forensic psychologist has a clear responsibility to try to protect the public from potential violence or other uncontrolled behavior of a dangerous examinee. Megargee (2006a) provided a valuable discussion on assessment of violence and detailed the challenges psychologists experience in this assessment.

Not Guilty by Reason of Insanity Pleas

In some cases, defendants who are being charged with murder use the insanity defense—also known as the not guilty by reason of insanity, or NGRI, plea—as a means of escaping the legally prescribed consequences of their crimes (Borum, 2003; L. Miller, Sadoff, & Dattillo, 2011; Zapf, Golding, & Roesch, 2006). These defendants claim that they were not legally responsible for their criminal acts and instead invoke the long-standing doctrine that their acts, although guilty ones (*actus rea*), lacked moral responsibility because these acts were not intentional. The claim is that these defendants did not possess their full mental faculties at the time of the crime and did not know what they were doing (*mens rea*). The underlying assumption is that "insanity" somehow precludes or absolves the guilty intent.

Although the insanity defense can be appealing to the defense when the known facts are strongly against the defendant, the NGRI defense has been employed with low frequency, in less than 2% of capital cases in the United States (Lymburner & Roesch, 1999; Steadman et al., 1998). The ultimate outcome of NGRI pleas is inconsistent and of questionable success. Some research has shown that persons acquitted on the basis of an NGRI plea spend less time in a psychiatric hospital than persons who are convicted of crimes spend in prison (Lymburner & Roesch, 1999). States differ widely in the amount of time that persons found not guilty by reason of insanity are actually confined. For example, Callahan and Silver (1998) reported that in some states nearly all persons acquitted as NGRI were released within 5 years, whereas in other states conditional release has been much more difficult to obtain. The rearrest rates for persons who have been freed on NGRI claims vary considerably, with some studies reporting recidivism rates as high as 50% (Callahan & Silver, 1998; Monson, Gunnin, Fogel, & Kyle, 2001; Wiederanders, Bromley, & Choate, 1997).

Forensic psychologists need to be aware of the controversy surrounding the use of the NGRI plea. The NGRI defense in capital murder trials has prompted criticism and generated some controversy (Steadman et al., 1998). Some critics have contended that the objection to the insanity defense in capital crimes might reflect negative social attitudes toward insane people (Perlin, 1996). There has also been great concern, particularly in high-visibility cases, that guilty defendants may feign mental disorder and hence avoid criminal responsibility. Goldstein and Bursztajn (2011) pointed out that the stakes are very high when experts conduct evaluations of defendants who are facing trials for capital offenses. The expert must understand the structure of the procedures followed in the trial process and assure that only the most acceptable psychological measures are used in the evaluation. It should also be kept in mind that no psychological tests allow the expert to go back in time and fully understand the mind and behavior of the defendant as they were before the crime was committed.

Presentencing Evaluation of Criminal Offenders

In some cases where psychological factors are considered central to the alleged crime to avoid harsh and unusual punishment, a psychological evaluation is conducted to provide information about the convicted individual. Providing an appropriate sentencing recommendation is an attempt to prevent crime through changing human behavior (i.e., by inhibition of criminal behavior through fear of punishment, actual punishment, or the reform of the individual; Roberts, 2001).

The United States Sentencing Commission (2008) allows for reduced sentences if the defendant is determined to have committed the offense while suffering from a significantly reduced mental capacity that may have had an impact on his or her understanding of the crime. If the defendant shows a significantly impaired ability to understand the wrongfulness of the behavior or could not control behavior that he or she knows is wrongful, the defendant can be viewed as having "diminished capacity." See Atkins and Watson (2011), Cooke and Bleier (2011), and Felthous (2007) for discussions of the referral process for a forensic mental health evaluation, timing of the evaluation, determination of the focus and scope of the evaluation, ethical issues related to the evaluation, data collection, data interpretation, and the communication process needed. For further considerations to address conducting evaluations in forensic assessments, see the guidelines in the American Association for Correctional Psychology, Standards Committee, (2000) and the American Psychological Association (2010a).

Assessment of Dangerousness

Some criminal offenders and demonstrably aggressive psychiatric patients, who are considered dangerous, may require close supervision and perhaps special confinement until they are no longer dangerous or potentially violent. Although the rates of assaultive behavior vary from setting to setting, the overall number of violent or assaultive psychiatric patients is relatively low. Most psychiatrically disturbed patients reportedly show no tendency toward violence (Lamberg, 1998; Pinard & Pagani, 2001). Hodgins and Lalonde (1999) pointed out that some types of mental disorder are associated with violence. For example, the disorders that have an increased risk for violent behavior include schizophrenia, mania, personality disorder, substance abuse, and the rarer conditions of organic brain injury and Huntington's disease. Eronen, Hakola, and Tiihonen (1996) found that homicidal behavior among former psychiatric patients was more frequent among patients with schizophrenia and even more common among patients with antisocial personality or alcoholism. Steadman et al. (1998) found that psychiatric patients who abused alcohol were more likely to engage in violent behavior.

Forensic psychologists are often called upon to evaluate the possibility that an inmate or psychiatric patient might be dangerous. Such an assessment can be difficult to make (Bauer et al., 2003). However, violence assessment is one of the most important responsibilities that forensic psychologists can have (Burke, 2010). A forensic psychologist has a clear responsibility to try to protect the public from potential violence or other uncontrolled behavior of dangerous examinees (Scott, 2010). Research has shown that mental health professionals can contribute substantially to the evaluation of potential violence among inmates and patients (Cunningham & Sorensen, 2007; Megargee, 2009; Quinsey et al., 2006), at least on a short-term basis (Binder, 1999).

Several factors can influence the outcome of a forensic evaluation. These factors include the circumstances of the evaluation, the situational context in which the examinee is living, the amount of external stress in which the examinee is involved, whether alcohol or drugs are likely to be involved, the length of time over which violence is to be predicted, and whether the examinee has a past history of violence (Burke, 2010; Megargee, 2009). Megargee, Carbonell, Bohn, and Sliger (2001) identified inmates who were most likely to be predatory and those most likely to be preyed upon so they could be housed in different dormitories. The MMPI–2 was found to be better at assessing offenders' attitudes, mental health, emotional adjustment, and need for treatment or other professional interventions (needs assessment) than it is at estimating how dangerous offenders are (Megargee, 2006b).

When asked to perform evaluations of dangerousness, a forensic psychologist may choose to "err in the positive direction" and predict a greater percentage of examinees to be more dangerous than they actually are in order to protect others from being involved in violent acts (Megargee, 2009, 2013). Some authorities have raised questions about the effectiveness of prediction of dangerousness based upon evaluations by mental health professionals (Krauss & Lieberman, 2007).

A broad range of the personality factors and mental health symptoms that are important in forensic evaluations is addressed by the MMPI–2 scales when the defendant cooperates with the evaluation (Megargee et al., 2001; Pope, Butcher, & Seelen, 2006).

Assessment of Criminals in Prison

One of the most extensive areas of research devoted to understanding criminal offenders has been the assessment of people who have been convicted of crimes and are serving time in prison. Sellbom (2014) recently concluded that

> among such tests, the Minnesota Multiphasic Personality Inventory—2 (Butcher, et al., 2001) is the most frequently used in correctional settings (e.g., Boothby & Clements, 2000), and research has shown that this instrument can be quite useful in screening for psychological problems in offenders (Black et al., 2004; Forbey, Ben-Porath, & Gartland, 2009; McNulty et al., 2003). (p. 293)

Much of the research, as cited below, involves efforts to classify and understand the personality and behavior of convicted felons in order to properly place them in appropriate prison populations or settings that would best aid them in reestablishing their lives (for example, to determine their level of dangerousness to prevent harm to themselves or others; Megargee, 2009). Another important area in which convicted criminals have been carefully evaluated (see Jacobson & Wirt, 1969) involves efforts to determine their need for and psychological openness to treatment in order to develop appropriate rehabilitation programs.

MMPI/MMPI–2 ASSESSMENT OF CRIMINAL OFFENDERS

Hundreds of articles have been published on the MMPI/MMPI–2 in various forensic applications since the instrument was introduced (see Pope et al., 2006, or go to the websites http://www.kspope.com or http://www1.umn.edu/mmpi). The following studies describe some of the special contributions that were made to assure that the scales on the test were appropriate, reliable, and valid in predicting behavior of criminal populations. Major research studies and valuable summary projects are highlighted and their findings and implications are noted here. The early journal publications on the MMPI by Hathaway and McKinley (1940, 1942b) and McKinley and Hathaway (1944) provided several empirical scales that serve as a basis for assessment of criminal offenders, particularly the *Pd, Pa, Sc,* and *Ma* scales.

Beginning in the 1940s, the MMPI was found to be an effective instrument for examining mental health or personality problems in people undergoing criminal investigations or being assessed in prison placement examinations. Fry (1949), J. H. Clark (1952), and Smith (1955) found that inmates across a wide variety of prison populations showed a number of mental health and personality problems, with prominence on the *Pd* scale. Rosen and Mink (1961) conducted an evaluation of male prisoners and a normal sample to evaluate the MMPI for self-appraisal of personality factors, personal desirability, and social desirability. The normal individuals and prisoners differed in several respects: (a) in personal and social desirability profiles, (b) in numerical increase of items consisting of admission of antisocial and psychopathological tendencies, and (c) in *D* and *Pd* scores. Lawton and Kleban (1965) reported that a group of prisoners who were psychopathic on the MMPI–2, as measured by the *Pd* scale, were unable to manipulate their responses to appear nonpsychopathic.

The acceptability of the MMPI/MMPI–2 became well established in forensic assessment. Borum and Grisso (1995) conducted a survey of psychological test use in criminal forensic evaluations and reported that the MMPI–2 was the most widely used personality test in criminal evaluations; 96% of psychologists who used testing reported using the MMPI–2. Moreover, Ogloff (1995) provided a review and overview of the admissibility of the MMPI–2 in forensic cases, concluding that courts have generally held that the MMPI–2 can be admitted in cases in which the mental health status of the examinee is addressed.

An important line of investigation in criminal assessment was initiated by Davis and Sines (1971). They described a narrowly defined MMPI profile type (4-3 profile pattern) and the behavior problems associated with it in a state hospital, a state prison, and a university medical center. The MMPI 4-3 profile with the *Pd* and *Hy* scales elevated in a particular configuration entailed a behavior pattern that includes hostile-aggressive acting out. The frequency of this profile pattern and the social and psychological importance of the behavior pattern are important to researchers and forensic psychologists. Persons and Marks (1971) replicated the study by Davis and Sines. They also found the MMPI high-point pattern of 4-3 is associated with commission of violent acts. A group of 48 male inmates with the 4-3 code type were compared with groups having the three most frequently occurring other MMPI code types in a prison and with the institutional base rate for commission of violent criminal offenses. The 4-3 inmates committed significantly more violent acts than any of the other personality groups and significantly more violence than the base rates of inmates in general. Of the 4-3 inmates, 85% had a history of violence.

Although prisoners, as a group, tend to have homogeneous MMPI scale scores with a prominent elevation on the *Pd* scale, Sutker and Moan (1973) conducted research to determine if subgroups of prisoners vary on some characteristics. Using a large sample of prisoners in Louisiana, they found that inmates who showed notable behavioral difficulties within the prison setting reflected by significantly more disciplinary write-ups were characterized by more elevated scales on the MMPI—particularly the *F* and *Ma* scales—than were those who had incurred no disciplinary write-ups during their incarceration. Both groups showed elevations on the *Pd* scale.

Extensive research on prison populations has been conducted by a number of psychologists. Panton (1976) compared a sample of male inmates sentenced to be executed with a large sample of inmates from the general prison population. He found that Death Row inmates presented significantly higher scores on the *Pa* and *Sc* scales than did other inmates. He concluded that the test revealed more feelings of resentment, hopelessness, failure, frustration, isolation, and social alienation than exhibited by other inmates.

Megargee (1977, 2006a) developed a quantitative system for the classification of MMPI profiles in assessing adult criminal offenders (Megargee, 1977). Ten profile clusters were found to identify discrete prison groups: Able, Baker, Charlie, Delta, Easy, Foxtrot, George, Howe, Item, and Jupiter. Rules were developed to classify prisoners in each profile type. The 10 MMPI-based groups were found to differ on a broad range of factors such as family background, behavioral correlates, and tendency toward repeat offenses. The Megargee typology has been replicated in numerous subsequent studies. For example, Megargee (2009) reported that a federal prison for youthful offenders, Bohn (1979) used the MMPI-based offender classification system (Megargee & Bohn, 1979; Megargee et al., 2001) to identify those persons who were most likely to prey on others and those who were most likely to be victimized. These groups were assigned to separate living quarters and the violence rates were evaluated. The study showed that using the assignments to place prisoners reduced the rate of serious assaults by 46%. Other researchers have found the Megargee system to be of value in classifying inmates (Archer, Stredny, & Wheeler, 2013; Graham, 2012; Nieberding et al., 2003; Sellbom, 2014). Moreover, the Megargee system has also been found to work well in classifying prisoners across cultures (Rossi & Sloore, 2008; Sirigatti, Giannini, Laura-Grotto, & Giangrasso, 2002). However, the system is likely to be more valuable for classification of inmates into distinctive personality groups in research studies than for use in making individual clinical decisions. Potential users of the system should be aware that the computer-based scoring for the Megargee system is no longer available through the test distributor's products; thus, its use in assessment must to be classified by the user. Psychologists interested in using the Megargee offender classification system should refer to the following sources for scoring information (Megargee et al., 2001). The best resource for interpreting the Megargee types is in Megargee (2006b).

Carmin, Wallbrown, Ownby, and Barnett (1989) conducted a factor analytic study of the MMPI on a large sample of criminal offenders. They found that there were five factors that are comparable to prior factor-based research. Carmin et al. concluded that the study supported the utility of the MMPI with an offender population.

A broad variety of topics within prison populations has been studied with the MMPI or MMPI–2. Examples include recidivism (Pavelka, 1986), malingering among insanity defendants (Steffan, Morgan, Lee, & Sellbom, 2010; Wasyliw, Grossman, Haywood, & Cavanaugh, 1988), dangerousness (Nieberding, Moore, & Dematatis, 2002), violent offenders (Jones, Beidleman, & Fowler, 1981), personality of murderers (Pennuto, 2010), and sexual offenders (Grover, 2011; Lanyon, 1993; Rader, 1977).

A number of studies have addressed psychological treatment of prison inmates. For example, Jacobson and Wirt (1969) conducted an extensive study of the effectiveness of group psychotherapy for improving the adjustment of men in prison. They tested all the men with the MMPI prior to treatment and obtained follow-up data to examine the effectiveness of treatment. They found that those men with more neurotic profile patterns made greater progress than those with antisocial behavior problems. Guy, Platt, Zwerling, and Bullock (1985) examined the mental health status of 486 inmates (mean age 25 years) admitted to the Philadelphia prisons, using a test battery that included the Structured Clinical Interview, MMPI, Wide Range Achievement Test, Quick Test, and a demographic questionnaire. One hundred and sixty-one inmates also completed the Rorschach, and 96 inmates completed a psychiatric diagnostic interview. Approximately two thirds of the inmates were identifiable by relatively stringent criteria as being psychiatrically disturbed and in need of specific mental health treatment, and one third of the inmates were identifiable by all indicators of psychopathology used.

Assessment of Malingering in Pretrial Evaluations

One of the most important questions to be addressed in any evaluation of defendants in court cases is whether the information they provide through self-report is credible. Without reliable and valid information about the individual's reporting of information about himself or herself, the forensic psychologist cannot make acceptable conclusions or recommendations on the case. As described in Chapter 2, the assessment of response credibility is one of the most researched and effective sources of information the MMPI–2 can provide. See the discussion by Pennuto (2010) illustrating the value of the MMPI–2 validity scale in assessment of criminal offenders.

The MMPI–2 validity profile shown in Figure 11.1 indicates clearly that the defendant was uncooperative with the assessment and attempted to present an overly pathological MMPI–2 pattern. He responded in a highly inconsistent and exaggerated manner in order to appear psychologically disturbed. His VRIN T score elevation of 84 shows a highly inconsistent pattern of responding; all of his infrequency scale scores (F [T = 97], FB [T = 87], and Fp [T = 80]) indicate a pattern of clearly exaggerated responding

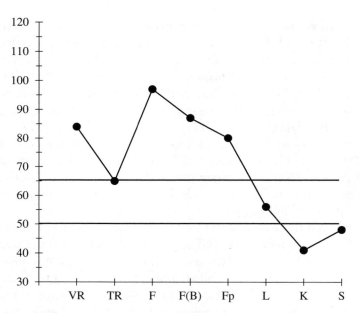

Figure 11.1. MMPI–2 profile of defendant who was uncooperative with the evaluation. Excerpted from the *MMPI®–2 (Minnesota Multiphasic Personality Inventory®—2) Manual for Administration, Scoring, and Interpretation, Revised Edition* by Butcher et al. Copyright © 2001 by the Regents of the University of Minnesota. Used by permission of the University of Minnesota Press. All rights reserved. "MMPI®" and "Minnesota Multiphasic Personality Inventory®" are trademarks owned by the Regents of the University of Minnesota.

throughout the test booklet. These validity scale elevations are interpreted as indicating an exaggerated pattern of endorsement that is not consistent with a cooperative and accurate portrayal of the defendant's symptoms and personality.

Common Scale Elevations and Code Types Among Criminal Offenders

As noted in the research, several MMPI clinical and content scales occur with great frequency in prison assessment settings: the *Pd, Pa,* and *Ma* scales (Hansen, Stokkeland, Johensen, Pallesen, & Wagge, 2013). The *Pd* scale, which was developed to detect empirically the personality problems in delinquent populations; the *Pa* scale, which addresses problems of suspicion and mistrust; and the *Ma* scale, which indicates acting-out and impulsivity, are three very prominent markers across correctional settings. The *Sc* scale is also prominent in some studies in which unusual thinking, chronic behavioral problems, cognitive problems, and social difficulties are reported. As noted above, the 4-3 code type is common among prison populations, as are 4-8, 4-6, and 4-9 code types.

CASE EXAMPLE

The defendant, Rachel, was a 23-year-old, married mother who was arrested and charged with neglect after her severely abused infant daughter was discovered alone in the house and dead in her crib by a family member. The child showed strong evidence of physical abuse: There were scars and bruises on her body, and she was found in a crib that had evidence of animal waste and trash. The defendant had left the scene of the crime and gone to a bar with friends; her husband was at work. Rachel was suspected of neglecting and smothering her child and underwent a psychological evaluation as part of the criminal investigation proceedings.

The MMPI–2 was administered as part of the psychological evaluation ordered by the court. The defendant's MMPI–2 validity profile was well within the normal range, indicating a valid performance on the test (see Figure 11.2). Her attitudes toward testing were open and appropriate and

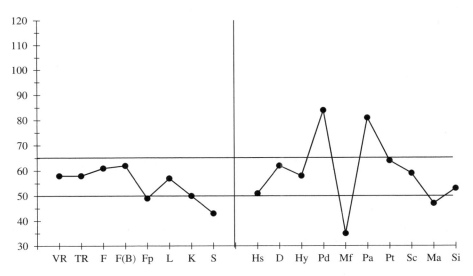

Figure 11.2. MMPI–2 basic validity and clinical scales profile for Rachel. Excerpted from the *MMPI®–2 (Minnesota Multiphasic Personality Inventory®–2) Manual for Administration, Scoring, and Interpretation, Revised Edition* by Butcher et al. Copyright © 2001 by the Regents of the University of Minnesota. Used by permission of the University of Minnesota Press. All rights reserved. "MMPI®" and "Minnesota Multiphasic Personality Inventory®" are trademarks owned by the Regents of the University of Minnesota.

showed no indication of falsely claiming problems. She freely admitted some psychological problems, which are described below.

The personality and behavioral descriptions for her very well defined MMPI–2 profile code, the *Pd* and *Pa* scales, are likely to clearly reflect the defendant's current personality functioning. Her profile is a good match with the empirical literature on which the 4-6 correlates have been derived. Individuals with this code type tend to show an extreme pattern of chronic psychological maladjustment. They are likely to be very immature and alienated, tending to manipulate others for their own gratification. The elevated scales also suggest that the defendant is quite self-indulgent, hedonistic, and narcissistic and has a grandiose conception of her capabilities. She may be quite aggressive with others, tends to be very impulsive, and acts out her problems. She rationalizes her difficulties and denies responsibility for her actions, preferring instead to blame other people. She tends to be very hostile, resentful, and irritable. She views the world as a threatening place, sees herself as having been unjustly blamed for others' problems, and feels that she is getting a raw deal out of life.

In addition to having elevations on the clinical scales, the defendant showed a high elevation on the content scale *ANG* that indicated a high degree of anger and a high potential for explosive behavior at times. She feels somewhat self-alienated and expresses some personal misgivings or a vague sense of remorse about past acts. She endorses statements that show some inability to control her anger. She may physically or verbally attack others when she is angry. The MMPI–2 clinical profile verified the severe personality and behavioral problems that were found in her past history of parental misbehavior.

SUMMARY

Psychological assessment, including personality evaluation, of people undergoing criminal investigations, those who have been convicted of crimes, or severely disturbed mental health patients, considered to be dangerous to themselves or others, is a prominent feature of forensic practice today. Conducting forensic psychological evaluations with examinees in criminal court cases is different in many respects from assessment in clinical settings, in which the examinee volunteers to undergo the self-disclosure required of a valid evaluation. It is important for forensic psychologists to keep in mind that the evaluations can be highly conflictual, and it is important to make certain that all the standards are followed as the evaluation proceeds.

As noted in this book, administration of psychological tests, such as the MMPI–2, requires careful monitoring to assure that the results are comparable to those employed in the normative data collection. This procedural requirement is particularly important in forensic evaluations, in which there is often a high degree of motivation for the examinee to appear different than he or she actually is. Deviations from standard procedures can result in inappropriate normative comparisons and invalid protocols. As noted in Chapter 1, many factors can influence examinees to produce invalid protocols in forensic settings. Assessment in court-ordered evaluations can be problematic indeed, with low levels of cooperation among examinees. The individual might be extremely disturbed, as in some civil commitment cases, and be unable to participate in responding to a self-report questionnaire.

This chapter provided an overview of the MMPI–2 scales that appear prominently in forensic evaluations. The *Pd*, *Pa*, *Ma*, and *Sc* scales and resulting code-type configurations that are encountered in forensic evaluations have a substantial research base to support the inclusion of the MMPI–2 in an assessment.

12

COMPUTER-BASED INTERPRETATION IN FORENSIC EVALUATIONS

Automated methods for scoring psychological tests have a long history in psychology (Atlis, Hahn, & Butcher, 2006; Butcher, Perry, & Dean, 2009). Computer-based systems for processing answers to psychological tests were developed in the 1950s in an effort to provide more efficient means of processing and summarizing the test takers' responses to the test items. In the 1960s, test developers began to use computers for scoring tests and analyzing data processing and to include test interpretation to explore more fully the interpretation of psychological tests (Meehl, 1954, 1956). One of the first computer-based systems for organizing and processing personality data was developed with the original Minnesota Multiphasic Personality Inventory (MMPI). Researchers at the Mayo Clinic in Rochester, Minnesota (Rome et al., 1962; Swenson & Pearson, 1964; Swenson, Rome, Pearson, & Brannick, 1965), developed a brief interpretive program for evaluating the MMPI responses of hospital patients being evaluated at the Mayo Clinic. This program provided a printout of clinical scale elevations in a profile along with

http://dx.doi.org/10.1037/14571-013
Using the MMPI–2 in Forensic Assessment, by J. N. Butcher, G. A. Hass, R. L. Greene, and L. D. Nelson

a listing of a number of personality correlates or symptoms that are typically associated with the highest scale elevations. The Mayo screening program printed out descriptive statements (from a total of 110 possibilities) that were correlated with particular scale elevations. This early scoring system enabled psychologists to provide needed consultation on large numbers of patients quickly and economically. This approach facilitated the psychological screening of individuals who otherwise might never have received a full psychological evaluation (Fowler, 1967).

Shortly after the Mayo MMPI interpretation program became operational, Raymond Fowler (1969) developed a more comprehensive and complex computer program with the Roche Psychiatric Service Institute (Fowler, 1964, 1965, 1967, 1969, 1972; Gehring & Blaser, 1972). The Roche program took computer interpretation to a more advanced level by creating a narrative report on the basis of the MMPI scale configurations. This program was developed to provide an assessment of the individual's cooperativeness by evaluating his or her response attitudes and to provide interpretive statements based on the highest clinical scale elevations. The computer output generated a three-page report to provide symptomatic information that could guide the practitioner's clinical evaluation.

Computer interpretation programs for the MMPI expanded further during the 1970s and usually included clinically useful narrative reports aimed at assisting psychiatrists and psychologists in arriving at clinical diagnoses and personality descriptions based on the MMPI item responses. Descriptions of these earlier MMPI interpretation systems can be found in Butcher (1987), Caldwell (1970), Lachar (1974), Finney, (1966), and Fowler (1987). Computer-based MMPI reports came to be widely used by practitioners during this period.

COMPUTER-BASED MMPI–2 SCORING AND INTERPRETATION SYSTEMS

This section provides a description of MMPI–2 interpretation by computer and uses a case example to illustrate the information that can be available in computer-based reports. The extensive range of the computer applications for MMPI–2 has been summarized by Butcher (2013b) and Butcher, Derksen, Sloore, and Sirigatti (2003).

MMPI Extended Score Report

The Extended Score Report was originally developed by Butcher (1982) to provide in-depth scoring information to accompany the Minnesota Report computerized interpretation system for the MMPI published by the University of Minnesota Press and distributed by National Computer Systems. A number of additional scales were scored beyond the validity, clinical, and Wiggins content scales and supplementary scales such as Dependency (*Dy*), Dominance (*Do*), Social Responsibility (*Re*), and MacAndrew Alcoholism (*MAC*). The Extended Score Report also included item-specific information with the Koss and Butcher (1973) critical items. The Koss–Butcher critical item sets were developed empirically from item content lists that keyed item responses to several diagnostic classification areas that enabled Minnesota Report users to focus upon specific symptom areas in follow-up interviews or in treatment sessions in order to seek out more specific personality information about examinees.

The basic features of the Extended Score Report were continued in the Minnesota Report system after the programs were revised when the MMPI was restandardized and the MMPI–2 was published in 1989. The name was changed to Supplementary Score Report. The Extended Score Report continued without the computer narrative report when the MMPI–2 publisher, the University of Minnesota Press, and the test distributor decided to publish the Extended Score Reports separately from the Minnesota Reports.

The Minnesota Report for the MMPI–2

Butcher (1982) developed the Minnesota Report, the official interpretation system for the MMPI–2 that is owned by the University of Minnesota and managed by the test publisher, the University of Minnesota Press, and distributed by Pearson Assessments, Minneapolis, Minnesota. This interpretation program is the most widely used computer interpretive system available and provides reports for clinical, forensic, personnel, and adolescent settings. Since its development, it has been geared toward clinical relevance and ease of use, with information based on empirical test correlates (Butcher, 1987). This computer interpretation system includes scores for validity, clinical, content, and many supplementary scales. The Minnesota Report was developed to provide test users with a comprehensive personality and symptomatic picture in a readable, user-friendly format. The Minnesota Report computer system is best viewed as an "electronic textbook" or correlate research that practitioners may consult to obtain the most likely personality and symptomatic data available and pertinent to the profile or scores in question (see http://www.umn.edu/mmpi for more information).

The Minnesota Report was developed as a conservative, research-based approach to automated MMPI–2 interpretation to provide the test user with the most validated and accepted personality and symptom descriptors for the examinee (Butcher, 2005). The goals for the Minnesota Report were to

- incorporate an extensive review of the individual's test-taking attitudes to assure that only valid protocols would be interpreted;
- use as basic descriptors the empirical scale and code-type correlates that are well validated by research findings;
- provide the practitioner with a broad range of personality and mental health symptom data available from the validity and clinical scales and on the MMPI–2 content scales, supplementary scales, critical items, rules, and indices;
- provide information about the relative frequency of the profile types that are used in interpretations typical in different clinical settings;
- focus on specific populations—mental health inpatients, mental health outpatients, general medical, chronic pain, alcohol and drug, college counseling, and correctional—taking into account demographic factors;
- expand the available information in the report in order to incorporate additional new scales, indices, or interpretive procedures that met high standards of validity, reliability, and utility when they become available; and
- provide periodic updates for the report in order to incorporate ongoing research and address the needs of the test user.

Illustrative Information Available in Minnesota Report Evaluations

The Minnesota Report provides information about the individual's response attitudes in taking the test as well as personality and symptom information that might characterize his or her clinical picture. This general information is provided, and special problem areas, such as substance abuse, marital problems, and hostility, are highlighted. The highlighted information includes the following categories: validity pattern; narrative report (including base-rate frequency information); basic and supplementary scales profile; content scales profile; supplementary score report; the *PSY-5* scales; content component scales; critical items; omitted items; and item responses (optional).

Readers may obtain sample reports for the Minnesota Reports for Forensic Settings from the Pearson website (see Pearson Assessments, n.d.).

INTERNATIONAL ADAPTATIONS OF COMPUTER REPORTS

Computer-based reports based upon the MMPI/MMPI–2 have been used effectively in a number of countries other than the United States. The Roche Psychiatric Service Institute, based in Switzerland, made efforts to expand its MMPI interpretation program, described earlier, for use in several European languages, in addition to English, during the 1970s. During this period, a computer-based MMPI interpretation system was developed in Italy by Pancheri and his colleagues (Pancheri, 1971; Pancheri & Liotti, 1968). They provided great impetus to the adaptation of the original MMPI in Italian, and their work on computer-based interpretation of the test went a long way in establishing the credibility of the MMPI for personality assessment in Italy.

The Minnesota Report has been adapted and researched empirically in a number of countries. Butcher et al. (1998) conducted a study in which MMPI–2 computerized reports were compared in a number of countries, such as Australia, Norway, Korea, Italy, Iran, Holland, and Israel. This study illustrated the broad generalizability of computer-based evaluations across cultures. The clinical utility of computer-based test interpretation of the MMPI—Adolescent was addressed in an extensive case analysis with adolescents in Butcher, Ellertsen, et al. (2000). The utility of the MMPI–2 in assessing response styles of examinees in Australia was demonstrated by Shores and Carstairs (1998). Finally, the Minnesota Report was translated into Dutch (referred to as the Nijmegen Report) and has been used successfully in evaluating examinees' mental health problems and personality in Holland and Belgium since 2006.

GENERAL ACCEPTABILITY OF COMPUTER-BASED ASSESSMENT

Although computer-based test interpretation has gained broad acceptance in practice, some questions have been raised concerning its use. One concern is that computer-based administration formats differ from traditional, paper-and-pencil administration methods. However, a number of studies have shown that differences between administrative formats are negligible in magnitude (Lambert, Andrews, Rylee, & Skinner, 1987; Schuldberg, 1988; Watson et al., 1990). Pinsoneault (1996), for example, concluded that there was "near perfect" correspondence between computer and booklet administrations on the basis of findings that were 92% to 97% in agreement. Jemelka, Wiegand, Walker, and Trupin (1992) administered several computer-based instruments to incarcerated felons; group administration of the MMPI was included in their battery. Forensic psychologists also interviewed the individuals and made their own independent diagnoses. The overall concordance between the two methods was 82%. Finger and Ones (1999) conducted a meta-analysis of 14 studies and concluded that administering the MMPI by computer instead of booklet had little negative impact on scale scores.

A second concern is whether computer reports dehumanize the assessment process. However, Fowler (1987) noted that computer reports are no more impersonal than other assessment methods. Computer reports are impartial to which examinee is being evaluated and will make the same comments about all examinees who have the same pattern of MMPI–2 scores. Many triers of fact find these comments useful.

A third concern is that computer-based psychological reports might ultimately replace forensic psychologists. Fowler (1967) discounted this view as well, pointing out that most authorities do not view computer-assisted assessment reports as being replacements for clinical assessments but as having been designed for use as "raw data" in the clinical report process. The reports should be considered additional information to augment data obtained by other means. Computer-based reports are not designed to serve as replacements for other clinical information (Butcher, 2011). It is important to ensure that computerized narratives are internally consistent and provide information that can be integrated with specific demographic and other contextual information.

A fourth concern is that practitioners might place too much trust in them because of their high-quality visual appearance. There might be a tendency for some people to place more confidence in computer-based reports because they appear professional and therefore are the "ultimate scientific word." In commercial test practice today, however, some publishers produce computer-based tests without sufficient empirical research support for the test. They might appear more trustworthy than they actually are. Thus, it behooves the psychologist to evaluate carefully the research underlying a particular computer-based product before using it in a forensic application.

Finally, forensic psychologists should not blindly rely upon computer test results or treat their conclusions as revealed truth. Computer reports are not intended to replace careful clinical observation and judgment or to allow forensic psychologists to circumvent the process of thoroughly integrating all available data, whether computer generated or not. Forensic psychologists should have sufficient working knowledge of the strengths and limitations of the personality instruments on which such reports are based to carefully evaluate the accuracy and usefulness of the results obtained.

COMPUTER-BASED INTERPRETATIONS IN COURT CASES

Overall, there has been a broader yet cautious acceptance of computer-based assessment as a means of providing personality and mental-health information in forensic assessments. As Greene (2005) concluded, "Computer scoring and computer interpretation of all psychological assessment techniques should become the basis for the psychological report" and "psychological assessment should become a computer-based field" (p. 6).

Computer-based MMPI–2 interpretations can reflect specific research-based correlates that are pertinent to the examinee if he or she has responded in a frank and open manner. However, as discussed in Chapter 2, many people being evaluated in forensic examinations may not report their behaviors and symptoms in an accurate manner. Therefore, it is critical that the validity scales are carefully evaluated in order to assure that the protocol is interpretable.

Computer interpretations generate extensive and research-based hypotheses about the individual and can substantially aid the psychologist conducting the examination. The computer-based report is a professional-to-professional consultation and serves as a source of hypotheses and descriptions that can be incorporated into a report. Computer reports are not considered a final product but a source of information that has been developed for the instrument. It is the responsibility of the forensic psychologist to evaluate the information the computer report generates and incorporate it into the final report in the context of other history, observations, and psychological information obtained in the evaluation. Thus, the narrative report is a source of hypotheses and not a final, stand-alone set of conclusions. Forensic psychologists need to be able to provide their rationale for information that is incorporated into the final report as well be as be prepared to defend the exclusion of portions that are not included (i.e., they cannot selectively choose only those points that support their position). They have to be able to explain their testing strategy in defense of their report. Forensic psychologists are ultimately responsible for any interpretations that are made of an assessment technique, even when automated or computerized interpretations are used (Ethical Principles of Psychologists and Code of Conduct, 9.06; American Psychological Association, 2010a).

USING COMPUTER-BASED MMPI–2 REPORTS IN FORENSIC CASES

In Chapter 13, we cover the topic of writing forensic reports. The potential contribution of computer-based psychological reports in forensic cases and in providing information for the forensic report is described below.

Computer-based psychological assessment can serve an important role in forensic evaluations. Computer reports should be considered to be preliminary or provisional working resources, analogous to hypotheses that forensic psychologists might collect by researching the published literature to find those that might be relevant to the profile at hand. Forensic psychologists who use computer reports need to be familiar with the research literature to be able to cite the background sources if questioned in cross-examination (Pope, Butcher, & Seelen, 2006). Blau (1984) noted that, "when relying on computer-based test interpretation, the forensic psychologist should be familiar with the rationale and validity of the interpretations and be prepared to justify their utilization in the judicial matter at hand" (p. 184).

The descriptions provided in computer interpretation of the MMPI–2 are typically summaries of correlates for a particular group of individuals that match the client's MMPI–2 scores. Most often, this group is based on the MMPI–2 code type, the two highest clinical scales at or above a T score of 65, but the group can be defined by more complex rules including several clinical, content, and supplementary scales, or profile analyses. It is important for the forensic psychologist to evaluate how well this specific person fits the profile of the group of individuals in the prototype and ways in which he or she might differ from the group profile. The psychologist should be familiar with the underlying research supporting which specific aspects of the automated or computerized interpretation are relevant for this particular person.

The psychologist should be able to provide a rationale for exclusions of report conclusions that are not included in his or her summary report. An important reason for the forensic psychologist to be knowledgeable about the information incorporated in computer-based reports is that there may be hypotheses or descriptions in the report that do not apply to a particular case. In such instances, the forensic psychologist may choose to use only those most likely statements from the report that are considered to match the case and to ignore the others. This approach is appropriate because it is the forensic psychologist who has the final responsibility for deciding what elements of a psychological evaluation are appropriate for a particular examinee. However, if the opposing counsel conducts an adequate discovery, the computer-generated printout will be available as a basis for cross-examination. Therefore, as described below, the psychologist may wish to include in the written forensic report the reasoning process that led him or her to reject certain hypotheses set forth by the computer program. A computerized report sometimes is entered directly into evidence and serves as the focus of direct and cross-examination.

Pope et al. (2006) pointed out that forensic psychologists may be faced with discordant test findings or with a computer-based report that includes statements that seem irrelevant or misleading in the specific case. As discussed, the forensic psychologist may need to introduce in direct examination or defend in cross-examination the decision not to interpret potentially discrepant findings or not to include tangential information in a computerized report. Shapiro (1991) advised expert witnesses to anticipate controversial issues and reduce the impact of potentially weak points during direct examination. The forensic psychologist needs to anticipate in advance what some of the challenges to the opinion will be and to make a frank assessment of the weakest parts of the evaluation and opinion. The psychologist must deal with these challenges in the forensic report and in direct examination, rather than create the impression that the psychologist is surprised by these challenges when they arise on cross-examination.

If the information used is provided in a computer-based report, the conclusions must be tailored to fit the client's situation. Pope et al. (2006) pointed out that using the personality descriptors as they appear in the computerized report is legitimate and appropriate (a) if they are relevant to the case at hand, (b) if the source is clearly and explicitly noted, and (c) if quotation marks are used around any phrases from the report that are taken verbatim as opposed to paraphrased. In all of these circumstances, the forensic psychologist retains the ultimate responsibility for any interpretations that are made of an assessment technique even when automated or computerized interpretations are used.

CASE EXAMPLE

The following case study provides an illustration of the computer-based interpretation of a client's MMPI–2 performance in a personal injury case that resulted from a stressful situation she experienced in the workplace.

Reason for the Evaluation

Beth V., age 52, married with two children, was recommended for a psychological assessment by her attorney as a result of her allegations of sexual harassment by her employer. She reported that there were a number of incidents in which her supervisor used explicit sexual terminology and invited her to come to his apartment over the past year. After she rejected his propositions, their working relationship became very strained and she became depressed and anxious about her future. She sought psychological treatment for her anxiety and depression through a psychotherapist. After discussion of the incidents, Ms. V. decided to file the lawsuit against her supervisor for workplace harassment.

Background

Ms. V. completed high school and worked in retail; she married her husband when she was 21 years of age. She and her husband have two children, ages 28 and 25, both of whom are currently employed and married. Ms. V. has worked during much of her adult life in retail or in secretarial/office management positions. Two years ago her husband was diagnosed with cancer and has undergone several surgical procedures. He has been unable to work full time for the past year, and Ms. V. has assumed more responsibility for her family's support.

Information From the MMPI–2

As in any forensic evaluation, it is important to determine if the client's test performance was valid and not an exaggerated, invalid protocol. The client's MMPI–2 performance has several scale elevations that require attention.

First, an examination of the client's MMPI–2 scores does not reflect exaggerated responding (see Figure 12.1).[1] All of the test validity indicators are within the valid and acceptable range of elevation. None of the infrequency scales suggest exaggerated responding or unusual response sets. Moreover, the K ($T = 30$), L ($T = 43$), and S ($T = 30$) scales, which measure test defensiveness, are not elevated in a T score range that raises concern. In fact, all of the defensiveness scales are extremely low in elevation, indicating a very frank and open response approach to the items. These scores are well below average, suggesting the possibility that she has low self-confidence and low self-esteem.

On the basis of the MMPI–2 results it can be concluded that the clinical, content and supplementary scales can be interpreted because the client's responses to the test items show valid and cooperative responding. The current MMPI–2 textbooks (Butcher, 2011; A. F. Friedman, Lewak, Nichols, & Webb, 2001; Graham, 2012; Greene, 2011; Nichols, 2011) support the conclusion that the client has produced a valid and interpretable pattern on the F ($T = 65$), FB ($T = 62$), and Fp ($T = 49$) scales and indicate that the MMPI–2 symptom scales can be interpreted to indicate mental health problems. The MMPI–2 test manual (Butcher et al., 2001) indicates that her infrequency scale T scores show that her performance is "likely valid.

---

[1]The psychologist for the defense inaccurately concluded that the client's MMPI–2 performance was invalid. The defense psychologist did not do an in-person assessment of the client or use the full MMPI–2 but based his conclusions on the MMPI–2–RF by excerpting the items from the full MMPI–2 that the client had completed. As described in Chapter 14, the MMPI–2–RF validity measures are not equivalent or comparable to those on the MMPI–2.

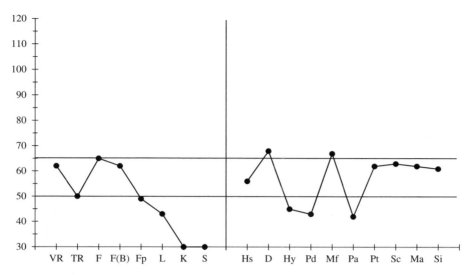

Figure 12.1. MMPI–2 basic validity and clinical scale profile for Ms. V. Excerpted from the *MMPI®–2 (Minnesota Multiphasic Personality Inventory®—2) Manual for Administration, Scoring, and Interpretation, Revised Edition* by Butcher et al. Copyright © 2001 by the Regents of the University of Minnesota. Used by permission of the University of Minnesota Press. All rights reserved. "MMPI®" and "Minnesota Multiphasic Personality Inventory®" are trademarks owned by the Regents of the University of Minnesota.

Test taker accurately reported a number of psychological problems" (p. 18). The validity interpretation of the Minnesota Report shown in Exhibit 12.1 provides the hypothesis that the client responded in a frank and open manner but may have been somewhat self-critical in her responding.

Second, the MMPI–2 clinical scales, as shown in Figure 12.1, and the MMPI–2 content scales, as shown in Figure 12.2, provide clear hypotheses concerning Ms. V.'s current mental health symptoms. The clinical scale Depression ($T = 68$) reflects a likely moderate depressive disorder along with symptoms of anxiety (ANX, $T = 66$; Pt, $T = 71$) and obsessive characteristics (OBS, $T = 75$) and cognitive difficulties (Sc, $T = 70$). The mental health symptoms she is presenting likely result from high stress, as reflected in the high elevation on the Keane Posttraumatic Stress Scale ($T = 70$) and the Pt scale.

Third, in addition to the clinical symptom pattern the client shows, several MMPI–2 scores indicate a number of possible personality factors that should be taken into consideration in evaluating her psychological adjustment and her likely success in management of the problems she is experiencing. The client also reported personality factors such as low self-esteem, difficult interpersonal relationships (Si, $T = 61$; Ma, $T = 66$), and cynical

EXHIBIT 12.1
Minnesota Report Narrative for Beth V.

Profile Validity
The client responded to the items in a frank and open manner, producing a valid MMPI–2 profile. She cooperated with the test administration and endorsed some psychological symptoms. She may tend to be overly self-critical. These hypotheses should be kept in mind when evaluating the clinical patterns reflected in the profile.

Symptomatic Patterns
The behavioral correlates included in the narrative report are likely to provide a good description of the client's current personality functioning. The clinical scale prototype used in the report, which incorporates correlates of *D*, is based on scores with high profile definition. The client has feelings of personal inadequacy and tends to view the future with uncertainty and pessimism. She tends to lack confidence in herself, is somewhat moody, is rather sensitive to criticism, and may tend to blame herself or things that go wrong. She seems to worry excessively, has low energy and a slow personal tempo, and is somewhat dissatisfied with her life. She is experiencing a depressed mood at this time. This profile may result from a stressful environment or a recent traumatic experience. The possibility of such circumstances should be evaluated.

In addition, the following description is suggested by the content of the client's item responses. According to her response content, there is a strong possibility that she has seriously contemplated suicide. The client's recent thinking is likely to be characterized by possessiveness and indecision. She reports some antisocial beliefs and attitudes, admits to rule violations, and acknowledges antisocial behavior in the past. She endorsed a number of unusual, bizarre ideas that suggest some difficulties with her thinking. The client's response content suggests that she feels intensely fearful about many objects and activities. This hypersensitivity and fearfulness appear to be generalized at this point and may be debilitating in social and work situations.

Profile Frequency
Profile interpretation can be greatly facilitated by examining the relative frequency of clinical scale patterns in various settings. The client's high-point clinical scale score (*D*) occurs in 7% of the MMPI–2 normative sample of women. However, only 4.4% of the women have *D* scale peak scores at or above a *T* score of 65, and only 2.1% have well-defined *D* spikes.

This high-point MMPI–2 score is relatively frequent in various samples of female medical patients. In the Pearson Assessments medical sample, the high-point clinical scale score on *D* occurs in 18.6% of the women. Moreover, 16.5% of the women have *D* as the peak score at or above a *T* score of 65 and 8.9% have well-defined peak *D* scores in that range. Her MMPI–2 profile peak score on the *D* scale occurs as a high point in 19% of women in chronic pain samples (L. S. Keller & Butcher, 1991).

This MMPI–2 profile peak score on the *D* scale occurs with modest frequency among individuals involved in personal injury litigation. Butcher (1997b) found that only 7.6% of personal injury litigants have *D* as a well-defined high-point score. Among litigants who produce an elevated *F* score relative to *L* and *K*, this MMPI–2 profile peak score on the *D* scale occurs with very high frequency (34.1%), but only 7.3% are well defined at or above a *T* of 65. This is one of the most frequent high-point profiles among nondefensive litigants.

EXHIBIT 12.1
Minnesota Report Narrative for Beth V. (*Continued*)

Profile Stability

The relative elevation of the highest scales in her clinical profile reflects high defini-tion. If she is retested at a later date, the peak scores are likely to retain their relative salience. Her high-point score on *D* is likely to remain stable over time. Short-term test–retest studies have shown a correlation of 0.77 for this high-point score.

Interpersonal Relations

Individuals with similar profiles tend to be hesitant and pessimistic about personal relationships and may feel rather inadequate in social situations. She is somewhat shy, with some social concerns and inhibitions. She is a bit hypersensitive about what others think of her and is occasionally concerned about her relationships with others. She appears to be somewhat inhibited in personal relationships and social situations, and she may have some difficulty expressing her feelings toward others. She appears to see herself as helpless and dependent, and she relies on her hus-band to take care of her.

The content of this client's MMPI–2 responses suggests the following additional information concerning her interpersonal relationships. She appears to have rather cynical views about life. Any efforts to initiate new behavior may be colored by her negativism. She may view relationships as threatening and harmful. Although she is experiencing some family conflict at this time, she does not consider it a major problem.

Mental Health Considerations

Symptoms of a mood disorder are prominent in her clinical picture. Her response content is consistent with the antisocial features in her history. These factors should be taken into consideration when arriving at a clinical diagnosis. Her unusual thinking and bizarre ideas should be taken into consideration in any diag-nostic formulation.

The item content she endorsed indicates attitudes and feelings that suggest a low capacity for change. Her potentially high resistance to change should be addressed early in treatment to promote a more treatment-expectant attitude.

In any intervention of psychological evaluation program involving occupational adjustment, her negative work attitudes could become an important problem to overcome. She has a number of attitudes and feelings that could interfere with work adjustment.

Personal Injury Considerations

She responded to the MMPI–2 validity items in a very open manner. She reported a number of mental health symptoms, which is relatively common in personal injury litigation in which the client openly describes problems.

Some problems are clearly evident in her MMPI–2 profile. The mood symp-toms she reported could affect her daily functioning. It is not clear from her profile whether these problems are reactive to negative life events or are more long-term in nature. However, she is presently depressed, unhappy, dysphoric, pessimistic, self-deprecating, guilt-prone, and lethargic. She reports numerous somatic complaints, such as weakness and fatigue. In addition, she reports feeling tense, worried, and indecisive. She lacks self-confidence and feels useless and unable to function effectively much of the time. She is likely to maintain a great deal of psychological distance from others and actively avoids interpersonal involvement.

(*continues*)

In addition to the problems indicated by her MMPI–2 clinical scale scores, she endorsed some items on the content scales that could reflect difficulties for her. Her proneness to experience problems with anxiety, fear, obsessive thinking, and unusual thoughts might make it difficult for her to think clearly or function effectively. The potential impact of her antisocial attitudes and behavior requires further assessment. Her likely irresponsible behavior should be assessed to determine if it is affecting her current situation.

attitudes toward others (CYN, $T = 75$). She reported having work adjustment problems (WRK, $T = 73$) that could have resulted from her negative experiences in the workplace. The Treatment Potential Scale ($T = 69$) provides an indication that the client might have difficulty making behavioral changes in therapy.

The Minnesota Report narrative, shown in Exhibit 12.1, highlights the mental health problems Ms. V. is currently reporting. The computer-based report was not designed to serve as the final product in a psychological evaluation but to develop a set of hypotheses based upon the most likely,

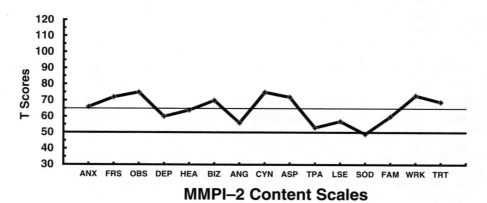

MMPI–2 Content Scales

Figure 12.2. MMPI–2 content scale profile for Ms. V. Excerpted from the *MMPI®–2 (Minnesota Multiphasic Personality Inventory®—2) Manual for Administration, Scoring, and Interpretation, Revised Edition* by Butcher et al. Copyright © 2001 by the Regents of the University of Minnesota. Used by permission of the University of Minnesota Press. All rights reserved. "MMPI®" and "Minnesota Multiphasic Personality Inventory®" are trademarks owned by the Regents of the University of Minnesota.

research-based, descriptors that summarize the client's self-description. The report summary provides an overview of the client's item response approach to the test. Ms. V's protocol was valid and interpretable and provided a cooperative and valid approach to the test. Based upon her honest and straightforward response to the items, the symptom scales provided a likely accurate self-portrayal of her mental health status.

How well did the computer-based Minnesota Report narrative perform in describing the personality and mental health problems acknowledged by the client? The Minnesota Report was designed to provide a summary of the most likely symptom pattern that describes the client's current mental health status. The report also incorporated personality factors that the MMPI–2 correlates reflect. Finally, the report includes information about the individual's mental health status that have been associated with the various item clusters that the client endorsed (in this case, for example, frequency data from relevant research populations, attitudes about work-related symptoms, and potential for benefiting from psychological intervention that can be gleaned from the literature).

SUMMARY

Computer-based methods for scoring and interpreting psychological tests have a long history in psychology. Computer scoring of examinee responses were developed in the 1950s. Efforts at processing and interpreting test results began in the 1960s, primarily with the MMPI because of its objective interpretive history and empirical base. More comprehensive and complex computer programs that provided computer-based narrative MMPI reports began in the United States in the 1960s. They have continued to evolve and provide psychologists with various system options. Computerized reports based upon the MMPI–2 have been developed or adapted for use in languages other than English and countries other than the United States.

Computer-generated MMPI and MMPI–2 interpretive reports have gained broad acceptance in the professional community and are commonly used in clinical, personnel screening, and forensic settings to provide information about examinees. The use of computer-based reports by an assessment professional is considered to be a professional-to-professional communication of information. Many forensic practitioners rely upon computer-based interpretive systems to provide the basic correlate information from the MMPI–2 or MMPI—Adolescent research database to develop their evaluations. Information from computerized narratives can provide an informative context for the evaluation, particularly with regard to response sets to evaluate the level of cooperation the examinee has engaged in during the assessment. If their protocols are sufficiently valid to allow test interpretation, the rich database of personality correlates can provide valuable information in a forensic evaluation. A case study in which the computer-based interpretation system, the Minnesota Report, was used in a personal injury case was included to illustrate how computer interpretation can provide summary reports that characterize client's personality and problems.

It is the responsibility of the forensic practitioner to integrate computer-based MMPI–2 information into the forensic report and have the necessary knowledge to support the information provided in court cases.

13

WRITING ASSESSMENT EVALUATION REPORTS IN FORENSIC SETTINGS

In their seminal article about conflict between forensic and therapeutic roles, Greenberg and Shuman (1997) clearly articulated the differences between being a care provider and being an expert to the court. In their view, "The role of a forensic examiner is, among other things, to offer opinions regarding historical truth and the validity of the psychological aspects of a litigant's claims" (p. 53). This role contrasts sharply not only with the role of a therapeutic psychologist but also with the role of the attorney who has requested the psychological evaluation in the first place. It sometimes contrasts with the court's expectations as well.

The tension between forensic psychology and law has been noted as including assumptions that forensic psychologists are "hired guns" and other, less kind epithets (Mossman, 1999) and that the law regards opinions of forensic experts with contempt (Melton, Petrila, Poythress, & Slobogin, 2007). Not only lawyers but also the law and the courts have difficulty dealing with the gray areas and nuance that forensic psychologists tend to present in their

http://dx.doi.org/10.1037/14571-014
Using the MMPI–2 in Forensic Assessment, by J. N. Butcher, G. A. Hass, R. L. Greene, and L. D. Nelson
Copyright © 2015 by the American Psychological Association. All rights reserved.

testimony and reports (Weinstein & Weinstein, 2010). The rigid objectivity to which forensic psychologists have to adhere, in contrast with the advocacy role of the attorneys, is another source of tension. No less important is that the struggle to communicate effectively in reports and testimony the work and opinions formed during a forensic assessment is never-ending for the profession. Forensic psychological practice is complex and like no other field in psychology. Because the stakes of a forensic assessment are so high, sometimes contributing to decisions of life and death, the focus on the level of practice and the continued systematic development of the profession is intense.

In 1996, Borum and Grisso wrote about the concern that many forensic evaluations have been faulted for not addressing the psycholegal issue at hand, providing opinions without supporting data or adequate reasoning, and falling short in their collection and communication of relevant information on which to base an opinion (p. 297). This argument continues to come up in the forensic psychology literature (Grisso, 2010) and includes growing concerns with the unreliability related to the examiner's agency, allegiance, and sometimes personality and attitudes in relation to decision making (T. M. S. Neal & Grisso, 2014).

It is important that forensic reports are workwise developed and consistent with ethical principles and published codes that guide forensic testimony (American Academy of Psychiatry and the Law, 2005; American Association for Correctional Psychology, 2010; American Psychiatric Association, 2013; American Psychological Association [APA], 2010a). In particular, the Specialty Guidelines for Forensic Psychology (APA, 2013b) include extensive guidelines around the issues that are at the core of forensic practice. The sentiment that high standards are required for forensic reports is illustrated by a maxim provided by Stan Brodsky (2013): "Excellent testimony is facilitated by precise, carefully written reports. Rewrite again and again to produce reports that are (almost) bulletproof" (p. 179).

This chapter addresses the structure of reports communicating tests results based on the Minnesota Multiphasic Personality Inventory—2 (MMPI–2) that are specifically prepared for forensic testimony in court cases. Special considerations to take when reporting MMPI–2 results are discussed.

RELEVANCE OF THE MMPI–2 IN THE FORENSIC REPORT

This book has described and illustrated the use of the MMPI–2 in different forensic contexts, including criminal, civil, family, and immigration law. The range of psycholegal concepts to fit the legal standards in these areas of forensic practice is extensive and diverse. Some of these fields, or aspects of them, have a rich and vast empirical support for the use of the MMPI–2 in the evaluations, whereas immigration, domestic violence, and parent capacity evaluations are still developing the empirical support of the MMPI–2 for the particular application. However, in all these areas of forensic practice, the MMPI–2 was relevant to understanding psychological constructs that underlie the expert opinion.

Given that the strength of the MMPI–2's psychometric properties and popularity meets criteria for evidence, as explained in Chapter 1, the only issue at stake is the MMPI–2's relevance to the legal issue at hand. As noted by Otto (2002), "The question is not whether it is appropriate to use the MMPI–2 in forensic settings, but rather, for what purposes may the MMPI–2 be used in forensic settings?" (p. 71).

The demand for the examiner in forensic reports is to establish the link between those underlying constructs and factors measured by the MMPI–2. The forensic psychologist is tasked in particular with connecting the data regarding psychopathology, behavioral style, and response style derived from the MMPI–2 with the psycholegal issue (e.g., parent capacity, mental state at the time of the offense, cause of emotional damage) in a manner that is contextual, logical, and empirically sound. The mere presence of psychopathology as identified by the MMPI–2 rarely is the ultimate issue. The examinee's strengths and deficits relevant to the psycholegal issue must be made explicit, along with the forensic psychologist's inferences and reasoning regarding the causes of the observed strengths and deficits.

Numerous books and articles have offered guidance to writing reports in forensic cases (Ackerman, 2006; Babitsky & Mangraviti, 2002; Brodsky, 2013; Greenfield & Gottschalk, 2009; Hoffman, 1986; Hoffman & Spiegel, 1989; Nicholson & Norwood, 2000; Ownby, 2009; Pope, Butcher, & Seelen, 2006; Tallent, 1993; Weiner, 2006; Weiner & Otto, 2013; M. A. Williams & Boll, 2000). Melton et al. (2007) offered forensic report samples in a chapter of their book. The overwhelming agreement among these authors on how to improve forensic reports can be summarized in the following points: (a) separate facts from inferences, (b) stay within the scope of the referral question, (c) avoid information under- or overkill, and (d) minimize clinical jargon.

Kwartner and Boccaccini (2008), who reviewed the empirical literature on which factors increased perceived credibility among expert witnesses, noted the importance of the clarity, clinical knowledge, case specificity, and certainty of the witness. These factors are essential in writing the forensic report, and they should be reflected in every forensic report. Reports should include only conclusions that are supported by research and contemporary practice guidelines. Bernet (2011) provided an excellent example of the need to avoid including inaccurate and "ridiculous" conclusions in testimony or in forensic reports and illustrated how such overstepping of the facts can adversely impact the expert's testimony and or reputation. The use of terminology that has clear behavioral or situational referents is preferred, including pertinent examples from the examinee's background, interview, collateral information, and so on.

A clear and useful report, of course, depends on a carefully planned and conducted psychological assessment. Chapter 1 discussed many of the issues that must be considered in planning and conducting a forensic assessment with the MMPI–2, and many of these issues represent topics to be covered in a report. The maxim in forensic assessment is that the rules of evidence shape the work of the examiner and the documentation of this work in the report (Otto, 2002). For instance, the Federal Rules of Evidence mandate that the psychologist needs to note the basis of his or her opinion. The psychologist needs to be clear about the legal issues that should be addressed and any collateral issues that the attorney may request.

Although the interpretation of the MMPI–2 should be comprehensive in scope, the report should focus on the MMPI–2 results that are relevant to the psycholegal issue that is under consideration with this specific examinee. The MMPI–2 has the potential to address, for example, the following major areas of functioning: affects/emotions, cognitive processes, interpersonal relations, impulsive acting-out behavior, physical/somatic symptoms, stress-related behavior, and substance use/abuse, to note some. The forensic psychologist needs to make the decision regarding which of them are relevant and warrant incorporating in the forensic report. The report should include a description of the code type, any clinical scales that are not in the expected range of the prominent the code type, and any differences that exist between the clinical and content scales assessing the same construct.

The inclusion of critical items and its follow-up through interview in the forensic report have to be carefully decided case by case. For clinical cases it is part of standardized procedure to review and follow up the critical items of the MMPI–2 (Butcher, Dahlstrom, Graham, Tellegen, & Kaemmer, 1989) because they can provide important clues for the practitioner to follow in personality test interpretation. However, the psychologist needs to be aware of the low reliability of item responses outside the context of the scale. Interpreting single items can be challenged as unreliable in a court of law. The strength of the MMPI–2 relies on grouping the items into scales. Some items may have lower content relevance than others, and if singled out they may detract from the overall value of the scale (Pope et al., 2006). It is for this reason that they are not highlighted or incorporated in the Minnesota Report for Forensic Settings computerized interpretation.

In addition, the report should include all relevant base rate information. One of the most valuable features of the MMPI–2 is that extensive research data—including base rates—support its interpretation. These base rates form an essential context for valid and meaningful interpretation.

Knowing the percentage of litigants in family custody cases who have primary, extreme elevations on various scales can assist the examiner in drawing conclusions about the client's MMPI–2 profile. For example, given that the *Pa* score is elevated at a moderate level in a large sample of child custody cases (e.g., 6.4%), Butcher (1997) informed the psychologist of a potential "situational" component of suspicion and mistrust that might influence the client's mental-health status and responses to the test. Sources of base-rate data on MMPI–2 patterns in different forensic settings include Bathurst, Gottfried, and Gottfried (1997); Butcher (1997); Butcher, Atlis, and Hahn (2004); Lees-Haley (1997); and Megargee (1994, 1997).

The forensic psychologist should also acknowledge and discuss discrepant findings, even with the knowledge that they will be a focus of cross-examination. The examiner cannot hide evidence; rather, he or she is responsible for presenting expert opinions and the basis for those opinions as truthfully, clearly, and fairly as possible. Acknowledging and explaining disparate information is the mark of an objective and scientific approach to test interpretation, and doing so fulfills the oath of telling the whole truth to the court. Biased test interpretation and biased presentation of results should be avoided.

Similarly, the forensic psychologist should not misrepresent what the MMPI–2 can and cannot do. Test-based psychological interpretations and conclusions are not perfect absolutes but probabilistic statements for specific situations interpreted by the examiner. The results of the MMPI–2 cannot establish whether the examinee was psychotic at the time of the alleged crime, is a sex offender, or is a fit parent. The MMPI–2 has not been validated to make these determinations.

To communicate results effectively and without jargon, forensic psychologists should avoid reporting the names of MMPI–2 scales and their *T* scores. They do not provide much useful information to nonprofessionals. In this vein, the reading level of the forensic report, including the MMPI–2 report, must be written at a level at which it will be easily understood by the individuals who have requested the evaluation. Harvey (2006) found that psychological reports are typically written at a 15- to 16-year educational reading level, which approximates the forensic psychologist's level of education rather than that of most examinees. (If the forensic psychologist is using Microsoft Word, the reading level of the report can be ascertained after a spelling check is conducted. For example, the Flesch–Kincaid reading level of this paragraph is 15.6.)

Finally, the psychologist should make clear the degree of confidence he or she has in the reliability of the interpretations and the basis of his or her assertions. The forensic report and testimony should ensure that the trier of fact understands the extent to which the data and interpretations are credible, reliable, accurate, and relevant.

GENERAL ISSUES TO BE INCLUDED IN THE FORENSIC REPORT OF MMPI–2 RESULTS

Competency and Consent

The examinee must be competent to understand the procedures and must consent to the evaluation process (APA, 2010a, 2013b). In order to consent to the evaluation, the examinee needs to have the basis for the evaluation and the potential uses of the report, if one is requested by the attorney, explained thoroughly. This explanation should include how the MMPI–2 is pertinent to the evaluation, because the mere presence of psychopathology is rarely the basis for the evaluation. The examinee also should be informed of whether he or she will see a copy of the report and of the limited confidentiality of the report. It is optimal, to be sure that the explanation has been understood, that the examinee states back to the psychologist the reason for the evaluation and signs a consent form.

Summary of the Interview

The examinee must be interviewed so that there is a context in which the MMPI–2 results can be interpreted. This interview must be comprehensive enough in length and breadth so that there is an adequate understanding of the examinee's history, background, and diagnostic symptoms and traits that are helpful for contextualizing the results of the MMPI–2. Keep in mind that the examiner may be prohibited from asking certain questions that may be considered prejudicial in certain forensic evaluations. The summary of the clinical interview should include any observations that were made during the psychological assessments. Special needs and circumstances should be identified, adequately addressed, and noted in the report. These factors are the examinee's vision, hearing, arm and hand movements; mobility and access; language, reading, and writing skills; physical illness; being under the influence of drugs, alcohol, or medications; and circumstances leading up to the testing. These issues may affect test performance to the point that they may make it invalid. Behavioral observations are relevant to contrast the examinee's response style during different aspects of the assessment, in particular the response style between tasks with more and less structure (i.e., MMPI–2 vs. Clinical Interview). Behavioral observations provide an understanding of the level of effort the examinee put forth in the assessment and whether the examinee was encumbered by excessive emotional or cognitive disruption that interfered with the ability to focus and coherently respond to the MMPI–2 items.

Examinee Preparation for the Evaluation

It is fruitful to ask the general question of whether the examinee read any material, searched the Internet, or talked to other people about the evaluation. Because of attorney–examinee privilege, the forensic psychologist cannot ask what preparation may have been suggested by the examinee's attorney. Any material that the examinee consulted should be noted, and the psychologist should make explicit if and how this information might have biased the obtained results. The impact of coaching in test response and performance has been noted in the Infrequency (F) scale (Storm & Graham, 2000).

Administration Issues

The MMPI–2 must be administered when using standard procedures, and the administration must be monitored constantly. The MMPI–2 cannot be sent home with the examinee or left with the examinee to be completed in the jail, prison, or waiting room. If this happens, the administration is invalid because there is no guarantee that the examinee completed the items or that he or she was not coached. In addition, the MMPI–2 booklet is a copyrighted instrument that has been authorized for the use of the professional psychologist. It should be utilized only under supervision. Further, the examiner needs to be there to ensure completeness and to remain alert to critical or urgent situations that may emerge during the administration of the MMPI–2.

The forensic psychologist needs to know or determine that the examinee has adequate reading and comprehension skills to take the MMPI–2. A taped administration is often very helpful for those examinees who have an adequate comprehension of oral English but have problems with reading per se. If the examinee asks what a specific item means, the forensic psychologist cannot provide a detailed explanation because of the potential of providing biasing information to the examinee. The examinee can consult a dictionary if desired. Any departure from the standard administration procedures must be noted in the report, along with the rationale for this departure. Instructions to the examinee have to be standardized, although there is empirical support for modified instructions that reduce defensiveness in personnel settings (Butcher, Morfitt, Rouse, & Holden, 1997; Cigrang & Staal, 2001; Gucker & McNulty, 2004) and in medical settings (Walfish, 2007, 2011). However, modified instructions have not been validated for forensic evaluations.

In addition, the examiner cannot ask the examinee to fill out the MMPI–2 as he or she remembers feeling at an earlier time (e.g., at the time of a crime or before a traumatic event). This is so because of the limitations of human memory, especially past emotions, and, more important, because the test was not standardized or validated for this use (Pope et al., 2006).

Review and Summary of Collateral Sources of Information

A forensic evaluation normally includes verification of the examinee's account against other information sources regarding the events in question. These sources may include collateral interviews with people relevant to the life and circumstances of the examinee and a review of relevant documents and any other possible sources of information about the litigant's pre- and post-incident thinking, emotional state, and behavioral patterns (Greenberg & Shuman, 1997), which also help contextualize the results of the MMPI–2.

Response Styles (Validity)

The variety of issues that arise in assessing the validity of the MMPI–2 was described in Chapter 2 and will not be repeated here. The report must explicitly address issues of item omissions, consistency of item endorsement, and any attempt by the examinee to present a more or less favorable description of his or her behaviors and symptoms. As explained earlier in this chapter, one of the major strengths of the MMPI–2 is the extensive literature on the assessing of validity in a variety of forensic settings. This literature will help the forensic psychologist put the response style in perspective.

Reporting the Basis of MMPI–2 Interpretation

One common error is to simply report the list of characteristics associated with elevations in the code type or single scales (A. F. Friedman, Lewack, Nichols, & Webb, 2001). This approach can seem disconnected or confusing, and it may be difficult to relate the list to the competencies or the opinion regarding how the specific psychopathological, emotional, and behavioral patterns contributed to the forensic opinion. An integrated description must begin with the most reliable and coherent picture of the examinee, as revealed in the MMPI–2 code type, and then integrate the rest of the scales and subscales in a manner that refines the hypotheses.

Code Type

The code type (including single-scale high points) provides the best validated information that can be provided by the MMPI–2. This code-type interpretation can be derived from the standard MMPI–2 references or a computer interpretive report. It is important to know how closely the examinee's profile

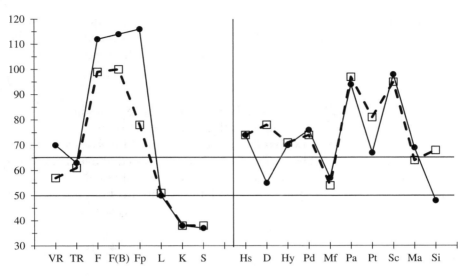

Figure 13.1. Illustration of matching an examinee's profile to the mean profile for the code type. Solid line denotes the examinee's MMPI–2 profile; dashed line denotes the mean MMPI–2 profile. Excerpted from the *MMPI®–2 (Minnesota Multiphasic Personality Inventory®—2) Manual for Administration, Scoring, and Interpretation, Revised Edition* by Butcher et al. Copyright © 2001 by the Regents of the University of Minnesota. Used by permission of the University of Minnesota Press. All rights reserved. "MMPI®" and "Minnesota Multiphasic Personality Inventory®" are trademarks owned by the Regents of the University of Minnesota.

matches the average profile for the code type; that is, the average score for all of basic validity and clinical scales. Greene (2011, Appendix A) provided the prototypic scores for all MMPI–2 code types that include all of the scales traditionally scored on the MMPI–2. He also showed that the average code type is very consistent across different settings (pp. 158–159; i.e., the profiles for the same code type in different settings are nearly identical). The frequency with which code types occur in these settings does vary considerably.

Figure 13.1 illustrates how an examinee's profile can deviate from the mean profile. Although the examinee has a 6-8/8-6 code type, Scales *D, Pt,* and *Si* are approximately two standard deviations lower than the mean profile, and Scales *F, FB,* and *Fp* are one, one and a half, and four standard deviations higher, respectively. This examinee is not reporting any general emotional or subjective distress, despite the presence of significant psychopathology and despite being evaluated in a forensic setting. This relative absence of distress is not expected, because the examinee is reporting more unusual and atypical symptoms, as measured by the family of *F* scales, than seen in the mean profile. Finally, the examinee is reporting on the *Si* scale that he is comfortable in social settings and likes being around people even though he is reporting a number of potential paranoid or psychotic behaviors. The forensic psychologist clearly must addresses these discrepancies from the mean profile and integrate them with the history and clinical interview.

Individual Scales

Individual MMPI–2 scales can be used to enhance or modify the code-type interpretation. The forensic psychologist will need to consider scales that are elevated as well as those that are not. For example, the absence of elevation on the D and Pt scales in Profile 13.1 was discussed above. Elevations on scales assessing paranoid and psychotic processes, physical and somatic symptoms, familial and interpersonal relations, and alcohol and drug use/abuse should be reviewed regardless of the code type because of the potential important information contained with them.

Item-Level Analyses

Forensic psychologists are cautioned about placing too much weight on individual MMPI–2 items because of the variety of interpretations that can be made about the meaning of any single item. This ambiguity in the understanding of the meaning of individual items led Hathaway and McKinley (1940) to develop the clinical scales empirically, which is one of the major strengths of the MMPI–2. However, items whose content is relevant directly to the psycholegal question may be reviewed. For example, Item 95, which inquires whether the person is happy all of the time, would be relevant for an examinee reporting serious depression as a result of a personal injury, particularly if the examinee endorsed this item as true.

Conclusion of MMPI–2 Interpretation

It is important to end with a summary paragraph indicating how the specific strengths and deficits identified by the MMPI–2 are relevant to the psycholegal issue under consideration. The forensic psychologist should make explicit the reasoning process from the MMPI–2 data to the conclusions reached. This reasoning should include recognition of any conflicting information from the MMPI–2 and how it was reconciled in reaching the conclusions.

USING COMPUTERIZED REPORT LANGUAGE IN FORENSIC EVALUATIONS

A number of concerns must be considered when deciding whether or how to include a computer interpretation of the MMPI–2 in the forensic report. The legitimacy of using the language or incorporating the computer interpretation of the MMPI–2 directly into the reports without referring to the source has been extensively addressed by one of the book authors (Butcher, 2009, 2013b; Pope et al., 2006).

In consideration of this issue it is important to remember that the MMPI–2 interpretation is based on using empirically supported behavioral descriptions reported in codebooks and research studies. When interpreting elevated scores, the psychologist is using reference sources for the given set of scale scores. Because of the reference to established correlated data, a psychologist can be confident that an elevation in a scale—for instance, a T score greater than 70 in scale Pa (6)—suggests symptoms of suspicion and mistrust. The goal of the computer-based MMPI–2 interpretation programs is to serve as an "electronic textbook" (Pope et al., 2006, p. 163) that contains the correlates for the various scale scores and indexes. The computer interpretation should be considered as if it were a professional-to-professional consultation. Each statement from the computerized interpretation is a prototype for the personality pattern obtained by the examinee, but the forensic psychologist needs to assess to what degree those personality descriptors match the examinee. If the statement matches the examinee closely, as revealed by its congruence with the rest of the assessment data, use of this language is appropriate.

SUMMARY

This chapter reviewed the different factors to consider when writing a forensic report that integrates MMPI–2 results. The establishment of the relevance of the MMPI–2 to the psycholegal question being addressed is key to the success of the instrument as an aid to the decision-making process in forensic evaluations. Guidelines for the manner in which the results can be reported were offered. The major point of this chapter is that the reader must understand that the MMPI–2 should not be interpreted as defining the complete answer to the psycholegal question but rather as providing the background information that must be considered when forming an expert opinion. The path that connects the MMPI–2 findings to the ultimate expert opinion has to be clearly drawn. Misuses and misrepresentations of what the MMPI–2 data can and cannot provide can have serious, unintended consequences that can hurt the psychologist, the examinee, the instrument, and the profession.

14

THE MMPI–2—RESTRUCTURED FORM

This chapter briefly describes the development of the MMPI–2—Restructured Form (MMPI–2–RF; Ben-Porath & Tellegen, 2008) and addresses a number of psychometric problems associated with its use in forensic evaluations.

DEVELOPMENT OF THE RESTRUCTURED FORM

The MMPI–2–RF (Ben-Porath & Tellegen, 2008) consists of 338 items selected to assess all possible clinically relevant variables contained within the 567 items from the Minnesota Multiphasic Personality Inventory—2 (MMPI–2; Butcher, Dahlstrom, Graham, Tellegen, & Kaemmer, 1989). The developers of the MMPI–2–RF used only 60% of the items from the MMPI–2. Many of the dropped items address personality problems and mental health

http://dx.doi.org/10.1037/14571-015
Using the MMPI–2 in Forensic Assessment, by J. N. Butcher, G. A. Hass, R. L. Greene, and L. D. Nelson
Copyright © 2015 by the American Psychological Association. All rights reserved.

symptoms that are important in forensic evaluations (e.g., 21 items related to antisocial attitudes, 21 items dealing with work functioning, 15 items assessing family problems, and 11 items dealing with negative life events). Thus, the broad coverage of problematic behaviors and symptoms in the MMPI–2 is not found in the MMPI–2–RF.

The general rationale and methodology for developing many of scales included on the MMPI–2–RF followed the same process that the authors used to develop the Restructured Clinical (RC) scales, which make up the core measures on the MMPI–2–RF (Tellegen et al., 2003). Tellegen et al. (2003) had two primary purposes in developing the RC scales: (a) minimizing the relationship among the MMPI–2 clinical scales caused by the general distress common to all of them and (b) identifying the "distinctive substantive core" of each clinical scale once the general distress had been removed. Demoralization (RCd) was the scale they developed to measure the general distress found in the clinical scales. They then identified the substantive component for each of the clinical scales, which became the restructured clinical scale: RC1 (Somatic Complaints); RC2 (Low Positive Emotions); RC3 (Cynicism); RC4 (Antisocial Behavior); RC6 (Ideas of Persecution); RC7 (Dysfunctional Negative Emotions); RC8 (Aberrant Experiences); and RC9 (Hypomanic Activation).

Tellegen and Ben-Porath (2008) factor analyzed the RC scales and identified three factors that they labeled Emotional/Internalizing Dysfunction (EID), Thought Dysfunction (THD), and Behavioral/Externalizing Dysfunction (BXD), which they subsequently designated as higher order scales. These three higher order scales can be conceptualized as broadband measures of the major divisions of psychopathology (general distress, psychoticism, acting out and problems with behavioral control). The specific problem scales provide a more refined description of these broadband measures. Excluding the nine validity scales, there are a total of 42 scales on the MMPI–2–RF: three higher order scales; nine RC scales; five somatic/cognitive scales; nine internalizing scales; four externalizing scales; five interpersonal scales; two interest scales; and five PSY-5–r scales derived from the PSY-5 scales developed by Harkness and McNulty (see Harkness & McNulty, 2006).

The specific problem scales on the MMPI–2–RF are short, ranging from four to 10 items. Their purpose is to identify very specific problems that are being reported by the person. For example, if the person elevates RC1, review of the somatic/cognitive scales (Malaise [MLS]; Gastrointestinal Complaints [GIC]; Head Pain Complaints [HPC]; Neurological Complaints [NUC]; Cognitive Complaints [COG]) can provide more specific details on the precise somatic symptoms being reported.

POTENTIAL PROBLEMS WITH USING THE RESTRUCTURED FORM IN FORENSIC SETTINGS

A number of problems, as discussed next, have been noted in the use of the MMPI–2–RF for making clinical decisions about clients since the test was published in 2008.

The Restructured Form Is Not a Revision of the MMPI–2

All five of the recent standard interpretive textbooks for the MMPI–2 arrived at the same conclusion that the MMPI–2–RF is not a revision of the MMPI–2. Rather, it is a new test, made from MMPI–2 items, that has to be researched and validated to establish its own merits and not just accepted as a newer version of the MMPI–2 (see Butcher, 2011; A. F. Friedman, Bolinskey, Lewak, & Nichols, 2014; Graham, 2012; Greene, 2011; Nichols, 2011). A. F. Friedman et al. (2014) stated,

> Despite the MMPI–2 designation for both the standard MMPI–2 and MMPI–2–RF versions, the RF form should be considered to be an essentially new instrument, as distinct from a mere revision or updating of the MMPI–2, as was the case in its transition from the original MMPI. . . . In short, the MMPI–2–RF is a new and, to this point, largely untested psychometric instrument and does not yet have the wealth of empirical support and interpretive data enjoyed by the MMPI–2. . . . (p. 593)

Graham (2012) pointed out that "the MMPI–2–RF is not intended as a replacement for the MMPI–2. Rather it should be viewed as another form of the test that has advantages and disadvantages compared with the MMPI–2" (p. 411). Greene (2011) stated that the MMPI–2 in the MMPI–2–RF is

> a misnomer because the only relationship to the MMPI–2 is its use of a subset of the MMPI–2 item pool, its normative group, and similar validity scales. The MMPI–2–RF should *not* be conceptualized as a revised or restructured form of the MMPI–2, but as a new self-report inventory that chose to select its items from the MMPI–2 item pool and to use its normative group. (p. 22)

The absence of the MMPI–2 clinical scales in the Restructured Form makes it impossible to utilize code-type interpretation, which has been at the core of MMPI/MMPI–2 interpretive process for over 50 years. None of the MMPI–2 content and supplementary scales can be scored on the MMPI–2–RF, so all of their research and clinical usage is also lost. Forensic psychologists who choose to use the MMPI–2–RF should realize that in doing so they have dropped the MMPI clinical scales and the related 70 years of clinical and research history, and they are learning a new self-report inventory.

Ben-Porath (2013b) pointed out in a recent publication that "calling this instrument (RF) anything but a restructured version of the MMPI–2 would, in fact, be misleading" (p. 475). However, the forensic psychologist who presents the MMPI–2–RF as a revision of the MMPI–2 and uses it in testimony should be able to document how it is a restructured version of the MMPI–2 by explaining how the MMPI–2 measures have been carried over into the MMPI–2–RF. For example, can one obtain the information available on the clinical, content, and supplementary scales of the MMPI–2 from the MMPI–2–RF, or what is the relationship between the new measures and the traditional scales?

Is the MMPI–2–RF Generally Accepted?

Use of a new self-report measure of psychopathology in forensic settings requires demonstration of acceptance by the professional community in addition to research demonstrating the measure's effectiveness. There have been no published surveys of the general usage of the MMPI–2–RF in comparison with the MMPI–2 since the introduction of the former measure in August 2007. The publisher of the MMPI–2–RF, the University of Minnesota Press, provides no information on how sales of the MMPI–2–RF compare with those of the MMPI–2. However, the publisher and its U.S. distributor, Pearson Assessments, have extensively marketed the MMPI–2–RF as the new standard in MMPI assessments since its release seven-plus years ago. In addition, they dropped MMPI–2 products from their offerings (e.g., the MMPI–2 Basic Score Report) while promoting the newcomer.

Information obtained in September 2014 from the University of Minnesota through a Data Practices Act request (Minnesota Statutes, Chapter 13) provides evidence about the general acceptance of the MMPI–2 over the MMPI–2–RF. During the first half of 2014, MMPI–2 products (i.e., hand-scored answer sheets, computer scoring and interpretive reports) accounted for 71% of the units sold.[1] In comparison, 29% of the units sold were MMPI–2–RF products (i.e., hand-scored answer sheets, computer scoring and interpretive reports). Practicing psychologists prefer the MMPI–2 to the MMPI–2–RF by a 3:1 margin, according to University of Minnesota Royalty Calculation records for the first half of 2014. In addition, of the available translations listed in September 2014 on the University of Minnesota

---

[1]The University's records indicate that computer scoring and interpretive reports are sold as individual units. However, in the University's records a unit sold of MMPI–2 hand-scored answer sheets is a packet of 50 answer sheets; similarly, a unit sold of MMPI–2–RF hand-scored answer sheets is a packet of 25. In order to make equivalent comparisons, a unit sold of MMPI–2 answer sheets was defined as the number of units sold according to University records multiplied by 50, and a unit sold of MMPI–2–RF answer sheets was defined as the number of units sold according to University records multiplied by 25.

website, 22 are of the MMPI–2 and only five are available for the MMPI–2–RF. In the seven years since the publication of the MMPI–2–RF, very few international publishers have accepted this version of the test. This is in clear contrast with the general acceptance of the MMPI–2 over the MMPI shortly after its introduction in 1989.

Moreover, other sources of information demonstrate that acceptance of the MMPI–2 remains high, given the large number of books and articles that continue to be published on it (http://www.umn.edu/mmpi). In addition, some test users do not accept the MMPI–2–RF in practice. For example, the Federal Aviation Administration (FAA), on the basis of research it conducted, requires inclusion of the MMPI–2 in its employment screening of air traffic controllers (FAA, 2013). The FAA explicitly prohibits the substitution of the MMPI–2–RF for the MMPI–2 in its screening procedures. Forensic psychologists are less likely to encounter challenges regarding general acceptance when using the MMPI–2 than they may face with use of the MMPI–2–RF.

Limited Validation Research for MMPI–2–RF Validity Scales

The MMPI–2–RF moved away from the empirical roots of the MMPI–2 and used factor analysis to identify sets of items that became the core of the higher order and Restructured Clinical scales. It has been criticized in several publications. For example, Nichols (2006b) and Ranson, Nichols, Rouse, and Harrington (2009) provided a detailed critique of the theory and methodology underlying the construction of the RC scales and pointed out that the development of the RC scales moved substantially from the original MMPI empirical development strategy. This developmental methodology results in scales that have rather clear, homogeneous content themes and that hence are more easily and conscientiously distorted, should a forensic client desire to do so. The forensic psychologist must consequently review the validity scales on the MMPI–2–RF very closely to assess for any potential distortion in responses to the items. For example, items with obvious symptom-related content can be readily manipulated. Moreover, it must be appreciated that the validity scales are designed to be sensitive to general, rather than specific, distorting trends within the response process. Such trends focused upon highly specific areas of item content (e.g., family problems, past delinquency, memory and concentration, obvious psychotic symptoms) that are essentially undetectable (Nichols & Greene, 1997).

Although the MMPI–2–RF validity scales have names similar to those of the MMPI–2 validity scales, the new validity scales have been changed substantially. For example, only 13 item pairs are common to both the *VRIN* scale (Butcher et al., 1989) and the *VRIN–r* scale, and Ben-Porath and Tellegen (2008) substantially changed the methodology used to select the item pairs on the MMPI–2–RF (pp. 11–14). The *F–r* scale consists of only 32 items that were endorsed rarely by the Restructured Form normative sample, whereas in the MMPI–2 the *F* scale item set contained 60 items. Additionally, there are 11 and 10 items on the *F–r* scale that overlap with the *F* and *FB* scales, respectively. The *Fp–r* scale consists of 21 items, 17 of which were selected from the 27 items on the *Fp* scale (Arbisi & Ben-Porath, 1995). Four of the deleted items were on the *L* scale. Another three items were not included among the Restructured Form items, so the rationale for their deletion is straightforward. The rationale for dropping the final three items and the methodology used to select the four additional items (40, 79, 157, 270) were not provided. The *L–r* scale consists of 14 items, 11 of which were selected from the *L* scale. Three of the four remaining items on the *L* scale were dropped on the MMPI–2–RF. One additional item was deleted from the *L* scale and three items were added to the *L–r* scale, but the rationale for these changes was not provided. The *K–r* scale consists of a subset of 14 items from the *K* scale. Once again, the rationale for the deletion of the remaining 16 items and the reversal of the scoring direction for one of the *K* scale items that was retained (202) on *K–r* was not provided.

An electronic search of the literature in September 2013 using *MMPI–2–RF* and *validity scales* in the title as search terms yielded a total of 15 publications. A similar search using *MMPI–2* or *MMPI* and not *MMPI–2–RF* and with *validity scales* in the title as search terms yielded 291 and 191 studies, respectively. Eleven of these 15 Restructured Form publications were authored by Ben-Porath and his colleagues. Several studies have reported that the MMPI–2–RF validity measures do not perform well at detecting malingering (Gass & Odland, 2012; Harp, Jasinski, Shandera-Ochsner, Mason, & Berry, 2011; Rogers, Gillard, Berry, & Granacher, 2011; P. Weiss, Bell, & Weiss, 2010). Rogers and Granacher (2011) concluded that "with minimal data on their effectiveness for assessing feigned mental disorders, it is likely to be years before the body of research justifies their use with suspected malingering in forensic cases" (p. 667). In a recent publication, Ben-Porath (2013a) noted that forensic validity information was lacking on the MMPI–2–RF. He acknowledged that "most of the peer-reviewed MMPI–2–RF publications did not focus specifically on forensic settings or samples, but many of those investigations can nonetheless inform forensic users of the inventory" (p. 75).

Limited Information on the Specific Problem Scales

There are psychometric weaknesses in the specific problem scales. First, Tellegen and Ben-Porath (2008, p. 18) did not report the particulars of scale derivation for the specific problem scales. Instead, they provided a narrative summary that leaves unexplained why items were assigned to one specific problem scale rather than another. Such an oversight in providing basic information is problematic. It would be interesting to know, for example, how items were assigned to the Helplessness/Hopelessness (*HLP*), Self-Doubt (*SFD*), and Inefficacy (*NFC*) scales, which appear to be very similar constructs.

Second, the specific problem scales tend to be very short, varying from four to 10 items. The internal consistencies of the scales are comparatively low, with standard errors of measurement varying from four to 11 *T*-score points (Tellegen & Ben-Porath, 2008, pp. 24–25). Emons, Sijtsma, and Meijer (2007) found that

> for scales consisting of 6–12 items, random measurement error exercised an unduly large influence on CC [classification consistency], even when items had the best quality encountered in test practice: That is, items had good discrimination power and locations at the cut-score. (p. 117)

Such short tests were found to classify, at most, 50% of a group consistently.

Third, there has been limited research on the specific problem scales. An electronic search of the literature in September 2013 using *MMPI–2–RF* and *specific problem scales* as search terms yielded a total of seven publications. These publications reported the descriptive statistics for the specific problem scales and how they conceptually related to the groups of individuals being evaluated.

It would be best to avoid the use of the specific problem scales entirely in a forensic setting, because of the lack of information on how the scales were developed, their limited number of items and resulting lower reliability, and the sparse research base.

Use of Nongendered Norms on the Restructured Form

The MMPI–2–RF uses the same normative group as the MMPI–2, except that 224 women were excluded randomly so as to equate the number of men (*N* = 1,138) and women (*N* = 1,138) in the Restructured Form normative group. Ben-Porath and Tellegen (2008) decided to use only nongender norms on the MMPI–2–RF. They reported minimal differences between the genders on the Restructured Form scales. Table 14.1 provides the descriptive statistics by gender using the MMPI–2 normative group for the Restructured Form scales with effect sizes (Cohen's *d*) greater than .20. Although these effect sizes are in the small to moderate range, there still are rather large differences between the genders on these scales (see Table 14.2). When nongendered *T* scores are used, men's scores are lowered on the Juvenile Conduct Problems (*JCP*) and Substance Abuse (*SUB*) scales, and women's scores are

TABLE 14.1
Gender Differences on Restructured Form Scales

Scale	Men		Women		Mean difference	d
	M	SD	M	SD		
MEC	3.96	2.11	1.35	1.42	2.61	.84
JCP	1.50	1.45	0.87	1.12	0.63	.39
SUB	1.53	1.52	0.96	1.28	0.57	.30
DISC–r	7.81	3.59	4.84	3.00	2.97	.28
MSF	2.45	2.08	4.40	2.39	−1.95	−.38
AES	2.44	1.72	3.39	1.67	−0.95	−.33
BRF	0.50	0.87	0.85	1.12	−0.34	−.33
AXY	0.34	0.68	0.52	0.83	−0.18	−.31
HPC	0.75	1.10	1.15	1.41	−0.40	−.24

Note. MEC = Mechanical-Physical Interests; JCP = Juvenile Conduct Problems; SUB = Substance Abuse; DISC–r = Disconstraint—revised; MSF = Multiple Specific Fears; AES = Aesthetic-Literary Interests; BRF = Behavior-Restricting Fears; AXY = Anxiety; HPC = Head Pain Complaints. Excerpted from the *MMPI–2–RF: Manual for Administration, Scoring, and Interpretation* by Yossef S. Ben-Porath and Auke Tellegen. Copyright © 2008, 2011 by the Regents of the University of Minnesota. Reproduced by permission of the University of Minnesota Press. All rights reserved. "Minnesota Multiphasic Personality Inventory–2—Restructured Form®" and "MMPI–2–RF®" are trademarks owned by the Regents of the University of Minnesota.

TABLE 14.2
Differences Between Gender and Nongendered *T* Scores on Specific Problem Scales

Anxiety (AXY)

	MMPI–2		RF
	Men	Women	Nongender
M	.34	.52	.43
SD	.68	.83	.76
Raw score	*T* score	*T* score	*T* score
5	119	104	100
4	104	92	91
3	89	80	80
2	74	68	70
1	60	56	59
0	45	44	44

Head Pain Complaints (HPC)

	MMPI–2		RF
	Men	Women	Nongender
M	.75	1.15	.95
SD	1.10	1.41	1.29
Raw score	*T* score	*T* score	*T* score
6	98	84	85
5	88	77	78
4	79	70	72
3	70	63	65
2	61	56	59
1	52	49	53
0	43	42	42

TABLE 14.2
Differences Between Gender and Nongendered *T* Scores on Specific Problem Scales *(Continued)*

	Juvenile Conduct Problems (*JCP*)		
	MMPI–2		RF
	Men	Women	Nongender
M	1.5	.87	1.17
SD	1.45	1.12	1.33
Raw score	*T* score	*T* score	*T* score
6	81	96	84
5	74	87	77
4	67	78	70
3	60	69	63
2	53	60	57
1	47	51	50
0	40	42	40

	Substance Abuse (*SUB*)		
	MMPI–2		RF
	Men	Women	Nongender
M	1.53	.96	1.26
SD	1.52	1.28	1.43
Raw score	*T* score	*T* score	*T* score
7	86	97	93
6	79	89	85
5	73	82	77
4	66	74	69
3	60	66	61
2	53	58	55
1	46	50	50
0	40	43	41

Note. RF = MMPI–2—Restructured Form. Excerpted from the *MMPI–2–RF: Manual for Administration, Scoring, and Interpretation* by Yossef S. Ben-Porath and Auke Tellegen. Copyright © 2008, 2011 by the Regents of the University of Minnesota. Reproduced by permission of the University of Minnesota Press. All rights reserved. "Minnesota Multiphasic Personality Inventory–2—Restructured Form®" and "MMPI–2–RF®" are trademarks owned by the Regents of the University of Minnesota.

raised about 10 *T* points at the higher raw scores. Thus, nongendered scores will underestimate the men's scores and overestimate the women's scores compared to gender scores, or, conversely, gender norms will overestimate men's scores and underestimate women's scores. It remains an empirical question as to which set of norms will yield higher correlates, but until such research is conducted, nongendered norms should be used cautiously with these scales. A similar pattern of raising and lower of men's and women's *T* scores is evident on the Anxiety (*AXY*) and Head Pain Complaints (*HCP*) scales but in the opposite direction.

Limited Research on the Potential Effects of Ethnicity

The normative sample that the MMPI–2–RF authors used for developing their norms included a 1990 census-matched sample of several ethnic groups developed for the MMPI–2 (see Butcher et al., 1989) in order to balance the normative sample for ethnicity. An electronic search of the literature in September 2013 using *MMPI–2–RF* and *ethnicity* as search terms yielded one publication and two unpublished dissertations. D'Orazio, Meyerowitz, Korst, Romero, and Goodwin (2011) reported the Restructured Form performance of 9 pregnant Latina women. However, there is a wealth of literature on the effects of ethnicity on the MMPI/MMPI–2 (cf. Greene, 2011, Chapter 11).

Low Sensitivity to Psychopathology for Restructured Clinical Scales

A number of recent studies have reported problems with the RC scales in the MMPI–2–RF in detecting psychopathology in various settings: persons with eating disorder (Erreca, 2010), clients with depression (Binford & Liljequist, 2008), Latinos with depression (Khouri, 2010), persons with posttraumatic stress disorder (Wolf et al., 2008), persons undergoing substance abuse treatment (VanPortfliet, 2012), persons with psychogenic nonepileptic seizures (Locke & Thomas, 2011), and Internet sex offenders (Lustig, 2011). Wallace and Liljequist (2005) reported that the average T scores of clinical patients on the restructured scales were significantly lower than the scores on their original MMPI–2. The majority of the profiles (56%) had fewer scale elevations when plotted with the restructured scales versus the original clinical scales.

As described in Chapter 9, the MMPI–2 results for the samples of parents being evaluated in parental competency and custody examinations in the United Kingdom (Carstairs, Richards, Fletcher, Droscher, & Ecob, 2012) were found to be largely consistent with those reported in studies in the United States, with a near-significant elevation on the L and peaks on the Pd and Pa scales. The elevations on the Pd and Pa scales in the British sample and the U.S. sample are noteworthy and highly similar to the results reported by Bathurst, Gottfried, and Gottfried (1997) and Stredny, Archer, and Mason (2006). However, a recent family custody study using the MMPI–2–RF (Archer, Hagan, Mason, Handel, & Archer, 2012) found that most of the average RC scales were below a T score of 50. The only RC scale that was elevated above a T score of 50 was RC6, which attained a mean score of 53.39. Only one of all the other Restructured Form scales was higher than 50 T, with an average scale score of 51.16.

Gordon, Stoffey, and Perkins (2013) conducted an empirical study comparing the sensitivity of the RC scales in detecting mental health problems in a sample of clinical patients. Most of the MMPI–2 scales have more clinical sensitivity than the RC scales at all levels of psychopathology and particularly at the less pathological levels. Gordon et al. also determined that the obtained differences did not result from the use of the *K* correction. Most of the RC scales added little to no incremental validity to the MMPI–2 clinical scales.

To illustrate the differences in sensitivity of the MMPI–2 clinical scales and the MMPI–2–RF scales in detecting psychopathology, we provide several examples from the recent literature. The first example is a clinical study of a well-known mass murderer, Theodore Kaczynski, also referred to as the Unabomber. Kaczynski received a PhD degree in mathematics from the University of Michigan in 1967. While teaching at the University of California, he encountered difficulties giving lectures and relating to students. After 2 years, he moved to rural Montana, where he built a sparse, isolated cabin and lived alone in the woods. He lived on vegetables that he grew and animals, such as rabbits, that he hunted. He lived the life of a survivalist and developed extreme antigovernment and antitechnology beliefs. For a number of years, Kaczynski mailed self-crafted bombs to people at several universities and American Airlines, killing three people and injuring 23.

Prior to his trial in 1998, Kaczynski refused to admit having mental-health problems and would not plead insanity for the crimes committed, although he attempted to commit suicide during the proceedings. Kaczynski was found to be guilty of murder, on the basis of all the evidence in the case, and was sentenced to life in prison.

During his imprisonment, Kaczynski was administered the MMPI–2 as part of his psychological evaluation (Hyman, Caldwell, & Nichols, 2013). Figure 14.1 illustrates his MMPI–2 clinical scale profile compared with the MMPI–2–RF profile. Kaczynski's performance on the MMPI–2 clinical scales shows a pattern of long-term psychological maladjustment. The prominent elevations on the *Pd* and *Pa* scales (4-6/6-4 code type) are indicative of features of a paranoid personality disorder. Kaczynski's MMPI–2 profile is highly consistent with past research on mass murderers (Craig, 2008; Nichols, 2006a). The only RC scale that reached a clinically interpretable range (*T* > 65) was *RC2* (Low Positive Emotions), suggesting mild to moderate dysphoric anhedonia. There was a slight elevation on the *RC1* (Physical Complaints) scale, but within the normal range. The RC scales did not detect the severe mental health and behavior problems that were noted in the MMPI–2 clinical scale elevations on *Pd* and *Pa* and in his actual life experiences involving severe paranoid thought disorder and strong potential for acting out his distorted belief system. The Restructured Form computer report indicated that Kaczynski showed no psychiatric problems, despite his demonstrated aggressiveness and his delusional belief system as established by his behavioral history and detected by the MMPI–2 clinical scales.

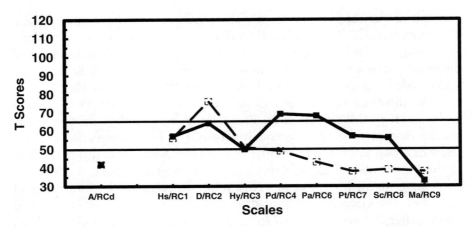

Figure 14.1. Unabomber clinical and restructured clinical scales profile. Solid line denotes clinical scales; dashed line denotes Restructured Clinical scales. A = Welsh Anxiety; Hs = Scale 1; D = Scale 2; Hy = Scale 3; Pd = Scale 4; Pa = Scale 6; Pt = Scale 7; Sc = Scale 8; Ma = Scale 9; RCd = Demoralization; RC1 = Somatic Complaints; RC2 = Low Positive Emotions; RC3 = Cynicism; RC4 = Antisocial Behavior; RC6 = Ideas of Persecution; RC7 = Dysfunctional Negative Emotions; RC8 = Aberrant Experiences; RC9 = Hypomanic Activation. Scale names and abbreviations are excerpted from the *MMPI–2–RF: Manual for Administration, Scoring, and Interpretation* by Yossef S. Ben-Porath & Auke Tellegen. Copyright © 2008, 2011 by the Regents of the University of Minnesota. Reproduced by permission of the University of Minnesota Press. All rights reserved. "Minnesota Multiphasic Personality Inventory–2—Restructured Form®" and "MMPI–2–RF®" are trademarks owned by the Regents of the University of Minnesota.

The inability of the RC scales to detect the well-documented personality problems of Kaczynski reflects flaws with the instrument that could result in failures in forensic evaluations for persons in court cases. This lack of sensitivity of the RC scales is shown further in studies described below.

Pizitz and McCullaugh (2011) reviewed the literature on personality factors among stalkers. They discussed the origins of stalking and reviewed laws related to stalking behavior. They conducted an empirical evaluation of the personality characteristics of stalkers using the MMPI–2 in a sample of 38 males who had been convicted of stalking-related offenses, stalking, terrorist threats, and restraining order violations. The victims were prior intimates, acquaintances, public figures, and strangers. Pizitz and McCullaugh evaluated the performance of the convicted stalkers on the MMPI–2 and the MMPI–2–RF (see profile comparison in Figure 14.2). They found that the MMPI–2 clinical scales show a prominent *Pd* elevation among stalkers; however, the *RC4* (Antisocial Behavior) scale shows no sensitivity toward detecting acting-out behavior. They concluded that

> the current findings present an area of concern to forensic psychologists. In completing a forensic evaluation, one must continuously assess the

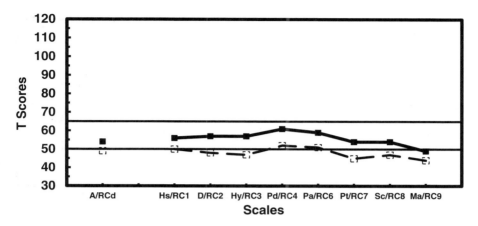

Figure 14.2. Clinical and restructured clinical scales profile of stalkers. Solid line denotes clinical scales; dashed line denotes Restructured Clinical scales. A = Welsh Anxiety; Hs = Scale 1; D = Scale 2; Hy = Scale 3; Pd = Scale 4; Pa = Scale 6; Pt = Scale 7; Sc = Scale 8; Ma = Scale 9; RCd = Demoralization; RC1 = Somatic Complaints; RC2 = Low Positive Emotions; RC3 = Cynicism; RC4 = Antisocial Behavior; RC6 = Ideas of Persecution; RC7 = Dysfunctional Negative Emotions; RC8 = Aberrant Experiences; RC9 = Hypomanic Activation. Scale names and abbreviations are excerpted from the *MMPI–2–RF: Manual for Administration, Scoring, and Interpretation* by Yossef S. Ben-Porath & Auke Tellegen. Copyright © 2008, 2011 by the Regents of the University of Minnesota. Reproduced by permission of the University of Minnesota Press. All rights reserved. "Minnesota Multiphasic Personality Inventory–2—Restructured Form®" and "MMPI–2–RF®" are trademarks owned by the Regents of the University of Minnesota.

validity of the existent measures and test data in order to make accurate clinical inferences. In the pursuit of forming accurate clinical inferences and opinions, psychologists must have supportive evidence from various sources to make determinations and conclusions. To date, multiple research studies have cautioned about the RC Scales' redundancy and problems with test validity; thus, forensic psychologists should be cautious in using the RC Scales with a stalker population until more empirical research has been conducted on this special sample, as well as in an effort to meet evidence admissibility standards such as *Frye* and *Daubert*. Moreover, the RC Scales may cause a psychologist to lose valuable bits of information and perhaps lessen the ability to make a fully informed clinical opinion. (Pizitz & McCullaugh, 2011, p. 43)

Saborío and Hass (2012) conducted an empirical evaluation, using the MMPI–2, of 167 women who had been sexually abused. They compared the performance of the assault victims on the MMPI–2 and MMPI–2–RF (see Figure 14.3) and found extreme differences in the ability of the RC scales to detect mental-health problems. The sexual assault victims showed extensive mental-health problems, including anxiety, depression, feelings of hopelessness,

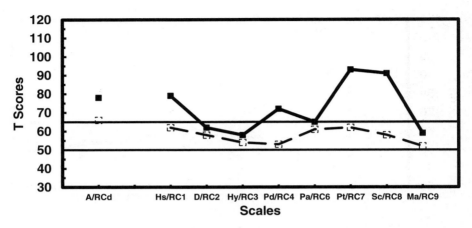

Figure 14.3. Clinical and restructured clinical scales for women victims of sexual assault. Solid line denotes clinical scales; dashed line denotes Restructured Clinical scales. A = Welsh Anxiety; Hs = Scale 1; D = Scale 2; Hy = Scale 3; Pd = Scale 4; Pa = Scale 6; Pt = Scale 7; Sc = Scale 8; Ma = Scale 9; RCd = Demoralization; RC1 = Somatic Complaints; RC2 = Low Positive Emotions; RC3 = Cynicism; RC4 = Antisocial Behavior; RC6 = Ideas of Persecution; RC7 = Dysfunctional Negative Emotions; RC8 = Aberrant Experiences; RC9 = Hypomanic Activation. Scale names and abbreviations are excerpted from the *MMPI–2–RF: Manual for Administration, Scoring, and Interpretation* by Yossef S. Ben-Porath & Auke Tellegen. Copyright © 2008, 2011 by the Regents of the University of Minnesota. Reproduced by permission of the University of Minnesota Press. All rights reserved. "Minnesota Multiphasic Personality Inventory–2—Restructured Form®" and "MMPI–2–RF®" are trademarks owned by the Regents of the University of Minnesota.

anger, isolation, and alienation, on the MMPI–2 clinical scales. These symptoms and behavior were consistent with interview and life event information the victims reported. However, the Restructured Form profile of the restructured clinical scales is well within the normal range except for the slight ($T = 65$) elevation on the *RCd* (Demoralization) scale. The RC scales failed to detect the broad range of mental health problems that these assault victims were experiencing, but the clinical scales more accurately reflected their psychopathology.

Sources of Insensitivity for the RC Scales

The decreased sensitivity of MMPI–2–RF scales compared with the MMPI–2 clinical scales likely results from a number of factors. First, the RC scales and other MMPI–2–RF scales contain substantially fewer items than do the clinical scales.

Second, the MMPI–2 clinical scales are heterogeneous measures comprising multiple item content groups. This item heterogeneity on clinical scales resulted from the empirical scale construction strategy used by Hathaway and McKinley (1940). Items were retained on the scale under development because they actually predicted the external behavior, not because they were congruent with other items in the scale. An item can validly be associated with and predict mental-health problems yet have low internal consistency with other items on the scale. That is, a set of items making up a scale does not have to conform to a single factor in order to be of value as a predictor of mental health problems. The Restructured Form scales were driven by a test construction strategy that focused upon unitary dimensions and was not dictated by behavioral prediction. Yet, mental-health problems and personality factors are often more complex and multifaceted and contain different problem areas or symptoms than does a single factorial dimension.

SUMMARY

Given that the MMPI–2–RF was advertised as the "new standard" in personality assessment when it debuted at the convention of the American Psychological Association in 2008, many psychologists were expecting that this new instrument would outperform the MMPI–2. The Restructured Form clearly has not been found to outperform the clinical scales in detecting psychopathology. It cannot serve as a replacement for the MMPI–2, which has been a valuable standard in forensic assessment for decades. This chapter has outlined a number of potential problems of which forensic psychologists need to be aware when they are deciding whether to use the MMPI–2–RF. The problems described include loss of information in several important assessment areas (items related to antisocial attitudes, items dealing with work functioning, items assessing family problems, and items dealing with negative life events), limited validation research, limited information on many of the new scales, reliance on nongendered norms, and low sensitivity to detecting mental health problems.

15

SUMMARY, CONCLUSIONS, AND FUTURE DIRECTIONS

Psychological assessment has been an important strategy for understanding the personality and behavior of people undergoing legal processes for many years, beginning with the pioneering work of Hugo Münsterberg in 1908. Over the past three decades, forensic psychologists have become increasingly involved in performing psychological evaluations of examinees in a broad range of forensic settings, such as personal injury litigation; evaluations of criminal and prison populations; mental health assessments in determining need for psychiatric commitment, capacity for parents to provide child care, and whether a parent should be allowed custody of children; and evaluation of immigrants. Psychological testing is an important component in evaluating human factors such as intelligence, cognitive impairment, mental health symptoms, behavioral problems, and personality functioning. The Minnesota Multiphasic Personality Inventory—2 (MMPI–2) is the self-report test most frequently used by forensic practitioners, as reported in several recent surveys.

http://dx.doi.org/10.1037/14571-016
Using the MMPI–2 in Forensic Assessment, by J. N. Butcher, G. A. Hass, R. L. Greene, and L. D. Nelson
Copyright © 2015 by the American Psychological Association. All rights reserved.

In this final chapter of the book, we provide an overview of the material that has been covered to describe these diverse forensic applications and provide a view of future developments in personality assessment.

SUMMARY

Forensic testimony, based on psychological tests, can be a more difficult application than areas of applied psychology such as conducting clinical, counseling, or health psychology examinations. Forensic psychologists reporting assessment results in court can find themselves in difficult cross-examinations over their results and conclusions. It is important for forensic psychologists to have a sound knowledge and current understanding of the ethical guidelines, norms, and policies that regulate them, as well as a solid grounding in the tests used, in order to deal with challenges to their evaluations (American Psychological Association, 2010a).

This book was developed to serve as a guide for interpreting the MMPI–2 in various forensic settings and to provide resource material on the MMPI–2 to assist forensic psychologists in preparing for testimony in court cases based upon the instrument. Several important questions should be addressed if psychologists are to make comfortable and effective use of the MMPI–2 in forensic case evaluations. Issues in the administration, scoring, and interpretation of the MMPI–2 in forensic evaluations have been highlighted in this book.

Many examinees being evaluated in forensic psychological assessments may approach the interview and testing in an uncooperative manner and may respond in an effort to influence the results in support of their case. Thus, a crucial consideration in forensic psychological assessment is the need to determine the extent of cooperation the examinee has shown in responding to the test. Examinees who are asked to describe their mental health condition or personality attributes on psychological tests may respond by endorsing symptoms they do not have in order to appear physically disabled in personal injury claims, by endorsing excessively severe psychiatric symptoms in order to appear mentally ill in a criminal trial, or by denying even minor and common attributes in order to appear highly virtuous in family custody evaluations. Honest and accurate self-portrayal of symptoms and behavior on the part of the examinee is crucial in personality evaluations. It is also important that forensic psychologists include an appraisal of the examinee's response strategies to assure that the test results are interpretable.

Chapter 2 presented a discussion of the effective ways in which the test interpreter can gain a perspective on the examinee's approach to the testing with the MMPI–2. The MMPI–2 provides one of the most comprehensive sets of measures to obtain information about an examinee's response sets.

These measures include various non-content-based response approaches, such as omitting items (*Cannot Say* scores), endorsing randomly (*VRIN*) or answering in an all true or all false pattern (*TRIN*), responding in an infrequent manner to claim a high degree of mental health or physical symptoms (*F, FB, Fp*), and defensive responding in order to make a good impression by appearing to have high virtue (*L, K,* or *S*).

Several issues concerning possible deviations from standard interpretive approaches for evaluating MMPI–2 scales in forensic evaluations should be considered to assure that the assessment meets accepted practices. It is important that standardized administration guidelines are followed and that validity scale interpretations are incorporated in the evaluation. Psychologists need to be aware that an examinee might have been coached on responding to test items in order to influence the outcome of the examinee's results. Moreover, psychologists need to be aware that multiple and conflicting approaches to validity evaluation might be included in a forensic evaluation. Some measures with insufficient research background or controversial results, such as the Fake Bad Scale (recently renamed the Symptom Validity Scale), might be challenged in court.

To provide readers with a readily available overview of what the MMPI–2 measures, we included a brief summary of high scores on each of the clinical, content, and supplementary scales in Chapter 3. A number of hypotheses about the examinee that can be derived from the MMPI–2 scales were presented. Information on the well-researched MMPI–2 code types was included to give readers an overview of this research for forensic applications. These hypotheses provide potential areas of interest about which the forensic examiner can further query the examinee to obtain additional information for the evaluation.

Substantial research supports the use of the MMPI–2 with African Americans, Hispanic Americans, and Native Americans, and there is adequate basis to use the MMPI–2 with Asian Americans, recent immigrants, individuals of mixed ethnicity, and other special populations. Cultural factors can play a role in some aspects of the forensic assessment with the MMPI–2, from the choice of language version to the administration and interpretation. The literature reviewed in Chapter 4 indicates that ethnically and culturally diverse examinees may interpret certain items in a different way than the normative sample did, and their profiles may vary slightly from the normative sample. The use of the MMPI–2 with ethnically diverse examinees requires that forensic psychologists consider the potential impact of diversity on testing results. Forensic psychologists have the responsibility to carefully determine when the profile elevations represent cultural factors and when they are a sign of bona fide psychopathology, as well as when there is a combination of both, and to integrate this information in the report. A case illustration was provided on the adaptation of a computerized MMPI–2 interpretive report in an international setting, Hong Kong. The examinee in the case, a convicted sexual predator, was being considered for mental-health treatment, and the psychologist was asked to evaluate his potential for rehabilitation.

The various forensic settings in which the MMPI–2 is used for examinee evaluations were described in detail in this book. Separate chapters were included for each application in order to address specifically the various contexts of assessment; special considerations in the application of MMPI–2, including research base for each; and interpretive hypotheses for the settings. Case illustrations were provided for most applications in order to highlight the utility of the test in these settings. The situations neuropsychologists face in conducting an independent medical examination were discussed in Chapter 5. Components of the evaluation take into consideration aspects of examination content and process. The MMPI–2 frequently plays an important role in ruling out malingering behavior, determining response validity, and measuring psychosomatic factors—all of which can contribute to a diagnosis and expert opinions. Several standards that a neuropsychologist may use as a basis for opinions of brain injury severity were described. The importance of underlying scientific and empirical bases for integrating results of the MMPI–2 was a point of emphasis. Utility of the MMPI–2 within a forensic neuropsychological examination was supported. A case example described a method by which neuropsychologists may build a case regarding the impact of brain injury on cognitive and emotional functioning, as well as the identification of malingering behavior, in a medicolegal context.

The research background on the MMPI–2 relevant for supporting the test in personal injury evaluations was described in Chapter 6. This chapter included summaries of some of the special contributions that assure the MMPI–2's utility in assessing behavior that is pertinent to evaluating examinees in compensation-seeking or personal injury litigation cases. Several areas in which the MMPI–2 can provide information on aspects of the examinee's test performance to assist the practitioner in developing interpretive hypotheses were included. A case study of a personal injury examinee's personality performance was included to illustrate the contribution that the MMPI–2 can make in evaluating personality characteristics of litigants.

Workers' compensation evaluations with the MMPI–2, though similar to the personal injury evaluations described in Chapter 6 in many respects, were addressed separately in Chapter 7. Workers' compensation is a form of insurance that provides wage replacement and medical benefits to injured employees or workers. Psychologists often serve as psychological examiners to contribute to information that is needed in work compensation decisions. The workers' compensation evaluation process includes a range of information, such as traditional psychological tests (often with the MMPI–2), a clinical interview, and ongoing behavioral observations of the claimant during the evaluation. Psychological examiners are responsible for developing a comprehensive analysis and description of the client's symptoms and behavior and may also contribute to determining causation of the alleged disability. The injured worker typically presents with multiple physical complaints associated with what he or she believes was an industrial injury incurred during the course of employment. Injuries may be physical or psychiatric in nature. A case study was included to highlight the utility of the MMPI–2 for understanding the symptomatic behavior of an injured worker in a workers' compensation case.

The MMPI–2 is an assessment instrument that offers a great deal of valuable data in different types of immigration evaluations. The MMPI–2 provides information on the impact on psychological adjustment in relation to psychological concepts such as extreme hardship, moral character, and issues of ineligibility in immigration assessment cases. In asylum cases, the MMPI–2 can be useful in assessing the impact of trauma, especially because it captures a wider range of trauma manifestations, which go beyond typical measures of posttraumatic stress disorder and depression, and may identify cultural variations of distress. The MMPI–2 allows the forensic psychologist to match the victim's account of the traumatic experience and the psychological findings and assess their consistency. It also provides an evaluation of response attitudes that helps the psychologist present an opinion of credibility, which is of paramount importance in these evaluations. A case example of an abused wife of an American man, who was being evaluated in a petition for U.S. residency case, was included in Chapter 8. The MMPI–2 was valuable in assessing her mental health problems caused by domestic violence, which qualified for a VAWA application. This personality-based information was very important in the success of her immigration case.

Factors that assist forensic psychologists in understanding the dynamics of family custody and child protection evaluations were discussed in Chapter 9. The assessment goals and evaluation strategies for these programs differ in several respects, and the distinctions were noted. The legal bases for psychological evaluations in custody and parental capacity evaluations were summarized, and the evaluation procedures and goals were detailed to assist the practitioner in knowing the testing context. Chapter 9 provided a historical perspective on the research basis of the MMPI–2 scales in evaluating parental custody evaluations. A number of these studies were highlighted to illustrate the empirical basis of the test in this application in a number of family-oriented contexts. Early research with the MMPI on parental behavior and problems established the MMPI–2's utility in understanding couple's problems. Hundreds of studies on personality and behavior of parents and their children that used the MMPI/MMPI–2 have been published over the past 75 years. The MMPI–2 can contribute substantially to a family custody or a parent capacity evaluation by providing the forensic psychologist with relevant information about the parent's mental health adjustment or personality characteristics. This information can give a valid perspective on the parent's likelihood of carrying out parental responsibilities. This chapter provided a discussion of several issues that are pertinent for forensic practitioners to consider in determining which psychological measures to include in a parental custody examination. An informative case study of parental neglect was included to illustrate issues in conducting child protection and custody evaluations.

The empirical research and legal perspective of the state of the intimate partner violence (IPV) field and the intricacies of interpreting the MMPI–2 with victims of partner violence were discussed in Chapter 10. Because partner violence trauma includes a range of diverse symptoms and signs that interact with personality traits and previous trauma, this field tends to be riddled with confusion and misinterpretation. However, when incorporated as part of a multimodal battery of interview and tests, IPV surveys, and actuarial instruments, the MMPI–2 provides an effective appraisal of the victim's credibility and psychological functioning. This perspective can be highly useful in forensic evaluations where the issue of partner violence is raised, because it provides empirically validated information that can assist the psychologist in formulating an opinion in a variety of psycholegal matters. A case study that illustrates the value of MMPI–2 assessment in the context of family violence concluded the chapter.

Personality assessments of people undergoing criminal investigations, those who have been convicted of crimes, or severely disturbed mental health examinees considered to be dangerous to themselves or others are prominent features of forensic practice today and were discussed in Chapter 11. Conducting forensic psychological evaluations of examinees in criminal court cases is quite different from assessment in clinical settings, in which the examinee volunteers to undergo the self-disclosure required for a valid evaluation. Evaluations of examinees who are being tried in a criminal case are often marked by defensive or uncooperative approaches to the items. Therefore, their test-taking style is an important aspect of the assessment. It is important for practitioners to keep in mind that the evaluations can be highly conflictual; thus, careful monitoring is required of the administration of psychological tests, such as the MMPI–2, to assure that the results are comparable to those employed in the normative data collection. This procedural requirement is particularly important in forensic evaluations, in which there may be a high degree of motivation for the examinee to appear different than he or she actually is. Deviations from standard procedures can result in inappropriate normative comparisons and invalid protocols. As noted in several chapters of this book, many factors can influence examinees to produce invalid protocols in forensic settings. Assessment in court-ordered evaluations can be problematic indeed, with low levels of cooperation among examinees. The examinee might be extremely disturbed, as in some civil commitment cases, and be unable to participate in responding to a self-report questionnaire. This chapter presented important descriptive information on the MMPI–2 scales that appear prominently in criminal evaluations. The Pd (4), Pa (6), Ma (9), and Sc (8) scales and resulting code-type configurations that are encountered in forensic evaluations have a substantial research base to support the inclusion of the MMPI–2 in an assessment. A psychological evaluation of a married mother who was arrested and charged with neglect, after her severely abused infant daughter was discovered alone and deceased in the house, provides a case example that illustrates the value of using the MMPI–2 in this setting.

Computerized scoring and interpretation of psychological tests have a long history in psychology. Computer scoring of the MMPI was developed in the 1950s, and computer-based interpretation systems began in the early 1960s. The development of more comprehensive and complex computer programs to provide narrative MMPI reports began in the 1960s and has continued to evolve, giving practitioners various system options. Computer-based reports based upon the MMPI/MMPI–2 have been developed or adapted for use in languages other than English and countries other than the United States. Chapter 12 provided a case illustration of a client in a workplace harassment personal injury claim.

Computer-generated interpretive reports have gained broad acceptance in the professional community and are commonly used in clinical, personnel screening, and forensic settings to obtain information about examinees. Many forensic practitioners rely upon computer-based interpretive systems to provide the basic correlate information from the MMPI–2 or MMPI—Adolescent research database in order to develop their evaluations. It is the responsibility of the forensic practitioner to integrate computer-based MMPI–2 information into the forensic report and to have the necessary knowledge to support the information provided in court cases. Developing MMPI–2 based forensic reports was described in Chapter 13. MMPI–2 evaluations should conclude with a summary of how the specific strengths and deficits identified by the MMPI–2 are relevant to the psycholegal issue under consideration in the expert witness's testimony. The forensic psychologist should make the reasoning process explicit from the MMPI–2 data to support the conclusions being reached. This reasoning process should include recognition of any conflicting information from the MMPI–2 and how it was reconciled in reaching the conclusions.

Given that the MMPI–2–RF was advertised as the "new standard" in personality assessment when it debuted at the convention of the American

Psychological Association in 2008, many psychologists expected that this new instrument would outperform the MMPI–2. This introduction was heralded and the test was heavily advertised, even though no research on the validity and utility of the scales had been published and a number of articles had criticized the core Restructured Clinical scales as being insensitive to psychopathology and as having a restricted range of information available.

As many recent studies have shown, the MMPI–2–RF clearly has not been found to perform as well as the clinical scales in detecting psychopathology. It cannot serve as a replacement for the MMPI–2, which has been a valuable standard in forensic assessment for decades. Chapter 14 described a number of potential problems of which forensic psychologists need to be aware if they are determining whether to use the MMPI–2–RF in court cases, in which a challenge on the use of new test is common.

CONCLUSIONS

We have provided an overview of the use of the MMPI–2 in assessing examinees in a broad range of forensic applications. We end this book with a number of summary conclusions concerning the use of the MMPI–2 in court:

1. The MMPI–2 has an extensive research base and broad professional usage as an objective personality measure that can contribute substantially to understanding the mental-health status of an individual undergoing a personality evaluation in a forensic context.
2. As an assessment measure used in legal cases, the MMPI–2 has gained broad acceptance. It provides the court with an objective, reliable, and valid personality picture of the examinee's mental-health status and personality characteristics.
3. Personality assessment of examinees in forensic evaluations can be quite different from assessments in clinical settings. The level of cooperation of the examinee in providing personal information can be low, and the test results can profoundly affect the examinee's conflictual life situation. In court cases, examinees usually feel the need to influence the outcome by responding in ways (often through coaching by their attorney) likely to be favorable to their outcome.
4. One of the most important aspects of a personality evaluation is the determination of whether the information obtained is credible. Of the personality assessment instruments available for evaluating examinees in forensic cases, the MMPI–2 has the

most comprehensive and research-based measures for evaluating a litigant's response attitudes that can address the common approaches to invalidating the test.

5. It is important for the forensic psychologist to be cognizant of the limitations of personality assessments in forensic cases resulting from the examinee's motivations as well as from the contextual requirements of test use in court. Psychologists need to be knowledgeable about the professional guidelines for forensic assessment. They must follow testing standards and carefully monitor test administration procedures to assure that the assessment has been conducted in a standard manner.

6. The MMPI–2 has been shown to be an effective instrument in providing personality and clinical symptom information in diverse populations, and it has been shown to be fair for evaluating minorities. The test is often used in forensic cases with examinees whose language skills do not allow them to read or understand English. Numerous MMPI–2 translations, along with appropriate norms from other countries, enable the practitioner to obtain MMPI–2 results for non-English-speaking examinees.

7. Research has shown that computer-based scoring of protocols is more accurate and reliable than hand scoring. Computer-based interpretation programs, at least those based on established empirical correlates, can provide useful summaries of MMPI–2 responses to include in a comprehensive forensic evaluation, although these reports cannot be considered to be complete assessments.

8. Forensic practitioners need to be aware that the recently published MMPI–2–RF is not a substitute for the MMPI–2. Even though the developers used a subset (60%) of the MMPI–2 items, it is a new and a different measure and has a limited research base. The scales were developed according to a different scale development approach and not according to the empirical scale construction of the original MMPI. Other than its having a similar name and the publisher making substantial efforts to market this new measure in the MMPI–2 tradition, it is a new test and requires substantial research before it can be trusted in forensic evaluations. The MMPI–2–RF has substantially lower sensitivity to mental-health problems than the MMPI–2. As noted in this book, experts on the MMPI–2 who have published recent textbooks warn the readers that the MMPI–2–RF is a new and relatively untested instrument for forensic use.

FUTURE DIRECTIONS

This book has been devoted to the contemporary use of the MMPI–2 in forensic assessments and has examined past research supporting its use in court testimony. We have also addressed, throughout this book, a number of challenges to personality assessment and to MMPI–2 use in the forensic assessment context that should be considered by test users. Current test use is driven by the information provided on an instrument's perceived applicability and by acceptance by the assessment field and the courts. The MMPI–2 remains the most viable instrument available today—even with the number of competitors that are available.

Other parts of the forensic field were not addressed in this book but will likely continue to accrue empirical support to receive greater attention in the field. Examples include issues around end of life; elder abuse; and abuse by teachers, clergy, and therapists. Nor did we dedicate space to discuss the issues surrounding the consultants who review the work product of experts, including their administration, scoring, and interpretation of the MMPI–2. This is an issue of upmost importance that merits some attention in the future. We have not addressed, in a substantial manner, the likely future forensic use of the MMPI–2. In the modern world, the future always holds a great deal of uncertainty. And one can never know for sure what the personality assessment world will look like in the years to come. Technological development and the electronic advancements that we witness nearly every few months will likely play an even greater role in appraising human behavior and mental health symptoms than they have in the past. But, we believe that what people think of themselves (and can describe about their feelings, emotions, and fears in self-report measures like the MMPI–2) will likely continue to play an important role in the future, as they have in the past. Client self-report will likely remain an important source of personality information in the future, no matter how it is obtained and processed. New developments will, as they have in the past, have to be verified and supported by research. Any assessment instrument method that is proposed to account for a client's personality characteristics and mental health symptoms will likely require that self-reported thoughts and behavior be an important component of successful measures. And, as in the past, substantial validity research of new instruments will be required in order to meet the high standards required by the forensic field.

REFERENCES

Abidin, R. R. (1990). *Parenting Stress Index* (3rd ed.). Charlottesville, VA: Pediatric Psychology Press.

Abraham, M. (2000). *Speaking the unspeakable: Marital violence among South Asian immigrants in the United States*. New Brunswick, NJ: Rutgers University Press.

Ackerman, M. J. (2006). Forensic report writing. *Journal of Clinical Psychology, 62,* 59–72. doi:10.1002/jclp.20200

Ackerman, M. J., & Ackerman, M. C. (1997). Custody evaluation practices: A survey of experienced professionals (revisited). *Professional Psychology: Research and Practice, 28,* 137–145. doi:10.1037/0735-7028.28.2.137

Adams, A., & Foulds, G. A. (1963). Personality and the paranoid depressive psychoses. *British Journal of Psychiatry, 109,* 273–278. doi:10.1192/bjp.109.459.273

Ahmad, F., Riaz, S., Barata, P., & Stewart, D. (2004). Patriarchal beliefs and perceptions of abuse among South Asian immigrant women. *Violence Against Women, 10,* 262–282. doi:10.1177/1077801203256000

Ainsworth, M. D. S., Blehar, M. C., Waters, E., & Wall, S. (1978). *Patterns of attachment: A psychological study of the Strange Situation*. Hillsdale, NJ: Erlbaum.

Allan, A. (2013). Ethics in correctional and forensic psychology: Getting the balance right. *Australian Psychologist, 48,* 47–56. doi:10.1111/j.1742-9544.2012.00079.x

Allard, G., Butler, J., Faust, D., & Shea, M. T. (1995). Errors in hand scoring objective personality tests: The case of the Personality Diagnostic Questionnaire—Revised (PDQ–R). *Professional Psychology: Research and Practice, 26,* 304–308. doi:10.1037/0735-7028.26.3.304

Allard, G., & Faust, D. (2000). Errors in scoring objective personality tests. *Assessment, 7,* 119–129. doi:10.1177/107319110000700203

Alwes, Y. R., Clark, J. A., Berry, D. T., & Granacher, R. P. (2008). Screening for feigning in a civil forensic setting. *Journal of Clinical and Experimental Neuropsychology, 30,* 133–140. doi:10.1080/13803390701260363

American Academy of Child and Adolescent Psychiatry. (2000). *Children of parents with mental illness*. Washington, DC: Author.

American Academy of Matrimonial Lawyers. (2011). *Child custody evaluation standards*. Retrieved from http://www.aaml.org/library/publications/

American Academy of Psychiatry and the Law. (2005). *Ethics guidelines for the practice of forensic psychiatry*. Bloomfield, CT: Author.

American Association for Correctional Psychology. (2010). Standards for psychology services in jails, prisons, correctional facilities, and agencies: International Association for Correctional and Forensic Psychology. *Criminal Justice and Behavior, 37,* 749–808. doi:10.1177/0093854810368253

American Association for Correctional Psychology, Standards Committee. (2000). Standards for psychological services in jails, prisons, correctional facilities, and agencies (2nd ed.). *Criminal Justice and Behavior, 27*, 433–494.

American Educational Research Association, American Psychological Association, & National Council of Measurement in Education. (2014). *Standards for educational and psychological testing.* Washington, DC: American Educational Research Association.

American Medical Association. (2012). *AMA guides to evaluation of permanent disability* (6th ed.). Washington, DC: Author.

American Psychiatric Association. (1980). *Diagnostic and statistical manual of mental disorders* (3rd ed.). Washington, DC: Author.

American Psychiatric Association. (2000). *Diagnostic and statistical manual of mental disorders* (4th ed., text rev.). Washington, DC: Author.

American Psychiatric Association. (2013). *Diagnostic and statistical manual of mental disorders* (5th ed.). Arlington, VA: American Psychiatric Publishing.

American Psychological Association. (1993). *Guidelines for providers of psychological services to ethnic, linguistic, and culturally diverse populations.* Washington, DC: Author.

American Psychological Association. (1996). *Report of the American Psychological Association Presidential Task Force on Violence and the Family.* Washington, DC: Author.

American Psychological Association. (2010a). *Ethical principles of psychologists and code of conduct (2002; amended June 1, 2010).* Retrieved from http://www.apa.org/ethics/code/index.aspx

American Psychological Association. (2010b). Guidelines for child custody evaluations in family law proceedings. *American Psychologist, 65*, 863–867. doi:10.1037/a0021250

American Psychological Association. (2013a). Guidelines for psychological evaluations in child protection matters. *American Psychologist, 68*, 20–31. doi:10.1037/a0029891

American Psychological Association. (2013b). Specialty guidelines for forensic psychology. *American Psychologist, 68*, 7–19. doi:10.1037/ a0029889

American Psychological Association, Presidential Task Force on Immigration. (2012). *Crossroads: The psychology of immigration in the new century. Report of the Presidential Task Force on Immigration.* Washington, DC: Author.

Americans With Disabilities Act of 1990, 42 U.S.C. § 12101 *et seq.* (2006).

Ammar, N. (2000). Simplistic stereotyping and complex reality of Arab-American immigrant identity: Consequences and future strategies in policing wife battery. *Islam and Christian-Muslim Relations, 11*, 51–70. doi:10.1080/095964100111517

Ammar, N., Orloff, L. E., Dutton, M. A., & Aguilar-Hass, G. (2005). Calls to police and police response: A case study of Latina immigrant women in the USA. *International Journal of Police Science & Management, 7,* 230–244. doi:10.1350/ijps.2005.7.4.230

Andersen, A. L., & Hanvik, L. J. (1950). The psychometric localization of brain lesions: The differential effect of frontal and parietal lesions on MMPI profiles. *Journal of Clinical Psychology, 6,* 177–180. doi:10.1002/1097-4679(195004)6:2<177::AID-JCLP2270060217>3.0.CO;2-2

Anderson, D. (2001). Use of the MMPI–2 in assessment of traumatic brain injury. *Australian Journal of Psychology, 53,* 185.

Anderson, D. K., Saunders, D. G., Yoshihama, M., Bybee, D. I., & Sullivan, C. M. (2003). Long-term trends in depression among women separated from abusive partners. *Violence Against Women, 9,* 807–838. doi:10.1177/1077801203009007004

Anderson v. E & S International Enterprises, No. RG05-211076 (Cal. Super. Ct. July 29, 2008).

Andreetto, U., & de Bertolini, C. (1999). Interactions between clinical and psychological factors during the adaptation period following liver transplantation. *Medicina Psicosomática, 44,* 199–221.

Arbisi, P. A., & Ben-Porath, Y. S. (1995). An MMPI–2 infrequent response scale for use with psychopathological populations: The Infrequency-Psychopathology Scale, *F(p)*. *Psychological Assessment, 7,* 424–431. doi:10.1037/1040-3590.7.4.424

Arbisi, P. A., Ben-Porath, Y. S., & McNulty, J. (2002). A comparison of MMPI–2 validity in African American and Caucasian psychiatric inpatients. *Psychological Assessment, 14,* 3–15. doi:10.1037/1040-3590.14.1.3

Arbisi, P. A., & Butcher, J. N. (2004). Relationship between personality and health symptoms: Use of the MMPI–2 in medical assessments. *International Journal of Clinical and Health Psychology, 4,* 571–595.

Archer, E. M., Hagan, L. D., Mason, J., Handel, R., & Archer, R. P. (2012). MMPI–2–RF characteristics of custody evaluation litigants. *Assessment, 19,* 14–20. doi:10.1177/1073191110397469

Archer, R. P., Buffington-Vollum, J. K., Stredny, R. V., & Handel, R. W. (2006). A survey of psychological test use patterns among forensic psychologists. *Journal of Personality Assessment, 87,* 84–94.

Archer, R. P., Fontaine, J., & McCrae, R. R. (1998). Effects of two MMPI–2 validity scales on basic scale relations to external criteria. *Journal of Personality Assessment, 70,* 87–102. doi:10.1207/s15327752jpa7001_6

Archer, R. P., Griffin, R., & Aiduk, R. (1995). MMPI–2 clinical correlates for ten common codes. *Journal of Personality Assessment, 65,* 391–407. doi:10.1207/s15327752jpa6503_1

Archer, R. P., Stredny, R. V., & Wheeler, M. A. (2013). Introduction to forensic uses of clinical assessment instruments. In R. P. Archer & M. A. Wheeler (Eds.),

Forensic uses of clinical assessment instruments (2nd ed., pp. 1–20). New York, NY: Routledge.

Archer, R. P., Stredny, R. V., & Zoby, M. (2006). Introduction to forensic uses of clinical assessment instruments. In R. P. Archer (Ed.), *Forensic uses of clinical assessment instruments* (pp. 1–18). Mahwah, NJ: Erlbaum.

Archer, R. P., & Wheeler, M. A. (Eds.). (2013). *Forensic uses of clinical assessment instruments* (2nd ed.). New York, NY: Routledge.

Arias, I., & Pape, K. T. (1999). Psychological abuse: Implications for adjustment and commitment to leave violent partners. *Violence and Victims, 14,* 55–67.

Armenian, H. K., Melkonian, A. K., & Hovanesian, A. P. (1998). Long-term mortality and morbidity related to degree of damage following the 1998 earthquake in Armenia. *American Journal of Epidemiology, 148,* 1077–1084. doi:10.1093/oxfordjournals.aje.a009585

Arnold, P. (1970). *Recurring MMPI two-point codes of marriage counselors and "normal" couples with implications for interpreting marital interaction behavior.* Unpublished manuscript.

Asgary, R. G., Metalios, E. E., Smith, C. L., & Paccioni, G. A. (2006). Evaluating asylum seekers/torture survivors in urban primary care: A collaborative approach at the Bronx Human Rights Clinic. *Health and Human Rights, 9,* 164–179. doi:10.2307/4065406

Association of Family and Conciliation Courts. (2006). *Model standards of practice for child custody evaluations.* Retrieved from http://www.afccnet.org/Portals/0/ModelStdsChildCustodyEvalSept2006.pdf

Atkins, E. L., & Watson, K. J. (2011). Sentencing. In E. Y. Drogin, F. M. Dattilio, R. L. Sadoff, & T. G. Gutheil (Eds.), *Handbook of forensic assessment: Psychological and psychiatric perspectives* (pp. 49–78). Hoboken, NJ: Wiley.

Atlis, M. M., Hahn, J., & Butcher, J. N. (2006). Computer-based assessment with the MMPI–2. In J. N. Butcher (Ed.), *MMPI–2: The practitioner's handbook* (pp. 445–476). Washington, DC: American Psychological Association.

Austin, W. G., & Drozd, L. M. (2012). Intimate partner violence and child custody evaluation, Part I: Theoretical framework, forensic model, and assessment issues. *Journal of Child Custody, 9,* 250–309. doi:10.1080/15379418.2012.749717

Azar, S. T. (2002). Adult development and parenthood. A social-cognitive perspective. In J. Demick & C. Andreoletti (Eds.), *Handbook of adult development* (pp. 391–415). New York, NY: Plenum Press.

Babcock, J. C., Costa, D. M., Green, C. E., & Eckhardt, C. I. (2004). What situations induce intimate partner violence? A reliability and validity study of Proximal Antecedents to Violent Episodes (PAVE) scale. *Journal of Family Psychology, 18,* 433–442. doi:10.1037/0893-3200.18.3.433

Babitsky, S., & Mangraviti, J. (2002). *Writing and defending your expert report: The step-by-step guide with models.* Falmouth, MA: SEAK.

Baer, R. A., & Miller, J. (2002). Underreporting of psychopathology on the MMPI–2: A meta-analytic review. *Psychological Assessment, 14*, 16–26. doi:10.1037/1040-3590.14.1.16

Baer, R. A., Wetter, M. W., & Berry, D. T. R. (1992). Detection of underreporting of psychopathology on the MMPI: A meta-analysis. *Clinical Psychology Review, 12*, 509–525. doi:10.1016/0272-7358(92)90069-K

Baer, R. A., Wetter, M. W., Nichols, D., Greene, R., & Berry, D. T. (1995). Sensitivity of MMPI–2 validity scales to underreporting of symptoms. *Psychological Assessment, 7*, 419–423. doi:10.1037/1040-3590.7.4.419

Bagby, R. M., Buis, T., & Nicholson, R. A. (1995). Relative effectiveness of the standard validity scales in detecting fake-bad and fake-good responding: Replication and extension. *Psychological Assessment, 7*, 84–92. doi:10.1037/1040-3590.7.1.84

Bagby, R. M., Marshall, M. B., Bury, A., Bacchiochi, J. R., & Miller, L. (2006). Assessing underreporting and overreporting styles on the MMPI–2. In J. N. Butcher (Ed.), *MMPI–2: The practitioner's handbook* (pp. 39–69). Washington, DC: American Psychological Association.

Bagby, R. M., Nicholson, R. A., Bacchiochi, J. R., Ryder, A. G., & Bury, A. S. (2002). The predictive capacity of the MMPI–2 and PAI validity scales and indexes to detect coached and uncoached feigning. *Journal of Personality Assessment, 78*, 69–86. doi:10.1207/S15327752JPA7801_05

Bagby, R. M., Nicholson, R. A., Buis, T., Radovanovic, H., & Fidler, B. J. (1999). Defensive responding on the MMPI–2 in family custody and access evaluations. *Psychological Assessment, 11*, 24–28. doi:10.1037/1040-3590.11.1.24

Bagby, R. M., Nicholson, R. A., Rogers, R., & Nussbaum, D. (1992). Domains of competency to stand trial: A factor analytic study. *Law and Human Behavior, 16*, 491–507. doi:10.1007/BF01044620

Bagby, R. M., Sellbom, M., Costa, P. T., Jr., & Widiger, T. A. (2008). Predicting *Diagnostic and Statistical Manual of Mental Disorders–IV* personality disorders with the five-factor model of personality and the personality psychopathology five. *Personality and Mental Health, 2*, 55–69. doi:10.1002/pmh.33

Baldwin, K., & Roys, D. T. (1998). Factors associated with denial in a sample of alleged adult sexual offenders. *Sexual Abuse, 10*, 211–226.

Bardenhagen, F. (2006). Assessing psychopathology in neuropsychological assessments: An introduction to the MMPI–2. *Australian Journal of Psychology, 58*, 224.

Barr, W. B., Larson, E., Alper, K., & Devinsky, O. (2005). Rates of invalid MMPI–2 responding in patients with epileptic and nonepileptic seizures. *Epilepsia, 46*(11), 60.

Barron, F. (1953). An ego-strength scale which predicts response to psychotherapy. *Journal of Consulting Psychology, 17*, 327–333. doi:10.1037/h0061962

Barth, J. T., Varney, N. R., Ruchinskas, R. A., & Francis, J. P. (1999). Mild head injury: The new frontier in sports medicine. In N. R. Varney & R. J. Roberts (Eds.), *The evaluation and treatment of mild traumatic brain injury* (pp. 85–86). Hillsdale, NJ: Erlbaum.

Barthlow, D. L., Graham, J. R., Ben-Porath, Y. S., Tellegen, A., & McNulty, J. L. (2002). The appropriateness of the MMPI–2 *K* correction. *Assessment, 9,* 219–229. doi:10.1177/1073191102009003001

Basile, K. C., Arias, I., Desai, S., & Thompson, M. P. (2004). The differential association of intimate partner physical, sexual, psychological, and stalking violence and posttraumatic stress symptoms in a nationally representative sample of women. *Journal of Traumatic Stress, 17,* 413–421. doi:10.1023/B:JOTS.0000048954.50232.d8

Bathurst, K., Gottfried, A. W., & Gottfried, A. E. (1997). Normative data for the MMPI–2 in child custody litigation. *Psychological Assessment, 9,* 205–211. doi:10.1037/1040-3590.9.3.205

Bauer, A., Rosca, P., Khawalled, R., Gruzniewski, A., & Grinshpoon, A. (2003). Dangerousness and risk assessment: The state of the art. *Israel Journal of Psychiatry and Related Sciences, 40,* 182–190.

Beck, A. T., & Beck, R. W. (1972). Screening depressed patients in family practice: A rapid technique. *Postgraduate Medicine, 52,* 81–85.

Beck, A. T., & Steer, R. A. (1993). *Beck Anxiety Inventory manual.* San Antonio, TX: Harcourt Brace.

Beck, A. T., Ward, C. H., Mendelson, M., Mock, J., & Erbaugh, J. (1961). An inventory for measuring depression. *Archives of General Psychiatry, 4,* 561–571. doi:10.1001/archpsyc.1961.01710120031004

Belanger, H. G., Vanderploeg, R. D., Curtiss, G., & Warden, D. L. (2007). Recent neuroimaging techniques in mild traumatic brain injury. *Journal of Neuropsychiatry and Clinical Neurosciences, 19,* 5–20. doi:10.1176/appi.neuropsych.19.1.5

Bennice, J. A., & Resick, P. A. (2003). Marital rape: History, research, and practice. *Trauma, Violence, & Abuse, 4,* 228–246. doi:10.1177/1524838003004003003

Benoit, D., Zeanah, C. H., Parker, K. C. H., Nicholson, E., & Coolbear, J. (1997). "Working model of the child interview": Infant clinical status related to maternal perceptions. *Infant Mental Health Journal, 18,* 107–121. doi:10.1002/(SICI)1097-0355(199721)18:1<107::AID-IMHJ8>3.0.CO;2-N

Ben-Porath, Y. S. (2013a). Forensic applications of the Minnesota Multiphasic Personality Inventory—2—Restructured Form. In R. P. Archer & E. M. A. Wheeler (Eds.), *Forensic use of clinical assessment instruments* (pp. 63–107). New York, NY: Routledge.

Ben-Porath, Y. S. (2013b). *Interpreting the MMPI–2–RF.* Minneapolis: University of Minnesota Press.

Ben-Porath, Y. S., Graham, J. R., & Tellegen, A. (2009). *The MMPI–2 Symptom Validity (FBS) Scale: Development, research findings, and interpretive recommendations.* Minneapolis: University of Minnesota Press.

Ben-Porath, Y. S., Greve, K. W., Bianchini, K. J., & Kaufmann, P. M. (2009). The MMPI–2 Symptom Validity Scale (FBS) is an empirically validated measure of overreporting in personal injury litigants and claimants: Reply to Butcher et al. (2008). *Psychological Injury and Law, 2*, 62–85. doi:10.1007/s12207-009-9037-4

Ben-Porath, Y. S., Greve, K. W., Bianchini, K. J., & Kaufmann, P. M. (2010). The MMPI–2 Symptom Validity Scale (FBS) is an empirically validated measure of overreporting in personal injury litigants and claimants: Reply to William et al. (2009). *Psychological Injury and Law, 3*, 77–80. doi:10.1007/s12207-009-9049-0

Ben-Porath, Y. S., & Sherwood, N. E. (1993). *The MMPI–2 content component scales: Development, psychometric characteristics, and clinical application.* Minneapolis: University of Minnesota Press.

Ben-Porath, Y. S., & Tellegen, A. (2008). *MMPI–2–RF: Manual for administration, scoring, and interpretation.* Minneapolis: University of Minnesota Press.

Bernet, W. (2011). Ridiculous statements by mental health experts. *Child and Adolescent Psychiatric Clinics of North America, 20*, 557–564. doi:10.1016/j.chc.2011.03.003

Berry, D. T. R., Adams, J. J., Smith, G. T., Greene, R. L., Sekirnjak, G. C., Wieland, G., & Tharpe, B. (1997). MMPI–2 clinical scales and 2-point code types: Impact of varying levels of omitted items. *Psychological Assessment, 9*, 158–160. doi:10.1037/1040-3590.9.2.158

Berry, D. T. R., Wetter, M. W., Baer, R. A., Youngjohn, J. R., Gass, C. S., Lamb, D. G., . . . Buchholz, D. (1995). Overreporting of closed-head injury symptoms on the MMPI–2. *Psychological Assessment, 7*, 517–523. doi:10.1037/1040-3590.7.4.517

Berry, J. W. (1995). Psychology of acculturation. In N. R. Goldberger & J. B. Veroff (Eds.), *The culture and psychology reader* (pp. 457–488). New York, NY: New York University Press.

Bigler, E. D. (2011). Structural imaging. In J. M. Silver, T. W. McAllister, & S. C. Yudofsky (Eds.), *Textbook of traumatic brain injury* (2nd ed., pp. 73–90). Arlington, VA: American Psychiatric Association.

Binder, R. L. (1999). Are the mentally ill dangerous? *Journal of the American Academy of Psychiatry and the Law, 27*, 189–201.

Binford, A., & Liljequist, L. (2008). Behavioral correlates of selected MMPI–2 clinical, content, and restructured clinical scales. *Journal of Personality Assessment, 90*, 608–614. doi:10.1080/00223890802388657

Biondi, M., Picardi, A., Pasquini, M., Gaetano, P., & Pancheri, P. (2005). Dimensional psychopathology of depression: Detection of an "activation" dimension in unipolar depressed outpatients. *Journal of Affective Disorders, 84*, 133–139. doi:10.1016/S0165-0327(02)00103-9

Black, M. S., Forbey, J. D., Ben-Porath, Y. S., Graham, J. R., McNulty, J. L., Anderson, S. V., & Burlew, A. (2004). Using the Minnesota Multiphasic Personality Inventory—2 (MMPI–2) to detect psychological stress and dysfunction in a state correctional setting. *Criminal Justice and Behavior, 31,* 734–751. doi:10.1177/0093854804268756

Blackburn, R. (1968). Emotionality, extraversion and aggression in paranoid and nonparanoid schizophrenic offenders. *British Journal of Psychiatry, 114,* 1301–1302. doi:10.1192/bjp.114.515.1301

Blake, D. D., Weathers, F. W., Nagy, L. M., Kaloupek, D. G., Gusman, F. D., Charney, D. S., & Keane, T. M. (1995). The development of a clinician-administered PTSD scale. *Journal of Traumatic Stress, 8,* 75–90. doi:10.1002/jts.2490080106

Blau, T. (1984). *The psychologist as expert witness.* New York, NY: Wiley.

Board of Immigration Appeals. (1978). Matter of Anderson, 16 I&N Dec 596.

Boerger, A. R., Graham, J. R., & Lilly, R. S. (1974). Behavioral correlates of single-scale MMPI code types. *Journal of Consulting and Clinical Psychology, 42,* 398–402. doi:10.1037/h0036689

Bohn, M. J., Jr. (1979). Inmate classification and the reduction of violence. *Proceedings of the 109th Annual Congress of Correction* (pp. 63–69). College Park, MD: American Correctional Association.

Bonnie, R. J. (1992). The competence of criminal defendants: A theoretical reformulation. *Behavioral Sciences & the Law, 10,* 291–316. doi:10.1002/bsl.2370100303

Boothby, J. L. & Clements, C. B. (2000). A national survey of correctional psychologists. *Journal of Criminal Justice and Behavior, 27,* 716–732. doi:10.1177/0093854800027006003

Borkosky, B. (2014). Who is the client and who controls release of records in a forensic evaluation? A review of ethics codes and practice guidelines. *Psychological Injury and Law, 7,* 264–289. doi:10.1007/s12207-014-9199-6

Borum, R. (2003). Not guilty by reason of insanity. In T. Grisso (Ed.), *Evaluating competencies: Forensic assessments and instruments* (2nd ed., pp. 193–227). New York, NY: Kluwer/Plenum.

Borum, R., & Grisso, T. (1995). Psychological test use in criminal forensic evaluations. *Professional Psychology: Research and Practice, 26,* 465–473. doi:10.1037/0735-7028.26.5.465

Borum, R., & Grisso, T. (1996). Establishing standards for criminal forensic reports: An empirical analysis. *Bulletin of the American Academy of Psychiatry and Law, 24,* 297–317.

Boscán, D. C., Penn, N. E., Velasquez, R. J., Reimann, J., Gomez, N., Gúzman, M., . . . Corrales de Romero, M. (2000). MMPI–2 profiles of Colombian, Mexican, and Venezuelan students. *Psychological Reports, 87,* 107–110. doi:10.2466/pr0.2000.87.1.107

Bosquet, M., & Egelund, B. (2000). Predicting parenting behavior from antisocial practices content scale scores of the MMPI–2 administered during pregnancy. *Journal of Personality Assessment, 74,* 146–162. doi:10.1207/S15327752JPA740110

Bow, J. N., Flens, J. R., & Gould, J. W. (2010). MMPI–2 and MCMI–III in forensic evaluations: A survey of psychologists. *Journal of Forensic Psychology Practice, 10,* 37–52. doi:10.1080/15228930903173021

Bow, J. N., Flens, J. R., Gould, J. W., & Greenhut, D. (2006). An analysis of administration, scoring, and interpretation of the MMPI–2 and MCMI–II/III in child custody evaluations. *Journal of Child Custody: Research, Issues, and Practices,* 2(4), 1–22. doi:10.1300/J190v02n04_01

Bradley, P. E. (1974). Parental MMPIs and certain pathological behaviors in children. *Journal of Clinical Psychology, 30,* 379–382. doi:10.1002/1097-4679(197407)30:3<379::AID-JCLP2270300349>3.0.CO;2-V

Brems, C., & Lloyd, P. (1995). Validation of the MMPI–2 Low Self-Esteem Content Scale. *Journal of Personality Assessment, 65,* 550–556. doi:10.1207/s15327752jpa6503_13

Bricklin, B. (1989). *Perception of Relationships Test manual.* Furlong, PA: Village.

Bricklin, B. (1990a). *Bricklin Perceptual Scales manual.* Furlong, PA: Village.

Bricklin, B. (1990b). *Parent Awareness Skills Survey manual.* Furlong, PA: Village.

Briere, J. (2001). *Detailed Assessment of Posttraumatic Stress (DAPS).* Lutz, FL: Psychological Assessment Resources.

Briere, J., & Scott, C. (2012). *Principles of trauma therapy: A guide to symptoms, evaluation, and treatment* (2nd ed.). Thousand Oaks, CA: Sage.

Brodsky, S. L. (2013). *Testifying in court: Guidelines and maxims for the expert witness* (2nd ed.). Washington, DC: American Psychological Association.

Bryant, R. A., Harvey, A. G., Dang, S. T., Sackville, T., & Basten, C. (1998). Treatment of acute stress disorder: A comparison of cognitive-behavioral therapy and supportive counseling. *Journal of Consulting and Clinical Psychology, 66,* 862–866. doi:10.1037/0022-006X.66.5.862

Budd, K. S. (2005). Assessing parenting capacity in a child welfare context. *Children and Youth Services Review, 27,* 429–444. doi:10.1016/j.childyouth.2004.11.008

Budd, K. S., Clark, J., & Connell, M. A. (2011). *Evaluation of parenting capacity in child protection.* New York, NY: Oxford University Press.

Budd, K. S., Poindexter, L. M., Felix, E. D., & Naik-Polan, A. T. (2001). Clinical assessment of parents in child protection cases: An empirical analysis. *Law and Human Behavior, 25,* 93–108. doi:10.1023/A:1005696026973

Bunnting, B. G., Wessels, W. H., Lasich, A. J., & Pillay, B. (1996). The distinction of malingering and mental illness in black forensic cases. *Medicine and Law, 15,* 241–247.

Bureau of Labor Statistics. (2010). *National Compensation Survey.* Washington, DC: United States Department of Labor.

Burgers, H. J., & Danelius, H. (1988). *The United Nations Convention Against Torture: A handbook on the Convention Against Torture and Other Cruel, Inhuman or Degrading Treatment or Punishment.* Dordrecht, the Netherlands: Nijhoff.

Burke, T. (2010). Psychiatric disorder: Understanding violence. In A. Bartlett & G. McGauley (Eds.), *Forensic mental health: Concepts, systems, and practice* (pp. 35–51). New York, NY: Oxford University Press.

Butcher, J. N. (1982). *User's guide for the MMPI–2 Minnesota Report: Adult clinical system.* Minneapolis, MN: National Computer Systems.

Butcher, J. N. (Ed.). (1987). *Computerized psychological assessment*. New York, NY: Basic Books.

Butcher, J. N. (1996). *International adaptations of the MMPI–2: Research and clinical applications*. Minneapolis: University of Minnesota Press.

Butcher, J. N. (1997). Frequency of MMPI–2 scores in forensic evaluations. *MMPI–2 News & Profiles, 8*, 1–2. Retrieved from http://www1.umn.edu/mmpi/documents/ FrequencyMMPI2Scores.pdf

Butcher, J. N. (2004). Personality assessment without borders: Adaptation of the MMPI–2 across cultures. *Journal of Personality Assessment, 83*, 90–104. doi:10.1207/s15327752jpa8302_02

Butcher, J. N. (2005). *User's guide for the Minnesota Clinical Report* (4th ed.). Minneapolis, MN: Pearson Assessments.

Butcher, J. N. (2009). How to use computer-based reports. In J. N. Butcher (Ed.), *Oxford handbook of personality assessment* (pp. 693–706). New York, NY: Oxford University Press.

Butcher, J. N. (2011). *A beginner's guide to the MMPI–2* (3rd ed.). Washington, DC: American Psychological Association.

Butcher, J. N. (2012). Personal injury references. Retrieved from http://www1.umn. edu/mmpi/documents/Reference-File5-Personal-Injury.pdf

Butcher, J. N. (2013a). Child custody related references. Retrieved from http:// www1.umn.edu/mmpi/documents/Reference_File_4_custody_refs_v1.pdf

Butcher, J. N. (2013b). Computerized psychological assessment. In J. R. Graham & J. Naglieri (Eds.), *Handbook of psychology* (2nd ed., Vol. 10, pp. 165–191). New York, NY: Wiley.

Butcher, J. N., Arbisi, P. A., Atlis, M. M., & McNulty, J. L. (2003). The construct validity of the Lees-Haley Fake Bad Scale: Does this scale measure somatic malingering and feigned emotional distress? *Archives of Clinical Neuropsychology, 18*, 473–485.

Butcher, J. N., Atlis, M. M., & Hahn, J. (2004). The Minnesota Multiphasic Personality Inventory—2 (MMPI–2). In M. J. Hilsenroth & D. L. Segal (Eds.), *Comprehensive handbook of psychological assessment: Vol. 2. Personality assessment* (pp. 30–38). Hoboken, NJ: Wiley.

Butcher, J. N., Berah, E., Ellertsen, B., Miach, P., Lim, J., Nezami, E., . . . Almagor, M. (1998). Objective personality assessment: Computer-based MMPI–2 interpretation in international clinical settings. In C. Belar (Ed.), *Comprehensive clinical psychology: Sociocultural and individual differences* (pp. 277–312). New York, NY: Elsevier.

Butcher, J. N., Cabiya, J., Lucio, E., & Garrido, M. (2007). *Assessing Hispanic clients using the MMPI–2 and the MMPI–A*. Washington, DC: American Psychological Association.

Butcher, J. N., & Cheung, F. M. (2006, May). Workshop on the MMPI–2 and foren-sic psychology. Chinese University of Hong Kong and the Hong Kong Social Welfare Department, Hong Kong.

Butcher, J. N., Cheung, F. M., & Lim, J. (2003). Use of the MMPI–2 with Asian populations. *Psychological Assessment, 15*, 248–256. doi:10.1037/1040-3590.15.3.248

Butcher, J. N., & Clark, L. A. (1979). Recent trends in cross-cultural MMPI research and application. In J. N. Butcher (Ed.), *New developments in the use of the MMPI* (pp. 69–111). Minneapolis: University of Minnesota Press.

Butcher, J. N., Coelho Mosch, S., Tsai, J., & Nezami, E. (2006). Cross-cultural applications of the *MMPI–2*. In J. N. Butcher (Ed.), *MMPI–2: A practitioner's guide* (pp. 505–537). Washington, DC: American Psychological Association.

Butcher, J. N., Dahlstrom, W. G., Graham, J. R., Tellegen, A., & Kaemmer, B. (1989). *Manual for the restandardized Minnesota Multiphasic Personality Inventory: MMPI–2. An administrative and interpretive guide.* Minneapolis: University of Minnesota Press.

Butcher, J. N., Derksen, J., Sloore, H., & Sirigatti, S. (2003). Objective personality assessment of people in diverse cultures: European adaptations of the MMPI–2. *Behaviour Research and Therapy, 41*, 819–840. doi:10.1016/S0005-7967(02)00186-9

Butcher, J. N., Ellertsen, B., Ubostad, B., Bubb, E., Lucio, E., Lim, J., . . . Elsbury, S. (2000). *International case studies on the MMPI–A: An objective approach.* Retrieved from http://www1.umn.edu/mmpi/adolescent.php

Butcher, J. N., Gass, C. S., Cumella, E., Kally, Z., & Williams, C. L. (2008). Potential for bias in MMPI–2 assessments using the Fake Bad Scale (FBS). *Psychological Injury and Law, 1*, 191–209. doi:10.1007/s12207-007-9002.

Butcher, J. N., Graham, J. R., & Ben-Porath, Y. S. (1995). Methodological problems and issues in MMPI/MMPI–2/MMPI–A research. *Psychological Assessment, 7*, 320–329. doi:10.1037/1040-3590.7.3.320

Butcher, J. N., Graham, J. R., Ben-Porath, Y. S., Tellegen, Y. S., Dahlstrom, W. G., & Kaemmer, B. (2001). *Minnesota Multiphasic Personality Inventory—2: Manual for administration and scoring* (Rev. ed.). Minneapolis: University of Minnesota Press.

Butcher, J. N., Graham, J. R., Williams, C. L., & Ben-Porath, Y. S. (1990). *Development and use of the MMPI–2 content scales.* Minneapolis: University of Minnesota Press.

Butcher, J. N., Gucker, D. K., & Hellervik, L. W. (2009). Clinical personality assessment in the employment context. In J. N. Butcher (Ed.), *Oxford handbook of personality assessment* (pp. 582–598). New York, NY: Oxford University Press.

Butcher, J. N., & Han, K. (1995). Development of an MMPI–2 scale to assess the presentation of self in a superlative manner: The S Scale. In J. N. Butcher & C. D. Spielberger (Eds.), *Advances in personality assessment* (Vol. 10, pp. 25–50). Hillsdale, NJ: Erlbaum.

Butcher, J. N., & Miller, K. (2005). Personality assessment in personal injury litigation. In A. Hess & I. B. Weiner (Eds.), *Handbook of forensic psychology* (2nd ed., pp. 104–126). New York, NY: Wiley.

Butcher, J. N., Morfitt, R., Rouse, S. V., & Holden, R. R. (1997). Reducing MMPI–2 defensiveness: The effect of specialized instructions on retest validity in a job applicant sample. *Journal of Personality Assessment, 68,* 385–401. doi:10.1207/s15327752jpa6802_9

Butcher, J. N., Mosch, S. C., Tsai, J., & Nezami, E. (2006). Cross-cultural applications of the MMPI–2. In J. N. Butcher (Ed.), *MMPI–2: A practitioner's guide* (pp. 505–537). Washington, DC: American Psychological Association.

Butcher, J. N., & Pancheri, P. (1976). *Handbook of cross-national MMPI research.* Minneapolis: University of Minnesota Press.

Butcher, J. N., & Perry, J. N. (2008). *Personality assessment in treatment planning: Use of the MMPI–2 and BTPI.* New York, NY: Oxford University Press.

Butcher, J. N., Perry, J., & Dean, B. L. (2009). Computer-based assessment. In J. N. Butcher (Ed.), *Oxford handbook of personality assessment* (pp. 163–182). New York, NY: Oxford University Press.

Butcher, J. N., Rouse, S. V., & Perry, J. N. (2000). Empirical description of psychopathology in therapy clients: Correlates of MMPI–2 scales. In J. N. Butcher (Ed.), *Basic sources on the MMPI–2* (pp. 487–500). Minneapolis: University of Minnesota Press.

Butcher, J. N., & Tellegen, A. (1978). MMPI research: Methodological problems and some current issues. *Journal of Consulting and Clinical Psychology, 46,* 620–628. doi:10.1037/0022-006X.46.4.620

Butcher, J. N., & Williams, C. L. (2000). *Essentials of MMPI–2 and MMPI–A clinical interpretation* (2nd ed.). Minneapolis: University of Minnesota Press.

Cabiya, J., Cruz, R., & Bayon, N. (2002, May). *MMPI–2 Hispanic normative project: Puerto Rican sample.* Paper presented at the Symposium on Recent Developments in the Use of the MMPI–2/MMPI–A, Minneapolis, MN.

Cabiya, J. J., Lucio, E., Chavira, D. A., Castellanos, J., Gomez, F. C., & Velasquez, R. (2000). MMPI–2 scores of Puerto Rican, Mexican, and U.S. Latino college students: A research note. *Psychological Reports, 87,* 266–268. doi:10.2466/pr0.2000.87.1.266

Caine, T. I. (1960). The expression of hostility and guilt in melancholic and paranoid women. *Journal of Consulting Psychology, 24,* 18–22. doi:10.1037/h0048476

Caldonazao, C. S. G. (1963). Observations on the diagnostic possibilities of Hathaway and McKinley's MMPI in the study of psychopathic paranoid development. *Rivista di Neuropsichiatria e Scienze Affini, 9,* 229–238.

Caldwell, A. B. (1970, May). *Recent advances in automated interpretation of the MMPI.* Paper presented at the Symposium on Recent Developments in the Use of the MMPI, Mexico City, Mexico.

Caldwell, A. B. (1997). Whither goest our redoubtable mentor, the MMPI/MMPI–2? *Journal of Personality Assessment, 68,* 47–68. doi:10.1207/s15327752jpa6801_5

Caldwell, A. B. J. (2005). How can the MMPI–2 help child custody examiners? *Journal of Child Custody, 2,* 83–117. doi:10.1300/J190v02n01_06

Cal. Labor Code (Bender 2014).

Callahan, L. A., & Silver, E. (1998). Factors associated with the conditional release of persons acquitted by reason of insanity: A decision tree approach. *Law and Human Behavior, 22,* 147–163. doi:10.1023/A:1025790003139

Campanella, S., Vanhoolandt, M. E., & Philippot, P. (2005). Emotional deficit in subjects with psychopathic tendencies as assessed by the Minnesota Multiphasic Personality Inventory—2: An event-related potentials study. *Neuroscience Letters, 373,* 26–31. doi:10.1016/j.neulet.2004.09.061

Campbell, J. C., Kub, J., Belknap, R. A., & Templin, T. (1997). Predictors of depression in battered women. *Violence Against Women, 3,* 271–293. doi:10.1177/1077801297003003004

Campbell, J. C., & Soeken, K. L. (1999). Women's responses to battering over time: An analysis of change. *Journal of Interpersonal Violence, 14,* 21–40. doi:10.1177/088626099014001002

Campbell, J. C., Webster, D. W., & Glass, N. (2009). The Danger Assessment: Validation of a lethality risk assessment instrument for intimate partner femicide. *Journal of Interpersonal Violence, 24,* 653–674. doi:10.1177/0886260508317180

Cantu, R. C. (1998). Return to play guidelines after a head injury. *Clinics in Sports Medicine, 17,* 45–60. doi:10.1016/S0278-5919(05)70060-0

Capaldi, D. M., & Owen, L. D. (2001). Physical aggression in a community sample of at-risk young couples: Gender comparisons for high frequency, injury, and fear. *Journal of Family Psychology, 15,* 425–440. doi:10.1037/0893-3200.15.3.425

Carmin, C. N., Wallbrown, F. H., Ownby, R. L., & Barnett, R. W. (1989). A factor analysis of the MMPI in an offender population. *Criminal Justice and Behavior, 16,* 486–494. doi:10.1177/0093854889016004008

Carr, G. D., Moretti, M. M., & Cue, B. J. H. (2005). Evaluating parenting capacity: Validity problems with the MMPI–2, PAI, CAPI, and ratings of child adjustment. *Professional Psychology: Research and Practice, 36,* 188–196. doi:10.1037/0735-7028.36.2.188

Carstairs, K. S., Richards, J. B., Fletcher, E. G., Droscher, H. K., & Ecob, R. (2012). Comparison of MMPI–2 trends in UK and USA parental competency examinees. *Journal of Child Custody, 9,* 195–200. doi:10.1080/15379418.2012.715548

Cassell, D., & Coleman, R. (1995). Parents with psychiatric problems. In P. Reder & C. Lucey (Eds.), *Assessment of parenting: Psychiatric and psychological contributions* (pp. 169–181). London, England: Routledge.

Cattell, R. B. (1948). The primary personality factors in women compared with those of men. *British Journal of Psychology, 1,* 114–130.

Cattell, R. B., Eber, H. W., & Tatsuoka, M. M. (1970). *Handbook for the Sixteen Personality Factor Questionnaire (16PF).* Champaign, IL: Institute for Personality and Ability Testing.

Cattell, R. B., & Stice, G. E. (1957). *The Sixteen Personality Factors Questionnaire*. Champaign, IL: Institute for Personality and Ability Testing.

Cervantes, R. C., Salgado de Snyder, V., & Padilla, A. M. (1989). Posttraumatic stress in immigrants from Central America and Mexico. *Hospital & Community Psychiatry, 40*, 615–619.

Chalus, G. A. (1976). Relationship between paranoid tendencies and projective behavior. *Psychological Reports, 39*, 1175–1181. doi:10.2466/pr0.1976.39.3f.1175

Chaney, H. S., Williams, S. G., Cohn, C. K., & Vincent, K. R. (1984). MMPI results: A comparison of trauma victims, psychogenic pain, and patients with organic disease. *Journal of Clinical Psychology, 40*, 1450–1454.

Chang, C.-H., & Wright, B. D. (2001). Detecting unexpected variables in the MMPI–2 Social Introversion scale. *Journal of Applied Measurement, 2*, 227–240.

Chaudry, A., Capps, R., Pedroza, J. M., Castañeda, R. M., Santos, R., & Scott, M. (2010). *Facing our future: Children in the aftermath of immigration enforcement*. New York, NY: Urban Institute.

Cheung, F. M. (1995). *Administration manual of the Minnesota Multiphasic Personality Inventory (MMPI), Chinese edition*. Hong Kong, China: Chinese University Press.

Cheung, F. M., Song, W. Z., & Butcher, J. N. (1991). An infrequency scale for the Chinese MMPI. *Psychological Assessment, 3*, 648–653. doi:10.1037/1040-3590.3.4.648

Cicchetti, D., & Olsen, K. (1990). The developmental psychopathology of child maltreatment. In M. Lewis & S. Miller (Eds.), *Handbook of developmental psychopathology* (pp. 261–279). New York, NY: Plenum Press.

Cigrang, J. A., & Staal, M. A. (2001). Readministration of the MMPI–2 following defensive invalidation in a military job applicant sample. *Journal of Personality Assessment, 76*, 472–481. doi:10.1207/S15327752JPA7603_08

Clark, J. H. (1952). The relationship between MMPI scores and psychiatric classification of Army general prisoners. *Journal of Clinical Psychology, 8*, 86–89. doi:10.1002/1097-4679(195201)8:1<86::AID-JCLP2270080117>3.0.CO;2-Q

Clark, M. E., Gironda, R. J., & Young, R. W. (2003). Detection of back random responding: Effectiveness of MMPI–2 and Personality Assessment Inventory validity indices. *Psychological Assessment, 15*, 223–234. doi:10.1037/1040-3590.15.2.223

Clark, S., Callahan, W. J., Lichtszajn, J., & Velasquez, R. J. (1996). MMPI performance of Central American refugees and Mexican immigrants. *Psychological Reports, 79*, 819–824. doi:10.2466/pr0.1996.79.3.819

Cocchiarella, L., & Andersson, G. B. (2001). *American Medical Association: Guides to the evaluation of permanent impairment* (5th ed.). Chicago, IL: AMA Press.

Cohen, R., Parmelee, D. X., Irwin, L., Weisz, J. R., Howard, P., Purcell, P., & Best, A. M. (1990). Characteristics of children and adolescents in a psychiatric hospital and a corrections facility. *Journal of the American Academy of Child & Adolescent Psychiatry, 29*, 909–913. doi:10.1097/00004583-199011000-00012

Collet, L., Cottraux, J. A., & Juenet, C. (1986). Tension headaches: Relation between MMPI paranoia score and pain and between MMPI hypochondriasis score and frontalis EMG. *Headache, 26*, 365–368. doi:10.1111/j.1526-4610.1986. hed2607365.x

Colligan, R. C., Osborne, D., Swenson, W. M., & Offord, K. P. (1983). *The MMPI: A contemporary normative study.* New York, NY: Praeger.

Colotla, V. A., Bowman, M. L., & Shercliffe, R. J. (2001). Test–retest stability of injured workers' MMPI-2 profiles. *Psychological Assessment, 13*, 572–576. doi:10.1037/1040-3590.13.4.572

Condie, L. O. (2003). *Parenting evaluations for the court: Care and protection matters.* New York, NY: Kluwer Academic.

Conrad, K. A., Amstadter, A. B., McCauley, J. L., Richardson, L., Kilpatrick, D. G., Tran, T. L., . . . Acierno, R. (2010). Examination of general health following Typhoon Xangsane: A pre–post analysis. *Psychological Trauma: Theory, Research, Practice, and Policy, 2*, 109–115. doi:10.1037/a0017943

Cook, W. W., & Medley, D. M. (1954). Proposed hostility and Pharisaic-virtue scales for the MMPI. *Journal of Applied Psychology, 38*, 414–418. doi:10.1037/h0060667

Cooke, G. (2010). MMPI-2 defensiveness in child custody evaluations: The role of education and socioeconomic level. *American Journal of Forensic Psychology, 28*, 5–16.

Cooke, G., & Bleier, D. M. (2011). Diminished capacity in federal sentencing. In E. Y. Drogin, F. M. Dattilio, R. L. Sadoff, & T. G. Gutheil (Eds.), *Handbook of forensic assessment: Psychological and psychiatric perspectives* (pp. 171–186). Hoboken, NJ: Wiley.

Costa, P. T., Zonderman, A. B., McCrae, R. R., & Williams, R. B. (1986). Cynicism and paranoid alienation in the Cook and Medley *Ho* Scale. *Psychosomatic Medicine, 48*, 283–285. doi:10.1097/00006842-198603000-00014

Craig, R. J. (2005). Assessing contemporary substance abusers with the MMPI MacAndrew Alcoholism Scale: A review. *Substance Use & Misuse, 40*, 427–450. doi:10.1081/JA-200052401

Craig, R. J. (2008). MMPI–based forensic-psychological assessment of lethal violence. In H. V. Hall (Ed.), *Forensic psychology and neuropsychology for criminal and civil cases* (pp. 393–416). Boca Raton, FL: CRC Press.

Craig, R. J., Ammar, A., & Olson, R. E. (1998). Psychological assessment (MMPI-2) of male African-American substance-abusing patients with and without histories of childhood physical abuse. *Journal of Substance Abuse, 10*, 43–51. doi:10.1016/S0899-3289(99)80139-4

Cripe, L. I. (1996). The ecological validity of executive function testing. In R. J. Sbordone & C. J. Long (Eds.), *Ecological validity of neuropsychological assessment* (pp. 129–146). Delray Beach, FL: GR/St. Lucie Press.

Cripe, L. I. (1999). Use of the MMPI with mild closed head injury. In N. R. Varney & R. J. Roberts (Eds.), *The evaluation and treatment of mild traumatic brain injury* (pp. 291–314). Hillsdale, NJ: Erlbaum.

Cronbach, L. (1970). Other characteristics desired in tests. In L. Cronbach (Ed.), *Essentials of psychological testing* (pp. 151–196). New York, NY: Harper & Row.

Cuéllar, I. (2000). Acculturation as a moderator of personality and psychological assessment. In R. H. Dana (Ed.), *Handbook of cross cultural and multicultural personality assessment* (pp. 113–129). Mahwah, NJ: Erlbaum.

Cuéllar, I., Arnold, B., & Maldonado, R. (1995). Acculturation Rating Scale for Mexican Americans—II: A revision of the original ARSMA scale. *Hispanic Journal of Behavioral Sciences, 17,* 275–304. doi:10.1177/07399863950173001

Cummings, E. M., & Davies, P. T. (1999). Depressed parents and family functioning: Interpersonal effects and children's functioning and development. In T. Joiner & C. James (Eds.), *The interactional nature of depression: Advances in interpersonal approaches* (pp. 299–327). Washington, DC: American Psychological Association.

Cunningham, M. D., & Sorensen, J. R. (2007). Capital offenders in Texas prisons: Rates, correlates, and an actuarial analysis of violent misconduct. *Law and Human Behavior, 31,* 553–571. doi:10.1007/s10979-006-9079-z

Dahlstrom, W. G. (1960). Characteristics of depressive and paranoid schizophrenic reactions on the Minnesota Multiphasic Personality Inventory. *Journal of Nervous and Mental Disease, 131,* 513–522. doi:10.1097/00005053-196012000-00005

Dahlstrom, W. G., Lachar, D., & Dahlstrom, L. E. (1986). *MMPI patterns of American minorities.* Minneapolis: University of Minnesota Press.

Dahlstrom, W. G., Welsh, G. S., & Dahlstrom, L. E. (1972). *An MMPI handbook: Vol. 1. Clinical interpretation* (Rev. ed.). Minneapolis: University of Minnesota Press.

Dana, R. H. (1988). Culturally diverse groups and MMPI interpretation. *Professional Psychology: Research and Practice, 19,* 490–495. doi:10.1037/0735-7028.19.5.490

Dana, R. H. (2000). *Handbook of cross cultural and multicultural personality assessment.* Mahwah, NJ: Erlbaum.

Daubert v. Merrell Dow Pharmaceuticals, 509 U.S. 579 (1993).

Davidson v. Strawberry Petroleum, No. 05-4320 (Fla. Hillsborough County Ct., May 30, 2007).

Davis, K. R., & Sines, J. O. (1971). An antisocial behavior pattern associated with a specific MMPI profile. *Journal of Consulting and Clinical Psychology, 36,* 229–234. doi:10.1037/h0030739

Dean, A. C., Boone, K. R., Kim, M. S., Curiel, A. R., Martin, D. J., Victor, T. L., . . . Lang, Y. K. (2008). Examination of the impact of ethnicity on the Minnesota Multiphasic Personality Inventory—2 (MMPI–2) Fake Bad Scale. *Clinical Neuropsychologist, 22,* 1054–1060. doi:10.1080/13854040701750891

Dearth, C. S., Berry, D. T. R., Vickery, C. D., Vagnini, V. L., Baser, R. E., Orey, S. A., & Cragar, D. E. (2005). Detection of feigned head injury symptoms on the MMPI–2 in head injured patients and community controls. *Archives of Clinical Neuropsychology, 20*, 95–110. doi:10.1016/j.acn.2004.03.004

De Jesús-Rentas, G., Boehnlein, J., & Sparr, L. (2010). Central American victims of gang violence as asylum seekers: The role of the forensic expert. *Journal of the American Academy of Psychiatry and the Law, 38*, 490–498.

de la Fuente, R. (1990). The mental health consequences of the 1985 earthquakes in Mexico. *International Journal of Mental Health, 19*, 21–29.

DeMatteo, D., Murrie, D. C., Anumba, N. M., & Keesler, M. E. (2011). *Forensic mental health assessments in death penalty cases*. New York, NY: Oxford University Press.

Department of Veterans Affairs, Department of Defense. (2009). *VA/DoD clinical practice guideline for management of concussion/mild traumatic brain injury (mTBI)*. Washington, DC: Author.

Derogatis, L. R., Lipman, R. S., & Covi, L. (1973). The SCL-90: An outpatient psychiatric rating scale. *Psychopharmacology Bulletin, 9*, 13–28.

Doehring, D. G., & Reitan, R. M. (1960). MMPI performance of aphasic and non-aphasic brain-damaged patients. *Journal of Clinical Psychology, 16*, 307–309.

Dong, Y. T., & Church, A. T. (2003). Cross-cultural equivalence and validity of the Vietnamese MMPI–2: Assessing psychological adjustment of Vietnamese refugees. *Psychological Assessment, 15*, 370–377. doi:10.1037/1040-3590.15.3.370

Donnelly, E. F., Murphy, D. L., & Waldman, I. N. (1980). Denial and somatization as characteristics of bipolar depressed groups. *Journal of Clinical Psychology, 36*, 159–162. doi:10.1002/1097-4679(198001)36:1<159::AID-JCLP2270360116>3.0.CO;2-Y

D'Orazio, L. M., Meyerowitz, B. E., Korst, L. M., Romero, R., & Goodwin, T. M. (2011). Evidence against a link between hyperemesis gravidarum and personality characteristics from an ethnically diverse sample of pregnant women: A pilot study. *Journal of Women's Health, 20*, 137–144. doi:10.1089/jwh.2009.1851

Downey, G., & Coyne, J. C. (1990). Children of depressed parents: An integrative review. *Psychological Bulletin, 108*, 50–76. doi:10.1037/0033-2909.108.1.50

Drozd, L. M., Kuehnle, K., & Walker, L. (2004). Safety first: A model for understanding domestic violence in child custody and access disputes. *Journal of Child Custody, 1*, 75–103. doi:10.1300/J190v01n02_04

DuAlba, L., & Scott, R. L. (1993). Somatization and malingering for workers' compensation applicants: A cross-cultural MMPI study. *Journal of Clinical Psychology, 49*, 913–917. doi:10.1002/1097-4679(199311)49:6<913::AID-JCLP2270490619>3.0.CO;2-1

Dush, D. M., Simons, L. E., Platt, M., & Nation, P. C. (1994). Psychological profiles distinguishing litigating and nonlitigating pain patients: Subtle, and not so subtle. *Journal of Personality Assessment, 62*, 299–313. doi:10.1207/s15327752jpa6202_10

Dutton, D. (2006). Domestic abuse assessment in child custody disputes: Beware the domestic violence research paradigm. *Journal of Child Custody, 2*(4), 23–42. doi:10.1300/J190v02n04_02

Dutton, M. A. (1992). *Empowering and healing the battered woman.* New York, NY: Springer.

Dutton, M. A., & Goodman, L. A. (2005). Coercion in intimate partner violence: Toward a new conceptualization. *Sex Roles, 52,* 743–756. doi:10.1007/s11199-005-4196-6

Dutton, M. A., Goodman, L. A., & Bennett, L. (1999). Court-involved battered women's responses to violence: The role of psychological, physical, and sexual abuse. *Violence and Victims, 14,* 89–104.

Dutton, M. A., Goodman, L., & Schmidt, R. J. (2005). *Development and validation of a coercive control measure for intimate partner violence: Final technical report* (NCJ 214438). Retrieved from https://www.ncjrs.gov/pdffiles1/nij/grants/214438.pdf

Dutton, M. A., Orloff, L., & Hass, G. A. (2000). Characteristics of help-seeking behaviors, resources, and service needs of battered immigrant Latinas: Legal and policy implications. *Georgetown Journal on Poverty Law & Policy, 7,* 30–49.

Edleson, J. (1999). The overlap between child maltreatment and woman battering. *Violence Against Women, 15,* 132–154.

Egeland, B., Erickson, M., Butcher, J. N., & Ben-Porath, Y. S. (1991). MMPI–2 profiles of women at risk for child abuse. *Journal of Personality Assessment, 57,* 254–263. doi:10.1207/s15327752jpa5702_5

Egeland, B., Jacobvitz, D., & Sroufe, L. A. (1988). Breaking the cycle of abuse. *Child Development, 59,* 1080–1088. doi:10.2307/1130274

Eisenman, R., & Coyle, F. A. (1965). Commonality in sociopathy and paranoia? *Psychological Reports, 17,* 704. doi:10.2466/pr0.1965.17.3.704

Elhai, J. D., Gold, P. B., Frueh, B. C., & Gold, S. N. (2000). Cross-validation of the MMPI–2 in detecting malingered posttraumatic stress disorder. *Journal of Personality Assessment, 75,* 449–463. doi:10.1207/S15327752JPA7503_06

Elhai, J. D., Gold, S. N., Mateus, L. F., & Astaphan, T. A. (2001). Scale 8 elevations on the MMPI–2 among women survivors of childhood sexual abuse: Evaluating posttraumatic stress, depression, and dissociation as predictors. *Journal of Family Violence, 16,* 47–57. doi:10.1023/A:1026576425986

Ellis, D., & Stuckless, N. (1996). *Mediating and negotiating marital conflict.* Thousand Oaks, CA: Sage.

Ellis, D., & Stuckless, N. (2006). Domestic violence, DOVE, and divorce mediation. *Family Court Review, 44,* 658–671. doi:10.1111/j.1744-1617.2006.00117.x

Elwood, R. W. (1993). The clinical utility of the MMPI–2 in diagnosing unipolar depression among male alcoholics. *Journal of Personality Assessment, 60,* 511–521. doi:10.1207/s15327752jpa6003_8

Emons, W. H. M., Sijtsma, K., & Meijer, R. R. (2007). On the consistency of individual classification using short scales. *Psychological Methods, 12,* 105–120. doi:10.1037/1082-989X.12.1.105

England, M. J., & Sim, L. J. (Eds.). (2009). *Depression in parents, parenting, and children: Opportunities to improve identification, treatment, and prevention.* Washington, DC: National Academy Press.

Englert, D. R., Weed, N. C., & Watson, G. (2000). Convergent, discriminant, and internal properties of the Minnesota Multiphasic Personality Inventory (2nd ed.) Low Self-Esteem Content Scale. *Measurement and Evaluation in Counseling and Development, 33,* 42–49.

Erickson, N. S. (2005). Use of the MMPI–2 in child custody evaluations involving battered women: What does psychological research tell us? *Family Law Quarterly, 39,* 87–108.

Eronen, M., Hakola, P., & Tiihonen, J. (1996). Mental disorders and homicidal behavior in Finland. *Archives of General Psychiatry, 53,* 497–501. doi:10.1001/archpsyc.1996.01830060039005

Erreca, K. (2010). *MMPI–2–RF profiles of women with eating disorders in an inpatient setting* (Doctoral dissertation). Available from ProQuest Dissertations and Theses database. (UMI No. 3437609)

Evans, B. F. (2004). Family violence, immigration law, and the Rorschach. *Rorschachiana, 26,* 147–157. doi:10.1027/1192-5604.26.1.147

Ezzo, F. R., Pinsoneault, T. B., & Evans, T. M. (2007). A comparison of MMPI–2 profiles between child maltreatment cases and two types of custody cases. *Journal of Forensic Psychology Practice, 7,* 29–43. doi:10.1300/J158v07n02_02

Fairbank, J. A., McCaffrey, R., & Keane, T. M. (1985). Psychometric detection of fabricated symptoms of post-traumatic stress disorder. *American Journal of Psychiatry, 142,* 501–503.

Family Preservation and Support Services Program Act of 1993, enacted as part of the Omnibus Budget Reconciliation Act of 1993, Pub. L. No. 103-66, 107 Stat. 312.

Faunce, G. J., Mapledoram, P. K., & Job, R. F. S. (2004). Type A behavior pattern and attentional bias in relation to anger/hostility, achievement, and failure. *Personality and Individual Differences, 36,* 1975–1988. doi:10.1016/j.paid.2003.07.016

Faust, D. (Ed.). (2012). *Coping with psychiatric and psychological testimony* (6th ed., pp. 511–518). New York, NY: Oxford University Press.

Federal Aviation Administration. (2013). *Guide for aviation medical examiners: Decision considerations, disease protocols, psychiatric and psychological evaluations.* Retrieved from http://www.faa.gov/about/office_org/headquarters_offices/avs/offices/aam/ame/guide/dec_cons/disease_prot/ppevals/

Federal Register Publications. (2007). *New classification for victims of criminal activity: Eligibility for "U" nonimmigrant status.* Retrieved from http://www.uscis.gov/ilink/docView/FR/HTML/FR/0-0-0-1/0-0-0-123038/0-0-0-133528/0-0-0-137708.html

Felthous, A. R. (2007). Criminal sentencing: The role of mental health professionals with special consideration for psychopathic disorders. In A. R. Felthous & H. Sass (Eds.), *International handbook of psychopathic disorders and the law: Vol. 2. Laws and policies* (pp. 317–327). New York, NY: Wiley.

Finger, M. S., & Ones, D. S. (1999). Psychometric equivalence of the computer and booklet forms of the MMPI: A meta-analysis. *Psychological Assessment, 11*, 58–66. doi:10.1037/1040-3590.11.1.58

Finney, J. C. (1966). Programmed interpretation of MMPI and CPI. *Archives of General Psychiatry, 15*, 75–81. doi:10.1001/archpsyc.1966.01730130077012

Flens, J. R. (2005). The responsible use of psychological testing in child custody evaluations: Selection of tests. *Journal of Child Custody, 2*, 3–27.

Forbey, J. D., Ben-Porath, Y. S., & Gartland, D. (2009). Validation of the MMPI–2 Computerized Adaptive Version (MMPI–2CA) in a correctional intake facility. *Psychological Services, 6*, 279–292. doi:10.1037/a0016195

Ford, J. D., Adams, M. L., & Dailey, W. F. (2007). Psychological and health problems in a geographically proximate population time-sampled continuously for three months after the September 11th, 2001 terrorist incidents. *Anxiety, Stress, and Coping, 20*, 129–146. doi:10.1080/10615800701303215

Fordyce, W. E., Bigos, S. J., Batti'e, M. C., & Fisher, L. D. (1992). MMPI scale 3 as a predictor of back injury report: What does it tell us? *Clinical Journal of Pain, 8*, 222–226. doi:10.1097/00002508-199209000-00006

Foster, R. P. (2001). When immigration is trauma: Guidelines for the individual and family clinician. *American Journal of Orthopsychiatry, 71*, 153–170. doi:10.1037/0002-9432.71.2.153

Fowler, R. D. (1964, September). *Computer processing and reporting of personality test data.* Paper presented at the meeting of the American Psychological Association, Los Angeles, CA.

Fowler, R. D. (1965, September). *Purposes and usefulness of the Alabama program for the automatic interpretation of the MMPI.* Paper presented at the meeting of the American Psychological Association, Chicago, IL.

Fowler, R. D. (1967). Computer interpretation of personality tests: The automated psychologist. *Comprehensive Psychiatry, 8*, 455–467. doi:10.1016/S0010-440X(67)80029-4

Fowler, R. D. (1969). Automated interpretation of personality test data. In J. N. Butcher (Ed.), *MMPI: Research developments and clinical applications* (pp. 105–126). New York, NY: McGraw-Hill.

Fowler, R. D. (1972). Automated psychological test interpretation: The status in 1972. *Psychiatric Annals, 2*, 10–28.

Fowler, R. D. (1987). Developing a computer-based test interpretation system. In J. N. Butcher (Ed.), *Computerized psychological assessment: A practitioner's guide* (pp. 50–63). New York, NY: Basic Books.

Fowler, R. D., & Athey, E. B. (1971). A cross-validation of Gilberstadt and Duker's 1-2-3-4 profile type. *Journal of Clinical Psychology, 27,* 238–240. doi:10.1002/1097-4679(197104)27:2<238::AID-JCLP2270270226>3.0.CO;2-O

Fracchia, J., Sheppard, C., Merlis, M., & Merlis, S. (1970). Atypical reasoning errors in sociopathic, paranoid, and schizotypic personality types. *Journal of Psychology: Interdisciplinary and Applied, 76,* 91–95. doi:10.1080/00223980.1970.9916825

Franklin, C. L., Repasky, S. A., Thompson, K. E., Shelton, S. A., & Uddo, M. (2003). Assessment of response style in combat veterans seeking compensation for posttraumatic stress disorder. *Journal of Traumatic Stress, 16,* 251–255. doi:10.1023/A:1023744023717

Frankowski, R. F., Annegers, J. F., & Whitman, S. (1985). Epidemiological and descriptive studies. Part I: The descriptive epidemiology of head trauma in the United States. In D. P. Decker & J. T. Powlishock (Eds.), *Central nervous system trauma status report 1985* (pp. 33–43). Bethesda, MD: National Institute of Neurological Disorders and Stroke.

Frederick, L. (2001). *Effective interventions in domestic violence cases: The context is everything.* Minneapolis, MN: Battered Women's Justice Project.

Frederick, R. I. (2012). Criminal competency of adults. In D. Faust (Ed.), *Coping with psychiatric and psychological testimony* (6th ed., pp. 229–247). New York, NY: Oxford University Press.

Freeman, W., & Watts, J. (1942). *Psychosurgery.* Springfield, IL: Thomas.

Friedman, A. F., Bolinskey, P. K., Lewak, R. W., & Nichols, D. S. (2014). *Psychological assessment with the MMPI–2/MMPI–2–RF* (3rd ed.). New York, NY: Routledge/Taylor.

Friedman, A. F., Lewak, R., Nichols, D. A., & Webb, J. T. (2001). *Psychological assessment with the MMPI–2.* Mahwah, NJ: Erlbaum.

Friedman, M., & Jaranson, J. (1994). The applicability of the posttraumatic stress disorder concept to refugees. In A. J. Marsella, T. Bornemann, S. Ekblad, & J. Orley (Eds.), *Amidst peril and pain: The mental health and well-being of the world's refugees* (pp. 207–227). Washington, DC: American Psychological Association.

Frueh, B. C., Gold, P. B., de Arellano, M. A., & Brady, K. L. (1997). A racial comparison of combat veterans evaluated for PTSD. *Journal of Personality Assessment, 68,* 692–702. doi:10.1207/s15327752jpa6803_14

Frueh, B. C., Smith, D. W., & Barker, S. E. (1996). Compensation seeking status and psychometric assessment of combat veterans seeking treatment for PTSD. *Journal of Traumatic Stress, 9,* 427–439. doi:10.1002/jts.2490090303

Frumkin, B. I., & Friedland, J. (1995). Forensic evaluations in immigration cases: Evolving issues. *Behavioral Sciences & the Law, 13,* 477–489. doi:10.1002/bsl.2370130404

Fry, F. D. (1949). A study of the personality traits of college students, and of state prison inmates as measured by the Minnesota Multiphasic Personality Inventory. *Journal of Psychology: Interdisciplinary and Applied, 28,* 439–449. doi:10.1080/00223980.1949.9916021

Gacano, C. B., & Meloy, J. R. (2009). Assessing antisocial and psychopathic personalities. In J. N. Butcher (Ed.), *Oxford handbook of personality assessment* (pp. 567–581). New York, NY: Oxford University Press.

Gandolfo, R. (1995). MMPI–2 profiles of workers' compensation claimants who present with complaints of harassment. *Journal of Clinical Psychology, 51,* 711–715. doi:10.1002/1097-4679(199509)51:5<711::AID-JCLP2270510517>3.0.CO;2-R

Ganellen, R. J. (1996). *Integrating the Rorschach and the MMPI–2 in personality assessment.* Mahwah, NJ: Erlbaum.

Garg, S., Dattilio, F. M., & Mazzo, P. (2011). Transcultural considerations. In E. Y. Drogin, F. M. Dattilio, R. L. Sadoff, & T. G. Gutheil (Eds.), *Handbook of forensic assessment: Psychological and psychiatric perspectives* (pp. 679–696). Hoboken, NJ: Wiley.

Garrett, M. T., & Pichette, E. F. (2000). Red as an apple: Native American acculturation and counseling with or without reservation. *Journal of Counseling and Development, 78,* 3–13. doi:10.1002/j.1556-6676.2000.tb02554.x

Gasquoine, P. G. (2000). Postconcussional symptoms in chronic back pain. *Applied Neuropsychology, 7,* 83–89. doi:10.1207/S15324826AN0702_3

Gass, C. S. (1996). MMPI–2 variables in attention and memory test performance. *Psychological Assessment, 8,* 135–138. doi:10.1037/1040-3590.8.2.135

Gass, C. S. (2009). Use of the MMPI–2 in neuropsychological evaluations. In J. N. Butcher (Ed.), *Oxford handbook of personality assessment* (pp. 432–456). New York, NY: Oxford University Press.

Gass, C. S., & Apple, C. (1997). Cognitive complaints in closed-head injury: Relation to memory test performance and emotional disturbance. *Journal of Clinical and Experimental Neuropsychology, 19,* 229–299. doi:10.1080/01688639708403858

Gass, C. S., & Brown, M. C. (1992). Neuropsychological test feedback to patients with brain dysfunction. *Psychological Assessment, 4,* 272–277. doi:10.1037/1040-3590.4.3.272

Gass, C. S., & Luis, C. A. (2001). The MMPI–2 short form: Psychometric characteristics in a neuropsychological setting. *Assessment, 8,* 213–219. doi:10.1177/107319110100800209

Gass, C. S., & Odland, A. P. (2012). Minnesota Multiphasic Personality Inventory—2 Revised Form Symptom Validity Scale—Revised (MMPI–2–RF *FBS-r*; also known as Fake Bad Scale): Psychometric characteristics in a nonlitigation neuropsychological setting. *Journal of Clinical and Experimental Neuropsychology, 34,* 561–570. doi:10.1080/13803395.2012.666228

Gass, C. S., & Odland, A. P. (2014). MMPI–2 Symptom Validity (*FBS*) Scale: Psychometric characteristics and limitations in a Veterans Affairs neuropsychological setting. *Applied Neuropsychology: Adult, 21*, 1–8. doi:10.1080/09084282. 2012.715608

Gass, C. S., & Wald, H. S. (1997). MMPI–2 interpretation and closed-head trauma: Cross-validation of a correction factor. *Archives of Clinical Neuropsychology, 12*, 199–205. doi:10.1093/arclin/12.3.199

Gass, C. S., Williams, C. L., Cumella, E., Butcher, J. N., & Kally, Z. (2010). Ambiguous measures of unknown constructs: The MMPI–2 Fake Bad Scale (aka Symptom Validity Scale, *FBS, FBS-r*). *Psychological Injury and Law, 3*, 81–85. doi:10.1007/s12207-009-9063-2

Gatchel, R. J., Polatin, P. B., & Kinney, R. K. (1995). Predicting outcome of chronic back pain using clinical predictors of psychopathology: A prospective analysis. *Health Psychology, 14*, 415–420. doi:10.1037/0278-6133.14.5.415

Gatchel, R. J., Polatin, P. B., & Mayer, T. G. (1995). The dominant role of psychosocial risk factors in the development of chronic low back pain disability. *Spine, 20*, 2702–2709. doi:10.1097/00007632-199512150-00011

Gaughwin, P. C. (1998). Ethics, duty of care and forensic psychiatric assessment: A legal perspective. *Australian and New Zealand Journal of Psychiatry, 32*, 722–727. doi:10.3109/00048679809113129

Gehring, A., & Blaser, P. (1972). A computer program for the evaluation and interpretation of the MMPI. *Psychologie, 31*, 292–297.

Geisinger, K. F. (Ed.). (1992). *Psychological testing of Hispanics*. Washington, DC: American Psychological Association.

Gelles, R. J., & Straus, M. A. (1988). *Intimate violence: The definite study of the causes and consequences of abuse in the American family*. New York, NY: Simon & Schuster.

Gerard, A. B. (1994). *Parent–Child Relationship Inventory manual*. Los Angeles, CA: Western Psychological Services.

Gervais, R. O., Ben-Porath, Y. S., Wygant, D. B., & Green, P. (2007). Development and validation of a Response Bias Scale (*RBS*) for the MMPI–2. *Assessment, 14*, 196–208. doi:10.1177/1073191106295861

Gervais, R. O., Ben-Porath, Y. S., Wygant, D. B., & Green, P. (2008). Differential sensitivity of the Response Bias Scale (*RBS*) and MMPI–2 validity scales to memory complaints. *Clinical Neuropsychologist, 22*, 1061–1079. doi:10.1080/13854040701756930

Gilberstadt, H. (1970). *Comprehensive MMPI codebook for males*. Minneapolis, MN: Veterans Administration Hospital.

Gilberstadt, H., & Duker, J. (1965). *A handbook for clinical and actuarial MMPI interpretation*. Philadelphia, PA: Saunders.

Gim Chung, R. H., Kim, B. S. K., & Abreu, J. M. (2004). Asian American Multidimensional Acculturation Scale: Development, factor analysis, reliability and validity. *Cultural Diversity and Ethnic Minority Psychology, 10*, 66–80. doi: 10.1037/1099-9809.10.1.66

Giza, C. C., Kutcher, J. S., Ashwal, S., Barth, J., Getchius, T. S., Gioia, G. A., . . . Zafonte, R. (2013). Summary of evidence-based guideline update: evaluation and management of concussion in sports: Report of the Guideline Development Subcommittee of the American Academy of Neurology. *Neurology, 80*, 2250–2257. doi:10.1212/WNL.0b013e31828d57dd

Gleason, W. J. (1993). Mental disorders in battered women: An empirical study. *Violence and Victims, 8*, 53–68.

Golden, Z., & Golden, C. J. (2003). Impact of brain injury severity on personality dysfunction. *International Journal of Neuroscience, 113*, 733–745. doi:10.1080/00207450390200044

Golding, J. M. (1999). Intimate partner violence as a risk factor for mental disorders: A meta-analysis. *Journal of Family Violence, 14*, 99–132. doi:10.1023/A:1022079418229

Goldstein, A. M., & Bursztajn, H. J. (2011). Capital litigation: Special considerations. In E. Y. Drogin, F. M. Dattilio, R. L. Sadoff, & T. G. Gutheil (Eds.), *Handbook of forensic assessment: Psychological and psychiatric perspectives* (pp. 145–170). Hoboken, NJ: Wiley.

Goldstein, R. Z., Alia-Klein, N., Leskovjan, A. C., Fowler, J. S., Wang, G., Gur, R. C., . . . Volkow, N. D. (2005). Anger and depression in cocaine addiction: Association with the orbitofrontal cortex. *Psychiatry Research: Neuroimaging, 138*, 13–22. doi:10.1016/j.pscychresns.2004.10.002

Gordon, R., & Peek, L. A. (1989). *The Custody Quotient: Research manual.* Dallas, TX: Wilmington Institute.

Gordon, R. M., Stoffey, R.W., & Perkins, B. L. (2013). Comparing the sensitivity of the MMPI–2 clinical scales and the MMPI–RC scales to clients rated as psychotic, borderline or neurotic on the Psychodiagnostic Chart. *Psychology, 4*(9B), 12–16. doi:10.4236/psych.2013.49A1003

Gough, H. G., McClosky, H., & Meehl, P. E. (1951). A personality scale for dominance. *Journal of Abnormal and Social Psychology, 46*, 360–366. doi:10.1037/h0062542

Gough, H. G., McClosky, H., & Meehl, P. E. (1952). A personality scale for social responsibility. *Journal of Abnormal and Social Psychology, 47*, 73–80. doi:10.1037/h0062924

Gould, J. (2005). Use of psychological tests in child custody assessment. *Journal of Child Custody, 2*, 49–69. doi:10.1300/J190v02n01_04

Gowensmith, W. N., Murrie, D. C., & Boccaccini, M. T. (2013). How reliable are forensic evaluations of legal sanity? *Law and Human Behavior, 37*, 98–106. doi:10.1037/lhb0000001

Graham, J. R. (2006). *Assessing personality and psychopathology* (4th ed.). New York, NY: Oxford University Press.

Graham, J. R. (2012). *MMPI–2: Assessing psychopathology and personality* (4th ed.). New York, NY: Oxford University Press.

Graham, J. R., Smith, R. L., & Schwartz, G. F. (1986). Stability of MMPI configurations for psychiatric inpatients. *Journal of Consulting and Clinical Psychology, 54,* 375–380. doi:10.1037/0022-006X.54.3.375

Graham-Kevan, N., & Archer, J. (2003). Intimate terrorism and common couple violence: A test of Johnson's predictions in four British samples. *Journal of Interpersonal Violence, 18,* 1247–1270. doi:10.1177/0886260503256656

Greenberg, S. A., & Shuman, D. W. (1997). Irreconcilable conflict between therapeutic and forensic roles. *Professional Psychology: Research and Practice, 28,* 50–57. doi:10.1037/0735-7028.28.1.50

Greenblatt, R. L., & Davis, W. E. (1999). Differential diagnosis of PTSD, schizophrenia, and depression with the MMPI–2. *Journal of Clinical Psychology, 55,* 217–223. doi:10.1002/(SICI)1097-4679(199902)55:2<217::AID-JCLP9>3.0.CO;2-I

Greene, R. L. (1987). Ethnicity and MMPI performance: A review. *Journal of Consulting and Clinical Psychology, 55,* 497–512. doi:10.1037/0022-006X.55.4.497

Greene, R. L. (2000). *The MMPI–2: An interpretive manual.* Boston, MA: Allyn & Bacon.

Greene, R. L. (2005). Computer scoring and interpretation in psychological report writing. *SPA Exchange, 17,* 6.

Greene, R. L. (2006). [MMPI–2 data research file for child-custody litigants]. Unpublished raw data.

Greene, R. L. (2011). *The MMPI–2/MMPI–2–RF: An interpretive manual* (3rd ed.). Boston, MA: Allyn & Bacon.

Greene, R. L., Robin, R. W., Albaugh, B., Caldwell, A., & Goldman, D. (2003). Use of the MMPI–2 in American Indians: II. Empirical correlates. *Psychological Assessment, 15,* 360–369. doi:10.1037/1040-3590.15.3.360

Greenfield, D. P., & Gottschalk, J. A. (2009). *Writing forensic reports: A guide for mental health professionals.* New York, NY: Springer.

Greiffenstein, M. F., Fox, D., & Lees-Haley, P. R. (2007). The MMPI–2 Fake Bad Scale in detection of noncredible brain injury claims. In K. Boone (Ed.), *Detection of noncredible cognitive performance* (pp. 210–235). New York, NY: Guilford Press.

Grisso, T. (2003). *Evaluating competencies: Forensic assessments and instruments* (2nd ed.). New York, NY: Kluwer Academic.

Grisso, T. (2010). Guidance for improving forensic reports: A review of common errors. *Journal of Forensic Psychology, 2,* 102–115.

Grisso, T., Cocozza, J. J., Steadman, H. J., Fisher, W. H., & Greer, A. (1994). The organization of pretrial forensic evaluation services. *Law and Human Behavior, 18,* 377–393. doi:10.1007/BF01499046

Gross, K., Keyes, M. D., & Greene, R. L. (2000). Assessing depression with the MMPI and MMPI–2. *Journal of Personality Assessment, 75,* 464–477. doi:10.1207/S15327752JPA7503_07

Grossman, L. S., & Cavanaugh, J. L. (1990). Psychopathology and denial in alleged sex offenders. *Journal of Nervous and Mental Disease, 178,* 739–744. doi:10.1097/00005053-199012000-00002

Grover, B. L. (2011). The utility of MMPI–2 scores with a correctional population and convicted sex offenders. *Psychology, 2,* 638–642.

Guarnaccia, P. J. (1993). *Ataques de nervios* in Puerto Rico: Culture-bound syndrome or popular illness? *Medical Anthropology, 15,* 157–170. doi:10.1080/01459740.1993.9966087

Gucker, D., & McNulty, J. L. (2004, May). *The MMPI–2 defensiveness and an analytic strategy.* Paper presented at the Symposium on Recent Developments in the Use of the MMPI–2/MMPI–A, Minneapolis, MN.

Guéz, M., Brännström, R., Nyberg, L., Toolanen, G., & Hildingsson, C. (2005). Neuropsychological functioning and MMPI–2 profiles in chronic neck pain: A comparison of whiplash and non-traumatic groups. *Journal of Clinical and Experimental Neuropsychology, 27,* 151–163. doi:10.1080/13803390490515487

Gurman, E. B., & Balban, M. (1990). Self-evaluations of physical attractiveness as a function of self-esteem and defensiveness. *Journal of Social Behavior and Personality, 5,* 575–580.

Guy, E., Platt, J. J., Zwerling, I., & Bullock, S. (1985). Mental health status of prisoners in an urban jail. *Criminal Justice and Behavior, 12,* 29–53. doi:10.1177/0093854885012001004

Gynther, M. D. (1972). White norms and Black MMPIs: A prescription for discrimination. *Psychological Bulletin, 78,* 386–402. doi:10.1037/h0033555

Gynther, M. D., Altman, H., & Sletten, I. W. (1973). Development of an empirical interpretive system for the MMPI: Some after-the-fact observations. *Journal of Clinical Psychology, 29,* 232–234. doi:10.1002/1097-4679(197304)29:2<232::AID-JCLP2270290222>3.0.CO;2-3

Gynther, M. D., Altman, H., & Warbin, R. W. (1972). A new empirical automated MMPI interpretive program: The 2-4/4-2 code type. *Journal of Clinical Psychology, 28,* 498–501. doi:10.1002/1097-4679(197210)28:4<498::AID-JCLP2270280417>3.0.CO;2-T

Gynther, M. D., Altman, H., & Warbin, R. W. (1973a). A new actuarial-empirical automated MMPI interpretive program: The 4-3/3-4 code type. *Journal of Clinical Psychology, 29,* 229–231. doi:10.1002/1097-4679(197304)29:2<229::AID-JCLP2270290221>3.0.CO;2-N

Gynther, M. D., Altman, H., & Warbin, R. W. (1973b). A new empirical automated MMPI interpretive program: The 2-7/7-2 code type. *Journal of Clinical Psychology, 29,* 58–59. doi:10.1002/1097-4679(197301)29:1<58::AID-JCLP2270290121>3.0.CO;2-N

Gynther, M. D., Altman, H., & Warbin, R. W. (1973c). A new empirical automated MMPI interpretive program: The 6-9/9-6 code type. *Journal of Clinical Psychology, 29,* 60–61. doi:10.1002/1097-4679(197301)29:1<60::AID-JCLP2270290122>3.0.CO;2-6

Hafner, A. J., Butcher, J. N., Hall, M. D., & Quast, W. (1969). Comparisons of MMPI studies of parents. In J. N. Butcher (Ed.), *Recent developments in the use of the MMPI* (pp. 297–322). New York, NY: McGraw-Hill.

Hagen, M. A., & Castagna, N. (2001). The real numbers: Psychological testing in custody evaluations. *Professional Psychology: Research and Practice, 32,* 269–271. doi:10.1037/0735-7028.32.3.269

Hale, L. R., Goldstein, D. S., Abramowitz, C. S., Calamari, J. E., & Kosson, D. S. (2004). Psychopathy is related to negative affectivity but not to anxiety sensitivity. *Behaviour Research and Therapy, 42,* 697–710. doi:10.1016/S0005-7967(03)00192-X

Hall, G. C. N., Bansal, A., & Lopez, I. R. (1999). Ethnicity and psychopathology: A meta-analytic review of 31 years of comparative MMPI/MMPI–2 research. *Psychological Assessment, 11,* 186–197. doi:10.1037/1040-3590.11.2.186

Hall, G. C. N., & Phung, A. H. (2001). Minnesota Multiphasic Personality Inventory and Millon Clinical Mutiaxial Inventory. In L. A. Suzuki, J. G. Ponterotto, & P. J. Meller (Eds.), *Handbook of multicultural assessment: Clinical, psychological and educational applications* (pp. 307–330). San Francisco, CA: Jossey-Bass.

Han, K., Park, H. I., Weed, N. C., Lim, J., Johnson, A., & Joles, C. (2013). Gender differences on the MMPI across American and Korean adult and adolescent normative samples. *Journal of Personality Assessment, 95,* 197–206. doi:10.1080/00223891.2012.754360

Han, K., Weed, N. C., Calhoun, R. F., & Butcher, J. N. (1995). Psychometric characteristics of the MMPI–2 Cook–Medley Hostility Scale. *Journal of Personality Assessment, 65,* 567–585. doi:10.1207/s15327752jpa6503_15

Hansen, A. L., Stokkeland, L., Johensen, B. H., Pallesen, S., & Wagge, L. (2013). The relationship between the Psychopathy Checklist—Revised and the MMPI–2: A pilot study. *Psychological Reports, 112,* 445–457. doi:10.2466/03.09.PR0.112.2.445-457

Hanson, R. K., & Harris, A. (2001). A structured approach to evaluating change among sex offenders. *Sexual Abuse, 13,* 105–122. doi:10.1177/107906320101300204

Hapidou, E. G., & Kritikos, S. M. (2010, August/September). *The MMPI–2 FBS scale in a chronic pain management program: Effects of funding, and is the FBS a tool for evaluating program outcome?* Paper presented at the World Congress of the International Association for the Study of Pain, Montreal, Canada.

Hare, R. D. (1985). Comparison of procedures for the assessment of psychopathy. *Journal of Consulting and Clinical Psychology, 53,* 7–16. doi:10.1037/0022-006X.53.1.7

Harkness, A. R., & McNulty, J. L. (2006). An overview of personality: The MMPI–2 Personality Psychopathology Five (PSY-5) scales. In J. N. Butcher (Ed.), *MMPI–2: The practitioner's guide* (pp. 73–97). Washington, DC: American Psychological Association.

Harp, J. P., Jasinski, L. J., Shandera-Ochsner, A. L., Mason, L. H., & Berry, D. T. R. (2011). Detection of malingered ADHD using the MMPI–2–RF. *Psychological Injury and Law, 4*, 32–43. doi:10.1007/s12207-011-9100-9

Harris, C., & Kiefer, M. (2011, May 25). Judge finds Jared Loughner not competent to stand trial. *The Arizona Republic*. Retrieved from http://www.azcentral.com

Harris, M., & Fallot, R. D. (Eds.). (2001). *Using trauma theory to design service systems: New directions for mental health services*. New York, NY: Jossey-Bass.

Harris, R. E., & Lingoes, J. C. (1955). *Subscales for the MMPI: An aid to interpretation*. Unpublished manuscript, Department of Psychiatry, University of California, San Francisco.

Harris, R. J., Wittner, W., Koppell, B., & Hilf, F. D. (1970). MMPI scales vs. interviewer ratings of paranoia. *Psychological Reports, 27*, 447–450. doi:10.2466/pr0.1970.27.2.447

Harvey, V. S. (2006). Variables affecting the clarity of reports. *Journal of Clinical Psychology, 62*, 5–18. doi:10.1002/jclp.20196

Hasemann, D. M. (1997). *Practices and findings of mental health professionals conducting workers' compensation examinations*. Unpublished doctoral dissertation, University of Kentucky.

Hass, G. A. (2014). Parenting coordination and domestic violence. In S. A. Higuchi & S. J. Lally (Eds.), *Parenting coordination in postseparation disputes: A comprehensive guide for practitioners* (pp. 201–228). Washington, DC: American Psychological Association.

Hass, G. A., Dutton, M. A., & Orloff, L. E. (2000). Lifetime prevalence of domestic violence against Latina immigrants: Legal and policy implications. *International Review of Victimology, 7*, 93–113. doi:10.1177/026975800000700306

Hathaway, S. R. (1956). Scales 5 (Masculinity–Femininity), 6 (Paranoia), and 8 (Schizophrenia). In G. S. Welsh & W. G. Dahlstrom (Eds.), *Basic readings on the MMPI in psychiatry and medicine* (pp. 104–111). Minneapolis: University of Minnesota Press.

Hathaway, S. R. (1975, February). *Comment on MMPI abbreviated forms*. Paper presented at the 10th Annual Symposium on Recent Developments in the Use of the MMPI, St. Petersburg, FL.

Hathaway, S. R., & McKinley, J. C. (1940). A multiphasic personality schedule (Minnesota): I. Construction of the schedule. *Journal of Psychology: Interdisciplinary and Applied, 10*, 249–254. doi:10.1080/00223980.1940.9917000

Hathaway, S. R., & McKinley, J. C. (1942a). *The Minnesota Multiphasic Personality Schedule*. Minneapolis: University of Minnesota Press.

Hathaway, S. R., & McKinley, J. C. (1942b). A multiphasic personality schedule (Minnesota): III. The measurement of symptomatic depression. *Journal of Psychology, 14*, 73–84. doi:10.1080/00223980.1942.9917111

Hatters-Friedman, S., Hrouda, D. R., Holden, C. E., Noffsinger, S. G., & Resnick, P. J. (2005). Filicide-suicide: Common factors in parents who kill their children and themselves. *Journal of the American Academy of Psychiatry and the Law, 33,* 496–504.

Hauff, E., & Vaglum, P. (1994). Chronic posttraumatic stress disorder in Vietnamese refugees: A prospective community study of prevalence, course, psychopathology, and stressors. *Journal of Nervous and Mental Disease, 182,* 85–90. doi:10.1097/00005053-199402000-00004

Hayama, T., Oguchi, T., & Shinkai, Y. (1999). Trial of the new psychological test MMPI–2 on the chronic schizophrenic patients: Investigation of the basic and content scales [Japanese]. *Kitasata Medicine, 29,* 281–297.

Haynes, J. P. (2010). Parenting assessment in abuse, neglect, and permanent wardship cases. In E. Benedek, P. Ash, & C. L. Scott (Eds.), *Principles and practice of child and adolescent forensic mental health* (pp. 157–170). Washington, DC: American Psychiatric Publishing.

Haywood, T. W., & Grossman, L. S. (1994). Denial of deviant sexual arousal and psychopathology in child molesters. *Behavior Therapy, 25,* 327–340. doi:10.1016/S0005-7894(05)80291-6

Heilbrun, A. B., & Norbert, N. (1972). Style of adaptation to aversive maternal control and paranoid behavior. *Journal of Genetic Psychology, 120,* 145–153. doi:10.1080/00221325.1972.10532226

Heilbrun, K. (2001). *Forensic mental health assessment.* New York, NY: Kluwer Academic.

Heilbrun, K., DeMatteo, D., Marczyk, G., & Goldstein, A. M. (2008). Standards of practice and care in forensic mental health assessment: Legal, professional, and principles-based considerations. *Psychology, Public Policy, and Law, 14,* 1–26. doi:10.1037/1076-8971.14.1.1

Helmes, E., & Reddon, J. R. (1993). A perspective on developments in assessing psychopathology: A critical review of the MMPI and MMPI–2. *Psychological Bulletin, 113,* 453–471. doi:10.1037/0033-2909.113.3.453

Hemphill, J. F., & Hart, S. D. (2003). Forensic and clinical issues in the assessment of psychopathy. In I. Weiner (Series Ed.) & A. M. Goldstein (Vol. Ed.), *Handbook of psychology: Vol. 11. Forensic psychology* (pp. 87–107). New York, NY: Wiley.

Hermansson, A. C., Timpka, T., & Thyberg, M. (2002). The mental health of war-wounded refugees: An 8-year follow-up. *Journal of Nervous and Mental Disease, 190,* 374–380. doi:10.1097/00005053-200206000-00005

Hersch, P. D., & Alexander, R. W. (1990). MMPI profile patterns of emotional disability claimants. *Journal of Clinical Psychology, 46,* 795–799. doi:10.1002/1097-4679(199011)46:6<795::AID-JCLP2270460617>3.0.CO;2-K

Hersen, M., & Sudik, E. (1971). Verbal conditioning as related to awareness, paranoia, and suspiciousness. *Journal of Clinical Psychology, 27,* 43–47.

Hessen, E., Anderson, V., & Nestvold, K. (2008). MMPI–2 profiles 23 years after paediatric mild traumatic brain injury. *Brain Injury, 22,* 39–50. doi:10.1080/02699050701846179

Hilton, N. Z., Harris, G. T., & Rice, M. E. (2010). *Risk assessment for domestically violent men: Tools for criminal justice, offender intervention, and victim services.* Washington, DC: American Psychological Association.

Hjemboe, S., Almagor, M., & Butcher, J. N. (1992). Empirical assessment of marital distress: The Marital Distress Scale (*MDS*) for the MMPI–2. In C. D. Spielberger & J. N. Butcher (Eds.), *Advances in personality assessment* (Vol. 9, pp. 141–152). Hillsdale, NJ: Erlbaum.

Hodgins, S., & Lalonde, N. (1999). Major mental disorders and crime: Changes over time? In P. Cohen, C. Slomkowski, & L. N. Robins (Eds.), *Historical and geographical influences on psychopathology* (pp. 57–83). Mahwah, NJ: Erlbaum.

Hoffman, B. F. (1986). How to write a psychiatric report for litigation following a personal injury. *American Journal of Psychiatry, 143,* 164–169.

Hoffman, B. F., & Spiegel, H. (1989). Legal principles in the psychiatric assessment of personal injury litigants. *American Journal of Psychiatry, 146,* 304–310.

Holtzworth-Munroe, A. (2005). Male versus female intimate violence: Putting controversial findings into context. *Journal of Marriage and Family, 67,* 1120–1125. doi:10.1111/j.1741-3737.2005.00203.x

Holtzworth-Munroe, A., Beck, C., & Applegate, A. G. (2010). The Mediator's Assessment of Safety Issues and Concerns (MASIC): A screening interview for intimate partner violence and abuse available in the public domain. *Family Court Review, 48,* 646–662. doi:10.1111/j.1744-1617.2010.001339.x

Hutton, H. E., Miner, M. H., Blades, J. R., & Langfeldt, V. C. (1992). Ethnic differences on the MMPI Overcontrolled Hostility scale. *Journal of Personality Assessment, 58,* 260–268. doi:10.1207/s15327752jpa5802_5

Hyman, E. J., Caldwell, A., & Nichols, D. S. (2013, March). *Three iterations of the MMPI–2: Reliability, validity, and homicide.* Paper presented at the meeting of the Society for Personality Assessment, San Diego, CA.

Immigration and Nationality Act, 8 U.S.C. § 1101 *et seq.* (1952).

Infrasca, R. (2003). Childhood adversities and adult depression: An experimental study on childhood depressogenic markers. *Journal of Affective Disorders, 76,* 103–111. doi:10.1016/S0165-0327(02)00076-9

International Test Commission. (2005). *ITC guidelines for adapting tests.* Retrieved from http://www.intestcom.org/upload/sitefiles/40.pdf

Jacobsen, T. (2004). Mentally ill mothers in the parenting role: Clinical management and treatment. In M. Göpfert, J. Webster, & V. Seeman (Eds.), *Parental psychiatric disorder: Distressed parents and their families* (2nd ed., pp. 112–122). New York, NY: Cambridge University Press.

Jacobson, J., & Wirt, R. D. (1969). MMPI profiles associated with outcomes of group psychotherapy with prisoners. In J. N. Butcher (Ed.), *Recent developments in the use of the MMPI* (pp. 191–206). New York, NY: McGraw-Hill.

Jaffe, P. G., Crooks, C. V., & Bala, N. (2005). *Making appropriate parenting arrangements in family violence cases: Applying the literature to identify promising practices*

(Family, Children and Youth Section Research Report No. 2005-FCY-3E). Ottawa, Ontario, Canada: Department of Justice Canada.

Jaffe, P. G., Johnston, J. R., Crooks, C. V., & Bala, N. (2008). Custody disputes involving allegations of domestic violence: Toward a differentiated approach to parenting plans. *Family Court Review, 46*, 500–522. doi:10.1111/j.1744-1617.2008.00216.x

James, J. A., & Boake, C. (1988). MMPI profiles of child abusers and neglecters. *International Journal of Family Psychiatry, 9*, 351–371.

Jara-Navaretta v. Immigration and Naturalization Service, 800 F. 2nd 1530 (9th Cir. 1986).

Jaranson, J. M., Butcher, J., Halcon, L., Johnson, D. R., Robertson, C., Savik, K., . . . Westermeyer, J. (2004). Somali and Oromo refugees: Correlates of torture and trauma history. *American Journal of Public Health, 94*, 591–598. doi:10.2105/AJPH.94.4.591

Jarvis, P. E., & Hamlin, D. (1984). Avoiding pitfalls in compensation evaluations. *International Journal of Clinical Neuropsychology, 6*, 214–216.

Jemelka, R. P., Wiegand, G. A., Walker, E. A., & Trupin, E. W. (1992). Computerized offender assessment: Validation study. *Psychological Assessment, 4*, 138–144. doi:10.1037/1040-3590.4.2.138

Johnson, M. P. (2006a). Apples and oranges in child custody disputes: Intimate terrorism vs. situational couple violence. *Journal of Child Custody, 2*, 43–52. doi:10.1300/J190v02n04_03

Johnson, M. P. (2006b). Conflict and control: Gender symmetry and asymmetry in domestic violence. *Violence Against Women, 12*, 1003–1018. doi: 10.1177/1077801206293328

Johnson, M. P., & Ferraro, K. L. (2000). Research on domestic violence in the 1990s: Making distinctions. *Journal of Marriage and the Family, 62*, 948–963. doi:10.1111/j.1741-3737.2000.00948.x

Johnston, J. R. (1992). *High-conflict and violent parents in family court: Findings on children's adjustment and proposed guidelines for the resolution of custody and visitation disputes.* San Francisco, CA: Judicial Council.

Johnston, J. R. (1994). High-conflict divorce. *Children and Divorce, 4*, 165–182.

Johnston, J. R., & Campbell, L. E. G. (1988). *Impasses of divorce: The dynamics and resolution of family conflict.* New York, NY: Free Press.

Johnston, J. R., & Campbell, L. E. G. (1993). A clinical typology of interparental violence in disputed custody divorces. *American Journal of Orthopsychiatry, 63*, 190–199. doi:10.1037/h0079425

Johnston, J. R., Lee, S., Olesen, N. W., & Walters, M. G. (2005). Allegations and substantiations of abuse in custody-disputing families. *Family Court Review, 43*, 283–294.

Jones, T., Beidleman, W. B., & Fowler, R. D. (1981). Differentiating violent and nonviolent prison inmates by use of selected MMPI scales. *Journal of Clinical*

Psychology, 37, 673–678. doi:10.1002/1097-4679(198107)37:3<673::AID-JCLP2270370340>3.0.CO;2-P

Jordan, R. G., Nunley, T. V., & Cook, R. R. (1992). Symptom exaggeration in a PTSD inpatient population: Response set or claim for compensation. *Journal of Traumatic Stress, 5,* 633–642. doi:10.1002/jts.2490050412

Juckett, G., & Rudolph-Watson, L. (2010). Recognizing mental illness in culture-bound syndromes. *American Family Physician, 81,* 206–210.

Kaser-Boyd, N. (2004). Battered woman syndrome: Clinical features, evaluation, and expert testimony. In B. J. Cling (Ed), *Sexualized violence against women and children: A psychology and law perspective* (pp. 41–70). New York, NY: Guilford Press.

Kay, T., Duerksen, C., Pike, P., & Anderson, T. (2003). The effects of gender and ethnicity on the Overcontrolled Hostility scale of the MMPI–2. *Journal of Articles in Support of the Null Hypothesis, 2*(3), 86–96.

Keane, T. M., Malloy, P. F., & Fairbank, J. A. (1984). Empirical development of an MMPI subscale for the assessment of posttraumatic stress disorder. *Journal of Consulting and Clinical Psychology, 52,* 888–891. doi:10.1037/0022-006X.52.5.888

Keilin, W. G., & Bloom, L. J. (1986). Child custody evaluation practices: A survey of experienced professionals. *Professional Psychology: Research and Practice, 17,* 338–346. doi:10.1037/0735-7028.17.4.338

Keller, A., Lhewa, D., Rosenfeld, B., Sachs, E., Aladjem, A., Cohen, I., & Porterfield, K. (2006). Traumatic experiences and psychological distress in an urban refugee population seeking treatment services. *Journal of Nervous and Mental Disease, 194,* 188–194. doi:10.1097/01.nmd.0000202494.75723.83

Keller, L. S., & Butcher, J. N. (1991). *Assessment of chronic pain patients with the MMPI–2.* Minneapolis: University of Minnesota Press.

Kelly, J., & Johnson, M. P. (2008). Differentiation among types of intimate partner violence: Research update and implications for intervention. *Family Court Review, 46,* 476–499. doi:10.1111/j.1744-1617.2008.00215.x

Khan, F. I., Welch, T. L., & Zillmer, E. A. (1993). MMPI–2 profiles of battered women in transition. *Journal of Personality Assessment, 60,* 100–111. doi:10.1207/s15327752jpa6001_7

Khouri, R. (2010). *MMPI–2 RF vs. MMPI–2: Latinos with depression* (Doctoral dissertation). Available from ProQuest Dissertations and Theses database. (UMI No. 3416813)

Kinder, B. N., Curtiss, G., & Kalichman, S. (1986). Anxiety and anger as predictors of MMPI elevations in chronic pain patients. *Journal of Personality Assessment, 50,* 651–661. doi:10.1207/s15327752jpa5004_11

King, H. E. (2012). Psychological testing in child custody evaluations. In J. Hansen (Ed.), *Handbook of psychological assessment* (pp. 587–605). Washington, DC: American Psychological Association.

Kisac, I. (2006). Stress symptoms of survivors of the Marmara region (Turkey) earthquakes: A follow-up study. *International Journal of Stress Management, 13*, 118–126. doi:10.1037/1072-5245.13.1.118

Kleinke, C. L. (1994). MMPI scales as predictors of pain-coping strategies preferred by patients with chronic pain. *Rehabilitation Psychology, 39*, 123–128. doi:10.1037/h0080308

Kleinmuntz, B. (1961). The College Maladjustment scale (*MT*): Norms and predictive validity. *Educational and Psychological Measurement, 21*, 1029–1033. doi:10.1177/001316446102100432

Knapp, S., & VandeCreek, L. (2001). Ethical issues in personality assessment in forensic psychology. *Journal of Personality Assessment, 77*, 242–254. doi:10.1207/S15327752JPA7702_07

Knaster, C. A., & Micucci, J. A. (2013). The effect of client ethnicity on clinical interpretation of the MMPI–2. *Assessment, 20*, 43–47. doi:10.1177/1073191112465333

Knisely, J. S., Barker, S. B., Ingersoll, K. S., & Dawson, K. S. (2000). Psychopathology in substance abusing women reporting childhood sexual abuse. *Journal of Addictive Diseases, 19*, 31–44. doi:10.1300/J069v19n01_03

Korbanka, J. E., & McKay, M. (2000). An MMPI–2 scale to identify history of physical abuse. *Journal of Interpersonal Violence, 15*, 1131–1139. doi:10.1177/088626000015011001

Koretzky, M. B., & Peck, A. H. (1990). Validation and cross-validation of the PTSD subscale of the MMPI with civilian trauma victims. *Journal of Clinical Psychology, 46*, 296–300. doi:10.1002/1097-4679(199005)46:3<296::AID-JCLP2270460308>3.0.CO;2-A

Koss, M. P., & Butcher, J. N. (1973). A comparison of psychiatric patients' self-report with other sources of clinical information. *Journal of Research in Personality, 7*, 225–236. doi:10.1016/0092-6566(73)90038-X

Krauss, D., & Lieberman, J. (2007). Expert testimony on risk and future dangerousness. In M. Costanzo, D. Krauss, & D. K. Pezdek (Eds.), *Expert psychological testimony for the courts* (pp. 227–249). Mahwah, NJ: Erlbaum.

Kropp, P. R., Hart, S. D., Webster, C. D., & Eaves, D. (1999). *Spousal Assault Risk Assessment Guide*. Toronto, Ontario, Canada: Multi-Health Systems.

Kwan, K.-L. K. (1999). MMPI and MMPI–2 performance of the Chinese: Cross-cultural applicability. *Professional Psychology: Research and Practice, 30*, 260–268. doi:10.1037/0735-7028.30.3.260

Kwartner, P., & Boccaccini, M. T. (2008). Testifying in court: Evidence-based recommendations for expert-witness testimony. In R. Jackson (Ed.), *Learning forensic assessment* (pp. 565–588). New York, NY: Routledge/Taylor.

LaBruzza, A. L., & Mendez-Villarrubia, J. M. (1994). *Using DSM–IV: A clinician's guide to psychiatric diagnosis*. Northvale, NJ: Aronson.

Lachar, D. (1974). *The MMPI: Clinical assessment and automated interpretation.* Los Angeles, CA: Western Psychological Services.

LaFortune, K. A., & Nicholson, R. A. (1995). How adequate are Oklahoma's mental health evaluations to determine competence in criminal proceedings? The bench and bar respond. *Journal of Psychiatry & Law, 23,* 231–262.

Lally, S. J. (2003). What tests are acceptable for use in forensic evaluations? A survey of experts. *Professional Psychology: Research and Practice, 34,* 491–498. doi:10.1037/0735-7028.34.5.491

Lamberg, L. (1998). Mental illness and violent acts: Protecting the patient and the public. *JAMA, 280,* 407–408. doi:10.1001/jama.280.5.407-JMN0805-3-1

Lambert, M. E., Andrews, R. H., Rylee, K., & Skinner, J. (1987). Equivalence of computerized and traditional MMPI administration with substance abusers. *Computers in Human Behavior, 3,* 139–143. doi:10.1016/0747-5632(87)90018-5

Land, H. M. (1986). Child abuse: Differential diagnosis, differential treatment. *Child Welfare, 65,* 33–44.

Landrine, H., & Klonoff, E. A. (1994). The African American Acculturation Scale: Development, reliability, and validity. *Journal of Black Psychology, 20,* 104–127. doi:10.1177/00957984940202002

Landwher, D. N., & Llorente, A. M. (2012). Forensic issues in neuropsychological assessment: Culture and language. In E. M. S. Sherman & B. L. Brooks (Eds.), *Pediatric forensic neuropsychology* (pp.163–181). New York, NY: Oxford University Press.

Lange, R. T., Sullivan, K. A., & Scott, C. (2010). Comparison of MMPI–2 and PAI validity indicators to detect feigned depression and PTSD symptom reporting. *Psychiatry Research, 176,* 229–235. doi:10.1016/j.psychres.2009.03.004

Lanyon, R. I. (1993). Validity of MMPI sex offender scales with admitters and no admitters. *Psychological Assessment, 5,* 302–306. doi:10.1037/1040-3590.5.3.302

Lanyon, R. I., & Almer, E. R. (2002). Characteristics of compensable disability patients who choose to litigate. *Journal of the American Academy of Psychiatry and the Law, 30,* 400–404.

Law, A., Schulz, I., Butcher, J. N., Lo, J. C., & Ng, J. M. (2014, June). *Exploring the clinical profiles of workers with confirmed traumatic brain injuries and high scores on the MMPI–2 FBS: A study.* Paper presented at the Canadian Psychological Association, Vancouver, British Columbia, Canada.

Lawton, M. P., & Kleban, M. H. (1965). Prisoners' faking on the MMPI. *Journal of Clinical Psychology, 21,* 269–271. doi:10.1002/1097-4679(196507)21:3<269::AID-JCLP2270210311>3.0.CO;2-N

Lees-Haley, P. R. (1988). Litigation response syndrome. *American Journal of Forensic Psychology, 6,* 3–12.

Lees-Haley, P. R. (1992). Efficacy of MMPI–2 validity scales and MCMI–II modifier scales for detecting spurious PTSD claims: F, F-K, Fake Bad Scale, Ego Strength, Subtle–Obvious subscales, DIS, and DEB. *Journal of Clinical*

Psychology, 48, 681–688. doi:10.1002/1097-4679(199209)48:5<681::AID-JCLP2270480516>3.0.CO;2-Q

Lees-Haley, P. R. (1997). Attorneys influence expert evidence in forensic psychological and neuropsychological cases. *Assessment, 4*, 321–324.

Lees-Haley, P. R., English, L. T., & Glenn, W. J. (1991). A Fake Bad Scale on the MMPI–2 for personal injury claimants. *Psychological Reports, 68*, 203–210. doi:10.2466/pr0.1991.68.1.203

Leib, R. (2006). MMPI–2 family problems scales in child-custody litigants. *Dissertation Abstracts International: Section B. Sciences and Engineering, 68*, 4879.

Lemmon, K. W. (1983). Chronic lower back pain: Differentiation of the real and imagined. *Medical Hypnoanalysis, 4*, 17–30.

Lewandowski, D., & Graham, J. R. (1972). Empirical correlates of frequently occurring two-point MMPI code types: A replicated study. *Journal of Consulting and Clinical Psychology, 39*, 467–472. doi:10.1037/h0034018

Lewis, G., Croft-Jeffreys, C., & David, A. (1990). Are British psychiatrists racist? *British Journal of Psychiatry, 157*, 410–415. doi:10.1192/bjp.157.3.410

Lezak, M. D., Howieson, D. B., & Loring, D. W. (2004). The neuropsychological examination: Procedures. In M. D. Lezak, D. B. Howieson, & D. W. Loring (Eds.), *Neuropsychological assessment* (4th ed., pp. 100–132). New York, NY: Oxford University Press.

Lichtenberg, P. A., Skehan, M. W., & Swensen, C. H. (1984). The role of personality, recent life stress and arthritic severity in predicting pain. *Journal of Psychosomatic Research, 28*, 231–236. doi:10.1016/0022-3999(84)90024-2

Lilienfeld, S. O. (1996). The MMPI–2 Antisocial Practices Content Scale: Construct validity and comparison with the Psychopathic Deviate Scale. *Psychological Assessment, 8*, 281–293. doi:10.1037/1040-3590.8.3.281

Lim, J., & Butcher, J. N. (1996). Detection of faking on the MMPI–2: Differentiation between faking-bad, denial, and claiming extreme virtue. *Journal of Personality Assessment, 67*, 1–25. doi:10.1207/s15327752jpa6701_1

Limbaugh-Kirker v. Dicosta, No. 06-CA-00706 (Fla. Cir. Ct., February 10, 2009).

Liverant, S. (1959). MMPI differences between parents of disturbed and nondisturbed children. *Journal of Consulting Psychology, 23*, 256–260. doi:10.1037/h0048657

Livingston, R. B., Jennings, E., Colotla, V. A., Reynolds, C. R., & Shercliffe, R. J. (2006). MMPI–2 code-type congruence of injured workers. *Psychological Assessment, 18*, 126–130. doi:10.1037/1040-3590.18.1.126

Locke, D. E. C., & Thomas, M. L. (2011). Initial development of Minnesota Multiphasic Personality Inventory—2—Restructured Form (MMPI–2–RF) scales to identify patients with psychogenic nonepileptic seizures. *Journal of Clinical and Experimental Neuropsychology, 33*, 335–343. doi:10.1080/13803395.2010.518141

Lockheed Martin v. Workers' Compensation Appeals Board, 117 Cal. Rptr. 2d 865, 96 Cal. App. 4th 1237 (Cal. Ct. App. 2002)

Loeb, J. (1966). The personality factor in divorce. *Journal of Consulting Psychology, 30,* 562. doi:10.1037/h0024025

Loeb, J., & Price, J. R. (1966). Mother and child personality characteristics related to parental marital status in child guidance cases. *Journal of Consulting Psychology, 30,* 112–117. doi:10.1037/h0023179

Long, B., Rouse, S. V., Nelson, R. O., & Butcher, J. N. (2004). The MMPI–2 in sexual harassment and discrimination cases. *Journal of Clinical Psychology, 60,* 643–657. doi:10.1002/jclp.10269

Lucenko, B. A., Gold, S. N., Elhai, J. D., Russo, S. A., & Swingle, J. M. (2000). Relations between coercive strategies and MMPI–2 scale elevations among women survivors of childhood sexual abuse. *Journal of Traumatic Stress, 13,* 169–177. doi:10.1023/A:1007785201112

Lucio, E., Ampudia, A., Durán, C., Léon, I., & Butcher, J. N. (2001). Comparison of the Mexican and American norms of the MMPI–2. *Journal of Clinical Psychology, 57,* 1459–1468. doi:10.1002/jclp.1109

Lucio, E., & Reyes-Lagunes, I. (1996). The Mexican version of the MMPI–2 in Mexico and Nicaragua: Translation, adaptation, and demonstrated equivalency. In J. N. Butcher (Ed.), *International adaptations of the MMPI–2: Research and clinical applications* (pp. 265–283). Minneapolis: University of Minnesota Press.

Lucio, E., & Valencia, M. (1997). Detección del perfil de los sujetos simuladores y de los sujetos honestos por medio de las escalas del MMPI–2 [Detection of the profile of simulating subjects and honest subjects using MMPI–2 scales]. *Salud Mental, 20*(4), 23–33.

Lucio, E. L., Reyes-Lagunes, I., & Scott, R. L. (1994). MMPI–2 for Mexico: Translation and adaptation. *Journal of Personality Assessment, 63,* 105–116. doi:10.1207/s15327752jpa6301_9

Luepnitz, R. R., Randolph, D. L., & Gutsch, K. U. (1982). Race and socioeconomic status as confounding variables in the accurate diagnosis of alcoholism. *Journal of Clinical Psychology, 38,* 665–669. doi:10.1002/1097-4679(198207)38:3<665::AID JCLP2270380338> 3.0.CO;2-R

Lundberg-Love, P. K., Marmion, S., Ford, K., & Geffner, R. (1992). The long-term consequences of childhood incestuous victimization upon adult women's psychological symptomatology. *Journal of Child Sexual Abuse, 1,* 81–102. doi:10.1300/J070v01n01_06

Lustig, L. (2011). *The MMPI–2–RF and the MCMI–III on Internet sex offenders* (Doctoral dissertation). Available from ProQuest Dissertations and Theses database. (UMI No. 3459245)

Lymburner, J. A., & Roesch, R. (1999). The insanity defense: Five years of research (1993–1997). *International Journal of Law and Psychiatry, 22,* 213–240. doi:10.1016/S0160-2527(99)00006-0

MacAndrew, C. (1965). The differentiation of male alcoholic outpatients from non-alcoholic psychiatric outpatients by means of the MMPI. *Quarterly Journal of Studies on Alcohol, 26,* 238–246.

Malgady, R. G., Rogler, L. H., & Constantino, G. (1987). Ethnocultural and linguistic bias in mental health evaluation of Hispanics. *American Psychologist, 42,* 228–234. doi:10.1037/0003-066X.42.3.228

Marks, P. A., Seeman, W., & Haller, D. L. (1974). *The actuarial use of the MMPI with adolescents and adults.* Baltimore, MD: William & Wilkins.

Martin, H., & Finn, S. (2014). *Masculinity and femininity in the MMPI–2 and MMPI–A.* Minneapolis: University of Minnesota Press.

Martin, M. A., Allan, A., & Allan, M. M. (2001). The use of psychological tests by Australian psychologists who do assessments for the courts. *Australian Journal of Psychology, 53,* 77–82. doi:10.1080/00049530108255127

Mason, S. N., Bubany, S., & Butcher, J. N. (2012). *Frequently asked questions: Gender differences on personality tests.* Retrieved from http://www.umn.edu/mmpi

Matsuoka, K., Kim, Y., Toshida, S., & Ohshima, N. (2000). Relationships between age of onset, antisocial history and general psychopathological traits in Japanese alcoholics. *Psychiatry and Clinical Neurosciences, 54,* 413–417. doi:10.1046/j.1440-1819.2000.00730.x

McAdoo, W. G., & Connolly, F. J. (1975). MMPIs of parents in dysfunctional families. *Journal of Consulting and Clinical Psychology, 43,* 270. doi:10.1037/h0076517

McGoldrick, M., Giordano, J., & Garcia-Preto, N. (2005). *Ethnicity and family therapy* (3rd ed.). New York, NY: Guilford Press.

McKenzie, K. (2004). Commentary: Ethnicity, race, and forensic psychiatry—Is being unblinded enough? *Journal of the American Academy of Psychiatry and the Law, 32,* 36–39.

McKinley, J. C., & Hathaway, S. R. (1940). A multiphasic personality schedule (Minnesota): II. A differential study of hypochondriasis. *Journal of Psychology: Interdisciplinary and Applied, 10,* 255–268. doi:10.1080/00223980.1940.9917001

McKinley, J. C., & Hathaway, S. R. (1944). The MMPI: V. Hysteria, hypomania, and psychopathic deviate. *Journal of Psychology, 28,* 153–174.

McLaughlin, J. L., & Kan, L. Y. (2014). Test usage in four common types of forensic mental health assessment. *Professional Psychology: Research and Practice, 45,* 128–135. doi:10.1037/a0036318

McNiel, D. E., & Binder, R. L. (1994). Screening for risk of inpatient violence: Validation of an actuarial tool. *Law and Human Behavior, 18,* 579–586. doi:10.1007/BF01499176

McNulty, J. L., Forbey, J. D., Graham, J. R., Ben-Porath, Y. S., Black, M. S., Anderson, S. V., & Burlew, A. (2003). MMPI–2 validity scale characteristics in a correctional sample. *Assessment, 10,* 288–298. doi:10.1177/1073191103255623

Mechanic, M. B., Weaver, T. L., & Resick, P. A. (2008). Mental health consequences of intimate partner abuse: A multidimensional assessment of four different forms of abuse. *Violence Against Women, 14,* 634–654. doi:10.1177/1077801208319283

Meehl, P. E. (1954). *Clinical versus statistical prediction: A theoretical analysis and a review of the evidence.* Minneapolis: University of Minnesota Press.

Meehl, P. E. (1956). Wanted: A good cookbook. *American Psychologist, 11,* 263–272. doi:10.1037/h0044164

Meehl, P. E., & Hathaway, S. R. (1946). The *K* factor as a suppressor variable in the Minnesota Multiphasic Personality Inventory. *Journal of Applied Psychology, 30,* 525–564. doi:10.1037/h0053634

Megargee, E. I. (1977). A new classification system for criminal offenders. *Criminal Justice and Behavior, 4,* 107–114. doi:10.1177/009385487700400201

Megargee, E. I. (1994). Using the Megargee MMPI-based classification system with MMPI–2s of male prison inmates. *Psychological Assessment, 6,* 337–344. doi:10.1037/1040-3590.6.4.337

Megargee, E. I. (1997). Using the Megargee MMPI-based classification system with the MMPI–2s of female prison inmates. *Psychological Assessment, 9,* 75–82. doi:10.1037/1040-3590.9.2.75

Megargee, E. I. (2006a). Using the MMPI–2 in correctional settings. In J. N. Butcher (Ed.), *MMPI–2: A practitioner's guide* (pp. 327–360). Washington, DC: American Psychological Association.

Megargee, E. I. (2006b). *Using the MMPI–2 in criminal justice and correctional settings: An empirical approach.* Minneapolis: University of Minnesota Press.

Megargee, E. I. (2009). Understanding and assessing aggression and violence. In J. N. Butcher (Ed.), *Oxford handbook of personality and clinical assessment* (pp. 542–566). New York, NY: Oxford University Press.

Megargee, E. I. (2013). Psychological assessment in correctional settings. In J. R. Graham & J. Naglieri (Eds.), *Handbook of psychology* (2nd ed., Vol. 10, pp. 394–424). New York, NY: Wiley.

Megargee, E. I., & Bohn, M. J., Jr. (with Meyer, J., Jr., & Sink, F.). (1979). *Classifying criminal offenders: A new system based on the MMPI.* Beverly Hills, CA: Sage.

Megargee, E. I., Carbonell, J. L., Bohn, M., & Sliger, G. L. (2001). *Classifying criminal offenders with MMPI–2: The Megargee system.* Minneapolis: University of Minnesota Press.

Megargee, E. I., Cook, P. E., & Mendelsohn, G. A. (1967). Development and validation of an MMPI scale of assaultiveness in overcontrolled individuals. *Journal of Abnormal Psychology, 72,* 519–528. doi:10.1037/h0025242

Meier, M. J. (1961). Interrelationships among personality variables, kinesthetic figure aftereffect, and reminiscence in motor learning. *Journal of Abnormal and Social Psychology, 63,* 87–94. doi:10.1037/h0047684

Meier, M. J. (1964). Caudality scale changes following unilateral temporal lobectomy. *Journal of Clinical Psychology, 20,* 464–467. doi:10.1002/1097-4679(196410)20:4<464::AID-JCLP2270200416>3.0.CO;2-M

Meier, M. J. (1965a). Changes in MMPI scale scores and an index or psychopathology following unilateral temporal lobectomy for epilepsy. *Epilepsia, 6,* 263–273. doi:10.1111/j.1528-1157.1965.tb03794.x

Meier, M. J. (1965b). Some personality correlates of unilateral and bilateral EEG abnormalities in psychomotor epileptics. *Journal of Clinical Psychology, 21*, 3–9. doi:10.1002/1097-4679(196501)21:1<3::AID-JCLP2270210102>3.0.CO;2-W

Meier, M. J. (1969). The regional localization hypothesis and personality changes associated with focal cerebral lesions and ablations. In J. N. Butcher (Ed.), *Recent developments in the use of the MMPI* (pp. 243–262). New York, NY: McGraw-Hill.

Melton, G., Petrila, J., Poythress, N. G., & Slobogin, C. (2007). *Psychological evaluations for the courts: A handbook for mental health professionals and lawyers.* New York, NY: Guilford Press.

Meredith, L. S., Wenger, N., Liu, H., Harada, N., & Khan, K. (2000). Development of a brief scale to measure acculturation among Japanese Americans. *Journal of Community Psychology, 28*, 103–113. doi:10.1002/(SICI)1520-6629(200001)28:1<103::AID-JCOP10>3.0.CO;2-E

Merrill, L. L., Hervig, L. K., & Milner, J. S. (1996). Childhood parenting experiences, intimate partner conflict resolution, and adult risk for child physical abuse. *Child Abuse & Neglect, 20*, 1049–1065. doi:10.1016/0145-2134(96)00094-4

Mettler, F. (1949). *Selective partial ablation of the frontal cortex.* New York, NY: Hoeber.

Meyers, J. E., Millis, S. R., & Volkert, K. (2002). A validity index for the MMPI–2. *Archives of Clinical Neuropsychology, 17*, 157–169. doi:10.1093/arclin/17.2.157

Micco, J. A., Henin, A., Mick, E., Kim, S., Hopkins, C. A., Biederman, J., & Hirschfeld-Becker, D. R. (2009). Anxiety and depressive disorders in offspring at high risk for anxiety: A meta-analysis. *Journal of Anxiety Disorders, 23*, 1158–1164. doi:10.1016/j.janxdis.2009.07.021

Michelson, M. (2001). The admissibility of expert testimony on battering and its effects after *Kumho Tire. Washington University Law Review, 79*, 367–402.

Miller, G. A., Galanter, E., & Pribram, K. H. (1960). *Plans and the structure of behavior.* New York, NY: Holt, Rinehart & Winston.

Miller, L. (2013). Psychological evaluations in the criminal justice system: Basic principles and best practices. *Aggression and Violent Behavior, 18*, 83–911. doi:10.1016/j.avb.2012.10.005

Miller, L., Sadoff, R. L., & Dattilo, F. M. (2011). Civil commitment. In E. Y. Drogin, F. M. Dattilio, R. L. Sadoff, & T. G. Gutheil (Eds.), *Handbook of forensic assessment: Psychological and psychiatric perspectives* (pp. 277–302). Hoboken, NJ: Wiley.

Milner, J. S. (1986). *The Child Abuse Potential Inventory: Manual* (2nd ed.). Webster, NC: Psytec.

Misdraji, E. L., & Gass, C. S. (2010). The Trail Making Test and its neurobehavioral components. *Journal of Clinical and Experimental Neuropsychology, 32*, 159–163. doi:10.1080/13803390902881942

Mittag, O., & Maurischat, C. (2004). A comparison of the Cook–Medley Hostility Scale (*Ho* scale) and the content scales "cynicism," "anger," and "type A" out of the MMPI–2: On the future assessment of hostility. *Zeitschrift für Medizinische Psychologie, 13*(1), 7–12.

Mollica, R. F., Caspi-Yavin, Y., Bollini, P., Truong, T., Tor, S., & Lavelle, J. (1992). The Harvard Trauma Questionnaire: Validating a cross-cultural instrument for measuring torture, trauma, and posttraumatic stress disorder in Indochinese refugees. *Journal of Nervous and Mental Disease, 180,* 111–116. doi:10.1097/00005053-199202000-00008

Mollica, R. F., Wyshak, G., de Marneffe, D., Khuon, F., & Lavelle, J. (1987). Indochinese version of the Hopkins Symptom Checklist-25: A screening instrument for psychiatric care of refugees. *American Journal of Psychiatry, 144,* 497–500.

Moniz, E. (1936). Prefrontal leucotomy in the treatment of mental disorder. *American Journal of Psychiatry, 93,* 1379–1385.

Monson, C. M., Gunnin, D. D., Fogel, M. H., & Kyle, L. L. (2001). Stopping (or slowing) the revolving door: Factors related to NGRI acquittees' maintenance of a conditional release. *Law and Human Behavior, 25,* 257–267. doi:10.1023/A:1010745927735

Morey, L. C. (1991). *The Personality Assessment Inventory: Professional manual.* Odessa, FL: Psychological Assessment Resources.

Moriconi, D. M., & Martinez, J. C. (1995). Roles of hypomania and intelligence in antisocial practices when self-esteem and family problems are considered. *Psychological Reports, 76,* 435–442. doi:10.2466/pr0.1995.76.2.435

Morrell, J. S., & Rubin, L. J. (2001). The Minnesota Multiphasic Personality Inventory–2, posttraumatic stress disorder, and women domestic violence survivors. *Professional Psychology: Research and Practice, 32,* 151–156. doi:10.1037/0735-7028.32.2.151

Mossman, D. (1999). "Hired guns," "whores," and "prostitutes": Case law references to clinicians of ill repute. *Journal of the American Academy of Psychiatry and the Law, 27,* 414–425.

Moyer, D. M., Burkhardt, B., & Gordon, R. M. (2002). Faking PTSD from a motor vehicle accident on the MMPI–2. *American Journal of Forensic Psychology, 20,* 81–89.

Mrad, D. M., & Watson, C. (2011). Civil commitment. In E. Y. Drogin, F. M. Dattilio, R. L. Sadoff, & T. G. Gutheil (Eds.), *Handbook of forensic assessment: Psychological and psychiatric perspectives* (pp. 479–501). Hoboken, NJ: Wiley.

Munley, P. H. (2002). Comparability of MMPI–2 scales and profiles over time. *Journal of Personality Assessment, 78,* 145–160. doi:10.1207/S15327752JPA7801_09

Munley, P. H., Bains, D. S., Bloem, W. D., & Busby, R. M. (1995). Post-traumatic stress disorder and the MMPI–2. *Journal of Traumatic Stress, 8,* 171–178. doi:10.1002/jts.2490080113

Munley, P. H., Busby, R. M., & Jaynes, G. (1997). MMPI–2 findings in schizophrenia and depression. *Psychological Assessment, 9,* 508–511. doi:10.1037/1040-3590.9.4.508

Münsterberg, H. (1908). *On the witness stand: Essays on psychology and crime*. New York, NY: McClure.

Murray, J. B. (1982). Psychological aspects of low back pain: Summary. *Psychological Reports, 50*, 343–351. doi:10.2466/pr0.1982.50.2.343

Murrey, G. J. (2008). Overview of traumatic brain injury: Issues in the forensic assessment. In G. J. Murrey & D. Starzinski (Eds.), *The forensic evaluation of traumatic brain injury: A handbook for clinicians and attorneys* (2nd ed., pp. 1–23). Boca Raton, FL: CRC Press.

Murstein, B. I., & Glaudin, V. (1968). The use of the MMPI in the determination of marital adjustment. *Journal of Marriage and the Family, 30*, 651–655. doi:10.2307/349512

Narayan, U. (1997). *Dislocating cultures: Identities, traditions, and third-world feminism*. New York, NY: Routledge.

Nardi, B., & Pannelli, G. (1997). Attachment patterns and developmental depression: A clinical and process-oriented cognitive investigation. *Rivista di Psichiatria, 32*, 157–164.

National Center for Injury Prevention and Control. (2003). *Report to Congress on mild traumatic brain injury in the United States: Steps to prevent a serious public health problem*. Atlanta, GA: Centers for Disease Control and Prevention.

National Council on Disability. (n.d.). *Chapter 7: The family law system: Custody and visitation*. Retrieved from http://www.ncd.gov/publications/2012/Sep272012/Ch7

Neal, L. A., Busuttil, W., Rollins, J., Herepath, R., Strike, P., & Turnbull, G. (1994). Convergent validity of measures of post-traumatic stress disorder in a mixed military and civilian population. *Journal of Traumatic Stress, 7*, 447–455. doi:10.1002/jts.2490070310

Neal, T. M. S., & Grisso, T. (2014). The cognitive underpinnings of bias in forensic mental health evaluations. *Psychology, Public Policy, and Law, 20*, 200–211. doi:10.1037/a0035824

Neighbors, H. W., Trierweiler, S. J., Munday, C., Thompson, E. E., Jackson, J. S., Binion, V. J., & Gomez, J. (1999). Psychiatric diagnosis of African Americans: Diagnostic divergence in clinician structured and semistructured interviewing conditions. *Journal of the National Medical Association, 91*, 601–612.

Nelson, L. D., Pham, D., & Uchiyama, C. (1996). Subtlety of the MMPI–2 Depression Scale: A subject laid to rest? *Psychological Assessment, 8*, 331–333. doi:10.1037/1040-3590.8.3.331

Nelson, N. W., Sweet, J. J., Berry, D. T., Bryant, F. B., & Granacher, R. P. (2007). Response validity in forensic neuropsychology: Exploratory factor analytic evidence of distinct cognitive and psychological constructs. *Journal of the International Neuropsychological Society, 13*, 440–449. doi:10.1017/S1355617707070373

Nichols, D. (2001). *Essentials of MMPI–2 assessment*. New York, NY: Wiley.

Nichols, D. S. (2006a). Tell me a story: MMPI responses and personal biography in the case of a serial killer. *Journal of Personality Assessment, 86,* 242–262. doi:10.1207/s15327752jpa8603_02

Nichols, D. S. (2006b). The trials of separating bath water from baby: A review and critique of the MMPI–2 Restructured Clinical Scales. *Journal of Personality Assessment, 87,* 121–138. doi:10.1207/s15327752jpa8702_02

Nichols, D. S. (2011). *Essentials of MMPI–2 assessment* (2nd ed.). New York, NY: Wiley.

Nichols, D. S., & Greene, R. L. (1997). Dimensions of deception in personality assessment: The example of the MMPI–2. *Journal of Personality Assessment, 68,* 251–266. doi:10.1207/s15327752jpa6802_3

Nichols, D. S., Greene, R., & Schmolck, P. (1989). Criteria for assessing inconsistent patterns of item endorsement on the MMPI: Rationale, development, and empirical trials. *Journal of Clinical Psychology, 45,* 239–250. doi:10.1002/1097-4679(198903)45:2<239::AID-JCLP2270450210>3.0.CO;2-1

Nichols, D. S., Williams, C. L., & Greene, R. L. (2009, March). *Gender bias in the MMPI–2 Fake Bad Scale* (FBS) *and the* FBS–r *in the MMPI–2–RF.* Paper presented at the conference of the Society for Personality Assessment, Chicago, IL.

Nicholson, R. A., & Norwood, S. (2000). The quality of forensic psychological assessments, reports, and testimony: Acknowledging the gap between promise and practice. *Law and Human Behavior, 24,* 9–44. doi:10.1023/A:1005422702678

Nicol-Harper, R., Harvey, A. G., & Stein, A. (2007). Interactions between mothers and infants: Impact of maternal anxiety. *Infant Behavior & Development, 30,* 161–167. doi:10.1016/j.infbeh.2006.08.005

Nieberding, R. J., Gacono, C. B., Pirie, M., Bannatyne, L. A., Viglione, D. J., Cooper, B., . . . Frackowiak, M. (2003). MMPI–2 based classification of forensic psychiatric outpatients: An exploratory cluster analytic study. *Journal of Clinical Psychology, 59,* 907–920. doi:10.1002/jclp.10192

Nieberding, R. J., Moore, J. T., & Dematatis, A. P. (2002). Psychological assessment of forensic psychiatric outpatients. *International Journal of Offender Therapy and Comparative Criminology, 46,* 350–363. doi:10.1177/03024X02046003008

Noh, S., & Avison, W. R. (1992). Assessing psychopathology in Korean immigrants: Some preliminary results on the SCL-90. *Canadian Journal of Psychiatry/Revue canadienne de psychiatrie, 37,* 640–645.

Novack, T. A., Daniel, M. S., & Long, C. J. (1984). Factors related to emotional adjustment following head injury. *International Journal of Clinical Neuropsychology, 6,* 139–142.

Novy, D. M., Nelson, D. V., Goodwin, J. R., & Rowzee, R. D. (1993). Psychometric comparability of the State–Trait Anxiety Inventory for different ethnic subpopulations. *Psychological Assessment, 5,* 343–349. doi:10.1037/1040-3590.5.3.343

Ogloff, J. R. P. (1995). The legal basis of forensic application of the MMPI–2. In Y. S. Ben-Porath, J. R. Graham, G. C. N. Hall, R. D. Hirschman, & M. S.

Zaragoza (Eds.), *Forensic applications of the MMPI–2* (pp. 18–47). Thousand Oaks, CA: Sage.

Okawa, J. B. (2008). Considerations for the cross-cultural evaluation of refugees and asylum seekers. In L. Suzuki & J. G. Ponterotto (Eds.), *Handbook of multicultural assessment: Clinical, psychological, and educational applications* (pp. 165–194). San Francisco, CA: Jossey-Bass.

Ollendick, D. G. (1984). Scores on three MMPI alcohol scales of parents who receive child custody. *Psychological Reports, 55,* 337–338. doi:10.2466/pr0.1984.55.1.337

Ollendick, D. G., & Otto, B. J. (1984). MMPI characteristics of parents referred for child-custody studies. *Journal of Psychology, 117,* 227–232. doi:10.1080/00223980.1984.9923682

Ollendick, D. G., Otto, B. J., & Heider, S. M. (1983). Marital MMPI characteristics: A test of Arnold's signs. *Journal of Clinical Psychology: Interdisciplinary and Applied, 39,* 240–245. doi:10.1002/1097-4679(198303)39:2<240::AID-JCLP2270390216>3.0.CO;2-U

Orloff, L. E., Dutton, M. A., Hass, G. A., & Ammar, N. (Fall, 2003). Battered immigrant women's willingness to call for help and police response. *UCLA Women's Law Journal, 13*(1), pp. 43–100.

Osborne, D. (1971). An MMPI index of disturbed marital interaction. *Psychological Reports, 29,* 852–854. doi:10.2466/pr0.1971.29.3.852

Otto, R. K. (2002). Use of the MMPI–2 in forensic settings. *Journal of Forensic Psychology Practice, 2*(3), 71–91. doi:10.1300/J158v02n03_05

Otto, R. K., Buffington-Vollum, J. K., & Edens, J. F. (2003). Child custody evaluation. In I. Weiner (Series Ed.) & A. M. Goldstein (Vol. Ed.), *Handbook of psychology: Vol. 11. Forensic psychology* (pp. 179–208). Hoboken, NJ: Wiley.

Otto, R. K., & Butcher, J. N. (1995). Computer-assisted psychological assessment in child custody evaluations. *Family Law Quarterly, 29,* 79–96.

Otto, R. K., Edens, J. F., & Barcus, E. H. (2000). The use of psychological testing in child custody evaluations. *Family Court Review, 38,* 312–340. doi:10.1111/j.174-1617.2000.tb00578.x

Ownby, R. L. (2009). Writing clinical reports. In J. N. Butcher (Ed.), *Oxford handbook of personality assessment* (pp. 684–692). New York, NY: Oxford University Press.

Pace, T. M., Robbins, R. R., Choney, S. K., Hill, J. S., Lacey, K., & Blair, G. (2006). A cultural-contextual perspective on the validity of the MMPI–2 with American Indians. *Cultural Diversity and Ethnic Minority Psychology, 12,* 320–333. doi:10.1037/1099-9809.12.2.320

Palau, N. (1981, August). *Battered women: A homogeneous group? Theoretical considerations and MMPI data interpretation.* Paper presented at the annual meeting of the American Psychological Association, Los Angeles, CA.

Palav, A., Ortega, A., & McCaffrey, R. J. (2001). Incremental validity of the MMPI–2 content scales: A preliminary study with brain-injured patients. *Journal of Head Trauma Rehabilitation, 16,* 275–283. doi:10.1097/00001199-200106000-00006

Pancheri, P. (1971). Mètodo per la valutazione quantitative della sintomatologia schizofrenica attraverso l'impiego del MMPI [A method for the quantitative evaluation of schizophrenic symptoms by means of the MMPI]. *Rivista di Psichiatria, 6*, 64–84.

Pancheri, P., & Liotti, G. (1968). Validità diagnòstica dell'associazione Rorschach–MMPI nella syndrome schizofrencia [Diagnostic validity of the relationship between the Rorschach and the MMPI in schizophrenic syndrome]. *Rivista di Psichiatria, 3*, 704–723.

Pancoast, D. L., & Archer, R. P. (1989). Original adult MMPI norms in normal samples: A review with implications for future developments. *Journal of Personality Assessment, 53*, 376–395. doi:10.1207/s15327752jpa5302_14

Panton, J. H. (1976). Personality characteristics of death-row prison inmates. *Journal of Clinical Psychology, 32*, 306–309. doi:10.1002/1097-4679(197604)32:2<306::AID-JCLP2270320224>3.0.CO;2-M

Patch, P. C., & Hartlage, L. C. (2003). Behavioral change following traumatic brain injury. In A. M. Horton & L. C. Hartlage (Eds.), *Handbook of forensic neuropsychology* (pp. 215–235). New York, NY: Springer.

Paulson, M. J., Afifi, A. A., Thomason, M. L., & Chaleff, A. (1974). The MMPI: A descriptive measure of psychopathology in abusive parents. *Journal of Clinical Psychology, 30*, 387–390. doi:10.1002/1097-4679(197407)30:3<387::AID-JCLP2270300352>3.0.CO;2-J

Pavelka, F. L. (1986). Psychosocial characteristics of parolees in forensic social work. *Journal of Psychiatry & Law, 14*, 217–223.

Pearson Assessments. (2007, January 11). *FBS (Symptom Validity Scale) added to MMPI–2 standard scoring materials: Scale helps identify non-credible reporting* [Press release].

Pearson Assessments. (n.d.). *MMPI–2 The Minnesota Report: Reports for Forensic Settings.* Retrieved from http://www.pearsonclinical.com/education/products/100000650/mmpi-2-the-minnesota-report-reports-for-forensic-settings.html

Pedersen, P. B. (1997). *Culture-centered counseling interventions: Striving for accuracy.* Thousand Oaks, CA: Sage.

Pelcovitz, D., Van der Kolk, B. A., Roth, S., Mandel, F., Kaplan, S., & Resick, P. (1997). Development of a criteria set and a structured interview for disorders of extreme stress (SIDES). *Journal of Traumatic Stress, 10*, 3–16. doi:10.1002/jts.2490100103

Peltzer, K. (1998). Ethnocultural construction of posttraumatic stress symptoms in African contexts. *Journal of Psychology in Africa, South of the Sahara, the Caribbean and Afro-Latin America, 1*, 17–30.

Penk, W. E., Rierdan, J., Losardo, M., & Robinowitz, R. (2006). The MMPI–2 and assessment of posttraumatic stress disorder (PTSD). In J. N. Butcher (Ed.), *MMPI–2: A practitioner's guide* (pp. 121–141). Washington, DC: American Psychological Association.

Pennuto, T. O. (2010). Murder and the MMPI–2: The necessity of knowledgeable legal professionals. *Golden Gate University Law Review, 34*, 340–391.

Perl, J. L., & Kahn, M. W. (1983). The effects of compensation on psychiatric disability. *Social Science & Medicine, 17*, 439–443. doi:10.1016/0277-9536(83)90349-0

Perlin, M. L. (1996). Myths, realities, and the political world: The anthropology of insanity defense attitudes. *Bulletin of the American Academy of Psychiatry and the Law, 24*, 5–26.

Perrin, S., Van Hasselt, V. B., Basilio, I., & Hersen, M. (1996). Assessing the effects of violence on women in battering relationships with the Keane MMPI-PTSD scale. *Journal of Traumatic Stress, 9*, 805–816. doi:10.1002/jts.2490090409

Perrin, S., Van Hasselt, V. B., & Hersen, M. (1997). Validation of the Keane MMPI–PTSD Scale against *DSM–III–R* criteria in a sample of battered women. *Violence and Victims, 12*, 99–104.

Persons, R. W., & Marks, P. A. (1971). The violent 4-3 MMPI personality type. *Journal of Consulting and Clinical Psychology, 36*, 189–196. doi:10.1037/h0030742

Petchprapai, N., & Winkelman, C. (2007). Mild traumatic brain injury: Determinants and subsequent quality of life: A review of the literature. *Journal of Neuroscience Nursing, 39*, 260–272. doi:10.1097/01376517-200710000-00002

Peterson, C. D., & Dahlstrom, W. G. (1992). The derivation of gender role scales GM and GF for MMPI–2 and their relationship to scale 5 (M*f*). *Journal of Personality Assessment, 59*, 486–499. doi:10.1207/s15327752jpa5903_5

Phinney, J. S. (1992). The Multigroup Ethnic Identity Measure: A new scale for use with diverse groups. *Journal of Adolescent Research, 7*, 156–176. doi:10.1177/074355489272003

Physicians for Human Rights. (2012). *Examining asylum seekers: A clinician's guide to physical and psychological evaluations of torture and ill treatment.* Cambridge, MA: Author.

Pianta, R., Egeland, B., & Erickson, M. F. (1989). The antecedents of maltreatment: Results of the Mother–Child Interaction Project. In D. Cicchetti & V. Carlson (Eds.), *Child maltreatment: Theory and research on the causes and consequences of child abuse and neglect* (pp. 203–253). New York, NY: Cambridge University Press.

Pianta, R. C., Egeland, B., & Adam, E. K. (1996). Adult attachment classification and self-reported psychiatric symptomatology as assessed by the Minnesota Multiphasic Personality Inventory—2. *Journal of Consulting and Clinical Psychology, 64*, 273–281. doi:10.1037/0022-006X.64.2.273

Pico-Alfonso, M. A., Echeburua, E., & Martinez, M. (2008). Personality disorder symptoms in women as a result of chronic intimate partner violence. *Journal of Family Violence, 23*, 577–588. doi:10.1007/s10896-008-9180-9

Pinals, D. A., Packer, I. K., Fisher, W., & Roy-Bujnowski, K. (2004). Relationship between race and ethnicity and forensic clinical triage dispositions. *Psychiatric Services, 55*, 873–878. doi:10.1176/appi.ps.55.8.873

Pinard, G. F., & Pagani, L. (Eds.). (2001). *Clinical assessment of dangerousness: Empirical contributions*. New York, NY: Cambridge University Press.

Pinsoneault, T. B. (1996). Equivalency of computer-assisted and paper-and-pencil administered versions of the Minnesota Multiphasic Personality Inventory—2. *Computers in Human Behavior, 12*, 291–300. doi:10.1016/0747-5632(96)00008-8

Pirelli, G., Gottdiener, W. H., & Zapf, P. A. (2011). A meta-analytic review of competency to stand trial research. *Psychology, Public Policy, and Law, 17*, 1–53. doi:10.1037/a0021713

Pizitz, T., & McCullaugh, J. (2011). An overview of male personality profiles using the MMPI–2. *American Journal of Forensic Psychiatry, 32*, 31–39.

Pollack, D. R., & Grainey, T. F. (1984). A comparison of MMPI profiles for state and private disability insurance applicants. *Journal of Personality Assessment, 48*, 121–125. doi:10.1207/s15327752jpa4802_2

Pollack, D., & Shore, J. H. (1980). Validity of the MMPI with Native Americans. *American Journal of Psychiatry, 137*, 946–950.

Ponterotto, J. G. (1996). Evaluating and selecting research instruments. In F. T. Leong & J. T. Austin (Eds.), *The psychology research handbook: A primer for graduate students and research assistants* (pp. 73–84). Thousand Oaks, CA: Sage.

Pope, K. S. (2012). Psychological evaluation of torture survivors: Essential steps, avoidable errors, and helpful resources. *International Journal of Law and Psychiatry, 35*, 418–426. doi:10.1016/j.ijlp.2012.09.017

Pope, K. S., Butcher, J. N., & Seelen, J. (2006). *The MMPI, MMPI–2, and MMPI–A in court: A practical guide for expert witnesses and attorneys* (3rd ed.). Washington, DC: American Psychological Association.

Pope, K. S., & Garcia-Peltoniemi, R. E. (1991). Responding to victims of torture: Clinical issues, professional responsibilities, and useful resources. *Professional Psychology: Research and Practice, 22*, 269–276. doi:10.1037/0735-7028.22.4.269

Pospisil, T., Kirsten, A., Chuplis, K. A., Conger, C., & Golden, C. J. (2002). Examination of the relationship between the MMPI Depression Scale and performance on the Halstead–Reitan Test Battery. *Archives of Clinical Neuropsychology, 17*, 863–864.

Posthuma, A. B., & Harper, J. F. (1998). Comparison of MMPI–2 responses of child custody and personal injury litigants. *Professional Psychology: Research and Practice, 29*, 437–443. doi:10.1037/0735-7028.29.5.437

Pottick, K. J., Kirk, S. A., Hsieh, D. K., & Tian, X. (2007). Judging mental disorder in youths: Effects of client, clinician, and contextual differences. *Journal of Consulting and Clinical Psychology, 73*, 1–8. doi:10.1037/0022-006X.75.1.1

Pribram, K. H. (1954). Toward a science of neuropsychology (method and data). In R. A. Patton (Ed.), *Current trends in psychology and the behavioral sciences* (pp. 115–142). Pittsburgh, PA: University of Pittsburgh Press.

Pribram, K. H. (1969). *The brain and behavior* (Vols. I–IV). London, England: Penguin.

Pribram, K. H., Lim, H., Poppen, R., & Bagshaw, M. H. (1966). Limbic lesions and the temporal structure of redundancy. *Journal of Comparative and Physiological Psychology, 61*, 368–373. doi:10.1037/h0023245

Pribram, K. H., & Mishkin, M. (1955). Simultaneous and successive visual discrimination by monkeys with inferotemporal lesions. *Journal of Comparative and Physiological Psychology, 48*, 198–202. doi:10.1037/h0049140

Pritchard, D. A., & Rosenblatt, A. (1980). Racial bias in the MMPI: A methodological review. *Journal of Consulting and Clinical Psychology, 48*, 263–267. doi:10.1037/0022-006X.48.2.263

Prokop, C. K., Bradley, L. A., Margolis, R., & Gentry, W. (1980). Multivariate analysis of the MMPI profiles of patients with multiple pain complaints. *Journal of Personality Assessment, 44*, 246–252. doi:10.1207/s15327752jpa4403_5

Psychologists for Social Responsibility. (n.d.). *PsySR's Political Asylum Project.* Retrieved from http://www.psysr.org/

Putzke, J. D., Williams, M. A., Daniel, F. J., & Boll, T. J. (1999). The utility of *K*-correction to adjust for a defensive response set on the MMPI. *Assessment, 6*, 61–70. doi:10.1177/107319119900600107

Quinnell, F. A., & Bow, J. N. (2001). Psychological tests used in child custody evaluations. *Behavioral Sciences & the Law, 19*, 491–501. doi:10.1002/bsl.452

Quinsey, V. L., Harris, G. T., Rice, M. E., & Cornier, C. A. (2006). *Violent offenders: Appraising and managing risk* (2nd ed.). Washington, DC: American Psychological Association.

Quinsey, V. L., Lalumière, M. L., Rice, M. E., & Harris, G. T. (1995). Predicting sexual offenses. In J. C. Campbell (Ed.), *Assessing dangerousness: Violence by sexual offenders, batterers, and child abusers* (pp. 114–137). Thousand Oaks, CA: Sage.

Rader, C. M. (1977). MMPI profile types of exposers, rapists, and assaulters in a court services population. *Journal of Consulting and Clinical Psychology, 45*, 61–69. doi:10.1037/0022-006X.45.1.61

Raj, A., & Silverman, J. (2002a). Intimate partner violence against south Asian women in greater Boston. *Journal of the American Medical Women's Association, 57*, 111–114.

Raj, A., & Silverman, J. (2002b). Violence against immigrant women: The roles of culture, context, and legal immigrant status on partner violence. *Violence Against Women, 8*, 367–398. doi:10.1177/10778010222183107

Ramji-Nogales, J., Schoenholtz, A. I., & Schrag, P. G. (2009). *Refugee roulette: Disparity in asylum adjudication and proposals for reform.* New York, NY: New York University Press.

Ranson, M., Nichols, D. S., Rouse, S. V., & Harrington, J. (2009). Changing or replacing an established personality assessment standard: Issues, goals, and problems, with special reference to recent developments in the MMPI–2. In J. N. Butcher (Ed.), *Handbook of personality assessment* (pp. 112–139). New York, NY: Oxford University Press.

Ready, R. E., & Veague, H. B. (2014). Training in psychological assessment: Current practices of clinical psychology programs. *Professional Psychology: Research and Practice, 45*, 278–282. doi:10.1037/a0037439

Rehabilitation Act of 1973, Pub. L. No. 93-112, 87 Stat. 355.

Reitan, R. M. (1955a). Affective disturbances in brain-damaged patients: Measurements with the Minnesota Multiphasic Personality Inventory. *Archives of Neurology and Psychiatry, 73*, 530–532. doi:10.1001/archneurpsyc.1955.02330110046005

Reitan, R. M. (1955b). Certain differential effects of left and right cerebral lesions in human adults. *Journal of Comparative and Physiological Psychology, 48*, 474–477. doi:10.1037/h0048581

Repko, G. R., & Cooper, R. (1983). A study of the average workers' compensation case. *Journal of Clinical Psychology, 39*, 287–295. doi:10.1002/1097-4679 (198303)39:2<287::AID-JCLP2270390228>3.0.CO;2-Z

Resendes, J., & Lecci, L. (2012). Comparing the MMPI–2 scale scores of parents involved in parental competency and child custody assessments. *Psychological Assessment, 24*, 1054–1059. doi:10.1037/a0028585

Rhodes, N. R. (1992). Comparison of MMPI Psychopathic Deviate scores of battered and nonbattered women. *Journal of Family Violence, 7*, 297–307. doi:10.1007/ BF00994620

Richard, L. S., Wakefield, J. A., & Lewak, R. (1990). Similarity of personality variables as predictors of marital satisfaction: A Minnesota Multiphasic Personality Inventory (MMPI) item analysis. *Personality and Individual Differences, 11*, 39–43. doi:10.1016/0191-8869(90)90166-O

Rissel, C. (1997). The development and application of a scale of acculturation. *Australian and New Zealand Journal of Public Health, 21*, 606–613. doi:10.1111/ j.1467-842X.1997.tb01764.x

Ritzler, B. (1981). Predicting offspring vulnerability to psychopathology from parents' test data. *Journal of Personality Assessment, 45*, 600–607.

Roberts, J. V. (2001). Sentencing, parole, and psychology. In R. A. Schuller & J. R. P. Ogloff (Eds.), *Introduction to psychology and law: Canadian perspectives* (pp. 188–213). Toronto, Ontario, Canada: University of Toronto Press.

Roberts, J., & Hawton, K. (1980). Child abuse and attempted suicide. *British Journal of Psychiatry, 137*, 319–323. doi:10.1192/bjp.137.4.319

Robin, R. W., Greene, R. L., Albaugh, B., Caldwell, A., & Goldman, D. (2003). Use of the MMPI–2 in American Indians: I. Comparability of the MMPI–2 between two tribes and with the MMPI–2 normative group. *Psychological Assessment, 15*, 351–359. doi:10.1037/1040-3590.15.3.351

Rodriguez, C. M. (2010). Parent–child aggression: Association with child abuse potential and parenting styles. *Violence and Victims, 25*, 728–741. doi:10.1891/ 0886-6708.25.6.728

Rodriguez, R. (2004). *Community partnership models addressing violence against migrant and seasonal farmworker women.* Rockville, MD: National Criminal Justice Reference Service.

Rodriguez v. Miller Coors, No. 1:10-cv-00919-RPM-CBS (D. Colo. September 7, 2012).

Rogers, R., Bagby, R. M., & Dickens, S. E. (1992). *SIRS: Structured Interview of Reported Symptoms: Professional manual*. Odessa, FL: Psychological Assessment Resources.

Rogers, R., Gillard, N. D., Berry, D. T. R., & Granacher, R. P. (2011). Effectiveness of the MMPI–2–RF validity scales for feigned mental disorders and cognitive impairment: A known-groups study. *Journal of Psychopathology and Behavioral Assessment, 33*, 355–367. doi:10.1007/s10862-011-9222-0

Rogers, R., & Granacher, R. P. (2011). Conceptualization and assessment of malingering. In E. Y. Drogin, F. M. Dattilio, R. L. Sadoff, & T. G. Gutheil (Eds.), *Handbook of forensic assessment: Psychological and psychiatric perspectives* (pp. 659–678). Hoboken, NJ: Wiley.

Rogers, R., Sewell, K. W., Martin, M. A., & Vitacco, M. J. (2003). Detection of feigned mental disorders: A meta-analysis of the MMPI–2 and malingering. *Assessment, 10*, 160–177. doi:10.1177/1073191103010002007

Rohrer, J. M. (2008). Battered women: A survey of forensic psychologists and psychiatrists. *Dissertation Abstracts International: Section B. Sciences and Engineering, 68*, 6980.

Rolda v. Pitney Bowes, 66 Cal. Comp. Cases 241 (2001) (en banc).

Rome, H. P., Swenson, W. M., Mataya, P., McCarthy, C. E., Pearson, J. S., Keating, F. R., & Hathaway, S. R. (1962). Symposium on automation techniques in personality assessment. *Proceedings of the Staff Meeting of the Mayo Clinic, 37*, 61–82.

Rosen, E., & Mink, S. H. (1961). Desirability of personality traits as perceived by prisoners. *Journal of Clinical Psychology, 17*, 147–151. doi:10.1002/1097-4679(196104)17:2<147::AID-JCLP2270170212>3.0.CO;2-A

Rosenfeld, B., Green, D., Pivovarova, E., Dole, T., & Zapf, P. (2010). What to do with contradictory data? Approaches to the integration of multiple malingering measures. *International Journal of Forensic Mental Health, 9*, 63–73. doi:10.1080/14999013.2010.499559

Rosewater, L. B. (1988). Battered or schizophrenic? Psychological tests can't tell. In K. Yllö & M. Bograd (Eds.), *Feminist perspectives on wife abuse* (pp. 200–215). Newbury Park, CA: Sage.

Rosich, K. J. (2007). *Race, ethnicity, and the criminal justice system*. Washington, DC: American Sociological Association.

Ross, S. R., Putnam, S. H., Gass, C. S., Bailey, D. E., & Adams, K. M. (2003). MMPI–2 indices of psychological disturbance and attention and memory test performance in head injury. *Archives of Clinical Neuropsychology, 18*, 905–906. doi:10.1093/arclin/18.8.905

Rossi, G., & Sloore, H. (2008). Cross-cultural reliability and generality of the Megargee Offender Classification System. *Criminal Justice and Behavior, 35*, 725–740. doi:10.1177/0093854808316300

Ruch, F. L., & Ruch, W. W. (1967). The K factor as a (validity) suppressor variable in predicting success in selling. *Journal of Applied Psychology, 51*, 201–204. doi:10.1037/h0024663

Ruttan, L. A., & Heinrichs, R. W. (2003). Depression and neurocognitive functioning in mild traumatic brain injury patients referred for assessment. *Journal of Clinical and Experimental Neuropsychology, 25,* 407–419. doi:10.1076/jcen.25.3.407.13812

Ryan, J. J., Dunn, G. E., & Paolo, A. M. (1995). Temporal stability of the MMPI–2 in a substance abuse sample. *Psychotherapy in Private Practice, 14,* 33–41.

S. 899, 2003–2004 Sess. (Cal. 2004).

Saborío, C., & Hass, G. (2012, March). *The psychological functioning of sexually assaulted women as seen through the MMPI–2 clinical and restructured clinical scales.* Paper presented at the meeting of the Society for Personality Assessment, Chicago, IL.

Sands, R. (1995). The parenting experience of low-income single women with serious mental disorders. *Families in Society, 76*(2), 86–89.

Santos, F. (2012, August 7). Life term for gunman after guilty plea in Tucson killings. *The New York Times.* Retrieved from http://www.nytimes.com

Scarpetti, W. L. (1973). The repression–sensitization dimension in relation to impending painful stimulation. *Journal of Consulting and Clinical Psychology, 40,* 377–382. doi:10.1037/h0034494

Schill, T., & Wang, T. (1990). Correlates of the MMPI–2 Anger Content Scale. *Psychological Reports, 67,* 800–802. doi:10.2466/PR0.67.7.800-802

Schinka, J. A., & LaLone, L. (1997). MMPI–2 norms: Comparisons with a census-matched subsample. *Psychological Assessment, 9,* 307–311. doi:10.1037/1040-3590.9.3.307

Schmidtgall, K., King, A., Zarski, J. J., & Cooper, J. E. (2000). The effects of parental conflict on later child development. *Journal of Divorce & Remarriage, 33,* 149–157. doi:10.1300/J087v33n01_09

Schuldberg, D. (1988). The MMPI is less sensitive to the automated testing format than it is to repeated testing: Item and scale effects. *Computers in Human Behavior, 4,* 285–298. doi:10.1016/0747-5632(88)90001-5

Scott, C. L. (Ed.). (2010). *Handbook of correctional mental health* (2nd ed.). Arlington, VA: American Psychiatric Publishing.

Scott, C. L., Quanbeck, C. D., & Resnick, P. J. (2003). Assessment of dangerousness. In R. E. Hales, S. C. Yudofsky, & G. O. Gabbard (Eds.), *The American Psychiatric Publishing textbook of psychiatry* (5th ed., pp. 1655–1672). Washington, DC: American Psychiatric Publishing.

Seeman, M. V., & Göpfert, M. (2004). Parenthood and adult mental health. In M. Göpfert, J. Webster, & V. Seeman (Eds.), *Parental psychiatric disorder: Distressed parents and their families* (2nd ed., pp. 8–21). New York, NY: Cambridge University Press.

Sellbom, M. (2014). A factor mixture model approach to elaborating on offender mental health classification with the MMPI–2–RF. *Journal of Personality Assessment, 96,* 293–305.

Shapiro, D. L. (1991). Informed consent in forensic evaluations. *Psychotherapy in Private Practice, 9*, 145–154.

Sharland, M. J., & Gfeller, J. D. (2007). A survey of neuropsychologists' beliefs and practices with respect to the assessment of effort. *Archives of Clinical Neuropsychology, 22*, 213–223. doi:10.1016/j.acn.2006.12.004

Sharp, C., & Fonagy, P. (2008). The parent's capacity to treat the child as a psychological agent: Constructs, measures and implications for developmental psychopathology. *Social Development, 17*, 737–754. doi:10.1111/j.1467-9507.2007.00457.x

Sher, K. J., & McCrady, B. (1984). The MacAndrew Alcoholism Scale: Severity of alcohol abuse and parental alcoholism. *Addictive Behaviors, 9*, 99–102. doi:10.1016/0306-4603(84)90013-3

Shercliffe, R. J., & Colotla, V. (2009). MMPI–2 profiles in civilian PTSD: An examination of differential responses between victims of crime and industrial accidents. *Journal of Interpersonal Violence, 24*, 349–360. doi:10.1177/0886260508316482

Shetty, S., & Kaguyutan, J. (2002). *Immigrant victims of domestic violence: Cultural challenges and available legal protections.* Retrieved from http://www.vawnet.org

Shiota, N. K., Krauss, S. S., & Clark, L. A. (1996). Adaptation and validation of the Japanese MMPI–2. In J. N. Butcher (Ed.), *International adaptations of the MMPI–2: A handbook of research and applications* (pp. 67–87). Minneapolis: University of Minnesota Press.

Shores, A., & Carstairs, J. R. (1998). Accuracy of the MMPI–2 computerized Minnesota Report in identifying fake-good and fake-bad response sets. *Clinical Neuropsychologist, 12*, 101–106. doi:10.1076/clin.12.1.101.1733

Sieber, K. O., & Meyers, L. (1992). Validation of the MMPI–2 Social Introversion subscales. *Psychological Assessment, 4*, 185–189. doi:10.1037/1040-3590.4.2.185

Siegel, J. C. (1996). Traditional MMPI–2 validity indicators and initial presentation in custody evaluations. *American Journal of Forensic Psychology, 14*, 55–63.

Siegel, J. C., Bow, J. N., & Gottlieb, M. C. (2012). The MMPI–2 in high conflict child custody cases. *American Journal of Forensic Psychology, 30*(3), 21–34.

Siegel, J. C., & Langford, J. S. (1998). MMPI–2 validity scales and suspected parental alienation syndrome. *American Journal of Forensic Psychology, 16*(4), 5–14.

Simons, R., Goddard, R., & Patton, W. (2002). Hand-scoring error rates in psychological testing. *Assessment, 9*, 292–300. doi:10.1177/1073191102009003008

Sines, J. O. (1966). Actuarial methods in personality assessment. In B. A. Maher (Ed.), *Progress in experimental personality research* (pp. 133–193). New York, NY: Academic Press.

Sines, L. K., Baucom, D. H., & Gruba, G. H. (1979). A validity scale sign calling for caution in the interpretation of MMPIs among psychiatric inpatients. *Journal of Personality Assessment, 43*, 604–607. doi:10.1207/s15327752jpa4306_7

Sines, L. K., & Silver, R. J. (1963). An index of psychopathology (*Ip*) derived from clinicians' judgments of MMPI profiles. *Journal of Clinical Psychology, 19*, 324–326. doi:10.1002/1097-4679(196307)19:3<324::AID-JCLP2270190323>3.0.CO;2-P

Sirigatti, S., & Giannini, M. (2000). Detection of faking good on the MMPI–2: Psychometric characteristics of the S scale. *Bollettino di Psicologia Applicata, 232*, 61–69.

Sirigatti, S., & Giannini, M. (2007). To detect underreporting of symptoms in an Italian sample: The MMPI–2 superlative scale (MMPI–2 S). *Bollettino di Psicologia Applicata, 251*, 13–21.

Sirigatti, S., Giannini, M., Laura-Grotto, R., & Giangrasso, B. (2002). Classificare i detenuti con il MMPI–2: Il sistema di Megargee. Primi dati su un campione italiano [Classifying prison inmates with the MMPI–2: The Megargee system. First data from an Italian sample]. *Bollettino di Psicologia Applicata, 238*, 17–23.

Sivák, S., Kurca, E., Jancovic, D., Petriscak, S., & Kucera, P. (2005). Nácrt súcasného pohl'adu na problematiku l'ahkých poranení mozgu so zameraním na dospelú populáciu [An outline of the current concepts of mild brain injury with emphasis on the adult population]. *Casopis Lekaru Ceskych, 144*, 445–450.

Slade, A. (2005). Parental reflective functioning: An introduction. *Attachment & Human Development, 7*, 269–281. doi:10.1080/14616730500245906

Slade, A., Aber, J. L., Bresgi, I., Berger, B., & Kaplan, M. (2004). *The Parent Development Interview, Revised*. Unpublished protocol, City University of New York.

Smart, C. M., Nelson, N. W., Sweet, J. J., Bryant, F. B., Berry, D. T., Granacher, R. P., & Heilbronner, R. L. (2008). Use of MMPI–2 to predict cognitive effort: A hierarchically optimal classification tree analysis. *Journal of the International Neuropsychological Society, 14*, 842–852. doi:10.1017/S1355617708081034

Smith, R. E. (1955). *Personality configurations of adult male penal populations as revealed by the MMPI* (Unpublished doctoral dissertation). University of Minnesota.

Smith, S. R., Gorske, T. T., Wiggins, C., & Little, J. A. (2010). Personality assessment use by clinical neuropsychologists. *International Journal of Testing, 10*, 6–20. doi:10.1080/15305050903534787

Smith, S. R., Hilsenroth, M. J., Castlebury, F. D., & Durham, T. W. (1999). The clinical utility of the MMPI–2 Antisocial Practices Content Scale. *Journal of Personality Disorders, 13*, 385–393. doi:10.1521/pedi.1999.13.4.385

Sopchak, A. L. (1952). Parental "identification" and "tendency toward disorders" as measured by the Minnesota Multiphasic Personality Inventory. *Journal of Abnormal and Social Psychology, 47*, 159–165. doi:10.1037/h0056247

Sparta, S. N., & Koocher, G. P. (Eds.). (2006). *Forensic mental health assessment of children and adolescents*. New York, NY: Oxford University Press.

Späte, H. F., & Schirmer, S. (1987). Medical ethics and forensic psychiatric assessment. *Psychiatrie, Neurologie und medizinische Psychologie, 39*, 17–23.

Spielberger, C. D., Diaz-Guerrero, R., & Strelau, J. (1990). *Cross-cultural anxiety* (Vol. 4). Washington, DC: Hemisphere.

Spielberger, C. D., Gorsuch, R. L., Lushene, R., Vagg, P. R., & Jacobs, G. A. (1983). *Manual for the State–Trait Anxiety Inventory*. Palo Alto, CA: Consulting Psychologists Press.

Srinivasan, S., & Ivey, S. (1999). Domestic violence. In S. Ivey & E. Kramer (Eds.), *Immigrant women's health* (pp. 178–189). San Francisco, CA: Jossey-Bass.

Stafford, K. P., & Sadoff, R. L. (2011). Competence to stand trial. In E. Y. Drogin, F. M. Dattilio, R. L. Sadoff, & T. G. Gutheil (Eds.), *Handbook of forensic assessment: Psychological and psychiatric perspectives* (pp. 3–24). Hoboken, NJ: Wiley.

Stahl, P. M. (2010). *Conducting child custody evaluations: From basic to complex issues*. Thousand Oaks, CA: Sage.

Stark, E. (2007). *Coercive control: The entrapment of women in personal life*. New York, NY: Oxford University Press.

Steadman, H. J., Mulvey, E. P., Monahan, J., Robbins, P. C., Appelbaum, P. S., Grisso, T., . . . Silver, E. (1998). Violence by people discharged from acute psychiatric inpatient facilities and by others in the same neighborhoods. *Archives of General Psychiatry, 55*, 393–401. doi:10.1001/archpsyc.55.5.393

Steffan, J. S., Morgan, R. D., Lee, J., & Sellbom, M. (2010). A comparative analysis of MMPI–2 malingering detection models among inmates. *Assessment, 17*, 185–196. doi:10.1177/1073191109359382

Stein, A., & Fairburn, C. G. (1996). Eating habits and attitudes to body shape and weight during the postnatal period. *Psychosomatic Medicine, 58*, 321–325. doi:10.1097/00006842-199607000-00004

Steinberg, M. (1994). *The Structured Clinical Interview for* DSM–IV *Dissociative Disorders—Revised (SCID–D)*. Washington, DC: American Psychiatric Press.

Stephenson, M. (2000). Development and validation at the Stephenson Multigroup Acculturation Scale (SMAS). *Psychological Assessment, 12*, 77–88. doi:10.1037/1040-3590.12.1.77

Sternbach, R. A., Wolf, S. R., Murphy, R. W., & Akeson, W. H. (1973). Traits of pain patients: The low back "loser." *Psychosomatics, 14*, 226–229. doi:10.1016/S0033-3182(73)71337-2

Stevens, M. J., Kwan, K.-L., & Graybill, D. (1993). Comparison of MMPI–2 scores of foreign Chinese and Caucasian-American students. *Journal of Clinical Psychology, 49*, 23–27. doi:10.1002/1097-4679(199301)49:1<23::AID-JCLP2270490104>3.0.CO;2-O

Stith v. State Farm Mutual Insurance, No. 03-CA-010945 (Fla. Cir. Ct. August, 28, 2008).

Storm, J., & Graham, J. R. (2000). Detection of coached general malingering on the MMPI–2. *Psychological Assessment, 12*, 158–165. doi:10.1037/1040-3590.12.2.158

Straus, M. A. (2007). Conflict Tactics Scales. In N. A. Jackson (Ed.), *Encyclopedia of domestic violence* (pp. 190–197). New York, NY: Taylor & Francis.

Straus, M. A., Hamby, S. L., Boney-McCoy, S., & Sugarman, D. B. (1996). The revised Conflict Tactics Scales (CTS2): Development and preliminary psychometric data. *Journal of Family Issues, 17,* 283–316. doi:10.1177/019251396017003001

Stredny, R. V., Archer, R. P., & Mason, J. A. (2006). MMPI–2 and MCMI–III characteristics of parental competency examinees. *Journal of Personality Assessment, 87,* 113–115. doi:10.1207/s15327752jpa8701_10

Streit, K., Greene, R. L., Cogan, R., & Davis, H. G. (1993). Clinical correlates of MMPI depression scales. *Journal of Personality Assessment, 60,* 390–396. doi:10.1207/s15327752jpa6002_14

Substance Abuse and Mental Health Services Administration. (2014). *A treatment improved protocol: Trauma informed care in behavioral health services (Tip 57).* Rockville, MD: Author.

Sutker, P. B., & Moan, C. E. (1973). Prediction of socially maladaptive behavior within a state prison system. *Journal of Community Psychology, 1,* 74–78. doi:10.1002/1520-6629(197301)1:1<74::AID-JCOP2290010121>3.0.CO;2-I

Svanum, S., & McAdoo, W. G. (1991). Parental alcoholism: An examination of male and female alcoholics in treatment. *Journal of Studies on Alcohol, 52,* 127–132.

Swenson, W. M., & Pearson, J. S. (1964). Automation techniques in personality assessment—A frontier in behavioral science and medicine. *Methods of Information in Medicine, 3,* 34–36.

Swenson, W. M., Rome, H. P., Pearson, J. S., & Brannick, T. L. (1965). A totally automated psychological test: Experience in a medical center. *JAMA, 191,* 925–927. doi:10.1001/jama.1965.03080110049012

Symonds, P. M. (1934). *Psychological diagnosis in social adjustment, including an annotated list of tests, questionnaires, and rating scales for the study of personality and conduct* (pp. 11–42). doi:10.1037/11043-002

Taft, C. T., Murphy, C. M., King, L. A., Dedeyn, J. M., & Musser, P. H. (2005). Posttraumatic stress disorder symptomatology among partners of men in treatment for relationship abuse. *Journal of Abnormal Psychology, 114,* 259–268. doi:10.1037/0021-843X.114.2.259

Tajima, E. A. (2004). Correlates of the co-occurrence of wife abuse and child abuse among a representative sample. *Journal of Family Violence, 19,* 391–402. doi:10.1007/s10896-004-0684-7

Tallent, N. (1993). *Psychological report writing* (4th ed.). Englewood Cliffs, NJ: Prentice-Hall.

Tellegen, A., & Ben-Porath, Y. S. (2008). *MMPI–2–RF technical manual.* Minneapolis: University of Minnesota Press.

Tellegen, A., Ben-Porath, Y. S., McNulty, J. L., Arbisi, P. A., Graham, J. R., & Kaemmer, B. (2003). *The MMPI–2 Restructured Clinical Scales: Development, validation, and interpretation.* Minneapolis: University of Minnesota Press.

Teodorescu, D. S., Heir, T., Hauff, E., Wentzel-Larsen, T., & Lien, L. (2012). Mental health problems and post-migration stress among multi-traumatized refugees attending outpatient clinics upon resettlement to Norway. *Scandinavian Journal of Psychology, 53*, 316–332. doi:10.1111/j.1467-9450.2012.00954.x

Thatte, S., Manos, N., & Butcher, J. N. (1987, July). *Cross-cultural study of abnormal personality in three countries: United States, India, and Greece.* Paper presented at the Conference on Personality Assessment, Brussels, Belgium.

The Human Smuggling and Trafficking Center (2006). *Fact sheet: Distinction between human smuggling and human trafficking.* Retrieved from www.state.gov/documents/organization/90541.pdf

Thomas, M. L., & Youngjohn, J. R. (2009). Let's not get hysterical: Comparing the MMPI–2 validity, clinical, and RC scales in TBI litigants tested for effort. *Clinical Neuropsychologist, 23*, 1067–1084. doi:10.1080/13854040902795000

Timbrook, R. E., & Graham, J. R. (1994). Ethnic differences on the MMPI–2. *Psychological Assessment, 6*, 212–217. doi:10.1037/1040-3590.6.3.212

Tolman, R. M. (1999). The validation of the Psychological Maltreatment of Women Inventory. *Violence and Victims, 14*, 25–37.

Trujillo, M. (2008). Multicultural aspects of mental health. *Primary Psychiatry, 15*(4), 65–71.

Tsai, D. C., & Pike, P. L. (2000). Effects of acculturation on the MMPI–2 scores of Asian American students. *Journal of Personality Assessment, 74*, 216–230. doi:10.1207/S15327752JPA7402_4

Tsai, J. L., Chentsova-Dutton, Y., & Wong, Y. (2002). Why and how researchers should study ethnic identity, acculturation, and cultural orientation. In G. C. N. Hall & S. Okazaki (Eds.), *Asian American psychology: The science of lives in context* (pp. 41–65). Washington, DC: American Psychological Association.

Tsai, J. L., Ying, Y., & Lee, P. A. (2001). Cultural predictors of self-esteem: A study of Chinese American female and male young adults. *Cultural Diversity and Ethnic Minority Psychology, 7*, 284–297. doi:10.1037/1099-9809.7.3.284

Tseng, W. S., Matthews, D. B., & Elwin, T. S. (2004). *Cultural competence in forensic mental health: A guide for psychiatrist, psychologists, and attorneys.* New York, NY: Brunner-Routledge.

Uluç, S. (2008). MMPI–2 depresyon, kaygi ve ofke icerik olceklerinin olcut gecerligi acisindan degerlendirilmesi [Examination of the criterion validity of the MMPI–2 Depression, Anxiety, and Anger Content scales]. *Turkish Journal of Psychiatry, 19*, 57–66.

Unif. Marriage and Divorce Act § 402, 9A U.L.A. 561(1987).

United Nations. (n.d.). *What is a refugee?* Retrieved from http://www.unrefugees.org/

United States Citizenship and Immigration Services. (n.d.). *Policy manual: Vol. 12. Citizenship and naturalization.* Retrieved from http://www.uscis.gov/ policymanual/html

United States Sentencing Commission. (2008). *The federal sentencing guidelines manual.* Washington, DC: Thompson/West.

University of Michigan School of Social Work. (n.d.). Downloadable versions of the PMWI. Retrieved from http://sitemaker.umich.edu/downloadable_versions_of_the_pmwi

University of Minnesota Press. (2011). Available translations. Retrieved from http://www.upress.umn.edu/test-division/translations-permissions/permissions

U.S. Const. amend XIV.

Vaccaro, T. P., & Hogan, J. D. (2004). The origins of forensic psychology in America: Hugo Münsterberg on the witness stand. *NYS Psychologist, 16*(3), 14–17.

Vaisman-Tzachor, R. (2012). Psychological evaluations in federal immigration courts: Fifteen years in the making—lessons learned. *Forensic Examiner, 21*(2), 42–53.

Vandergracht v. Progressive Express, No. 02-04552 (Fla. Hillsborough County Ct. March 9, 2007).

VanPortfliet, P. (2012). *The MMPI–2–RF and the prediction of completion of a substance abuse rehabilitation program* (Doctoral dissertation). Available from ProQuest Dissertations and Theses database. (UMI No. 3517595)

Varela, J. G., & Conroy, M. A. (2012). Professional competencies in forensic psychology. *Professional Psychology: Research and Practice, 43*, 410–421. doi:10.1037/a0026776

Velasquez, R. J., Chavira, D. A., Karle, H. R., Callahan, W. J., Garcia, J. A., & Castellanos, J. (2000). Assessing bilingual and monolingual Latino students with translations of the MMPI–2: Initial data. *Cultural Diversity and Ethnic Minority Psychology, 6*, 65–72. doi:10.1037/1099-9809.6.1.65

Velligan, D., Christensen, A., Goldstein, M. J., & Margolin, G. (1988). Parental communication deviance: Its relationship to parent, child, and family system variables. *Psychiatry Research, 26*, 313–325. doi:10.1016/0165-1781(88)90126-6

Vendrig, A. A. (2000). The Minnesota Multiphasic Personality Inventory and chronic pain: A conceptual analysis of a long-standing but complicated relationship. *Clinical Psychology Review, 20*, 533–559. doi:10.1016/S0272-7358(00)00053-2

Ver Steegh, N. (2005). Differentiating types of domestic violence: Implications for child custody. *Louisiana Law Review, 65*, 1379–1431.

Ver Steegh, N., & Dalton, C. (2008). Report from the Wingspread Conference on Domestic Violence and Family Courts. *Family Court Review, 46*, 454–475. doi:10.1111/j.1744-1617.2008.00214.x

Vestre, N. D., & Watson, C. G. (1972). Behavioral correlates of the MMPI Paranoia scale. *Psychological Reports, 31*, 851–854. doi:10.2466/pr0.1972.31.3.851

Victims of Trafficking and Violence Protection Act of 2000, Pub. L. No. 06-386, 114 Stat. 1464.

Vilariño, M., Arce, R., & Fariña, F. (2013). Forensic-clinical interview: Reliability and validity for the evaluation of psychological injury. *European Journal of Psychology Applied to Legal Context, 5*(1). Retrieved from http://scielo.isciii.es/scielo.php

Violence Against Women Act of 1994, Pub. L. No. 103-322,108 Stat. 1902.

Violence Against Women Act of 2013, Pub. L. No. 113-114, § 802, 127 Stat. 24.

Violence Against Women Reauthorization Act of 2005, Pub. L. No. 109-162, 119 Stat. 2960 (2006).

Vojvoda, D., Weine, S. M., McGlashan, T., Becker, D. F., & Southwick, S. M. (2008). Posttraumatic stress disorder symptoms in Bosnian refugees 3½ years after resettlement. *Journal of Rehabilitation Research and Development, 45*, 421–426. doi:10.1682/JRRD. 2007.06.0083

Walfish, S. (2007). Reducing Minnesota Multiphasic Personality Inventory defensiveness: Effect of specialized instructions on retest validity in a sample of preoperative bariatric patients. *Surgery for Obesity and Related Diseases, 3*, 184–188. doi:10.1016/j.soard.2007.01.001

Walfish, S. (2011). Reducing MMPI–defensiveness in professionals presenting for evaluation. *Journal of Addictive Diseases, 30*, 75–80. doi:10.1080/10550887.2010. 531666

Wallace, A., & Liljequist, L. (2005). A comparison of the correlational structures and elevation patterns of the MMPI–2 Restructured Clinical (RC) and Clinical Scales. *Assessment, 12*, 290–294. doi:10.1177/1073191105276250

Walters, G. D., Rogers, R., Berry, D. T., Miller, H. A., Duncan, S. A., McCusker, P. J., . . . Granacher, R. P. (2008). Malingering as a categorical or dimensional construct: The latent structure of feigned psychopathology as measured by the SIRS and MMPI–2. *Psychological Assessment, 20*, 238–247. doi:10.1037/1040-3590.20.3.238

Wangberg, D. K. (2000). Child custody evaluation practices: A survey of experienced clinical psychologists. *Dissertation Abstracts International: Section B. Sciences and Engineering, 61*, 1100.

Ward, C., & Rana-Deuba, A. (1999). Acculturation and adaptation revisited. *Journal of Cross-Cultural Psychology, 30*, 422–442. doi:10.1177/0022022199030004003

Ward, L. C. (1997). Confirmatory factor analyses of the Anxiety and Depression Content Scales of the MMPI–2. *Journal of Personality Assessment, 68*, 678–691. doi:10.1207/s15327752jpa6803_13

Ward, L. C. (1998). Measurement of social introversion by the MMPI–2. *Journal of Personality Assessment, 70*, 171–182. doi:10.1207/s15327752jpa7001_11

Warriner, E. M., Rourke, B. P., Velikonja, D., & Metham, L. (2003). Subtypes of emotional and behavioral sequelae in patients with traumatic brain injury. *Journal of Clinical and Experimental Neuropsychology, 25*, 904–917. doi:10.1076/jcen.25.7.904.16494

Wasyliw, O. E., Grossman, L. S., Haywood, T. W., & Cavanaugh, J. L. (1988). The detection of malingering in criminal forensic groups: MMPI validity scales. *Journal of Personality Assessment, 52*, 321–333. doi:10.1207/s15327752jpa5202_13

Watson, C. G., Manifold, V., Klett, W. G., Brown, J., Thomas, D., & Anderson, D. (1990). Comparability of computer- and booklet-administered Minnesota Multiphasic Personality Inventories among primarily chemically dependent patients. *Psychological Assessment, 2*, 276–280. doi:10.1037/1040-3590.2.3.276

Weaver, T. L., & Clum, G. A. (1995). Psychological distress associated with inter-personal violence: A meta-analysis. *Clinical Psychology Review, 15,* 115–140. doi:10.1016/0272-7358(95)00004-9

Weed, N. C. (1993). An evaluation of the efficacy of MMPI–2 indicators of validity. *Dissertation Abstracts International, 53,* 3800.

Weed, N. C., Butcher, J. N., McKenna, T., & Ben-Porath, Y. S. (1992). New measures for assessing alcohol and drug abuse with the MMPI-2: The APS and AAS. *Journal of Personality Assessment, 58,* 389–404. doi:10.1207/s15327752jpa5802_15

Weiner, I. B. (2006). Writing forensic reports. In I. B. Weiner & A. K. Hess (Eds.), *Handbook of forensic psychology* (3rd ed., pp. 631–651). New York, NY: Wiley.

Weiner, I. B., & Otto, R. K. (Eds.). (2013). *The handbook of forensic psychology* (4th ed.). New York, NY: Wiley.

Weinstein, R., & Weinstein, J. (2010). Culturally competent criminal forensic psychological evaluations. In L. Ramirez (Ed.), *Criminal issues in criminal defense* (3rd ed., pp. 213–239). Huntington, NY: Juris.

Weisaeth, L. (1989). The stressors and post-traumatic stress syndrome after an industrial disaster. *Acta Psychiatrica Scandinavica Supplementum, 355,* 25–37.

Weiss, P., Bell, K., & Weiss, W. (2010). Use of the MMPI–2 Restructured Clinical (RC) scales in detecting criminal malingering. *Journal of Police and Criminal Psychology, 25,* 49–55. doi:10.1007/s11896-009-9056-9

Weiss, R. A., & Rosenfeld, B. (2012). Navigating cross-cultural issues in forensic assessment: Recommendations for practice. *Professional Psychology: Research and Practice, 43,* 234–240. doi:10.1037/a0025850

Welsh, G. S. (1956). Factor dimensions *A* and *R.* In G. S. Welsh & W. G. Dahlstrom (Eds.), *Basic readings on the MMPI in psychology and medicine* (pp. 264–281). Minneapolis: University of Minnesota Press.

Wetter, M. W., Baer, R. A., Berry, D. T. R., & Reynolds, S. (1994). The effect of symptom information on faking on the MMPI–2. *Assessment, 1,* 199–207. doi:10.1177/1073191194001002010

Wetter, M. W., Baer, R. A., Berry, D. T. R., Robinson, L. H., & Sumpter, J. (1993). MMPI–2 profiles of motivated fakers given specific symptom information: A comparison to matched patients. *Psychological Assessment, 5,* 317–323. doi:10.1037/1040-3590.5.3.317

Wetter, M. W., & Corrigan, S. K. (1995). Providing information to clients about psychological tests: A survey of attorneys' and law students' attitudes. *Professional Psychology: Research and Practice, 26,* 474–477. doi:10.1037/0735-7028.26.5.474

Wettstein, R. M. (2008). Ethical practice in forensic psychology: A systematic model for decision making forensic ethics and the expert witness. *Journal of the American Academy of Psychiatry and the Law, 36,* 595–598.

Wheatley, R. D. (1984). *Psychometric evaluation of head injury among fliers referred to the USAF School of Aerospace Medicine* (Tech. Rep. 84-47). Brooks Air Force Base, TX: USAF School of Aerospace Medicine.

White, A. (2005). *Assessment of parenting capacity: Research report*. Ashfield, New South Wales, Australia: Centre for Parenting and Research.

Whitworth, R. H., & McBlaine, D. C. (1993). Comparison of the MMPI and MMPI–2 administered to Anglo- and Hispanic-American university students. *Journal of Personality Assessment, 61*, 19–27. doi:10.1207/s15327752jpa6101_2

Wiederanders, M. R., Bromley, D. L., & Choate, P. A. (1997). Forensic conditional release programs and outcomes in three states. *International Journal of Law and Psychiatry, 20*, 249–257. doi:10.1016/S0160-2527(97)00006-X

Wiener, D. N. (1948). Subtle and obvious keys for the MMPI. *Journal of Consulting Psychology, 12*, 164–170. doi:10.1037/h0055594

Williams, C. L., Butcher, J. N., Gass, C. S., Cumella, E., & Kally, Z. (2009). Inaccuracies about the MMPI–2 Fake Bad Scale in the Reply by Ben-Porath, Greve, Bianchini, and Kaufmann (2009). *Psychological Injury and Law, 2*, 182–197. doi:10.1007/s12207-009-9046-3

Williams, J. L. (1971). Personal space and its relation to extraversion-introversion. *Canadian Journal of Behavioural Science/Revue canadienne des sciences du comportement, 3*, 156–160. doi:10.1037/h0082257

Williams, M. A., & Boll, T. J. (2000). Report writing in clinical neuropsychology. In G. Groth-Marnat (Ed.), *Neuropsychological assessment in clinical practice: A guide to test interpretation and integration* (pp. 575–605). Hoboken, NJ: Wiley.

Williams v. CSX Transportation, No. 04-CA-008892 (Fla. Cir. Ct. August 24, 2007).

Wolf, E. J., Miller, M. W., Orazem, R. J., Weierich, M. R., Castillo, D. T., Milford, J., . . . & Keane, T. M. (2008). The MMPI–2 Restructured Clinical Scales in the assessment of posttraumatic stress disorder and comorbid disorders. *Psychological Assessment, 20*, 327–340. doi:10.1037/a0012948

Wooten, A. J. (1984). Effectiveness of the *K* correction in the detection of psychopathology and its impact on profile height and configuration among young adult men. *Journal of Consulting and Clinical Psychology, 52*, 468–473. doi:10.1037/0022-006X.52.3.468

Workman, M., & Beer, J. (1992). Aggression, alcohol dependency, and self-consciousness among high school students of divorced and nondivorced parents. *Psychological Reports, 71*, 279–286.

Wright, L. (1976). The "sick but slick" syndrome as a personality component of parents of battered children. *Journal of Clinical Psychology, 32*, 41–45.

Wygant, D. B. (2008). Validation of the MMPI–2 infrequent somatic complaints (FS) scale. *Dissertation Abstracts International: Section B. Sciences and Engineering, 68*(10), 6989.

Wygant, D. B., Sellbom, M., Ben-Porath, Y. S., Stafford, K. P., Freeman, D. B., & Heilbronner, R. L. (2007). The relation between symptom validity testing and MMPI–2 scores as a function of forensic evaluation context. *Archives of Clinical Neuropsychology, 22*, 489–499.

Youngjohn, J. R., Davis, D., & Wolf, I. (1997). Head injury and the MMPI–2: Paradoxical severity effects and the influence of litigation. *Psychological Assessment, 9,* 177–184.

Zapata-Sola, A., Kreuch, T., Landers, R. N., Hoyt, T., & Butcher, J. N. (2009). Personality assessment in personnel selection using the MMPI–2: A cross-cultural comparison. *International Journal of Clinical and Health Psychology, 9,* 287–298.

Zapf, P. A., Boccaccini, M. T., & Brodsky, S. L. (2003). Assessment of competency for execution: Professional guidelines and an evaluation checklist. *Behavioral Sciences & the Law, 21,* 103–120.

Zapf, P. A., Golding, S. L., & Roesch, R. (2006). Criminal responsibility and the insanity defense. In R. B. Weiner & A. K. Hess (Eds.), *The handbook of forensic psychology* (3rd ed., pp. 332–363). Hoboken, NJ: Wiley.

Zea, M. C., Asner-Self, K. K., Birman, D., & Buki, L. P. (2003). The Abbreviated Multidimensional Acculturation Scale: Empirical validation with two Latino/Latina samples. *Cultural Diversity and Ethnic Minority Psychology, 9,* 107–126. doi:10.1037/1099-9809.9.2.107

Zoccolillo, M., & Cloninger, C. R. (1985). Parental breakdown associated with somatisation disorder (hysteria). *British Journal of Psychiatry, 147,* 443–446.

INDEX

Daubert v. Merrell Dow Pharmaceuticals, 74, 194

Davis, D., 121

Davis, K. R., 213

Dearth, C. S., 104

Defendants, 21

Defensiveness (*K*) scale
in child custody evaluations, 183
on MMPI–2–RF, 254
overview, 36–37

De la Fuente, R., 155

Department of Homeland Security (DHS), 147, 148, 158

Depression, 174, 178, 182, 197

Depression scale. *See D* scale

DEP (Depression) scale, 58

Diagnostic and Statistical Manual of Mental Disorders (DSM–III), 199

Diagnostic and Statistical Manual of Mental Disorders (DSM–IV–TR), 96, 134, 136

Diagnostic and Statistical Manual of Mental Disorders (DSM–5)
cultural formulation in, 157
diagnostic categories in, 96
elimination of Global Assessment of Functioning in, 135
Factitious Disorder in, 28, 97
gender differences noted in, 17
hypochondriasis in, 52
neurocognitive disorder in, 93

Disability, 173

Discrimination, 147

Divorcing families, 170

Doehring, D. G., 102

Dole, T., 46

Domestic violence. *See* Intimate partner violence

Domestic Violence Evaluation (DOVE), 195

Dong, Y. T., 162

D'Orazio, L. M., 258

Do (Dominance) scale, 63

DOVE (Domestic Violence Evaluation), 195

Droscher, H. K., 180

D (Depression) scale
and battered women, 198
in child custody evaluations, 182

cultural differences with, 79
neuropsychological correlates of, 100, 109
overview, 52–53
and personal injury evaluations, 118–120

DSM. *See Diagnostic and Statistical Manual of Mental Disorders* headings

DuAlba, L., 119

Dush, D. M., 119

Ecob, R., 180

Egeland, B., 178

Ego Strength (*Es*) scale
in child custody evaluations, 183
overview, 62–63

Elhai, J. D., 122

Ellertsen, B., 225

Emons, W. H. M., 255

Emotion, 93

Emotional attunement, 175

English, L. T., 40

Erickson, M., 178

Erickson, N. S., 199

Eronen, M., 211

Es (Ego Strength) scale
in child custody evaluations, 183
overview, 62–63

Ethnicity. *See* Cultural factors

Evaluation reports. *See* Assessment evaluation reports

Evans, B. F., 164

Expert witness roles, 157–158

Extended Score Report, 222–223

FAA (Federal Aviation Administration), 253

Factitious Disorder, 28, 97

Fairbank, J. A., 121

Fake Bad Scale (*FBS*)
construct validity of, 41
gender differences with, 17
response set assessment with, 40–44

FAM (Family Problems) scale, 60

Fariña, F., 122

FB (Back F) scale, 35, 40, 41

Fears (*FRS*) scale, 57

Federal Aviation Administration (FAA), 253

on MMPI–2–RF, 258
neuropsychological correlates of, 100
overview, 54
and personal injury evaluations, 118,
125
Paulson, M. J., 178
PDRS (Permanent Disability Rating
Schedule), 135
Pd (Psychopathic Deviate) scale
and battered women, 198
in child custody evaluations, 179,
183, 184
in criminal offender assessments,
213–214, 216
cultural differences with, 76, 77, 79
on MMPI–2–RF, 258
overview, 50, 53
Pearson Assessments, 223, 224, 252
Perceptions of Relationship Test, 176
Perkins, B. L., 258–259
Permanent Disability Rating Schedule
(PDRS), 135
Perrin, S., 199
Personal injury evaluations, 115–131
case example, 129–131
cooperation with examinee in, 118
and credibility of forensic expert,
116–117
of examinees with traumatic brain
injury, 127–128
examining personality characteristics
in, 128–129
guiding resources for, 116
and MMPI–2 based testimony,
122–125
MMPI–2 research relevant to,
125–126
and psychometric understanding of
tests, 117
standard administration procedures
for, 117
and uses of test data, 118
value of MMPI–2 in, 118–122
Personality Assessment Inventory, 17
Personality Factor Questionnaire, 16
Persons, R. W., 213
Physicians for Human Rights, 159
Pinsoneault, T. B., 225
Pirelli, G., 207
Pivovarova, E., 46

Pizitz, T., 260
PK (Posttraumatic Stress Disorder—
Keane) scale
assessment of stress with, 126
in child custody evaluations, 182
and intimate partner violence, 199
overview, 63
Platt, M., 119
PMWI (Psychological Maltreatment of
Women Inventory), 194
Polatin, P. B., 119
Pollack, D. R., 118
Pope, K. S., 24, 159, 161, 228–229
Postconcussive syndrome. *See* Brain
damage
Posttraumatic stress disorder (PTSD)
in immigrant populations, 153–156
with intimate partner violence, 197,
199
personal injury cases related to,
121–122, 126
Pottick, K. J., 77
Prejudice, 147
Presentencing evaluation, 210
Pribram, Karl, 99
Price, J. R., 178
Prosecution (plaintiff), 21
Psychological Maltreatment of Women
Inventory (PMWI), 194
Psychologists for Social Responsibility,
146
Pt (Psychasthenia) scale
and battered women, 198
in child custody evaluations, 182
cultural differences with, 77, 79
neuropsychological correlates of,
100, 109
overview, 54–55
PTSD. *See* Posttraumatic stress disorder

Quanback, C. D., 208
Quick Test, 215
Quinnell, F. A., 177

Ranson, M., 253
RC (Restructured Clinical) scales, 250,
259, 261, 262
Recidivism, 215
Referrals, 210
Reflective functioning, 175

ABOUT THE AUTHORS

James N. Butcher, PhD, is a professor emeritus in the Department of Psychology at the University of Minnesota. He was awarded honorary doctorates for his international personality assessment research (Doctor Honoris Causa) from the Free University of Brussels, Belgium, in 1990 and from the University of Florence, Italy (Laurea ad Honorem in Psychology), in 2005. He received the Bruno Klopfer Award from the Society for Personality Assessment in 2004 for long-standing contributions to personality assessment. He has maintained an active research program in the areas of personality assessment, abnormal psychology, cross-cultural personality factors, and computer-based personality assessment. He has conducted extensive research on the Minnesota Multiphasic Personality Inventory (MMPI) in a broad range of contexts. His publications include basic research works in abnormal psychology, personality assessment, and the MMPI, including research methodology and computer applications of psychological tests. Dr. Butcher is a coauthor of *The MMPI, MMPI–2, and MMPI–A in Court: A Practical Guide for Expert Witnesses and Attorneys, Third Edition* (2006; with K. S. Pope & J. Seelen). Dr. Butcher's forensic testimony, the source of much material included in this book, has been extensive and covers many types of legal cases. His court testimony almost always focuses on the interpretation of MMPI–2 scores. Issues concerning technical aspects of the test, the likely meaning of a particular MMPI configuration, or the assessment of symptom validity are common themes in his court testimony.

Giselle A. Hass, PsyD, is a forensic expert and consultant for local and national family and immigration courts. She is a native of Costa Rica and was a forensic psychologist in her own country before she immigrated to the United States. She earned a doctorate in clinical psychology from Nova Southeastern University and is licensed both in Virginia and Washington, DC. Dr. Hass is currently an adjunct professor of law at Georgetown University Law Center, Center for Applied Legal Studies; a forensic psychologist for the Assessment Center, Washington DC Department of Behavioral Health; and a psychologist for the Ainsworth Attachment Clinic, Charlottesville, Virginia. She has coauthored articles and book chapters on assessment, immigration and culture, parenting, and divorce issues.

Roger L. Greene, PhD, is a Distinguished Emeritus in the Pacific Graduate School of Psychology at Palo Alto University in Palo Alto, California, where he worked for over 20 years. Dr. Greene has worked in a variety of clinical settings and with different types of patients in his clinical career. His particular area of interest clinically is in the assessment and treatment of alcohol and drug abuse. He has written a number of texts and articles on the use of the MMPI–2 both clinically and forensically and has developed computer interpretation programs on both the MMPI–2 and the MMPI–2–RF. His most recent book, *The MMPI–2/MMPI–2–RF: An Interpretive Manual* (3rd ed.), was published in 2011. He recently received the Bruno Klopfer Award from the Society for Personality Assessment for lifetime contributions to the field of assessment. His books on the MMPI–2 have been among the standard references for over two decades.

Linda D. Nelson, PhD, has a thriving private practice in Santa Monica, California, where she evaluates and treats patients with neurological and psychiatric problems. She is a qualified medical evaluator for the State of California and is regularly called on to perform independent medical examinations on individuals with suspected head injury. After serving as vice chair of neurology for 16 years at the University of California, Irvine, Dr. Nelson assumed a faculty position at the University of California, Los Angeles. As Professor Emerita, UCLA, she currently conducts research on the link between Alzheimer's disease and Down syndrome and maintains an active teaching role in undergraduate neuroscience. Dr. Nelson received her doctorate in clinical psychology from the Ohio State University, where she studied with MMPI expert Philip Marks. She also worked with James N. Butcher and Alex Caldwell on the MMPI during her early career. She published extensively on the MMPI and later went on to complete postdoctoral training in clinical neuropsychology from the University of California, Los Angeles. Her professional career has emphasized evaluation and assessment, with the MMPI and later the MMPI–2, remaining a staple in her adult forensic test batteries.